Reverend James T. O'Connor

THE HIDDEN MANNA

Reverend James T. O'Connor

THE HIDDEN MANNA

A Theology of the Eucharist

IGNATIUS PRESS   SAN FRANCISCO

Cover by Roxanne Mei Lum

With ecclesiastical approval
© 1988 Ignatius Press, San Francisco
All rights reserved
ISBN 0–89870–288–7 (HC)
ISBN 0–89870–255–9 (SC)
Library of Congress catalogue number 88–82477
Printed in the United States of America

CONTENTS

FOREWORD

It doesn't surprise me that Father O'Connor would use Flannery O'Connor's reverential irreverence to comment on the Eucharist as Mystery. It is typical of both the whimsy of his writing and the brilliance of his teaching.

He is speaking of the shock created at Capharnaum by Jesus' words: "My flesh is meat indeed, my blood is drink indeed. Whoever eats of my flesh and drinks of my blood will never die." Jesus anticipated the shock, Father O'Connor tells us, and knew well that it would be for many simply too much to accept. The scandal of the Mystery has never gone away. Flannery O'Connor talks about it in one of her letters in *The Habit of Being*, in recalling a visit she had made to another well-known author and former Catholic:

> [She] said that when she was a child and received the Host, she thought of it as the Holy Ghost, He being the "most portable" person of the Trinity; now she thought of it as a symbol and implied that it was a pretty good one. I then said, in a very shaky voice, "Well, if it's a symbol, to hell with it." That was all the defense I was capable of but I realize now that this is all I will ever be able to say about it, outside of a story, except that it is the center of existence for me; all the rest of life is expendable.

That just happens to be one of my own favorite Flannery O'Connor stories. Much more importantly, it tells us a great deal about Father O'Connor's thinking and his book. In a day of far too much ambiguity about both the meaning of the Mass and the Real Presence of Christ in the tabernacle, he gives us a ringing affirmation of the Church's traditional and unmistakable teaching. His scholarliness is indisputable, his own faith unshakeable, yet his arguments are straightforward and uncomplicated, and his understanding of the difficulties of those neither schooled as is he nor gifted with his faith is sensitive and authentic.

As he does so carefully in his Christological study, *The Father's Son*, Father O'Connor respects modern scriptural exegesis and studies in the development of doctrine. He is no fundamentalist. *The Hidden Manna* is rooted in exhaustive study of scripture, commentaries and sermons of the Church Fathers and insights of modern theologians. He gives us nothing less than a comprehensive study of the Church's meditation on the Mystery of the Eucharist from the first centuries to our own times. I suspect that he would summarize his own convictions about this Mystery of Faith in the words of Pope John Paul II's "Message to the Eucharistic Congress at Lourdes" (July 21, 1981).

> The sacrifice of the Cross is so decisive for the future of man that Christ did not carry it out and did not return to the Father until he had left us the means to take part in it as if we had been present. Christ's offering on the Cross—which is the real Bread of Life broken—is the first value that must be communicated and shared. The Mass and the Cross are but one and the same sacrifice. Nevertheless the eucharistic breaking of bread has an essential function, that of putting at our disposal the original offering of the Cross. It makes it actual today for our generation. By making the Body and Blood of Christ really present under the species of bread and wine, it makes—simultaneously—the Sacrifice of the Cross actual and accessible to our generation, this Sacrifice which remains, in its uniqueness, the turning point of the history of salvation, the essential link between time and eternity.

I find myself touched particularly by Father O'Connor's dedicating this work to Mary and its overall Marian orientation. He is, after all, one of the outstanding Mariologists in the United States, and his recognition of Mary's role in giving us the Eucharist is both moving and insightful.

For the lay reader who wants a rich understanding of the Eucharist, for either teacher or student of the theology of the

Eucharist, for the preacher who, as in my own case, is always seeking deeper insight to share with God's People, *The Hidden Manna* is a superb work. I am personally most grateful to its author.

+ John Cardinal O'Connor

PREFACE

"If it's worth doing, it's worth doing poorly", wrote G. K. Chesterton, attempting to combat our tendency to use that other famous dictum "If it's worth doing, it's worth doing well" as an excuse for doing nothing. Now, having completed this work on the Eucharist, I am sadly aware of how well I have followed Chesterton's advice. What we really need in the English language is an updated version of Darwell Stone's monumental two volume work, from which I have learned so much. Long out of print, it is a study that still leaves one amazed at the breadth of Stone's scholarship and the balance of his judgments. Even the admirable synthesis of the history of Eucharistic doctrine that is found throughout the four volumes of *The Christian Tradition,* written by Jaroslav Pelikan, another non-Catholic scholar, is not able to replace Stone's work, simply because Pelikan has endeavored, successfully, to provide us with a study that encompasses so much more than the doctrine on the Eucharist, thereby limiting the space he might spend on any one theme. If one must at times question something reported as a specific fact or disagree with a particular interpretation of these men, it can be done only with the recognition of the lasting value of their achievements.

We also need in English a work on the Eucharist that would be written with the love and fervor of an Ignatius of Antioch or of Chrysostom or Augustine or Aquinas. And so, on the counts of both scholarship and fervor, this present book is most deficient. Nonetheless, Aquinas, anticipating Chesterton, wrote that the theme of the Eucharist is so special that we must take a risk in offering our praise and do as much as we are capable of accomplishing.

I have made no attempt to deal with the history of the Eucharistic liturgies. There is, as well, no direct treatment of the sources of the theme as found in Sacred Scripture, since I trust that the abundant references to the Scriptures by the Fathers of the Church and the great theologians will be more than adequate to present the Bible as it is read and meditated upon by the Church.

Like Mr. Dick of *David Copperfield*, who discovered that King Charles' head kept creeping into his never completed Memorial, so I recognize that certain authors appear repeatedly in what follows. Augustine and Aquinas are everywhere. For this, however, I offer no apology. Whatever of value there is to be found here is due in very great measure to them.

Completed in the year which Pope John Paul II proclaimed particularly Mary's own, this book is dedicated to her who, in Augustine's words, "gave milk to our Bread". The treatment on Our Lady and the Eucharist as found in Chapter Four is an edited version of a paper previously published in *Marian Studies,* vol. 39. I pray that it is to her honor.

I want to express my gratitude to Mother Mary of the Blessed Sacrament, O.P., whose prayers for me before the Host I shall never be able to repay, to Fr. Bertrand de Margerie, S.J., who read and offered helpful advice on the section dealing with the Fathers of the Church, and to Sr. Ellen Gaffney, R.D.C., and Mrs. Barbara Carey of the Library of St. Joseph's Seminary, Dunwoodie for their prompt, patient, and generous assistance. And, in a particular way, thanks is owed to Cardinal John O'Connor who kindly agreed to write the Foreword, and whose own love for and preaching on the Eucharist has been a source of edification.

I

Lauda, Sion

Prelude

The Wisdom of God creates poets. How evidently this is so can be seen by considering Mary of Nazareth. When she had given to the Lord of Hosts the Flesh that would become our Bread, Wisdom caused her to break into a poem of praise, a song repeated by more people than probably any other ever composed. The Presence within stirred her to exult and proclaim the One "who has filled the hungry with good things". And the praise owed to the Presence of embodied Wisdom among us has never ceased in the Church from that day until this. So great is his power that he has even made the dumb, the mute, speak. In that regard one thinks particularly of St. Thomas Aquinas, so taciturn by nature that his classmates named him the "dumb ox". Yet the Eucharist made this very prosaic man a poet, perhaps the greatest of Eucharistic troubadours after Our Lady. In the awesomely beautiful Office that he composed for the Feast of the Body and Blood of the Lord, Thomas began the Sequence of the Mass with the following words:

Lauda, Sion, Salvatorem
Lauda Ducem et Pastorem
In hymnis et canticis.
Quantum potes, tantum aude:
Quia major omni laude,
Nec laudare sufficis.

O Sion, praise your Savior,
Praise your Leader and
* Shepherd*
In hymns and canticles.
Dare to praise as much as you
* are able,*
Because he is greater than all
* praise,*
Indeed no praise is sufficient.

I

The *Lauda Sion* is an injunction to the Church (Sion) to praise the Eucharistic Presence, joined with the realization that no praise is or can be sufficient. The theme surpasses our ability. Yet both before and since Aquinas, the Eucharist has been the inspiration for innumerable compositions of great beauty in prose, poetry, art, and music, all of it a sign of the depth of feeling aroused in the faithful by this Mystery.

The praise is not always literally poetry, at least not in poetic form. Often it is prose that is as beautiful as poetry. Consider, for example, the poetic nature of the following words of St. Augustine as he preached to the faithful, commenting on the sixth chapter of St. John, which contains the Eucharistic discourse of the Lord. Commenting on verse 44 ("No one can come to me unless the Father draws him . . . "), Augustine says:

> Do not think that you are drawn unwillingly, because the mind is also drawn by love. Nor should we be afraid of men who weigh words but are far removed from understanding realities, especially divine realities and who perhaps reprove us in respect to this Gospel word as found in Holy Scripture, saying to us: "How am I to believe willingly, if I am drawn?" I respond, "It is a little thing, since you are also drawn willingly by pleasure." What does it mean to be drawn by pleasure? "Delight in the Lord and he will grant your heart's requests" (Ps 37:4). There is a certain pleasure of the heart to which this heavenly Bread is sweet. Indeed if the poet can say, "His pleasure draws each man" (Virgil, *Eclogues* 2), it is not necessity but pleasure; not obligation but delight. Should we not then say more forcefully that a man is drawn to Christ, who delights us with truth, delights us with happiness, delights us with justice, delights us with eternal life—all of which Christ himself is? Or is it to be that the senses of the body have their pleasures while the mind is deprived of its own pleasures? If the mind does not have its own pleasure, how is it said, "The sons of men shall hope under the protection of your wings; they will be inebriated by the fullness of your house, and you will give them to drink from the torrent of your pleasure; because with you is the fountain of life, and in your light we see the light" (Ps 36:8–9)? Give me a man in love and he'll know what I am talking about. Give me one who is

desirous and hungry and traveling as a pilgrim in this wilderness, one who is thirsting and yearning for the fountain of our eternal homeland, give me such a man and he'll know what I am talking about. But if I speak to someone who is frigid, he will not know what of I am speaking. Such were those who murmured among themselves, and so Jesus says, "Whomever the Father shall have drawn will come to me."[1]

Thus, says Augustine, the Father draws us by the sweet appeal that this heavenly Bread makes to our minds. Although not speaking of the Eucharistic Mystery, the Apostle John, too, had sung the praises of the Word of life: "That which was from the beginning, which we have heard, which we have seen with our eyes, which we have looked at and our hands have touched—this we proclaim concerning the Word of life" (1 Jn 1:1).

What we have heard, looked at, and touched with our hands is what we proclaim. In this way one can sum up the testimony of Christians—beginning with the Fathers of the Church—to the Word of life who has made himself the Bread of life.

There are many aspects from which one may approach the writings of the Fathers of the Church. They can be viewed as privileged depositories of Christian Tradition, and thus one can read and present them as witnesses to the continuity and development of Catholic doctrine. This perspective is certainly an essential one. In respect to their writings on the Eucharist, it enables one to see how quickly some insights into the "mystery of faith" manifested themselves and how others developed only gradually and often enough with that lack of clarity in expression or thought that accompanies any initial efforts to probe the riches contained in what God has revealed. This lack of clarity can at times be a cause of wonder or concern to someone who would expect to find a fully elaborated presentation of the Church's doctrine on the Eucharist in the Patristic writings. In fact, however, no such expectation should exist at all. Most of the literature that remains

---

[1] *Tractatus In Jo. 26*, 4; *CCSL*, 36, pp. 261–62.

for us to examine exists in the form of letters, sermons, or works of Christian apology whose direct concerns were other than a presentation of a Eucharistic theology. Indeed, the first full treatise on the Eucharist was produced only in the ninth century. Nonetheless, granted the limitations imposed by the nature and purpose of the writings, the extant works of the Church Fathers give ample testimony to almost all the facets of the Eucharistic Mystery that are treated in a systematic theological study.

There is, also, another perspective from which one can approach the writings of the Fathers on the Eucharist, namely, as examples and expressions of a truth we have already mentioned: Sion's desire to praise her Savior. Reading the Fathers can be compared to listening to a sustained hymn of praise for the Eucharistic gifts. It is a chorus of many voices, in different languages, from various times and places, each seeking to exalt or explain or defend or merely wonder at this Bread that has been given to us from heaven. No one voice is sufficient, no particular insight comprehensive enough, yet all together form a Christian "Canticle of Canticles" to a love that is both divine and human in a relationship more intimate than even that of marriage. Read from that point of view — while still searching precisely for the truths expressed — the writings of the Patristic age are basically an invitation to prayer and meditation.

The Patristic literature on the Eucharist covers, of course, almost nine centuries, and so it is impossible to treat it in any way that is nearly adequate in a book of this size. All one can attempt to do is to choose those Fathers and texts that are most significant and most beautiful, trying to make the selection truly representative. Normally the selections will be left to speak for themselves, the commentary being limited to indicating matters of major importance for the Church's understanding of this memorial of the New Covenant in Christ's Blood.

The *Didache*

One of the oldest of Christian documents still in existence is the *Didache*, the so-called Teaching of the Twelve Apostles. The exact date of its writing is disputed, with estimates ranging from 50 to 150 A.D. Internal evidence, not perhaps absolutely conclusive but nonetheless very strong, suggests that parts of it, including Sections 9 and 10, which are of immediate concern here, are to be dated somewhere between 30 and 100 A.D.[2] Its words on the Eucharist, frequently cited and in part well known through being adapted for use in modern Christian hymns, are as follows:

(9) As far as concerns the Eucharist [Gk. *eucharistias*], give thanks in this fashion. First, in respect to the cup: We give you thanks [Gk. *eucharistoumen*], Our Father, for the holy vine of your servant [Gk. *paidos*] David, which you made known to us through your servant [Gk. *paidos*], Jesus; yours is the glory forever and ever. Then, in respect to the broken bread: We give you thanks, Our Father, for the life and knowledge that you made known to us through your servant Jesus; yours is the glory forever and ever. As this broken bread was scattered on the mountains and, having been gathered together, became one, so may your Church be gathered into your Kingdom from the ends of the earth, for yours is the glory and the power through Jesus Christ forever and ever. However, let no one eat or drink of this Eucharist unless he has been baptized

---

[2] A good discussion of the question of dating the *Didache* is to be found in the critical edition published in *Sources Chrétiennes*, 248, pp. 47 and 96 in particular. The editors, agreeing essentially with Audet, who dates it ca. 50 A.D. (cf. article "Didache" in *New Catholic Encyclopedia*), date the Eucharistic sections to the first century. With this position J. A. T. Robinson, *Redating the New Testament*, is in agreement. Lightfoot and Kleist place its composition in the first or at the beginning of the second century, as does Funk. Staniforth holds that it is a composite document, its final form no later than 150. There does not appear to be any compelling evidence for a specific date, but because of internal indications the dates between 30 and 100 A.D., at least for the Eucharistic sections, seem to be more likely.

in the name of the Lord; for concerning this the Lord also said: "Do not give to dogs what is holy."

(10) After it has been completed, give thanks in this fashion: Holy Father, we give you thanks for your holy Name, which you have made dwell in our hearts, and for the knowledge and faith and immortality that you have made known to us through your servant Jesus. Yours is the glory forever. Almighty Master, you created all things for your Name's sake and gave man food and drink for enjoyment so that they might give thanks to you, but you gave us spiritual food and drink [Gk. *pneumatiken trophen kai poton*] and eternal life through your Servant.... Remember, Lord, your Church and deliver her from all evil and make her perfect in your love, and gather your holy Church from the four winds into your Kingdom, which you have prepared for her; for yours are the power and the glory forever.... Let the prophets indeed give thanks as they wish.

. . .

(14) And on the Lord's own day gather together and break bread and give thanks, first confessing [Gk. *proexomologesamenoi*] your sins so that your sacrifice may be pure. And let no man having a dispute with his companion join your assembly until they have been reconciled so that your sacrifice may not be defiled; for this is that sacrifice spoken of by the Lord: "In every place and time offer me a pure sacrifice [Gk. *thusian*]; for I am a great king, says the Lord, and my Name is wonderful among the nations" [cf. Malachi 1:11].[3]

The prophets mentioned are the "high priests" of the Christian community, the ones who offer the Eucharist (cf. *Didache,* 13, 3), but the task of the overseers or bishops (Gk. *episkopoi*) is identical with theirs (cf. *Didache,* 15).[4]

Several things are to be noted in the above citation from the *Didache.*

---

[3] *Didache,* 9, 10, and 14. Critical editions of the Greek are to be found in F. X. Funk, vol. 1, and in the *Sources Chrétiennes* series, vol. 248.

[4] Cf. n. 14 below under Clement of Rome.

1. It is possible to interpret the opening words as a reference to no more than a "thanksgiving" that is not the specific Eucharistic liturgy of Christians but perhaps the "agape" meal, or even to simple Christian table blessings.[5] It is thought by many that, like the early Christian Eucharistic celebrations, Christian prayers at such meals would have derived from the *beraka* (thanksgiving, blessing) prayers of Judaism, especially as these were used at Jewish meals and at the Passover commemoration.[6] We are familiar with this type of prayer from the words of Jesus himself ("Blessed are you, Father, Lord of heaven and earth": Mt 11:25) and from our own Eucharist when the bread and wine are offered ("Blessed are you, Lord, God of all creation"). The sections of the *Didache* cited above could reflect this tradition. However, in the light of the third paragraph of the citation, which clearly refers to the Sunday assembly and uses the same terminology as the previous sections, and the reference to "spiritual food and drink", the notion that the prayers of the *Didache* are (non-Eucharistic) table prayers must be reckoned as a possibility without any real likelihood.[7]

---

[5] Cf. Jungmann, *The Mass of the Roman Rite*, I, pp. 12–13.

[6] A detailed study of the *beraka/berakoth* formularies and their influence on the Christian liturgy can be found in L. Bouyer's *Eucharist*, chaps. 2–5. It must be noted, however, that recently reservations have been expressed concerning the relationship between the *berakoth* prayers and the Christian Eucharist. Footnote no. 1 of the Vatican document *Response to WCC Document: Baptism, Eucharist, and Ministry: An Appraisal* reads: "Is it appropriate to classify the Eucharist as *berakah* or even to explain . . . that it is derived 'from the Jewish tradition of the *berakah*'? At the present stage of investigation of the history of *berakah* and its relation to Eucharistic prayers, many questions remain open" (*Origins*, vol. 17, no. 23, p. 416). Similar reservations are expressed by Joseph Ratzinger in the article "Form and Content in the Eucharistic Celebration", with its postscripts 1 and 2 (*Feast of Faith*, pp. 33–61).

[7] On the possibility that the citation from the *Didache* refers to a "thanksgiving" that is not the specific Christian Eucharist, Quasten's remarks should still be judged appropriate. "The opinion advanced more than once, that we have here no specific Eucharistic prayers but simply table prayers, is untenable. The discussion of the Eucharist is closely connected with that of Baptism, and the two are evidently associated in the author's mind. Unbaptized persons are moreover expressly excluded from the reception of the Eucharist" (1, p. 32).

Viewing the citation as simply a reference to a thanksgiving
that is not the liturgical Eucharist would eliminate a difficulty that
many have found with the *Didache*'s instruction, viz., the lack of
any mention of the Lord's words of Eucharistic Institution—words
that later theology and the Church's teaching came to recognize
as among the necessary elements for a true or valid Eucharistic
celebration.[8] Some who admit that the *Didache*'s references are
truly Eucharistic have drawn the conclusion—from the lack of
any words of Institution—that at least certain communities in the
primitive Church celebrated a Eucharist without including the
dominical words, and that, at least for that period of Church
history, the words of Institution were not necessary for a valid
Eucharist. As further evidence for such a conclusion, appeal is
made to another liturgical text, the "Eucharistic Prayer", or *Anaphora
of Addai and Mari*. This document, probably deriving originally
from those Christian communities centered around Edessa and
Nisibis and whose tradition today is carried on in part by the
Catholic Churches of the Chaldean and Malabar Rites in the
Middle East and India, is surely an important and interesting one,
although it is surrounded by much uncertainty. We possess no
manuscript of the *Anaphora* that predates the tenth or eleventh
centuries. Therefore, the speculated original date of the work
ranges from the second to the seventh centuries. It is possible, too,
that the *Anaphora* represents a heterodox form of Christianity,
since, during the aftermath of the Nestorian controversy and the
Council of Ephesus, theological dissension and poor communica-
tions separated some of the Churches that may have given birth to
the *Anaphora* from the Church of Rome and from the patriarchal
Sees of Constantinople and Alexandria. Also, it is known from
manuscripts of other Eucharistic prayers that the words of Institution were not always included in the text even when it is certain
that they were used and considered necessary. Their exclusion was
due in part to the fact that they existed in so fixed a form that

[8] See below, p. 203–5.

the celebrant was expected to know them by memory.[9] These general difficulties are compounded by the fact that a number of the experts on the text are of the opinion that it originally did contain a narrative of Institution. They have reconstructed the text accordingly.[10] The state of the question being such, it would be precipitous to appeal to this document as proof—along with the *Didache*—that there was indeed a time when the Eucharist was celebrated with an anaphora or canon or prayer that did not include the institutional words of Jesus. As far as the *Didache* is concerned, it is quite possible that the instructions given refer to the prayers to be said *after* the Institution narrative.

The Epistle of Clement of Rome

Another ancient piece of Christian literature—perhaps the oldest outside the New Testament, depending on the dates assigned to the *Didache* and to the *Odes of Solomon*—is the letter of the Church in Rome to the Church in Corinth. In it the Romans rebuke the Corinthians for having "deposed" some of the leaders of their local Church. The epistle was held in great repute by the early Church and was universally attributed to Clement, the third Bishop of Rome after St. Peter.[11] It was written sometime between 70 and 96 A.D.[12]

---

[9] Cf. Bouyer, *Eucharist,* pp. 143–82, esp. pp. 150–52.

[10] For information on the *Anaphora of Addai and Mari,* cf. Bryan D. Spinks, *Addai and Mari—The Anaphora of the Apostles: A Text for Students,* New York: Grove Books, 1980; Thomas M. O'Hagan, *The Anaphora of the Apostles, Mar Addai and Mar Mari: A Reexamination of the Problems,* Rome: Pontificium Athenaeum Anselmianum, 1978.

[11] The critical Greek text of Clement's letter used here is to be found in Funk, I, pp. 98–184. *Sources Chrétiennes,* vol. 167 (1971) also has a critical text of the Greek and a French translation.

[12] Because of the dates for Clement's reign given by the Church historian Eusebius (ca. 325), the references in the first paragraph of the letter to "the

Some have raised the possibility that the long prayer found in sections 59 to 61 of Clement's letter is drawn from the Eucharistic liturgy as celebrated in Rome at that time.[13] This is certainly not impossible, but it is a conjecture that cannot be verified by any other evidence presently available to us. What is clear, however, is that Clement makes a distinction between the leaders of the community, and the faithful in general. The former he calls presbyters (elders) and bishops (overseers) without apparently making any further distinction between them;[14] the latter Clement, using the word in Christian literature for the first time, calls "laity".[15] Working from this distinction, he draws the con-

---

sudden and successive events and misfortunes" that had occurred, and the reference in *Clement,* 63, 3 to men of the Roman Church who have grown old as Christians, the letter of Clement is almost universally dated as having been written around 96 A.D. at the end of reign of the Emperor Domitian, who, Eusebius tells us, persecuted the Christians. The difficulty with the date, however, is that the first paragraph does not mention persecutions whereas the letter explicitly mentions the "recent" persecutions under the Emperor Nero (cf. *Clement,* 5). The "sudden and successive events" referred to may in fact be the great fire and subsequent plague in the city—perhaps related to the eruption of Vesuvius in the same year—all of them recorded for the years 79–80 in Suetonius' treatment of the reign of Titus in his *The Twelve Caesars.* Such a date does not contradict Eusebius' dating of Clement's reign as bishop since Clement could have written the letter before he became bishop when he may have served the Roman Church as "secretary for foreign correspondence" (cf. *The Shepherd of Hermas,* Vision II, no. 4). Some few would date the work earlier, around 70 A.D. Cf. Thomas Herron, *The Dating of the First Epistle of Clement.*

[13] Funk, I, p. 175, states that "one can suspect" some borrowing from the Roman liturgy in this section.

[14] The difficulties with the nomenclature for Church offices and the holders of Church office in some of the primitive documents are well known and have been cause for much discussion. Clement, for example, appears to use the terms for presbyter and bishop interchangeably. Nevertheless, he seems to distinguish between presbyters and those who are rulers of the community (*Clement,* I, 3). It is too often concluded from the lack of specificity in nomenclature that there was a corresponding lack of specificity in function.

[15] *Clement,* 40, 5: "The layman is held to the rules for the layman." Op. cit., p. 150.

clusion that "each one of us, brothers, in his own order should fittingly give thanks to God with a good conscience, not transgressing the assigned rule of his ministry" (Gk. *mē parekbainōn ton horismenon tēs leitourgias autou kanona*).[16] He thus gives evidence of a rule for liturgical service that will appear again and again in the documents of the Church. When he comes to speak of the ministry proper to the presbyter-bishops, he refers to it as the "offering of the gifts": "Our sin will not be a light one if we expel those who worthily and blamelessly have offered the gifts of [proper to?] the episcopacy."[17] In the light of Matthew 5:23 and Leviticus 1:2 and 7:38, it seems quite clear that the offering of gifts referred to by Clement is the equivalent of calling the Eucharistic liturgy a sacrifice.

The *Odes of Solomon*

Until 1909 the *Odes of Solomon* were known only through scattered references in other early Christian writings. In 1905 a Syriac manuscript was found, and all forty-two *Odes* were published in 1909. Although scholars differ, it would appear that they were originally written in Syriac and represent an orthodox and often very moving example of poetry that derives from Christians of a Jewish background.

---

[16] *Clement,* 40, 1. Op. cit., p. 150.

[17] *Clement,* 44, 4. Op. cit., p. 156. The Greek of 44, 4, offers two possibilities for translation. One can read the Greek as saying: "Our sin will not be a light one if we expel from the episcopacy those who worthily and blamelessly have offered the gifts." This translation is taken from Funk, p. 157; Staniforth, p. 46; Richardson, p. 64; the *Sources Chrétiennes,* 167, p. 173; Jurgens, 1, p. 11. Lightfoot I–II, p. 76, and Kleist, p. 36, however, read the *tes episkopes* with *dora.* I think this decision is the correct one and have followed it. It is worth noting, too, that Kleist, Jurgens, and Richardson have translated the Greek *prosenegkontas dora* as "offering the sacrifices". This is most probably a correct interpretation of what Clement means, but it goes beyond the literal Greek, which here does not use the technical word for sacrifice (viz., *thusia*).

There is a possible reference to the Eucharist in the daring imagery of *Ode* 19.

Ode 19

A cup of milk was offered to me,
and I drank it in the sweetness of the Lord's kindness.

The Son is the cup,
and the Father is he who is milked;
and the Holy Spirit is she who milked him;
Because his breasts were full,
and it was undesirable that his milk should be released without purpose.
The Holy Spirit opened her bosom
and mixed the milk of the two breasts of the Father.
Then she gave the mixture to the generation without their knowing,
and those who have received it are in the perfection of the right hand.
The womb of the Virgin took it,
and she received conception and gave birth.
And she labored and bore the Son but without pain
because it did not occur without purpose.
And she did not seek a midwife,
because he caused her to give life.[18]

The "cup of milk" is the Son, milked by the Spirit from the breasts of the Father. Although the imagery is bold in that it depicts feminine attributes of the Father, its intentions are clear and perfectly orthodox. The Son is of the substance of the Father, a truth that the Council of Nicaea in 325 would capture by its use of the term *homoousios,* one in being. The action of the Spirit in milking is a reference to the later credal statement "conceived by the Holy Spirit", since the action of the Spirit results in the reception of the Milk in the womb of the Virgin Mary, whose parturition is virginal. Mary acts as the servant through whom

[18] Charlesworth, James H., *The Odes of Solomon* (Scholars Press, 1977), pp. 752–53.

the Milk is passed to us "to drink in the sweetness of the Lord". Thus, the Father's Milk becomes our nourishment; we feed on and drink of his substance.

St. Ignatius of Antioch

The references of St. Ignatius of Antioch (d. 107) to the Eucharist in the seven authentic letters he wrote while on his way to Rome to suffer martyrdom are sufficient to indicate that the Mystery of the Lord's Body and Blood was a most significant aspect in his thought and in his own spiritual life. In his letter to the Christians of Tralles, for example, he apparently compares the virtues of faith and love to the Eucharistic Mystery when he writes: "Therefore, arming yourselves with gentleness, renew yourselves in faith, which is the Flesh of the Lord, and in charity, which is the Blood of Jesus Christ. Hold nothing against your neighbor."[19] His letter to the Romans is almost mystical in its Eucharistic allusions. He compares his own coming tortures to the process that the wheat must undergo (a comparison later taken up and used by St. Augustine with great effect).[20] In facing death, Ignatius states that his only remaining desire is to encounter him who has made himself the food and drink of Christians. He writes:

> I am God's grain, and I am being ground by the teeth of wild beasts in order that I may be found [to be] pure bread for Christ.
> My [earthly] love [lit. *eros*] has been crucified, and there is in me no fire of material love, but rather a living water, speaking in me and saying within me, "Come to the Father". I take no pleasure in corruptible food or in the delights of this life. I want the Bread of God, which is the Flesh of Jesus Christ, who is of the seed

[19] Tralles, 8. The text of Ignatius' letters in a critical Greek edition with a French translation can be found in *Sources Chrétiennes,* vol. 10, 2nd ed. On the Eucharistic interpretation of the text, cf. p. 54.

[20] For the Augustinian reference, cf. below, p. 60.

of David; and as drink I want his Blood, which is incorruptible love.[21]

The above passages are filled with allusions, intended or not by Ignatius it is difficult to say, although the surest hypothesis would hold that they were. The "living water" that speaks within him recalls the words of Christ to the Samaritan woman (Jn 4:10) and is a reference to the Holy Spirit (cf. Jn 7:38–39). The Spirit's words are an invitation to the Father, who will feed the one who accepts that invitation with "the Bread of God", an allusion to John 6:32–33, where Jesus is recorded as saying: "It is not Moses who has given you the Bread from heaven, but it is my Father who gives you the true Bread from heaven. For the Bread of God is he who comes down from heaven and gives life to the world." And, following Christ, Ignatius identifies "the Bread of God" with the Flesh and Blood of Jesus himself. For emphasis Ignatius refers to Jesus' Davidic descent, thereby stressing—as he does so often throughout his letters—the historical and material reality of the Incarnation.

Ignatius' words are clearly an example of his own desire to imitate Christ. In expressing this desire, the Bishop of Antioch is responding to an explicit invitation of the Lord himself, who had said, "Learn from me, for I am meek and humble of heart" (Mt 11:29), an injunction seconded by St. Paul when he wrote: "Your attitude should be the same as that of Christ Jesus" (Phil 2:5) and "By the meekness and gentleness of Christ, I appeal to you" (2 Cor 10:1). In Ignatius this idea of the imitation of Christ (which was to have so central a place in Christian spirituality) passed, by a natural progression, from the imitation of Christ as he had manifested himself in Palestine to an imitation of the Eucharistic Lord as he continues to reveal himself in the Mystery of his Flesh and Blood. Indeed, it is probably true to say that the Eucharist served as model not only for Ignatius' view of his own approaching death but also for the marked Christocentric nature of all his spirituality.

---

[21] Romans, 4 and 7., op. cit., pp. 130, 136.

What I need is the meekness by which the prince of this world is destroyed.[22]

Without him we do not have true life.[23]

Let me be no more than a libation [cf. Phil 2:17] for God while an altar of sacrifice [Gk. *thusiasterion*] is still at hand.[24]

I greet you in the Blood of Jesus Christ, which is eternal and abiding joy.[25]

Let me be an imitator of the Passion of my God.[26]

Let us do all things as [having] him dwelling in us.[27]

I pray that there may be in them [i.e., the Churches] a union of the Flesh and Spirit of Jesus Christ.[28]

Remember me as Jesus Christ [remembers] you.[29]

The last words of the citation from Ignatius' letter to the Romans ("I want his Blood, which is incorruptible love") offer differing possibilities to the translator. The words in Greek are *ho estin agapē aphthartos,* and they may be translated as "love immortal", thereby indicating the undying love of Christ for us as he feeds us with his Flesh and Blood. Or the "agape" referred to may be an allusion to the "supper" celebrated by Christians in conjunction with the Eucharist (cf. 1 Cor 11). The former interpretation, however, is to be preferred.[30]

Ignatius' desire for God's Bread is grounded in the realism with which he identifies that Bread with the Flesh and Blood of Christ. That such an identification is not merely something of his own invention but rather the teaching of the Christian community in

[22] Tralles, 4. Idem, p. 115.

[23] Idem, 9, p. 118.

[24] Romans, 2. Idem, p. 128.

[25] Philadelphia, salutation. Idem, p. 140.

[26] Romans, 6. Idem, p. 134.

[27] Ephesians, 15. Idem, p. 84.

[28] Magnesians, 1. Idem, p. 94.

[29] Ephesians, 21. Idem, p. 92.

[30] Lightfoot and Staniforth opt for the translation "love imperishable"

general is clearly seen, although in an indirect fashion, when Ignatius comments on the beliefs of some who call themselves Christians but who stay away from the Christian Eucharist. Of them he writes:

> Observe well those who are heterodox in respect to the grace of Jesus Christ that has come to us; see how they are opposed to the mind of God. Charity is of no concern to them, nor are widows and orphans or the oppressed, either those in prison or at liberty, or the hungry or the thirsty. They abstain from the Eucharist and from prayer, because they do not confess that the Eucharist is the Flesh of our Savior Jesus Christ, which suffered for our sins and which, in his goodness, the Father raised. . . . It would be better for them to show love in order they [also] might rise.[31]

The people Ignatius is referring to are those who manifest some of the tendencies that later would be grouped under the generic term *Gnostic*. A common trait of the various Gnostic or proto-Gnostic groups was a disdain for material reality. Therefore, those marked by such an outlook in Ignatius' time rejected Eucharistic fellowship because it meant participating in a Mystery all too material for their views, namely, the eating of the very Flesh that had suffered and been raised. Their rejection of Eucharistic fellowship indicates that the orthodox Christian communities held for an *identity* between the Eucharist and the crucified and risen Body of the Lord. Such an identity carried clear notions of materiality, since the Eucharistic and risen Body is, in fact, the identical Flesh that had suffered Crucifixion, as Ignatius affirms in the same letter when he writes: "For I know and believe

---

(Staniforth, p. 106) or "incorruptible" (Lightfoot, p. 78). Camelot in the *Sources Chrétiennes* edition (vol. 10) (p. 137) adopts the same rendering. Richardson, however, chooses "an immortal love feast indeed" (p. 105). The evidence that the "agape" as a meal united with the Eucharistic celebration survived N.T. times is very meager.

[31] Smyrna, 7. Idem, p. 160.

that after the Resurrection he exists [lit., is] in the flesh."[32] Perceiving that this was what the orthodox Christians were maintaining, they separated themselves from so "carnal" an understanding of the Eucharistic reality. Such a realistic understanding of what the Christians were saying about the Eucharist was that not only of Gnostic-type fellow Christians but also of pagans, one of whose frequent charges against the Christians was that of cannibalism.[33]

It is evident, then, that both Ignatius and his opponents offer strong evidence for that aspect of the Eucharistic Mystery that would, in later times, be called the Real Presence. It is, moreover, the identity between the crucified and risen Body and the Eucharistic Body that underlies the unity of the Church. Ignatius teaches this explicitly:

> Be careful to observe [only] one Eucharist; for there is only one Flesh of Our Lord Jesus Christ and one cup of union with his Blood, one altar of sacrifice [Gk. *thusiasterion*], as [there is] one bishop with the presbyters and my fellow-servants, the deacons.[34]

With allusions to St. Paul's words in 1 Corinthians 10:17, Ignatius urges his fellow Christians to assemble in common, obeying the bishop, and "breaking one bread that is the medicine of immortality and the antidote against dying that offers life for all in Jesus Christ".[35] In this way, he unites the notions of ecclesial unity, the role of the bishop, and the medicinal and eschatological effects of the Eucharist. It is the "medicine of immortality and the antidote to death", beautiful words serving almost as a synopsis of the teaching of the Lord himself (cf. Jn 6:51, 54–58) and of his apostle (cf. 1 Cor 11:30–32). Important, too, in the above citation is Ignatius' reference to the "altar of sacrifice", the altar, that is,

---

[32] Smyrna, 3. Idem. p. 156.

[33] On the charge of "cannibalism" against the Christians and its significance, cf. below pp. 29, 43.

[34] Philadelphia, 4. Idem, pp. 142–43.

[35] Ephesians, 20. Idem, p. 90.

on which the Eucharist is offered. As did the author(s) of the *Didache*, Ignatius views the Eucharist as a sacrifice, and he uses technical sacrificial language for the Mystery. Indeed, by a kind of metonyomy, Ignatius applies the term "altar of sacrifice" to the Church (cf. Eph 5 and Tralles 7), and "it seems that the conception of the Eucharist as the sacrifice of the Church suggested this designation".[36]

In summary, one may say that St. Ignatius reflects in his letters all the major Eucharistic themes that would appear again and again throughout Christian history. The Eucharist is Jesus himself; it is sacrifice, thanksgiving, the cause of the unity of the Church, spiritual medicine, pledge of Resurrection, and model for Christians to imitate. The only later theme not to be found explicitly in Ignatius is that concerning the change that takes place in the elements of bread and wine, the change, that is, that would in subsequent Catholic theology be called transubstantiation by which they become the Flesh and Blood of Christ. Ignatius nowhere mentions such a change. Yet, as one non-Catholic theologian has justly observed, he came close to doing so.[37]

The First Chorus

St. Justin Martyr

St. Justin was born about 110 A.D. in Palestine. He was converted to Christianity around 135 and turned his skills as a philosopher to a defense of the Faith. In the year 150 he wrote his great *Apology*. Although he was not an outstanding writer (his periodic Greek style tends to use what we would call "run-on" sentences), the work is of great interest because we find in it our first extant description of the Mass as it was celebrated in Rome in the second century.

[36] Quasten, *Patrology* I, p. 66.
[37] Pelikan, I, p. 167.

The First Apology

(65) After we have washed in this way the one who has believed and has assented to our doctrine, we bring him to the place where those who are called brethren are assembled, in order that we may offer heartfelt prayers in common for ourselves and for the one who has been illuminated, and for all others in every place, so that, now that we have learned the truth, we may be counted worthy, doing good works and obeying the Commandments, to be saved with an everlasting salvation. Having finished the prayers, we greet one another with a kiss. There is then brought to the one who presides over the brethren bread and a cup of water and a cup of wine mixed with water; and, taking them, he gives praise and glory at great length to the Father of the universe, through the name of the Son and of the Holy Spirit, because he has considered us worthy of these things. And when he has concluded the prayers and thanksgiving, all the people present cry out saying Amen. This word *Amen* in the Hebrew means "Let it be". And when the one who is presiding has given thanks, and all the people have cried out, those whom we call deacons give the bread and wine and water over which the thanksgiving was made [lit., "the eucharistized bread and wine and water"] to be received by each of those present, and then they carry it to those who are absent.

(66) This food we call Eucharist, which no one is allowed to share except the one who believes that our teaching is true, and who has been washed with the washing that is for the remission of sins, and unto regeneration, and so lives as Christ has handed down. For we do not receive these as common bread and common drink; but just as Jesus Christ our Savior, having been made flesh by the word of God, had both flesh and blood for our salvation, so likewise have we learned that the food over which thanks has been given by the prayer of the word which comes from him, and by which our blood and flesh are nourished through a change [Gk. *kata metabolen*], is the Flesh and Blood of the same incarnate Jesus. For the Apostles in the memoirs composed by them and that are called Gospels have thus handed on what was commanded them; namely, that Jesus took bread, and when he had given thanks, said, "Do this in remembrance of me; this is my Body"; and that, in like manner, having taken the cup and given thanks, he said, "This is

my Blood", and gave it to them alone. The wicked devils have handed on the same thing to be done in the mysteries of Mithras; for you either know or can learn that bread and a cup of water are set forth with certain incantations when one is being initiated in the rites.

(67) After these things [are done], we continually remember them among ourselves; and the wealthy among us help the needy; and we are always in harmony. And we bless the Maker of all through his Son Jesus Christ and through the Holy Spirit for all the things that we have eaten. On the day called Sunday all who live in cities or in the country assemble in one place, and the memoirs of the Apostles or the writings of the prophets are read, as long as time permits. Then, when the reader has ceased, the one who presides instructs with his word and admonishes and exhorts us to imitate these good things. Then we all rise together and pray; and, as we said before, when our prayer is ended, bread and wine and water are brought, and the one who presides in like manner offers prayers and thanksgivings according to his ability, and the people cry out saying Amen; and there is a distribution to each, and a sharing in that over which thanks has been given, and through the deacons they are sent to the absent. Those who are rich and willing give as seems right to each of them, and what is collected is deposited with the one who presides. He helps the orphans and widows and those who, because of sickness or any other cause, are in need, as well as those who are in prison or who are visitors among us, and then all in need. Sunday is the day on which we all hold our common assembly, because it is the first day, the one on which God, changing darkness and matter, made the world; and Jesus Christ our Savior rose from the dead on that day; for they crucified him on the day before that of Kronos [Saturday]; and on the day after Saturday, which is the day of the sun, having appeared to his Apostles and disciples, he taught them these things that we have submitted for all of you to examine.[38]

[38] Justin Martyr, *The First Apology*, 65–67. Greek text and a Latin translation are found in J. Th. Eques de Otto, ed., *Justini, Phil. et Mar., Opera,* Tome I, vol. 1, pp. 176–89.

A careful reading of Justin's account will help one to discern the structure of the Mass so familiar to us: the coming together of the faithful; the Biblical readings, including the Gospels, which Justin calls the "memoirs of the Apostles"; the homily; the Intercessions or Prayer of the Faithful; the Kiss of Peace; the bringing forward of the gifts (bread, wine, and water); the Prayer of the Celebrant (later called the Canon or Eucharistic Prayer), which ends with the Amen of the faithful; the reception of Communion; and, of course, the collection.

It is not clear whether the Eucharistic Prayer offered by the celebrant already had some fixed form or whether it was composed more or less spontaneously by the celebrant. Some would interpret the words "according to his ability", which are used in reference to the celebrant's prayer, as indicating spontaneity. This is surely possible, but they may simply mean that, as we would say, "he put his heart and soul into it".[39] Whether spontaneous or fixed, it would appear that the Lord's words of Institution were used, since Justin explicitly cites them in the context of the thanksgiving prayer offered over the bread and wine. This thanksgiving prayer brings it about that the bread and wine are no longer "common bread" and "common drink" but the very Body and Blood of Christ, which then nourish our body and blood. This nourishment, says Justin, takes place "through a change", by which he would seem to be referring to the digestive processes by which the Eucharistic Mystery is assimilated by the believer. It is interesting to note, however, that the Greek word *metaballo* that Justin uses in this context will soon be found used to describe what takes place in the elements themselves when they become the Lord's Body and Blood. From its use in the context of digestion, one is able to gather some of the significance the word will have when used of the change that takes place in the bread and wine when they are sanctified or consecrated. From the word *metaballo* we

[39] Eques de Otto, op. cit., n. 10, p. 187, understands it as being the equivalent of the celebrant's putting "his heart and soul" into the prayer.

derive our English word metabolism, which *Webster's Dictionary* describes as "the chemical and physical processes continuously going on in living organisms". It is a process that involves a total change in the elements undergoing the process as they are assimilated in the human body. The elements lose their own being or reality and become part of the organism into which they are absorbed. This is the very sense apparently intended by Justin. *Metaballo* will carry the same realistic sense when it comes to describe what happens to the elements of bread and wine when the all-powerful and creative Spirit of God is invoked over them.

St. Justin also has references to the sacrificial aspect of the Eucharist. In his *Dialogue with Trypho the Jew,* he writes:

> Concerning the sacrifices once offered by you Jews, God, as I have already said, has spoken through Malachi the prophet, who was one of the Twelve [minor prophets]: "I have no pleasure in you," says the Lord, "and I do not accept your sacrifices from your hands, because from the rising of the sun to its setting my Name has been glorified among the Gentiles. And in every place incense and a pure sacrifice are offered to my Name, because my Name is great among the Gentiles, says the Lord, while you have profaned it" (Malachi 1:10–12). Already, then, did he prophesy about those sacrifices that are offered to him in every place by us Gentiles, speaking, that is, about the Bread of the Eucharist and the cup of the Eucharist. And he added that his Name is glorified by us and profaned by you.[40]

The Eucharist, then, has replaced the sacrifices of the Temple in Jerusalem, a replacement, says Justin, that was already predicted by the prophet Malachi. This appeal to Malachi was something done very early by Christians, since, as seen above, it is already referred to in the *Didache.* After Justin's time it became a kind of "proof text" for the prediction of the Eucharistic Sacrifice, and one often mentioned by the Fathers of the Church.

---

[40] Justin, *Dialogus cum Tryphone,* 41; Eques de Otto, op. cit., pp. 138–39.

St. Irenaeus

St. Irenaeus, the Bishop of Lyons, France, was born around 130 A.D., probably in the city of Smyrna in modern-day Turkey. He himself tells us that it was there, as a young boy, that he was accustomed to listen to the preaching of St. Polycarp, the disciple of the Apostle John. Having become Bishop of Lyons, he wrote his great work, the *Adversus Haereses*,[41] in the 180s and 190s. In it he speaks of the Eucharist as follows.

(Bk. V, 2, 2) Vain in every respect are they who reject the entire dispensation [Lat. *dispositionem;* Gk. *oikonomian*] of God, and deny the salvation of the flesh, and spurn its regeneration, saying that it is not capable of incorruption. But if this flesh is not saved, then neither did the Lord redeem us by his Blood, nor is the cup of the Eucharist the Communion of his Blood, or the bread that we break the Communion of his Body. For blood can only come from veins and flesh, and whatever else makes the human substance. Having truly become this human substance, the Word of God redeemed us by his own Blood, as his Apostle says: "In him we have redemption through his Blood, the remission of sins" (Col 1:14). And because we are his members and are nourished by means of the creation—a creation that he himself offers to us, making the sun to rise and letting it rain as he wills—he has declared that the cup that is taken from creation is his own Blood, from which he makes our blood increase, and he has decreed that the bread, taken from creation, is his own Body, by means of which our bodies grow.

3. When, therefore, the cup that has been mixed and the bread that has been made receive the Word of God and become the Eucharist and the Body of Christ [Gk. *artos epidechetai ton logon tou*

---

[41] *Adversus Haereses,* V, 2, 2–3. The critical text of the Latin and the surviving Greek fragments are to be found in *Irenée de Lyon: Contre les Hérésies,* Livre V, vol. 153 of *Sources Chrétiennes,* pp. 28–32.

Theou kai ginetai eucharistia kai sōma Christou], [42] from which the substance of our flesh is increased and supported, how can they affirm that the flesh is incapable of receiving the gift of God, which is life eternal, which flesh is nourished from the Body and Blood of the Lord and is a member of him? . . . And just as the vine planted in the ground fructifies in its season, and as a grain of wheat falling into the earth and decomposing rises with manifold increase by the Spirit of God who contains all things and then, through the wisdom of God, serves for the use of men, and having received the Word of God become the Eucharist [Gk. *kai proslambanomena ton logon tou Theou eucharistia ginetai;* Latin, . . . *et percipientia verbum Dei Eucharistia fiunt*], which is the Body and Blood of Christ; so also our bodies, having been nourished by this Eucharist and then placed in the earth and suffering decomposition there, shall rise at their time, the Word of God granting them resurrection unto the glory of God the Father.

Irenaeus has another important passage referring to the Eucharist in Book IV of his *Adversus Haereses.*

---

[42] In the translation we have followed the text of the Greek of fragment no. 4, which is found in St. John Damascene. The Latin reads: "panis percipit verbum Dei et fit Eucharistia sanguinis et corporis Christi". Idem, p. 34.

On this crucial sentence, Jurgens (1, p. 104, n. 68) makes the following pertinent observations: "A very considerable theological point hinges somewhat upon whether we spell *word* with a capital or a lowercase *W*. If the passage be read with a lowercase *W*, the *word of God* will refer to the words of institution, and the passage will readily admit of interpretation in accord with the Catholic doctrine of transubstantiation; if with a capital *W*, however, the *Word of God* must be the eternal and personal Word, and the passage will be more in accord with the concept of impanation, which Catholic theology rejects." He holds that it should be read with an uppercase *W* and notes, to support his contention, that the Greek *epidechetai* "might as readily be translated *receives in addition* or *admits of*". Richardson, p. 388, also employs the capital *W*.

Both Jurgens and Richardson are working from the critical edition done by W. W. Harvey in 1857. The critical edition found in the *Sources Chrétiennes* employs the lowercase *w* (or *logos* for the Greek and *verbum* for the Latin) and defends its editorial position in op. cit., vol. 152, in its note for p. 35, n. 2. In the translation I have followed this decision and reasoning, and this is reflected in the text.

Therefore the offering [Gk. *prosphora*] which the Lord taught to be offered throughout the whole world is considered by God a pure sacrifice [Gk. *thusia*] and is acceptable to him[43] (cf. Malachi 1:10–12).

Again, moreover, how do they [i.e., heretics] say that the flesh will end in corruption and not receive life, that flesh that is nourished by the Body and Blood of the Lord? Therefore let them either change their opinion or cease to assert such things. Our opinion is in conformity with the Eucharist, and the Eucharist confirms our opinion. . . . Just as the bread from the earth, receiving the invocation of God [Gk. *artos proslambomenos ten epiklesin tou Theou*], is no longer common bread but rather the Eucharist consisting of two things, the earthly and the heavenly, so our bodies, receiving the Eucharist, are no longer corruptible but have the hope of resurrection to eternal life.[44]

It can readily be seen that, in his writing, Irenaeus is striving to answer the arguments of those Gnostics who deny the value of the body and consider it unworthy of resurrection on the Last Day. This tendency is the one already combated by Ignatius, although it had, by the time of Irenaeus, come to full flower. And, just as Ignatius has proclaimed the Eucharist "medicine of immortality" and "antidote to death", so Irenaeus uses the Church's doctrine on the Eucharist to defend the value of the human body and its vocation to everlasting resurrection. The bread and wine of creation, says Irenaeus, become [Gk. *ginetai*] the very Body and Blood of Christ. Stating this, he is the first to mention explicitly the change that takes place in the bread and wine when they become Eucharist. By this change, earthly creation is raised to a new dignity in order to become the food and drink of Christians. Since this is the case, Irenaeus asks rhetorically, who can possibly deny that, having given Christian bodies so great a dignity, God will also give them eternal life. "Our bodies, receiving the Eucharist, are no longer corruptible but have the hope of resurrection to eternal life." By

---

[43] *Adversus Haereses,* IV, 18, 1. Op. cit., vol. 100, p. 596.
[44] *Adversus Haereses,* IV, 18, 5. Op. cit., vol. 100, pp. 611–12.

his words Irenaeus is urging his readers to remember the teaching of Jesus himself: "Whoever eats my Flesh and drinks my Blood has eternal life, and I will raise him up at the last day" (Jn 6:54). Thus, following the Lord and Ignatius, Irenaeus begins the centuries-long meditation on the "fruits of the Eucharist", i.e., the consequences or results that accrue to the person who has received the Eucharist worthily.

Irenaeus tells us that the dignity conferred on the bread and wine that makes them become the Body and Blood of Christ is something that occurs when the bread and wine "receive the word of God". A careful reading of Irenaeus reveals that the "word of God" received by the bread and wine is a reference to the *epiclesis,* the invocation of the Spirit. In Book V, he writes of the bread and wine: "Having received the word of God, it becomes the Eucharist" (Gk. *kai proslambanomena ton logon tou Theou eucharistia ginetai*). In Book IV, he has already used the identical phrase, with one significant difference. There he wrote: "The bread, receiving the invocation of God" [Gk. *artos proslambomenos ten epiklesin tou Theou*]. The word *epiclesis* (the invocation of the Spirit) is used instead of *logos* (word) but quite evidently carries the same significance. Receiving the word of God and receiving the invocation are equivalent terms for Irenaeus. The sense of Irenaeus' statements then is: the bread and wine receive the *w*ord of God in order to become the Body and Blood of the *W*ord of God.

St. Hilary of Poitiers

St. Hilary (c. 315–68) is best known as the Western Church's great opponent to Arianism and for *De Trinitate,* his work on the Trinity. He has left us in that work several rich passages that refer to the divinization of our nature by the share given to us in Christ's nature through the Eucharist.

If indeed the Word has become Flesh and if indeed we receive the Word made Flesh in the Eucharist [*cibo dominico*], how can it be thought that he does not remain in us by his nature since, by

becoming man, he took to himself our fleshy nature in an inseparable way and has mingled his fleshy nature with his divine nature
to be communicated to us in the Sacrament? Truly, then, we are all
one, because the Father is in Christ and Christ is in us. Therefore,
whoever denies that the Father is, by nature, in Christ must first
deny that he is by nature in Christ or Christ by nature in him.
. . . Therefore, if Christ truly assumed the flesh of our body and if
Christ is truly that man born of Mary, and if we truly receive the
Flesh of his Body in the Mystery, how is anyone going to assert
that we are speaking merely of a union of wills . . . ?

About the truth of his Flesh and Blood there is left no room for
doubt. For by the Lord's own word and by our faith [we know]
that it is truly flesh and truly blood. And when we have received
and drunk these realities it comes about that we are in Christ and
Christ in us. Is this not the truth? Let it happen that those who
deny that Christ is God deny this also. He is in us through his
Flesh, and we are in him, and that by which we are with him is
in God.[45]

The *Mystagogic Catechesis*

From the Church in Jerusalem of the late fourth or very early fifth
centuries there survive a series of five catechetical sermons apparently
given to the recently baptized. The authorship of these talks has
always been disputed, sometimes heatedly, but most commentators,
attribute them to St. Cyril of Jerusalem or to his immediate

---

[45] St. Hilary of Poitiers, *De Trinitate*, 8, 13 and 14; *PL*, 10, 246–47.
Reflections like those of St. Hilary on our divinization because of the Eucharist are also found in St. Cyril of Alexandria's *Commentary on the Gospel of John*,
which was written around 428. Commenting on the text "I in you, and you in
me, that they may be perfected in truth", he wrote: "The Son as man is in us
bodily, mixed and united with us through the mystic Eucharist [Gk. *sunanchir-
namenos te kai sunenoumenos di eulogias tes mustiches*]" (*PG*, 74, 564). The whole
of chap. 11 of Book XII of this commentary is an exposition of how the
Eucharist makes the Church Christ's Body and makes us become one with the
Father (*PG*, 74, 557–62).

successor, John.[46] For our purposes, the question of authorship is of secondary importance, since the general agreement on their date of composition and their origin allows us to see in them an expression of the Eucharistic faith of the oldest Christian See at a time when, because of Constantine, the Christian Church had become a recognized participant in the society of the Roman Empire. The fourth and fifth catechetical lectures treat of the Eucharist, and from them the following selections are drawn.

(1) . . . Therefore, when he has spoken and says about the bread, "This is my Body", who will have the nerve to doubt any longer? And, when he affirms clearly, "This is my Blood", who will then doubt, saying that it is not his Blood?

(2) Once, by his own will, he changed water into wine at Cana of Galilee; is he not worthy of belief when he changes [Gk. *metabalon*] wine into blood? . . .

(3) Therefore with all confidence we receive this as the Body and Blood of Christ. For in the type [Gk. *tupo*] of bread the Body is given to you, and in the type of wine the Blood is given to you, so that, partaking of the Body and Blood of Christ, you may become one Body and one Blood with Christ. And so we become Christ-bearers, when his Body and his Blood have been diffused in our members. Thus, according to the Blessed Peter, we become "partakers of the Divine Nature" (2 Pet 1:4).

(4) At the time when Christ was speaking to the Jews, he said, "Unless you eat my Flesh and drink my Blood, you do not have life in you." They, not understanding his words spiritually and being scandalized, went away thinking that the Savior was asking them to eat flesh [Gk. *sarkophagian*].

(5) In the Old Covenant there were the loaves of proposition, but they, being of the Old Covenant, have come to an end. In the New Covenant there is a heavenly bread and a cup of salvation

---

[46] A critical edition of the *Mystagogic Catechesis* can be found in the *Sources Chrétiennes* series, vol. 126. There as well (pp. 18–40) one can read a dispassionate discussion concerning the problem of authorship, which, although generally favorable to the arguments that support authorship by Cyril, concludes that we cannot be certain.

that sanctify soul and body. For, as the bread exists for the body, so the Word is in harmony with the soul.

(6) Therefore do not consider them as bare bread and wine; for, according to the declaration of the Master, they are Body and Blood. If even the senses suggest this to you [viz., that they are bare bread and wine], let faith reassure you. Do not judge the reality by taste but, having full assurance from faith, realize that you have been judged worthy of the Body and Blood of Christ.

. . .

(9) Having learned these things, you have complete certitude that the visible bread is not bread [Gk. *hōs ho phainomenos artos ouk artos estin*], even if it is such to the taste, but the Body of Christ; and the visible wine [Gk. *ho phainomenos oinos ouk oinos estin*] is not wine, even if taste thinks it such, but the Blood of Christ. You know that it was of this which David sang of old, saying, "Bread strengthens the heart of man, and his face is joyful with oil" (Ps 104:15).[47]

Notable in these selections from the fourth Catechesis are various elements common to the writers of both the Eastern and Western Churches during the fourth and fifth centuries. In addition to the ever-present challenge offered by the Scriptural reading of John 6:52 ("Then the Jews began to argue sharply among themselves, 'How can this man give us his flesh to eat?'"), there still remains the Christian sensitivity to the pagan charges of cannibalism. Both factors were sufficient warrant for the Christian preacher to stress the spiritual nature of Christ's words, without, however, reducing their meaning to the merely symbolic. The preacher of the *Mystagogia* in Jerusalem tries to achieve this balance in several ways. He recalls the scandal that the Lord's words provoked among those who heard him and points out that they did not have faith sufficient to understand that he was not speaking of cannibalism (which is what the Greek *sarkophagian* intends to say); he reminds his hearers that the bread and wine are received "as" (Gk. *hos*) the Body and Blood "in the type of bread" (Gk. *typos-*

---

[47] *Mystagogic Catechesis*, 1–6, 9, in *Sources Chrétiennes*, 126, pp. 134–39, 144.

typo), an expression about which comment will be made later. Having combated such a misunderstanding of the Lord's words, the catechist, however, speaks in very realistic language of the Mystery. The visible bread is not bread and the visible wine is not wine, despite what the senses say.[48] What is present is actually the Body and Blood of the Lord. Here we find by anticipation that which would be later expressed by Aquinas in the hymn *Adoro Te: "Visus, tactus, gustus in te fallitur, sed auditu solo tuto creditur"* ("sight, touch, and taste are here deceived; only hearing is safely believed").

Moreover, the Jerusalem catechist goes beyond a simple affirmation of the Presence. Unlike the oil of chrism, of which the words "type" and "antitype" are also used (cf. *Mystagogic Catechesis,* III, 1, 7) and which, by an explicit comparison with the Eucharist (*Mystagogic Catechesis,* III, 3), is even spoken of as "visible oil" (Gk. *to men phainomeno muro*) that is not "mere oil" (Gk. *muron ouk eti psilon*), the Eucharistic elements are said to be not only "sanctified by the invocation of the Holy Spirit" but also changed in a manner not attributed to the chrism. The Eucharistic change is compared with what the Lord did to the water at Cana of Galilee, where a change of *kind* took place; one thing was changed into another. And the comparison is emphasized by the use in both cases of the same verb, the Greek *metaballo* (to change, transform), which is never used by the catechist when referring to the water of Baptism or to the sacred chrism. Although the language is more refined philosophically than the catechist's, to speak of a "substantial

---

[48] In line with the catechist's use of the word in the *Mystagogic Catechesis,* I, 4, where he speaks of the West as the "place of visible darkness" (Gk. *Epeide tou phainomenou skotous topos . . .*), I have translated *ho phainomenos artos,* etc., in paragraph 9 as "visible bread" and "visible wine". I am convinced, however, that Quasten's translation ("That what seems bread is not bread . . . and what seems wine is not wine"; *Patrology,* 3, p. 375) as well as that of the French in *Sources Chrétiennes,* vol. 126 ("ce qui paraît du pain . . . ce qui paraît vin n'est pas du vin") more accurately capture the sense of paragraph 9, viz., "what appears to be bread is not bread . . . what appears to be wine is not wine".

change", a change in the elements of bread and wine, expresses accurately what is being taught.[49]

The fifth sermon of the *Mystagogic Catechesis* is in effect an extended commentary on the liturgical celebration of the Eucharist as it was enacted in the late fourth century in the Church at Jerusalem. The commentary begins at that part of the liturgy where the celebrant, presumably having received the offerings of bread and wine, washed his hands. It then proceeds to comment on each part of the Eucharistic Prayer in the following order:

1. The Kiss of Peace
2. The Dialogue or Invitation ["Lift up your hearts"; "We have lifted them to the Lord"; "Let us give thanks to the Lord"; "It is right and just"]

---

[49] Quasten writes: "It is in his Eucharistic doctrine that Cyril makes a more definite advance on his predecessors. He expresses himself more clearly.... According to Cyril this Real Presence is brought about by a changing of the substances of the elements, and thus he is the first theologian to interpret this transformation in the sense of a transubstantiation" (*Patrology*, 3, p. 375). The commentary in the *Sources Chrétiennes*, 126, p. 136, cites the Quasten remark and notes that he speaks judiciously. The editor of the English translation in *The Fathers of the Church* series (cf. bibliography under McCauley and Stephenson), who used the *Sources Chrétiennes* edition and so presumably was aware of the reference to Quasten, nowhere averts to Quasten's remarks as he offers an interpretation of the *Mystagogia*'s teaching, which defends the simultaneous Presence of the Body and Blood of Christ and the bread and wine (*The Works of Saint Cyril of Jerusalem*, vol. 2, n. 21, pp. 185–86, and appended note C, pp. 186ff.). This translation was published in 1970 and, for all the erudition evidenced in the notes, manifests a polemical intent vis-à-vis the notion of change that is captured in the final remarks: "Other Fathers, however, from ca. 380, use language hardly if at all distinguishable from that of transubstantiation: transelement, *metousioun, metastoicheioun, metarrhythmizein*, suggesting a change in what we would call the invisible atomic or nuclear structure of the bread—a regrettable concession, one may think, to the literalist piety of the simpler faithful" (op. cit., pp. 189–90). If transubstantiation is understood by the author to mean a change in the "invisible atomic or nuclear structure", then he has misunderstood not only the *Mystagogia* and the other Fathers but the doctrine of transubstantiation as well.

3.   A Thanksgiving Prayer, which ends with the *Sanctus*
4.   The *Epiclesis*

When we have sanctified ourselves through these spiritual hymns, we beg God, the Lover of mankind, to send the Holy Spirit upon what has been set forth, so that he may make the bread the Body of Christ and the wine the Blood of Christ; for whatever the Holy Spirit touches is sanctified and changed [Gk. *metabebletai*]. [50]

5.   Prayer of the Faithful

Then, after the spiritual sacrifice [Gk. *ten pneumatiken thusian*], our unbloody worship [Gk. *ten anaimakton latreian*], has been accomplished over that sacrifice of propitiation, we beg God for the common peace of the Church. [51]

6.   Commemoration of the Saints and of the Dead

Then we make remembrance of those who have fallen asleep, and do so first of all of the patriarchs, the prophets, the Apostles, and the martyrs so that, by their prayers and intercessions, God may favorably accept our prayer. Then we pray for all the holy Fathers and bishops who have fallen asleep and for all those in general among us who have fallen asleep. We do this trusting that it will be of great benefit to the souls for whom our prayer is offered while the holy and awesome sacrifice is present [Gk. *tes hagias kai phrikodestates prokeimenes thusias*].

I want to convince you by an example, since I know that many are saying, "What good is it for a soul with or without sins to be remembered at the Eucharistic offering once that soul has departed from this world?" Well, if a king has exiled some people who have offended him, and then their relatives, making a crown, present it to him on behalf of those exiled, will he not grant a remission of their punishment? In like manner we also, offering our prayers to him on behalf of those who have fallen asleep, even if they be sinners, although we are making no crown, are offering the slain Christ [Gk. *alla Christon esphagiasmenon huper ton hemeteron hamar-*

---

[50] *Mystagogic Catechesis,* V, 7; op. cit., p. 154.
[51] *Mystagogic Catechesis,* V, 8; op. cit., p. 156.

tematon prospheromen], propitiating God, the Lover of mankind, for ourselves and for them.[52]

The commemoration of the dead, with its either implicit or explicit belief in the doctrine of Purgatory, is found in other ancient texts as well as in this one from the Jerusalem catechesis. From a time earlier in the fourth century than the *Mystagogic Catechesis* we have the *Euchologion* or *Sacramentary* of Serapion, who was Bishop of Thumis in Egypt. This Sacramentary probably dates from ca. 350 A.D. and contains the prayer:

> We beg you also for all the dead whose memory we now keep [then the names of the dead are mentioned]: make these souls holy, for you know them all; make holy all those who sleep in the Lord [Gk. *hagiason pasas tas en kurio koimetheisas*] and number them with all your holy angels [lit., powers, *dunamesin*] and give them a place and a mansion in your kingdom.[53]

A similar reference is found in *Homily XV* of Theodore of Mospsuestia (d. 428).[54]

7. The Our Father
8. Communion

After these things, you hear a chanter invite you with divine music to the Communion in the holy Mysteries, singing, "Taste and see that the Lord is good" (Ps 34:8). Do not entrust your judgment to the bodily senses but rather to undoubted faith. For when you are eating, you are not eating bread and wine but the antitype of the Body and Blood of Christ.

Therefore when you come to receive, do not approach with hands extended and fingers open wide. Rather make of your left hand a throne for your right as it is about to receive the King, and receive the Body of Christ in the fold of your hand, responding,

---

[52] *Mystagogic Catechesis*, V, 10–11; op. cit., pp. 158–59.

[53] "Preces Missae Euchologii Serapionis", in Quasten, *Monumenta*, I, p. 63.

[54] Theodore of Mopsuestia, *Homily XV (First on the Mass)*, 43, *Studi e Testi*, pp. 527–29; Mingana, p. 105.

"Amen"... Take care that you lose not even one piece of that which is more precious than gold or precious stones.[55]

St. Gregory of Nyssa

St. Gregory was born in Asia Minor around 335, and was a younger brother of St. Basil. In 371 he became bishop of Nyssa and played a prominent role in the First Council of Constantinople (381), which completed the work of the Council of Nicaea. He died in 394. *The Great Catechism,* from which the following sections on the Eucharist are taken, was probably written soon after the Council of Constantinople.

Having spoken of Baptism in the previous chapters, St. Gregory treats of the Eucharist in Chapter XXXVII of *The Great Catechism.*[56]

But since human nature is twofold, composed of body and soul, it is necessary that both of these make contact with the author of life... (3) What then is the remedy [for the body]? it is none other than that Body that has been shown to be stronger than death and has become [the source] of life for us. Just as a little yeast—as the Apostle says [1 Cor 5:6]—assimilates the whole batch of dough to itself, so that Body raised by God to immortality, when it enters our bodies, changes [Gk. *metapoiei*] and transforms [Gk. *metatithesin*] them into itself... (4)... Since only the Body in which the Divinity became incarnate has received the grace [of immortality] and since it has been demonstrated that it is not possible for our body to become immortal unless it share in incorruptibility through communion with the Immortal Body, it is necessary to consider how it is possible for that One Body, although it is distributed continually to so many thousands of the faithful throughout the world, to remain whole when it is allotted to each individual through a portion while still remaining whole in itself... (8)... Since each body gets its existence from nourishment, from eating and

---

[55] *Mystagogic Catechesis,* V, 20–21; op. cit., pp. 168–73.

[56] For the text of *The Great Catechism,* we have used J. R. Strawley's critical text of 1903 as found in *Grégoire de Nysse: Discours Catéchètique.*

drinking ... (9) so, if a person sees bread, he sees, in a certain sense, the human body, because the bread that enters the body becomes the body itself. So, too, the Body into which God entered, by being nourished with bread, was in like manner identical with the bread.... This Body, by the indwelling of God the Word, has been changed [Gk. *metapoiethe*] to divine dignity. Rightly then do we believe that the bread consecrated by the word of God has been changed [Gk. *metapoieisthai*] into the Body of God the Word. (10) For that Body was bread in power, but it has been sanctified by the dwelling there of the Word, who pitched his tent in the flesh. The change that elevated to divine power the bread that had been transformed into that Body causes something similar now. In that case, the grace of the Word sanctified that Body whose material being [Gk. *ho ek tou artou he sustasis en*] came from bread and was, in a certain sense, bread itself. In this case, the bread "is sanctified by God's word and by prayer" [1 Tim 4:5], as the Apostle says, not becoming the Body of the Word through our eating but by being transformed [Gk. *metapoioumenos*] immediately into the Body by means of the word, as the Word himself said, "This is my Body".... (12) ... He shares himself with every believer through that Flesh whose material being [Gk. *sustasis*] comes from bread and wine ... in order to bring it about that, by communion with the Immortal, man may share in incorruption. He gives these things through the power of the blessing by which he transelements [Gk. *metastoikeiosas*] the nature of the visible things [Gk. *ton phainomenon ten phusin*]. [57]

What St. Gregory is saying is this: a man is what he eats, since food (in this case, bread and wine) nourishes the body. Indeed, by metonymy, the body is the bread and wine it eats and drinks. This was true even of the Body of the incarnate Word. Just as the union of the divine and human in Christ sanctified his humanity, so that union sanctified the bread and wine that his Body assimilated, uniting them with the Divine. And, just as he assimilated bread and wine in this way during his earthly life, so he now assimilates the Eucharistic elements into himself and then feeds us with what

---

[57] Gregory of Nyssa, *The Great Catechism,* 37, pp. 173–83.

has become himself through assimilation. Thereby he passes on to us the immortality that is proper to his risen and glorified Body.

The thought expressed by St. Gregory is reflected in a poem entitled "Transubstantiation" by Francis Thompson.

> Man's body was ordained to tell
> The tale of this sweet miracle.
> For bread and wine, and all his food,
> Are turned to Flesh, are turned to Blood;
> And all men, at their common feasts,
> Are transubstantiating priests.
>
> Christ, as in Cana's miracle,
> Generous, his creatures would excel,
> So gave to men ordained the power
> With his own Flesh and Blood to dower
> The altar Bread, the altar Wine—
> O daring plagiary divine!
>
> Then walk awarely mid the corn
> That will as human flesh be worn—
> 'Tis holy ground that thou dost tread.
> And be indeed a worshipper,
> Discerning in our daily bread
> The Eucharist's biographer.[58]

The Word's assimilation of the Eucharistic elements to himself— an assimilation by which they become his Body and Blood—is described by the forceful Greek word *metastoikeiosas*, transelementation. It actually means a restructuring of the elements, since the Greek *stoikeia* means "fundamental elements or principles". Stone's conclusion on this matter is still valid:

> The idea is parallel to, but different from, the later Western doctrine of transubstantiation, according to which the change is in the "substance" of the elements. The differences between St.

---

[58] Francis Thompson, quoted in Terence L. Connolly's *Francis Thompson: In His Paths*, pp. 71–72.

Gregory's view and this later doctrine, real as they are, pertain rather to different methods of philosophical thought than to essential theological principle.[59]

Gregory also clearly teaches that this "transelementation" occurs immediately at the Consecration, "through the power of the blessing", as he phrases it. The fact that this happens at the Consecration and not "through our eating" indicates that it is not the faith of the believer that makes Christ present: his Presence is due to the power of the sanctification or Consecration (the same Greek word, *hagiazo,* can be translated as either of these), apart from the faith of the believer, as later theological reflection will make even clearer.

It should be noted that St. Gregory raises and then sets out to answer the profound question: How is the whole Christ received entirely by the thousands who partake of the Eucharist throughout the world; how, that is, is Christ not divided when the Eucharistic elements are multiplied and subsequently consumed by many? He apparently thought he had answered the question by his explanation of the change that takes place in the elements, i.e., by their total assimilation into the Body of Christ—analogous with the assimilation of bread and wine into his Body while he walked the earth. Although that is surely the beginning of the answer—inasmuch as any answer can be given to what is a strict Mystery and must be accepted on faith—it is not all that later reflection will say. Nonetheless, it is to Gregory's credit that he raised and attempted an explanation of so mysterious an aspect of the Christian's participation in the Eucharist.

[59] Stone, I, p. 104.

The Second Chorus

St. Ambrose

St. Ambrose was born at Trier (today in Germany) between 335 and 340. He became a lawyer and a Roman administrator in Milan. There he was chosen as bishop by popular acclamation, although he was only a catechumen. He thus received all the Sacraments of Initiation and the episcopate within one week. He died in Milan in 397. Ambrose, who may well be the first to refer to the Eucharistic Mystery as the "Mass",[60] has left us two great works that deal with the Eucharist: the *De Sacramentis* and the *De Mysteriis,* both of them published around 390. The following selections are taken from the *De Mysteriis.*

(48) Now consider which is more excellent, the bread of angels [i.e., the manna] or the Flesh of Christ which is indeed the Body of life. That manna was from heaven; this is from above the heavens. The former was from heaven, the latter from the Lord of the heavens; the former was subject to corruption if it was preserved for a second day, the latter foreign to all corruption so that whoever shall have piously tasted it will not be able to experience corruption. For the people of Israel water flowed from the rock; for you Blood flows from Christ. The water satisfied them for a while; Blood washes you for eternity. The Jew drinks and is thirsty again; when you drink you will not be able to thirst. The former was given as an image [*in umbra*]; the latter is given as the reality [*in veritate*].

(49) If that which you marvel at is an image, how much greater is the reality whose image you marvel at? Listen and learn that

---

[60] Ambrose, in *Epistola,* 20, 4 (*PL,* 16, 995), remarks, "I, however, remained at my task and began to offer the Mass" (*Ego tamen mansi in munere, missam facere coepi*). Some would dispute this and say that he is merely speaking of the dismissal of the catechumens. An undisputed reference to the Eucharistic liturgy as "Mass" is found in Gregory of Tours (died 594), who writes of "celebrating daily the solemnity of the Mass" (*celebrans quotidie missarum solemnia*), *PL,* 71, 875.

what was done for the Fathers was an image: "They drank", he says, "from the rock following them, and the Rock was Christ; but with many of them God was not pleased, for they were laid low in the desert. These things moreover were done as a type [*in figura*] for us" (1 Cor 10:4–6). You have come to know the more excellent things, for the light is more excellent than the shade, reality more excellent than image, the Body of the Giver more excellent than the manna from heaven.

(50) Perhaps you will say, "What I see is different from what you speak of; how is it that you assert that I receive the Body of Christ?" And so it still remains for us to prove this. And thus we use manifold examples so that we may prove that this is not what nature formed but what the blessing consecrated [*ut probemus non hoc esse, quod natura formavit, sed quod benedictio consecravit*], and that there is greater power in the blessing than in nature because by the blessing nature itself is changed [*maioremque vim esse benedictionis quam naturae, quia benedictione etiam natura ipsa mutatur*].

(51) [Ambrose then cites the examples of Moses in Exodus 15 and of Elisha in 1 Kings 18, the former making the bitter water sweet by his blessing, the latter making the axe float on the water.]

(52) We note, therefore, that grace is more powerful than nature, even when we are only speaking of the grace that comes from the blessing of a prophet. But if a human blessing had such power so as to be able to change nature, what do we say about the divine Consecration itself in which the very words of Our Lord and Savior are at work? For that Sacrament which you receive is brought about by the word of Christ [*Christi sermone conficitur*]. If the word of Elijah had such power as to call down fire from heaven, will not the word of Christ have the power to change the nature of the elements [*ut species mutet elementorum*]? You have read about the creation of the whole world: "He spoke and they were made; he gave a command and they were created" (Ps 33:9). Therefore can not the word of Christ, which was able to create out of nothing that which did not exist, change those things that do exist into that which they were not? To create new things is no lesser thing than to change natures.

(53) ... It is clear that the Virgin conceived beyond the order of nature. And this that we effect is the Body that comes from the Virgin [*Liquet igitur, quod praeter naturae ordinem virgo generavit. Et*

hoc quo conficimus corpus ex virgine est]. . . . Indeed it is the true Flesh of Christ that was crucified and buried: therefore truly this is the Sacrament of that Flesh [*Vera utique caro Christi, quae crucifixa est, quae sepulta est: vere ergo carnis illius sacramentum est*].

(54) The Lord himself cries out, "This is my Body". Before the blessing of the heavenly words, another species is named; after the Consecration the Body is signified. He himself says that it is his Blood. Before the Consecration it is called something else; after the Consecration it is named Blood. And you say, "Amen", which means "it is true". What the mouth speaks, let the soul confess internally; let the soul experience what speech proclaims.

. . .

(58) What we eat and drink the Holy Spirit has spoken of through the prophet in another place, saying: "Taste and see that the Lord is sweet: blessed is the man who trusts in him" (Ps 34:8). It is Christ in that Sacrament, because it is the Body of Christ. Therefore it is not corporeal food, but spiritual food. And so the Apostle says about its type: "Our fathers ate the spiritual food and drank the spiritual drink"; for the body of God is a spiritual body; the Body of Christ is the body of a divine spirit because Christ is spirit, as we read: "The spirit before our face is Christ the Lord" [Lam 4:20 in the Latin version used by Ambrose]. And we read in the Epistle of Peter, "Christ died for us" (1 Peter 2:21). Finally, this food strengthens our heart, and this drink gives joy to the heart of man, as the prophet has recalled (cf. Ps 103:15).[61]

Having shown how the Eucharist was prefigured in the manna and water given to the Jews in the desert, Ambrose proceeds to strengthen the faith of the Christian who asks, "How can it be Christ, since it only looks like bread and wine?" He appeals to the power of God, who created everything out of nothing, who empowered the prophets by their word to effect wonders in nature, and who caused the Virgin to conceive. From such reminders of God's power, Ambrose draws his conclusions: the power of Christ is greater than that of any prophet; his blessing consecrates

[61] Ambrose, *De Mysteriis; CSEL*, 73, pp. 109–15.

what nature has formed, namely, the bread and wine. Indeed, Christ's blessing is more powerful than nature itself, since, by his blessing, "the nature of the elements itself is changed": bread and wine become his Body and Blood. Ambrose had previously expounded the same teaching in his work *De Fide* (On the Faith), published around 380. Commenting on John 6:55, he wrote there:

> Then he added, "For my Flesh truly is food and my Blood truly is drink." You hear of flesh, you hear of blood, and you are aware of the Sacraments of the Lord's death. . . . For as often as we receive the Sacraments, which, through the Mystery of the sacred prayer, are transfigured [*transfigurantur*] into Flesh and Blood, "we announce the death of the Lord".[62]

The *transfigurantur* means that a thing ceases to be what it was and becomes what it was not. This is the sense already given to the word by Tertullian, who used it when speaking of the Incarnation. Tertullian had written:

> it must be asked how the Word became Flesh. Was he transfigured [*transfiguratus*] into Flesh, or did he put on Flesh? We have to say "put on Flesh", since it is necessary to believe that God is immutable . . . as well as eternal. Transfiguration [*tranfiguratio*] is the making an end of [*interemptio*] what was formerly there: for everything that is transfigured [*transfiguratur*] into something else ceases to be what it was and begins to be what it was not.[63]

Thus, says Ambrose, the sacraments (i.e., the bread and wine) are transfigured into Flesh and Blood. It is a strong expression, and by it Ambrose is affirming the same truth seen in the text from the *De Mysteriis:* a real change in the very nature of the bread and wine—a change so profound that what becomes present is the "Body that comes from the Virgin" and "that was crucified and buried". With this statement, Ambrose teaches the identity between the Eucharist and the natural and glorified Body of Christ, a truth long before witnessed to by St. Ignatius of Antioch.

---

[62] Ambrose, *De Fide,* bk. IV, 10, 124; *CSEL,* 78, 7, p. 201.
[63] Tertullian, *Adversus Praxean,* 27, 6–7, *CCSL,* I, p. 1199.

Some have always interpreted the words that follow in the *De Mysteriis* to be a modification of what Ambrose has just affirmed. For he writes: "Therefore truly this is the Sacrament of that Flesh." His words quite naturally raise the question: Is the Eucharist the Flesh born of Mary, or is it [merely] the Sacrament of that Flesh? Or is there no difference? The difficulty is essentially the same one posed by the terminology of the Greek Fathers, who sometimes speak quite simply of the "Body and Blood of the Lord" and at other times refer to the "figure or type or antitype of the Lord's Body and Blood". As we shall see below, this difficulty did not escape the notice of the Greek Fathers themselves. Already, Ambrose's contemporary, Theodore of Mopsuestia, insists that the Eucharist is not a "type" or symbol, and John Damascene will teach that the Eucharist can only be called a "type" when one is speaking of the elements before the Consecration.

The reflections of Darwell Stone—made after his exhaustive study of the Patristic texts—are still of value as an aid to put the difficulty in context. He wrote:

> Careful attention to the use of the words "figure" and "symbol" in the early Church and to the general teaching of writers who employ these terms in regard to the Eucharist elicits that such a description of the Eucharistic elements does not indicate that they are regarded as, in the modern sense, simply figurative or symbolical of the Body and Blood. Consideration of the idea of their heightened efficacy shows that it does not imply that a change in use and power and effect is alone indicated. Those writers who speak of the elements as "symbols" or as having heightened power are seen also to believe that they are that which they symbolize and convey. This view of the elements as the Body and Blood of Christ is connected in different parts of the Church with the act of Consecration, whether the crucial moment of this be represented as the recitation of the words of Christ, the invocation of God the Word, the invocation of God the Holy Ghost, or the invocation of the Holy Trinity.[64]

[64] Stone, I, p. 131. Stone's conclusions are reaffirmed in our own day by Pelikan, I, pp. 167–70. Speaking of the writings of the second and third

The difficulty may be seen to have arisen from three factors: an effort on the part of the Fathers to combat the pagan charge that the Christians engaged in cannibalism; the theological necessity to account for the fact that Christ was truly present but, to all appearances, the bread and wine also remained; and an inadequacy or fluidity in terminology and in the concepts that lay behind the terminology.

The charge of cannibalistic feasts is one that the Christians had to combat from very early times. Already in the 170s Athenagoras, a contemporary of St. Irenaeus, notes that the pagans are accusing the Christians of celebrating "Thyestean feasts", i.e., dinners like those where the mythological Atreus, motivated by revenge, killed the children of his brother Thyestes and subsequently served them to Thyestes for dinner.[65] "The Christians eat flesh." It can be seen how the Christian doctrine of the Eucharist could lead even the well-intentioned pagan to make this charge against what was, in those days, nothing more than a strange new sect originating in the East. The danger of misunderstanding that was intrinsic to the Mystery was augmented by the reticence with which the Christians surrounded their celebrations. Partly out of reverence for the gifts given to them and partly to protect themselves from false pagan charges, many of the early Christian communities exercised what is called the *disciplina arcani,* a self-imposed discipline in respect to the Mysteries that hid them even from the catechumens. It is for this reason that many of our early references to the Eucharist are found in catechetical instructions given to the newly baptized only during the Easter Vigil, when they were about

---

centuries, Pelikan concludes: "The theologians did not have adequate concepts within which to formulate a doctrine of the Real Presence that evidently was already believed by the Church even though it was not yet taught by explicit instruction or confessed by creeds" (1, p. 168). For a more analytical study that reaches essentially the same conclusion, cf. Henri de Lubac, *Corpus Mysticum,* n. (Appendix) B, pp. 351–57.

[65] Athenagoras, *Supplication [Plea] for Christians,* 3. The Greek and an English translation can be found in William Schoedel, *Athenagoras, Legatio and De Resurrectione,* pp. 8–9.

to receive the Eucharist for the first time. References to this discipline are found frequently in St. Augustine's sermons, indicating that in some places Christian reticence in respect to the Eucharist lasted even into the fifth century.

To all appearances the bread and wine, after the Consecration, remained what they were previously. Even St. Paul had referred to the Eucharist as "this bread and this cup" (cf. 1 Cor 11:26) and as "one loaf" (1 Cor 10:17). Any effort to explain the Eucharist had to account for these facts without simultaneously reducing the Eucharist to a mere symbol. Furthermore, the elements of bread and wine carried with them a rich symbolism that Christians perceived as being an important facet of the Mystery. The process by which bread and wine are made symbolized the unity of the Church: they were part of the material creation, signifying the esteem held for that creation by the Creator: they were food, signifying the sustenance derived from the Eucharist: they reflected the toil and labor of mankind for its daily bread, a toil and labor offered back to God to represent the creature's dependence on him.

Finally, and perhaps most importantly, Christianity needed time to develop the concepts and terminology to express the various levels of the Mystery. The Middle Ages would develop a sacramental terminology that spoke of the *sacramentum tantum,* the *res et sacramentum,* and the *res tantum.* By this they would mean "the sign considered in itself", the "reality that was contained in the sign", and "the reality alone". In respect to the Eucharist, this would lead to calling the bread and wine and the consecratory words the "sign considered in itself"; the Body and Blood of Christ would be the "reality contained in the sign"; and either the Body and Blood of the Lord or the unity of the Church would be spoken of as "the reality alone". The distinctions were somewhat artificial and were not used in the same way by all, but at least they were a way of preserving all the manifold aspects of the doctrine. Lacking such terminology, the Fathers were left to do what they could. Therefore one must study them in a manner that seeks to avoid imposing later categories and language upon them, as well as striving to avoid the danger of reading them only in light of post-Reformation problems concerning the Eucharist. But one must also attempt to take into account *all* that they affirm, without forcing their entire Eucharistic thought into a category suggested by one word or phrase, especially as seen in the light of how we later understand that word or phrase. A careful reading of them will indicate that frequently their references to Eucharist as "Sacrament" or "symbol" or "type-antitype" is simply an anticipation of the later *sacramentum tantum.* They are, that is, merely referring to the sign value of the elements. That the elements, after the Consecration, contained what they signified (the *res et sacramentum* of later theology) was a truth taught by the Fathers in other and various ways. The elements were not "common" bread and wine; they were not "mere" bread and wine; they were not simply what they appeared to be. They were in fact the Body and Blood of the Lord. Indeed, the elements had become something else; they were changed, transelemented. In Ambrose's words, the blessing had changed the nature of the elements.

St. Jerome

The Eucharistic Mystery, then, was the Body of Christ. Indeed, Ignatius and Ambrose explicitly stated what is found implicitly in all the Fathers (with the possible exceptions of Clement of Alexandria and Origen): the Eucharist is the same Body born of Mary, raised on the Cross, and raised into glory. Even the notion of "raised in glory", however, posed questions. Was there a difference between pre-Easter and post-Easter Body? The Gospels themselves indicated some difference, and St. Jerome made explicit mention of it:

> Indeed, the Blood and Flesh of Christ are to be understood in two ways, either that spiritual and divine Flesh and Blood of which he himself said: "My Flesh is real food, and my Blood is real drink" (Jn 6:56) and "Unless you eat my Flesh and drink my Blood, you will not have eternal life"; or that Flesh which was crucified and that Blood which poured forth by the work of the

soldier's lance. According to this distinction, a difference of flesh and blood is also to be understood in the case of the saints, such that one kind is the flesh that will see the salvation of God, another kind that which cannot inherit the Kingdom of God.[66]

Jerome's remark has sometimes been taken as evidence that he did not defend the identity between the Eucharist and the body of Christ born of Mary. Such an assertion is wide of the mark, however. As noted, his observation is concerned with the nature of the change that takes place in a resurrected Body. In fact, his statement is an affirmation that the Eucharistic Body is the risen Body of Christ—a statement fully in harmony with that of St. Ignatius of Antioch. Ignatius, however, simply asserted the identity between the pre- and post-Easter Body of the Lord; Jerome attempted to indicate that there is a difference. Later theology will be able to express the difference as one of *modality,* not of identity. But that clarification awaited further reflection. Meanwhile, that and further questions remained. What, if anything, then differentiated the Eucharistic Body from the risen Body? And how does the Body of Christ that is the Church differ from the Eucharistic and risen Body of the Lord? To all these questions no explicit answer can be found until after the close of the Patristic period. Before then, however, there were other voices yet to be heard.

St. John Chrysostom

Born around 350 and dying in exile from his See, Constantinople, in 407, Chrysostom, contemporary of Ambrose and Augustine, is the great figure of the Eastern Church in the fourth century. His doctrine on the Eucharist was marked by its very realistic references to the Presence of Christ in the Sacrament and to his many references to the sacrificial nature of the Lord's Supper. His words on the theme are abundant. Typical of them are the following

---

[66] Jerome, *Commentary on Ephesians,* chap. I, v. 7; *PL,* 26, 451.

from his *Homily 82 on the Gospel of Matthew,* where he comments on the institution of the Eucharist as found in Matthew 26.

> Let us therefore everywhere be attentive to God. Let us not contradict him although what he says appears to be contrary to our reasoning and understanding. Thus we carry out in the Mysteries not only what appears to our senses but what his words tell us. For his word is not able to deceive; our senses are easily deceived. Because the Word says, "This is my Body", let us be attentive, let us believe, let us look upon him with the eyes of the spirit. For Christ did not give us something sensible; even in the sensible things, all is spiritual. . . . How many there are who still say, "I want to see his shape, his image [Gk. *ton tupon*], his clothing, his sandals." Behold, you do see him, you touch him, you eat him! You want to see his clothing. He gives himself to you, not just to be seen but to be touched, to be eaten, to be received within. . . . Let all of you be ardent, fervent, enthusiastic. If the Jews stood, shoes on, staff in hand, and eating in haste, how much more vigilant should you be. They were about to go to Palestine; . . . you are about to go to heaven.
>
> Therefore let everyone be vigilant. No small punishment hangs over him who communicates unworthily. Think of how angry you become against the traitor and against those who crucified Christ. And so beware lest you yourself be guilty of the Body and Blood of Christ. They killed that all-holy Body; after so many graces you receive him with a stained soul. . . . What purity should that man have who enjoys this sacrifice? How much purer than the rays of the sun should be the hand that touches this Flesh, the mouth which is filled with spiritual fire, the tongue tinted with the awe-inspiring Blood?
>
> . . .
>
> This work does not come about by human power. He who once did these things at the Supper is the One who does them now. We have the ministry of Orders [lit., the order of ministers], but he who makes holy and transforms [Gk. *hagiazon auta kai metaskeuazon*] these things is Christ himself.[67]

[67] John Chrysostom, *In Matthaeum Homil.,* 82, *PG,* 57–58, 741–44.

He gives himself to you, not just to be seen but to be touched, to be eaten." The words are very like those that the Church will later use to refute the heresy of Berengarius. St. John's reverence for the Eucharist manifested itself also in the holiness he expected for the ministers of the Sacrament. Indeed, his concept of the priesthood was an exalted one because of the connection between the sacrament of Orders and the "awe-inspiring Blood" to which it ministered.

> Though the office of the priesthood is exercised on earth, it ranks, nevertheless, in the order of celestial things—and rightly so. It was neither man nor an angel nor an archangel nor any other created power but the Paraclete himself who established this ministry and who ordained that men abiding in the flesh should imitate the ministry of the angels. For that reason it behooves the bearer of the priesthood to be as pure as if he stood in the very heavens amidst those powers. . . . If anyone examine the things which pertain to the workings of grace, he will find them, small as they are, to be of fearsome and awful import; for that which was spoken concerning the Old Law is true also of the New: *for though the former was made glorious, yet in this it is without glory, by reason of the overwhelming glory of the latter* (cf. 2 Cor 3:10). When you see the Lord immolated and lying upon the altar, and the priest bent over that sacrifice praying, and all the people empurpled by that precious Blood, can you think that you are still among men and on earth? Or are you not lifted up to heaven? Is not every carnal affection deposed? Do you not with pure mind and clean heart contemplate the things of heaven?[68]

For Chrysostom the earthly liturgy is itself but a veil that covers a reality taking place in heaven. At times he speaks as if the veil were removed and the Realities are no longer even hidden. The Lord is seen immolated on the altar; the people are stained red, or "empurpled", with the very Blood of the Lord; with pure mind and heart we contemplate the things of heaven. It is, of course, the

---

[68] John Chrysostom, *On the Priesthood,* 3, 4, translated by W. A. Jurgens, *The Priesthood,* pp. 31–32.

language of oratory and of a great orator. Nonetheless, it is language that flows from a conception of the Mysteries that is very "realistic", one in which faith is so strong that it pierces through appearances to grasp what is actually happening. For Chrysostom it is the appearances that are insubstantial; the Realities are concrete, practically visible, and tangible.

St. Augustine

In the Apostolic Letter that Pope John Paul II issued on the occasion of the sixteen-hundredth anniversary of the Baptism of Augustine, the Pope made his own the following words of his predecessor, Paul VI:

> Indeed, over and above the shining example he gives of the qualities common to all the Fathers, it may be said that all the thought currents of the past meet in his works and form the source that provides the whole doctrinal Tradition of succeeding ages.[69]

The statement is hardly an exaggeration. The person and work of Augustine have always played so large a part in the Church's theology, especially in the West, that one can run the risk of overlooking the other Fathers. His thought is so faithful to the Tradition, so rich in insight, so persuasively expressed that, by way of imitation or reaction, he has influenced theologians up to and including our own day. Often men of totally opposed theological positions have appealed to the authority of Augustine to substantiate their own opinions.

In respect to the Eucharist, Augustine has left us a fairly extensive record of the liturgical practices with which he was familiar. This he does in a letter, written around 400, to a friend named Januarius. He records, for example, that the forty days of Lent should be observed, and he finds its meaning rooted in Scripture; that Easter was already celebrated with an octave of eight days;

---

[69] John Paul II, *Augustine of Hippo,* Boston: St. Paul Editions, 1986, p. 1.

that Pentecost was a solemnity (or *sacramentum*), while Christmas was not. While admitting that it is not a universal custom, he encourages daily Eucharist and expresses his personal preference for a noble simplicity in the Liturgy. He also gives it as his opinion that the essentials of the Liturgy are to be governed by the practice of the entire Church, while the nonessentials may vary according to time and place. "For that which is not against faith or good morals should be considered as something indifferent and observed for the sake of social harmony [*societatem*] with those among whom one is living."[70] This principle does not mean that he thought all liturgical or paraliturgical practices were of equal value. He did not, and of some of them he disapproved, but unless they violated the principles of faith and good morals they were to be tolerated. "For the Church of God, situated among much chaff and many weeds, tolerates many things, although she neither approves nor is silent about nor does those things that are contrary to faith and a moral life."[71] Practices that are not sinful or against the Faith but are, nonetheless, abuses or capable of leading to problems with faith and good morals should be changed tactfully. He gives us an example of this in his approach to the "feasts of the dead", a practice common and popular in North Africa in his time. It consisted of devout (sometimes superstitious) Christians visiting the tombs of the dead (especially those venerated as martyrs), holding a prayer service, and having a meal there. In time these meals began to be occasions for the excesses witnessed earlier in the agape meal. In a letter of response to Bishop Aurelius of Carthage, Augustine advises that the practice be eliminated, but in a kindly and gentle manner. "In my opinion it should be done away with, but in a manner that is not severe, or hard or

---

[70] *Epistola 54: Ad Inquisitiones Januarii,* 2; *CSEL,* 34, 1–2, p. 160. "quod enim neque contra fidem neque contra bonos mores esse convincitur, indifferenter habendum et pro eorum inter quos vivitur, societate servandum est."

[71] *Epistola 55: Ad Inquisitiones Januarii,* 19; *CSEL,* 34, 1–2, p. 210. "sed ecclesia dei inter multam paleam multaque zizania constituta multa tolerat et tamen, quae sunt contra fidem vel bonam vitam, nec adprobat nec tacet nec facit."

imperious. Let it be abolished more by teaching than commanding, more by warning than threatening."[72] The entire manner of approach and the principles that he lays down reveal a very wise, tolerant, and prudent man. And his principles in these matters can be said to reflect also the practice of the Church of Rome, willing like Augustine to tolerate that which is not directly a danger to faith or morals. On the other hand, how much useless bickering and how many quarrels that wound charity has the Church witnessed because of liturgical matters down through the centuries, and even in our own day—disputes that arise from a failure to observe the principles set down by the great teacher of the Western Church.

It is to be noted, in the same letter to Bishop Aurelius, that Augustine makes a reference to those sins that make it mandatory not to receive Holy Communion. Drawing Aurelius' attention to Romans 13:13, with its references to orgies and drunkenness (which Augustine applied to the "feast for the dead") and to fornication and impurity (*impudicitiis* in his Latin version), he noted that these last two, by everyone's admission, excluded one from reception of the Eucharist, while the seriousness of the other sins sometimes failed to be recognized.[73]

In respect to the nature of the presence of Christ in the Eucharist, St. Augustine's doctrine has always presented certain difficulties. F. van der Meer, in his renowned study *Augustine the Bishop,* writes:

[72] *Epistola 22*: 5; *CSEL,* 34, 1–2, p. 58. "non ergo aspere, quantum existimo, non duriter, non modo imperioso ista tolluntur, magis docendo quam iubendo, magis monendo quam minando."

[73] *Epistola 22*: 3, *CSEL,* 34, 1–2, p. 56. From the point of view of the history of the Sacrament of Penance it is interesting to note that Augustine apparently does not think that these two sins—which excluded one from reception of the Eucharist—were matter for the public penitential system, as were adultery and murder, for example. They probably were to be submitted to the private penitential system, called *correptio,* a practice of the sacrament like the one we are familiar with.

It is perfectly true, however, that there is nowhere any indication of any awareness of the Real Presence of Christ in the Sacrament,
or that he thought very much about this subject or made it the
object of devotion; that was alien to the people of that age—at any
rate in the West.[74]

That rather strong assertion is not van der Meer's final word on
the matter, because he immediately proceeds to take into account
some strong statements of Augustine that touch upon the Real
Presence. Even then, however, he concludes: "These occasional
flashes are, however, really secondary to the idea which time and
again illumines his mind—namely, that through the eating of
Christ's Body and the drinking of his Blood, we become one with
him and with each other."[75] Indeed, at first glance Augustine
does appear to hold for a merely symbolic presence of Christ in
the Eucharist. Thus, in his letter to Bishop Boniface, written
around 408, we read:

Frequently we speak in such a way as to say, [for example,]
when Easter draws near, "Tomorrow or the next day will be the
Passion of the Lord", and we say this although he suffered many
years ago and although that Passion occurred once and for all.
Likewise on a Sunday we say, "The Lord rose today"—even though
very many years have passed since he rose. Now no one is so inept
as to call us liars when we speak this way, because we are referring
to these days according to the similitude they bear to those in
which such events happened.... Was not Christ immolated in
himself once and for all? Nevertheless is he not immolated for the
people in the Sacrament not only at the Paschal solemnities but
every day, so that anyone who replies to a questioner that he is
immolated does not lie? For if the sacraments did not bear a certain
similarity [Lat. *quandam similitudinem*] to those things for which
they are sacraments, they would not be sacraments at all. Therefore as the Sacrament of the Body of the Lord is in a certain way
the Body of the Lord [*Sicut ergo secundum quandam modum sacramentum
corporis Christi corpus Christi est*] and the Sacrament of the Blood of

---

[74] F. van der Meer, *Augustine the Bishop*, p. 313.
[75] *Augustine the Bishop*, p. 315.

Christ is the Blood of Christ, so the Sacrament of the Faith is the Faith. Believing is nothing else than having faith. And so when it is replied that the little child believes, even though he does not yet have an experience of the Faith, the response is given because he has the Sacrament of the Faith and has converted himself to God because of the sacrament of conversion.[76]

An even stronger argument for a symbolic understanding can be made from his remarks in the *De Doctrina Christiana*. In book 3 of that work he sets forth rules for the proper reading and understanding of Sacred Scripture. Not everything, he writes, is to be understood at face value. There are various types of writing. Among them, says Augustine, is the figurative or symbolic. Thus:

> If a word is prescriptive, forbidding a thing that is disgraceful or evil or ordering some good thing, it is not to be understood figuratively. If however it appears to order something which is disgraceful or evil or to forbid something which is good, then the language is figurative. The Lord says, "Unless you eat the Flesh of the Son of Man and drink his Blood, you will not have life in you." This appears to order us to do something disgraceful or evil. Therefore it is symbolic [lit., "a figure": *Figura ergo est*], commanding us to communicate in the Passion of the Lord and to remember pleasantly and usefully that his flesh was crucified and wounded for us.[77]

Another example can be found in his commentary on Psalm 3, in which he speaks of the "banquet in which the Lord entrusted and handed over to his disciples the symbol of his Body and Blood [*in quo corporis et sanguinis sui figuram discipulis commendavit et tradidit*]".[78]

It must be admitted that the prima facie evidence—as reflected in the above statements, which are the strongest but not the only ones that can be adduced—would seem to support the conclusion of those who find only a symbolic understanding of the Eucharistic

---

[76] Augustine, *Letter 98, to Boniface,* 9; *CSEL,* 34, 1-2, pp. 530-31.

[77] *De Doctrina Christiana,* 55; *CSEL,* 80, pp. 93-94.

[78] *Ennar. In Psalmos,* 3, 1; *CCSL,* 38, p. 8.

Mystery in Augustine's writings. Such a conclusion, however, would indicate that Augustine's Eucharistic teaching was at variance with that of St. Ambrose, from whom Augustine himself had received his catechesis on the Eucharist prior to his Baptism. There is nothing, however, in his own writings or those of his contemporaries or in the age immediately following his death that indicates that anyone perceived any difference between the teachings of these two men. And apart from the attempts of Berengarius to use Ambrose as well as Augustine to support his novel teaching, there has never been any serious doubt about the "realism" of Ambrose's teaching. That extrinsic consideration aside, however, it can be demonstrated by means of the following reflections that Augustine did not teach a symbolic or merely spiritual doctrine in respect to the Eucharistic Presence.

Augustine does not use the word *sacrament* in a manner identical with that of later theology. For him, it was the equivalent of the phrase *sacred sign* or *figure* and referred to the *visible element* in a holy action or activity or gesture. Thus, he writes: "Signs that pertain to divine things are called sacraments";[79] "The signs of divine things are visible, but what we honor in them are realities that are invisible."[80] "They are called sacraments because in them one thing is seen, another is understood. That which is seen has a bodily appearance [*speciem habet corporalem*]; that which is understood has spiritual fruit."[81] The visible element, of course, if it was really to be a sign, must have some kind of natural similarity to the holy reality or power for which it was a sign. This natural similarity, together with the word spoken over the visible element (one remembers his famous dictum: "The word comes to the element and it becomes Sacrament"),[82] is what raises the visible element from its status as being simply any sign and making of it a "sacred sign". In all this, his usage was equivalent to St. Ambrose's

---

[79] Augustine, *Ep. 138*, 1, 7; *CSEL*, 44, p. 131.
[80] Augustine, *De Catechizandis Rudibus*, 26, 50; *CCSL*, 46, p. 173.
[81] Augustine, *Sermon 272; PL*, 38, 1247.
[82] *In Jo.* Tract 80, 3; *CCSL*, 36, p. 529.

use of the word *sacramentum,* and to that of the Greek Fathers when they used the words "type-antitype". Indeed, for Augustine, the word *sacrament* was much wider than our notion, since it could be applied to many holy rites or gestures that were not sacraments in our sense of the Seven. Thus, in the passage cited above from his letter to Januarius, he calls the Feast of Pentecost a *sacramentum,* i.e., a visible sign of something sacred. From this visible element, Augustine always distinguished what he called the "reality" (the *res*) and the "power" (*virtus*) of the Sacrament. Nevertheless, for him this reality and power were not something that, in the Christian dispensation, existed *apart* from the sacramental sign.[83] As one can see by reading his commentary on John 6, Augustine held that both Jews and Christians had "sacraments". Those sacraments (e.g., the manna and the Eucharist), although they were different in visible appearance or sign value, nonetheless signified the same Reality, viz., Christ. *But the Christian received the Reality in truth, the Jews only in figure. "The manna was a shadow; this is the truth."* We would say, in our later terminology: the Christian sacraments contain what they signify. Thus, as we have seen above when considering the word in Ambrose, the word *sacramentum* for Augustine was the equivalent of what later theology would call the *sacramentum tantum,* the visible element considered by itself. To understand his thought about the "sacrament" in our sense of the word, one must consider not only what he says when using that word but also what he says concerning the reality or power present to us in or through the visible element.

[83] Berengarius interpreted Augustine as holding that the *res* of the Sacrament was not contained in the Sacrament. In our own day Johannes Betz follows the same interpretation of Augustine. He writes: "This doctrine, that is, that the true reality (*res*), the Body and the Blood of Jesus, are not contained directly in the consecrated signs but rather remain apart from them is again repeated by Augustine implicitly when he says that evil persons, heretics, and unworthy Catholics receive the Body and Blood of Christ only in sign, not in truth, *solo sacramento,* but not in *re ipsa,* not in *re vera*" (*Mysterium Salutis,* IV/2, p. 225). And so Betz concludes, "As shown, the teacher of Hippo does not go as far as the full Faith of the Church in the matter of the Real Presence" (idem,

If one examines again the texts cited above, which apparently support a merely symbolic understanding of the Eucharist, one can see the different perspective obtained by bearing in mind his notion of the word *sacrament*. The sacraments (i.e., the visible elements) bear a certain similarity to those things of which they are sacraments. Since Christ himself is our heavenly food, the sign or Sacrament of his Body and Blood is itself in a certain way Christ, i.e., since they are food and he is food. So too Baptism. The visible elements, the Sacrament, bear a certain resemblance to faith, which cleanses from sin and makes us belong to God.

This understanding illuminates, too, his words from the *De Doctrina Christiana* and his commentary on Psalm 3. When the Lord spoke of eating his Flesh and drinking his Blood, he was not encouraging cannibalism, "something disgraceful or evil"; the eating (in the actual physical sense of that word) referred to the "figure" or symbol or sacrament that bears a similarity to the heavenly food, the Body and Blood of Christ himself, which are the reality (the *res*) eaten but are also "the food that eating does not diminish".[84]

It must be said further that the above understanding is required unless one chooses, without reason, to hold that Augustine consistently contradicts himself. This is so because there are other texts where his remarks on the Eucharistic Presence are quite realistic.

Thus, in one of his sermons to the newly baptized, when he was no longer bound by the *disciplina,* Augustine says:

---

p. 227). This misunderstanding, beginning with Ratramnus and Berengarius, continued by Wyclif, Zwingli, and followed by many others since them, comes from a reading of Augustine that is overly literal and at that only partial. Moreover, even before the time of Ratramnus, Faustus of Riez and Gregory the Great read Augustine's teaching in a realistic sense, and the list of Augustine's disciples, from Paschasius to Aquinas to Portalie, who have followed Faustus and Gregory would necessitate a special bibliography. As in so many other areas where Augustine is variously interpreted, we will probably never see unanimous agreement.

[84] *Confessions*, Bk. 10, 6; *CCSL*, 27, p. 159.

I remember my promise. For last night I promised you who have been baptized a sermon in which I would explain the Sacrament of the Lord's table, which you now behold and which you became partakers of last night. You should understand what you have received, what you will receive, indeed what you should receive daily. That bread that you see on the altar and that has been sanctified by the word of God is the Body of Christ. That chalice—rather, that which the chalice contains—has been sanctified by the word of God and is the Blood of Christ. Through these things the Lord Christ wished to entrust to us his Body and his Blood, which he shed for us unto the remission of sins. If you receive them well, you are that which you receive. The Apostle says, "One bread and we, the many, are one body" (1 Cor 10:17).[85]

He says in another place:

[Christ has healed us Gentiles.] We did not know him in the flesh, yet we have deserved to eat his Flesh and to be his members in his Flesh.[86]

One of his clearest statements is found in his commentary on Psalm 33 (34). The inscription states that it is a Psalm of David composed by him at the time of the episode recounted in 1 Samuel 21:10–15. Attempting to give this background to his hearers, Augustine came across an exegetical difficulty. His Old Latin translation of 1 Samuel 21:13 was a very poor one, and the verse read, *"Ferebatur in manibus suis"* ("He carried himself in his own hands"). Having raised the difficulty, Augustine was left to explain how anyone could carry himself in his own hands.

And he was carried in his own hands. Now, brothers, who can understand how this can happen to a man? Who can be carried in his own hands? A man is able to be carried in the hands of others,

---

[85] Augustine, *Sermo CCXXVII: On Easter Sunday; PL,* 38, 1099. Augustine mentions here the idea of the bread being sanctified by the word of God. This is an idea not often found in him, but for a further text, cf. below, p. 209.

[86] Augustine, *In Johannis Evan.,* 31, 11, p. 299.

but no one is carried in his own hands. How this is to be understood in a literal way of David himself we cannot discover; however,
we can discover how this happened in the case of Christ. For
Christ was carried in his own hands when, entrusting to us his
own Body, he said: "This is my Body." Indeed he was carrying
that Body in his own hands.[87]

His daring statement, Christ carried himself in his own hands at
the Last Supper, coming at the end of the sermon, is quite under-
standable in context. His method of interpreting the Psalms was
to see them as always speaking of Christ in some way: either
Christ himself as an individual or what Augustine called the
"Whole Christ", i.e., Christ in his members, the Church. Much of
his commentary on Psalm 33 (34) speaks of Christ as victim, High
Priest, his sacrifice, and the Sacrifice of the Eucharist. Thus, by a
logical step when he came to a passage difficult to interpret, he
returned to the theme of the Eucharist, not in its aspect as sacrifice
but as Presence, concluding that Christ at the Last Supper carried
himself in his own hands. That it was not an offhand or nonreflective
remark on his part can be seen from the fact that Augustine
returned to the idea the following day, when he gave his second
sermon on the same Psalm.

And he carried himself in his own hands: How was he carried in
his own hands? Because, when he entrusted his own Body and
Blood, he took into his hands that which the faithful are aware of;
and he carried himself in a certain way when he said, "This is my
Body."[88]

[87] *Ennar. In Ps. 33,* 1st sermon, 10; *CCL,* 38, pp. 280–81.

[88] *Ennar. In Ps. 33,* 2nd sermon, 2, *CCL,* 38, p. 283. In the same sermon,
10, Augustine has a strong statement on the identity of the Victim on Calvary
with the Victim in the Eucharist: "They approached him in order to crucify
him; we approach him in order to receive his Body and Blood. They were
made darkness by the Crucified; by eating and drinking the Crucified we are
illuminated" (*CCL,* 38, pp. 288–89).

His language is more circumspect here. There is an allusion to the *disciplina arcani* in the "when . . . he took into his hands that which the faithful are aware of". The "in a certain way" is a statement like those seen above and is intended to avoid the ridiculous picture of the Lord actually holding himself in his hands according to his natural mode of being.

There are other clear indications of his Eucharistic realism. He tells us, for example, that the Eucharist is to be *adored* (it is, he says, a sin not to adore it) and that Christians would not communicate at all unless it was the Flesh of Christ. Indeed, he repeats the teaching already expressed by St. Ignatius and St. Ambrose: the Flesh we receive is the very flesh born of Mary.

> He took earth from earth, because flesh is from the earth, and he took Flesh of the flesh of Mary. He walked on earth in that same Flesh, and gave that same Flesh to us to be eaten for our salvation. Moreover no one eats that Flesh unless he has first adored it [*nemo autem illam carnem manducat, nisi prius adoraverit*] . . . and we sin by not adoring.[89]

> Who is the Bread of heaven except Christ? But in order that man might eat the bread of angels, the Lord of the angels became a man. If this had not happened, we would not have his Flesh: if we did not have his Flesh, we would not eat the Bread of the altar.[90]

A beautiful Eucharistic sermon attributed to Augustine but considered spurious by many is *Denis 3*. Part of it follows:

> Therefore Christ Our Lord, who by suffering offered for us that which, by being born, he had received from us, and who has been made High Priest forever, has given to us the rite [Lat. *ordinem*] of sacrificing that which you see, namely, his Body and Blood. Struck by the spear, his Body gave forth water and Blood, by which he took away our sins. Mindful of this grace, approach and share in this altar, working out your salvation in fear and trembling because it is God who works in you. Recognize in the

[89] *Ennar. In Ps. 98*, 9; *CCL*, 39, p. 1385.
[90] *Sermon 130*; PL, 38, 726.

Bread that which hung on the Cross; recognize in the chalice what flowed from his side. . . .

Therefore take and eat the Body of Christ, all of you who have already been made members of Christ in the Body of Christ. Take and drink the Blood of Christ. . . . Just as this is changed into you when you eat and drink, so you will be turned into the Body of Christ when you live obediently and worthily.[91]

To defend the "Eucharistic realism" of St. Augustine is not to deny the delight he took in elaborating on the directly symbolic aspects of the Mystery. A particularly striking example of his approach (if not his exact words, since the authenticity of the sermon is questioned) can be found in the sermon reported as given at the Easter Vigil and listed in the manuscripts as *Denis 6*.[92] In it Augustine compares the laborious preparation of the catechumens for their Baptism to the process by which wheat is planted, grown, threshed, and baked into bread for the Eucharist. As the process undergone by the wheat was ultimately to make of it the Body of Christ, so too with the preparation of those who would become members of Christ.

---

[91] Augustine, *Sermon Denis 3*; *PL*, 46, 827, or G. Morin, *Miscellanea Agostiniana*, p. 19. On the vivid expression "recognize in the chalice what flowed from his side", cf. the similar statement in an undoubtedly authentic text from the *De Trinitate* found below, p. 209. The authenticity of the sermon is much disputed. It forms part of Michael Denis' collection, made in the late eighteenth century. Van der Meer in his great work on Augustine prints it in full (pp. 376ff.) but notes the dispute on its authenticity; Sheerin is of the opinion that "it is definitely not the work of Augustine" (p. 102). On the whole, however, it is so "Augustinian" in tone that I would tend to credit its authenticity except for the reference to the Eucharist being turned into the recipient. Augustine frequently speaks of the recipient being converted into that which is received but never, as far as I am aware, of the Eucharist being transformed into the communicant. This could be possibly the exception to the rule, but it may just as well be an interpolation (with others?) in an otherwise authentic sermon. As we shall see below, this sermon is cited in the ninth century by St. Paschasius Radbertus as being a work of Augustine.

[92] *Denis 6*. A translation of all or large parts of this work can be found in Sheerin, pp. 105ff., and van der Meer, p. 372. Both men consider the sermon authentic.

Finally, the realism with which Augustine viewed the reality of Christ's Presence in the sacrifice, in which Christ "is immolated every day" (cf. *Letter 98, to Boniface,* note 76 above), can be measured by what was produced in the faithful who received the Eucharist: it made them what they received. Indeed, this is the very core of Augustine's teaching on the Eucharist. As "sacrament of piety and sign of unity", it was also the "bond of charity". It produced and symbolized the unity of the Church as Body of Christ, a truth attested to by Augustine many times and in many ways, some of them as daring as they are beautiful.

If, therefore, you are the Body of Christ and his members, it is your Mystery placed on the Lord's table; it is your Mystery that you receive.[93]

He who suffered for us has entrusted to us in this Sacrament his Body and Blood, which indeed he has even made us. For we have been made his Body, and, by his mercy, we are that which we receive.[94]

Not only do we become Christians; we become Christ. . . . If he is the Head and we the members, then together he and we are the whole man.[95]

And there will be One Christ, loving himself. For when the members love one another, the Body loves itself.[96]

Augustine left to us series of sermons that comprise a commentary on the Gospel of John. His preaching on John 6 is almost a compendium of his thought on the Eucharistic Mystery. We say "almost" because his frequent references to the sacrificial aspect of

[93] *Sermon 272; PL,* 38, 1246–48. The very reality with which Augustine spoke of the Church as Body of Christ argues for his realistic doctrine on the Eucharistic Body, and helps explain the apparently ambiguous statements to be found in him. Cf. below, p. 181, note 18 for Henri de Lubac's comments on this matter.

[94] *Sermon 229; PL,* 38, 1103.

[95] *In Jo.,* Tract 21, 8; *CCSL,* 36, pp. 216–17.

[96] *In Epis. ad Parthos,* Tract. 10, 3; *PL,* 35, 2055.

the Eucharist play no part in his commentary on John 6. Because no English translation of this work has been done since the 1880s, and because it played so influential a role in later theology, we have taken the liberty to include the following lengthy excerpt from that work.

On the Gospel of John 6:48–58

(Tract 26, 10) "Amen, amen I say to you, whoever believes in me has eternal life." He willed to reveal what he was; he might have said in summary, "Whoever believes in me has me." For Christ himself is true God and eternal life. Therefore, "whoever believes in me", he says, "comes to me"; "and whoever comes to me has me". What does this "to have me" mean? It means to have eternal life. Eternal life took on death; eternal life willed to die. Nevertheless he did this out of what is yours, not his own; he received from you that in which he might die for you. For he received Flesh from men, although not in the manner that men receive it. Having a Father in heaven, he chose a Mother on earth; born in heaven without a mother, born here without a father. Therefore life assumed death so that life might kill death. "Whoever believes in me", he says, "has eternal life", not that life which is apparent but that which is hidden. For eternal life is the Word who "in the beginning was with God, and the Word was God and was the Life that was the life of men". Being himself eternal life, he gave eternal life to the Flesh he had received. He came to die but rose on the third day. Between the Word receiving the Flesh and rising in the Flesh, death, which intervened, was consumed.

(11) He says, "I am the Bread of life." Why were the Jews proud? "Your fathers", he says, "ate the manna in the desert, and they have died." Whence the source of your pride? "They ate the manna, and have died." Why did they eat and die? Because they believed in that which they saw; they did not understand what they did not see. Therefore they are your fathers because you are like them. Now, my brothers, in what pertains to this visible, bodily death do we not also die, even we who eat the Bread come down from heaven? They died just as we shall die as far as pertains, as I have said, to the visible and carnal death of this body. But what about that death that the Lord warns about and in which their

fathers died? Moses ate the manna; Aaron ate the manna; Phineas
ate the manna; indeed, many ate the manna who were pleasing to
the Lord and have not died. Why? Because they understood the
visible food in a spiritual manner. They hungered spiritually,
tasted spiritually so that they might be satisfied spiritually. Even
we today receive visible food; but the Sacrament is one thing, the
power of the Sacrament another [*sed aliud est sacramentum, aliud
virtus sacramenti*]. How many receive from the altar and die, and
die by receiving? Therefore the Apostle says, "He eats and drinks
judgment unto himself." It was not the Lord's piece of bread [lit.,
bucella Dominica; cf. Jn 13:26–27] that was poison for Judas. And
nevertheless he took it, and when he took it the enemy entered
into him; not because he received an evil thing, but because, being
evil, he received a good thing in an evil manner. Therefore,
brothers, see that you eat the heavenly Bread spiritually; bring
innocence to the altar. Although your sins are daily, may they not
be deadly. "Forgive us our debts as we forgive our debtors." You
forgive and you are forgiven; approach the altar with confidence;
it is Bread, not poison. But see to it that you forgive; because if
you do not forgive, you are lying, and if you lie you do so to him
whom you cannot deceive. You can lie to God, but you cannot
deceive God. He knows what you do. He beholds you within, he
examines you within, he inspects you within, he judges you within,
and he damns or rewards you according to what is within you.
The Lord speaks of their fathers, that is, evil fathers of evil men,
unfaithful fathers of unfaithful men, murmuring fathers of murmuring men. For it is said that in nothing did that people more
offend God than in their murmuring against God. And therefore
the Lord, wanting to show them that they were sons of that type
of men, begins to address them, saying, "Why do you murmur
among yourselves", murmurers and sons of murmurers? "Your
fathers ate the manna and have died", not because the manna was
evil but because they ate it in an evil manner.

(12) "This is the Bread which has come down from heaven."
The manna was a sign of this Bread; the altar of God was a sign of
this Bread. They were sacraments, different as signs but equal in
respect to the reality that was signified. Listen to the Apostle: "I do
not want you to be ignorant, brothers, of the fact that all our
fathers were under the cloud and all passed through the sea and all

were baptized into Moses in the cloud and in the sea, and all ate the same spiritual food." Notice "the same spiritual food". It was different corporeally because they ate the manna, we eat something else; spiritually it was the same as we eat. But I speak of our fathers, those whom we are like, not of their fathers whom they were like. And Paul adds, "All drank the same spiritual drink." They drank one thing, we drink another in respect to its visible appearance, but each of them was a sign of the same thing in respect to its spiritual power. How was it they drank the same spiritual drink we do? Paul says, "They drank from the spiritual rock which followed them, and the Rock was Christ." From him the Bread, from him the drink. The rock was a sign of Christ, the true Christ in word and Flesh. And how did they drink? The rock was twice struck by a rod. The double striking signified the two wooden beams of the Cross. Therefore, "this is the Bread coming down from heaven, so that if anyone eats of it he shall not die." But he is speaking of what belongs to the power of the Sacrament, not what belongs to the visible Sacrament [*Sed quod pertinet ad virtutem sacramenti, non quod pertinet ad visibile sacramentum*]; it belongs to him who eats within, not without; to the one who eats in the heart, not to the one who chews with his teeth.

(13) "I am the living Bread who have come down from heaven." Living because I have come down from heaven. The manna also came down from heaven; but the manna was a shadow, this is the truth. "If anyone shall have eaten of this Bread, he will live forever; and the Bread which I will give is my Flesh for the life of the world." When will flesh understand this Flesh which he called Bread? That is called Flesh which flesh does not understand, and because it is called Flesh, so all the more does flesh not understand.[97] Many were horrified at this. They said it was too much; they thought it could not be. He says, "It is my Flesh for the life of the world." The faithful will know the Body of Christ if they do not neglect to be the Body of Christ. Let them be the Body of Christ if they wish to live by the Spirit of Christ. Only the Body of Christ

---

[97] There is a marvelous and typically Augustinian play on words in these lines, with much thought compacted into few words. In Latin the lines read, "Hoc quando caperet caro, quod dixit panem, carnem? Vocatur caro, quod non capit caro, et ideo magis non capit caro, qui vocatur caro."

lives by the Spirit of Christ. My brothers, understand what I am saying. You are a man and have a spirit and a body. I call spirit that which is called the soul, by which it comes about that you are a man. Therefore you have an invisible spirit, a visible body. Tell me which lives from which: Does your spirit live because of your body or your body because of your spirit? Let everyone who lives reply. (Indeed I am not sure whether anyone who cannot answer this is really alive.) And what does every living person reply? My body truly lives because of my spirit. Therefore wish to live from the Spirit of Christ. Be in the Body of Christ! My body does not live because of your spirit, does it? My body lives by my spirit and your body from your spirit. The Body of Christ cannot live except from the Spirit of Christ. Hence it is that Paul, commenting on this Bread for us, says, "One Bread [and] we many are one Body" (1 Cor 10:17). O Sacrament of piety! O sign of unity! O bond of charity! Whoever wants to live possesses where to live and whence to live. Let him approach; let him believe; let him be incorporated so that he may live. Let him not shrink back from the joining of members; let him not be a rotten member that deserves to be cut off; let him not be deformed so that he blushes; let him be beautiful, suitable, healthy; let him cling to the Body; let him live from God unto God; let him labor now on earth so that afterward he may reign in heaven.

(14) "Therefore the Jews argued with one another, saying, 'How can he give us his Flesh to eat?'" Surely they argued with one another because they did not understand the Bread of harmony. They did not wish to eat it because all who eat such Bread as this do not argue among themselves, inasmuch as the "one Bread makes us who are many one Body". And through this bread "God makes us to dwell in harmony in one home" (Ps. 67 [68]:6).

(15) Moreover they do not get an answer to that which they look for while arguing among themselves, viz., how the Lord can give his Flesh to eat: rather it is said to them, "Amen, amen I say to you, unless you shall have eaten the Flesh of the Son of Man and drunk his Blood, you will not have life in you." You do not know indeed how this Bread is eaten or in what manner it is eaten; nevertheless, "unless you shall have eaten the Flesh of the Son of Man and drunk his Blood, you will not have life in you." He spoke these words not to corpses but to living men. Therefore, lest they think he was

talking about this life and argue about that, he added what follows: "Whoever eats my Flesh and drinks my Blood has eternal life." Therefore whoever does not eat this Bread or drink this Blood will not have this eternal life. Men are able to have temporal life without him, but by no means can they have eternal life without him. Therefore whoever does not eat his Flesh or drink his Blood does not have life in him; and whoever eats his Flesh and drinks his Blood has life. However, the word *eternal* that he spoke of pertains to both. This is not the case in respect to that food that we eat to sustain this temporal life. For in this case whoever does not eat does not have life; and whoever does eat it nevertheless does not live. For it can happen that because of age or sickness or some other cause many who have eaten it still die. That is not the case with this true food and drink, which are the Body and Blood of the Lord. Those who do not eat it do not have life; and those who eat it have life, indeed, everlasting life. Therefore this food and drink he wants to be understood as the society of his Body and members that is the holy Church found in those who are predestined and called and justified and glorified, namely, his saints and faithful ones. Of these qualities, the first has already happened, namely, predestination; the second and third have happened, are happening, and will happen, namely, the call and justification; the fourth, namely, glorification, now exists in hope and in the future will exist in fact. The Sacrament of this reality, namely, of the Body and Blood of Christ, is prepared at the table of the Lord and is eaten from the Lord's table in some places daily, in others after a certain interval of days. For some it is eaten unto life, for some unto damnation; the Reality itself, however, of which it is the Sacrament, is for every man who shall have been a sharer in it a cause for life and for no one a cause of damnation.

. . .

(18) Finally he now expounds how that of which he speaks comes to be and what it means to eat his Body and drink his Blood. "Whoever eats my Flesh and drinks my Blood remains in me and I in him." This therefore is what it means to eat this food and drink this drink, viz., to remain in Christ and to have him remaining in the recipient. Thus whoever does not remain in Christ and in whom Christ does not remain certainly does not eat his Flesh or drink his

Blood. Rather he eats and drinks the Sacrament of so great a reality unto his own condemnation because, being unclean, he presumes to approach the Sacraments of Christ, which no one eats worthily unless he is clean. Of those who are clean it is said, "Blessed are the clean of heart, for they shall see God" (Mt 5:8).[98]

(27,5) What does it mean when he adds, "It is the Spirit who gives life; the Flesh profits nothing" (Jn 6:63)? Let us say to him (for he permits us to ask, not to contradict him but rather desirous to know): O Lord, good Master, how is it that the "Flesh profits nothing" since you say, "Unless anyone shall have eaten my Flesh and drunk my Blood he will not have life in him"? Is it that life is of no value? And why are we what we are except for the purpose of having eternal life, which you promise to us by your Flesh? Therefore why do you say, "The Flesh profits nothing"? It profits nothing as they understood it: for they understood the flesh as it is when cut up in a corpse or sold in a meat market, not as it is when animated by spirit. And therefore it is said, "The Flesh profits nothing", just as it is also said, "knowledge puffs one up" (1 Cor 8:1). On that account are we supposed to hate knowledge? Far from it. Then what does it mean to say "knowledge puffs one up"? It does that when it is alone, without charity. And so it is added, "charity indeed edifies". Therefore add charity to knowledge and knowledge is useful, not of itself but through charity. And so in this case where it is said, "Flesh profits nothing". It refers to flesh by itself. Let spirit be added to flesh—as charity is added to knowledge—and the flesh profits very much. For, if flesh profited nothing, the Word would not have become Flesh so that he might dwell among us. If Christ has been such profit to us through the flesh, how is it that flesh profits nothing? Rather, through the Flesh the Spirit has acted for our salvation. The Flesh was a vessel. Pay attention to what it held, not to what it was. The Apostles were sent forth. Was their flesh of no profit to us? And if the flesh of the Apostles was of profit to us, can it be said that the Flesh of the Lord is of no profit? How would the sound of a word come to us except through the voice of the flesh? How would pen be

[98] *Tractatus In Jo. 26,* 13–18; *CCSL,* 36, pp. 266–68.

moved and writing done by us except by means of the flesh? All these are works of the flesh, but used by the spirit as its instrument. Thus, it is "the Spirit who gives life, the Flesh profits nothing" —as they understood flesh—but that is not the way I give my Flesh to eat.[99]

Theodore of Mopsuestia

Theodore was born around 350, was ordained a priest in Antioch, under the influence of his friend John Chrysostom, in 383, and became bishop of Mopsuestia around 392. He died in 428, thus being a full contemporary of St. Augustine. Theodore was recognized in his own lifetime as a great theologian and preacher, and there seems no reason to doubt that, in all his works, he attempted to be a faithful disciple of the Christian Faith as Tradition had passed it to him. Although he died in full communion with the Church, his works soon became suspect of containing by anticipation the Nestorian heresy, which denied the unity of the Person of Christ. Both he and some of his writings were condemned as heretical by the ecumenical Council of Constantinople in 553, and, as a consequence, many of his works were neglected and lost. In 1932, however, there was discovered a Syriac translation of his *Catechetical Homilies,* only fragments of which had been previously available. Published and translated into English by A. Mingana, who discovered them, Homilies 5 (15) and 6 (16) are an extensive and frequently profound commentary on the Christian liturgy as used in and near Antioch in the fourth century. In them, Theodore very clearly expresses the traditional Faith in the reality of the Lord's Presence.

Indeed, he gave us the bread and the cup because it is with food and drink that we maintain ourselves in this world, and he called

---

[99] *Tractatus In Jo. 27,* 5; *CCSL,* vol. 36, p. 271–72. A fine new translation of Augustine's commentary on John is being done by John W. Rettig for *The Fathers of The Church* series. The first ten Treatises have already appeared (*The Fathers of the Church,* vol. 78, The Catholic University of America, Washington, D.C., 1988).

the bread "Body" and the cup "Blood", because, as it was his Passion that affected his Body which it tormented and from which it caused blood to flow, he wished to reveal, by means of these two objects . . . the immortal life in which we expect to participate when we perform this Sacrament. From it we believe we derive a strong hope for the things to come. It is with justice, therefore, that when he gave the bread he did not say, "This is the symbol of my Body", but, "This is my Body"; likewise, when he gave the cup he did not say, "This is the symbol of my Blood", but, "This is my Blood", because he wished us to look upon these [elements] after their reception of grace and the coming of the Spirit, not according to their nature, but to receive them as being the Body and the Blood of Our Lord.[100]

It is interesting to note that Theodore will himself often call the elements the "symbol" of the Lord's Body and Blood. As we have seen, this is a usage in conformity with other Eastern Fathers of the time, and, as is evident from Theodore's insistence on what Jesus himself actually said, the words are not used to indicate that the Presence of Christ is only symbolic. The Body and Blood of Christ are, according to Theodore, truly present in the elements, and in each part of the elements.

Although he comes to us after having divided himself, all of him is nevertheless in every portion, and he is near to all of us, and gives himself to each one of us, in order that we may hold him and embrace him with all our might and make manifest our love for him.[101]

Theodore sees the elements as being transformed by the *epiclesis,* the invocation and coming of the Holy Spirit who works upon the elements of bread and wine in a way analogous to the way

[100] Theodore, *Catechesis 5,* in Mingana, pp. 74–75. I have used the Mingana translation, adapting it slightly to conform with the French translation done by Tonneau and Devreesse in 1949, *Studi E Testi,* 144–45, pp. 474–75. While in Mingana the Eucharistic discourses are numbered as 5 and 6, they are listed in the Tonneau work as 15 and 16.

[101] Theodore, *Catechesis 6,* Mingana, p. 112; Tonneau, p. 577.

he worked in the humanity of Christ. The first citation above continues:

> Indeed, even the Body of our Lord does not possess immortality and the power of bestowing immortality in its own nature, but rather as something given to it by the Holy Spirit; at its Resurrection from the dead it received close union with divine nature and became immortal and instrumental for conferring immortality on others.
>
> ... And in order to show whence these things [i.e., immortality and the power of bestowing the same] came to him he added quickly: "It is the Spirit that gives life; the Flesh profits nothing" (Jn 6:63), as if he were saying: these things will come to it [Christ's human nature] from the nature of the vivifying Spirit, and it is through him that it will be given [the power] to become immortal and to confer immortality on others. These things it did not possess, and was not, therefore, in a position to confer upon others ... because the nature of the flesh is not able by itself to grant a gift and a help of this kind. If, therefore, the nature of the vivifying Spirit made the Body of our Lord into what its nature did not possess before, we, who have received the grace of the Holy Spirit through the symbols of the Sacrament, ought not regard the elements merely as bread and cup but as the Body and the Blood of Christ, into which they were so transformed by the descent of the Holy Spirit.[102]

---

[102] Theodore, *Catechesis 5,* Mingana, pp. 75–76; Tonneau, p. 477. There is a parallel text in *Catechesis 6* that emphasizes even more clearly the role of the *epiclesis.* It reads: "Indeed, the body of our Lord, which is from our own nature, was previously mortal by nature, but through the Resurrection it moved to an immortal and immutable nature. When the priest, therefore, declares them to be the Body and Blood of Christ, he clearly reveals that they have so become by the descent of the Holy Spirit, through whom they have also become immortal, inasmuch as the Body of Our Lord, after it was anointed and had received the Spirit, was clearly seen so to become. In this same way, after the Holy Spirit has come here also, we believe that the elements of bread and wine have received a kind of an anointing from the grace that comes upon them, and we hold them to be henceforth immortal, incorruptible, impassible, and immutable by nature, as the Body of Our Lord was after the Resurrection." Mingana, p. 104.

We know from a parallel text preserved in Greek that Theodore used the Greek word *metaballo* for what is translated above as "transformed".[103] The word as we saw above is a forceful expression of the change that takes place in the elements. However, unlike the clear contextual evidence found in the *Jerusalem Catechesis,* there is little indication to help one determine further the exact nature of the change or transformation spoken of by Theodore. A reading of the sermons would suggest that Theodore envisioned a change by which the elements of bread and wine would remain truly bread and wine, while serving as the medium through which Christ's Body and Blood became present. If that be the case, then Theodore's view of the change wrought by the *epiclesis* is quite similar to his Christology—which itself is an area of disagreement. While he may never have actually taught that the divine and human natures in Christ were so distinct as to constitute what could be considered two persons, his language at times was not sufficiently precise to remove the suspicion that this was in fact what he was teaching. Like all the great theologians of the Antiochene tradition, Theodore was intent on defending the truth and integrity of the Lord's human nature. Indeed, he won a great part of his theological reputation in defending the reality of the Lord's human nature against those who denied or undervalued it. He may, then, have considered the Eucharistic change to be modeled on that of the hypostatic union. Just as the human nature of the Eternal Son remains a complete human nature after the Incarnation, so the Eucharistic elements remained what they had been, truly bread and wine, while becoming the instrument through which the Lord's own Body and Blood were communicated.

A similar view is found in a letter attributed to Pope Gelasius I (Pope from 492 to 496). In it the author writes:

> Sacred Scripture, testifying that this Mystery began at the start of the blessed Conception, says; "Wisdom has built a house for itself" (Prov 9:1), rooted in the solidity of the sevenfold Spirit. This Wisdom ministers to us the food of the Incarnation of Christ

---

[103] Cf. *Fragment on Matthew 26:26; PG,* 66, 713.

through which we are made sharers of the divine nature. Certainly the sacraments of the Body and Blood of Christ that we receive are a divine reality, because of which and through which we "are made sharers of the divine nature" (2 Pet 1:4). Nevertheless the substance or nature of bread and wine does not cease to exist. And certainly the image and likeness of the Body and Blood of Christ are celebrated in the carrying out of the Mysteries.

Therefore it is shown to us with sufficient clarity that we ought to think about Christ himself as we think about that which we profess, celebrate, and receive in his image, namely, that by the work of the Holy Spirit they pass over into the divine substance while nevertheless remaining in their own nature [Lat. *in hanc, scilicet divinam, transeant sancto Spiritu perficiente substantiam, permanentes tamen in suae proprietate naturae*]. Thus, they show us that this principal Mystery, Christ himself, whose efficacy and power they truly represent, remains one, because he is entire and true, in the duly remaining [natures] in which he exists.[104]

As is obvious, the letter is not directly concerned with the Eucharist but rather with the Christological Mystery of the two natures in the One Person of the Lord. This Mystery was attacked by both Nestorians and Monophysites and was the subject for two Church councils, Ephesus and Chalcedon. The letter seeks to use the Eucharistic Mystery as an illustration for the Christological truths. It works from the implicit assumption, accepted by all parties, that the Eucharist is Christ. But, says the author, it is also bread and wine, thereby illustrating how Christ's Person is One, his natures two. It is easy to see how the comparison could be made, and it indicates that the notion of a total change in the

---

[104] Gelasius, *Tractatus De Duabus Naturis Adversus Eutychen et Nestorium; PL,* 224 (*Supplementum* 3), 773–74. Text also found in J. Solano, *Textos Eucaristicos Primitivos,* vol. 2, nos. 953–54, pp. 557–58. Aloys Grillmeier, S.J., who, along with most experts, attributes the letter to Gelasius, remarks: "We ought not gauge his conception against the Tridentine teaching of transubstantiation" (*Christ in Christian Tradition,* vol. 2, pt. 1, p. 303). This is certainly true. However, it can be judged against the more accurate understanding of the Eucharistic change already to be found in some of Gelasius' contemporaries.

elements was not yet so fixed in Christian thought that alternative solutions did not present themselves. One alternative, that of a type of "hypostatic union" between the bread and wine and the Body and Blood of the Lord, would be particularly agreeable to the Antiochene school of theology (which stressed the reality of Christ's two natures) and to those who had to defend Catholic doctrine against Monophysitism. It was an alternative, however, that found but few supporters and one that was destined to disappear, as further reflection on the Eucharistic Mystery would show that, for all its similarities to the Mystery of the Incarnation, an exact equivalence could not be drawn between the two. It also indicates that the Mystery involved in the Eucharistic change was not simply—as many would have it—the natural consequence of a firm belief in the true, corporeal Presence of Christ in the Eucharist. It was—at least concretely—possible to hold the latter without adopting the former.

If Theodore's own view was the same as that of the letter apparently authored by Gelasius, he was mistaken, and did not comprehend the profundity of the transformation that the Spirit's action worked on the bread and wine. To that extent his Eucharistic thought, beautiful as it is, falls short of what was being at least implied by some of his predecessors and what others of his contemporaries were explicitly teaching in more precise language.

If, however, his thought on the nature of the transformation may not be adequate, his thoughts on the Eucharist as sacrifice manifest a depth rarely reached by his predecessors or contemporaries. For Theodore, the Eucharistic celebration was a true sacrifice, offered by the priests—a sacrifice that makes present and commemorates the "once and for all" sacrifice of the Cross that is now being offered by Christ in heaven.

> We must first of all realize that we perform a sacrifice of which we eat. Although we remember the death of our Lord in food and drink . . . we nevertheless perform, in the liturgy, a sacrifice; and it is the office of the priest of the New Testament to offer this sacrifice, as it is through it that the New Covenant is seen to consist. It is indeed evident that it is a sacrifice, but not a new one

or one that the priest performs as his own, but as a remembrance of that other real sacrifice.[105]

. . .

As often, therefore, as the liturgy of this awe-inspiring sacrifice is performed, which is clearly the likeness of heavenly things and of which, after it has been enacted, we become worthy to partake through food and drink, as a true participation in the good things to come—we must picture in our mind, as in a dream [Fr. *comme en* "*phantasmes*"], that we are in heaven, and, through faith, picture in our imagination the image of heavenly things, while thinking that Christ, who is in heaven and who died for us, rose, and ascended into heaven, is now being immolated through the medium of these types. In contemplating with our eyes, through faith, the facts that are now being reenacted, viz., that he is again dying, rising, and ascending into heaven, we shall be led to the vision of the things that have taken place beforehand on our behalf.[106]

Theodore is very clear on the need to receive the Eucharist worthily. He distinguishes clearly between involuntary sins, those that come to us against our will,[107] and those that are grave. In the case of the latter, Penance is required before reception of the Eucharist.

If a great sin, contrary to the Commandments, is committed by us, and if we do not induce ourselves to turn away from sins of this kind, it behooves us to refrain always and without reservation from receiving the Communion, because what utility can come to us from this act if we are seen to persist in these sins? We must first induce our conscience with all our power to make haste and fittingly repent of our sins, and not permit any other medicine to ourselves. Let us know that as God gave to our body, which he made passible, medicinal herbs of which the experts make use for our healing, so also he gave penitence, as a medicine for sins, to our soul, which is changeable. Regulations for this penitence were laid down from the beginning, and the priest and the experts, who

[105] Theodore, *Catechesis 5,* Mingana, p. 79; Tonneau, p. 485.
[106] Theodore, *Catechesis 5,* Mingana, p. 83; Tonneau, p. 497.
[107] Theodore, *Catechesis 6,* Mingana, pp. 117–18.

heal and care for the sinners, bring medicine to the mind of the penitents who are in need, according to the ecclesiastical ordinance and wisdom, which is regulated in accordance with the measure of the sins....

This is the medicine for sins, which was established by God and delivered to the priests of the Church who, in making use of it with diligence, will heal the afflictions of men. The blessed Paul also said thus: "Teach in season and out of season, reprove, rebuke, and comfort" (2 Tim 4:2). He ordered that the sinners should be reproved . . . so that they should reveal their sins to the priests; and the "rebuke" is administered so that they may receive correction by some ordinances, and obtain help therefrom for themselves....

. . .

Since you are aware of these things, and also of the fact that because God greatly cares for us he gave us penitence and showed us the medicine of repentance and established some men, who are the priests, as physicians of sins, so that if we receive in this world through them healing and forgiveness of sins . . . it behooves us to draw near to the priests with great confidence and to reveal our sins to them, and they, with all diligence, pain, and love and according to the rules laid down above, will give healing to sinners. And they will not disclose the things that are not to be disclosed, but they will keep to themselves the things that have happened, as befits true and loving fathers, bound to safeguard the shame of their children while striving to heal their bodies.[108]

Not only do Theodore's words throw light on the relationship envisioned between the sacraments of the Eucharist and Penance, but they also tell us something about the form or manner in which Penance was administered. Theodore is not speaking here of the public system of Penance, which plays so large a part in the Patristic literature of the Western Church. He speaks, rather, of what was known in the West as the *correptio* (the "rebuke"), which we today would call private Penance (i.e., the system in which not only the confession but also the doing of the satisfaction-penance

---

[108] Theodore, *Catechesis 6,* Mingana, pp. 120–23; Tonneau, pp. 597–603.

and the reconciliation-absolution were private). Theodore, in the passage cited, also gives us the first explicit reference we have in the early Christian literature to what came to be called the Seal of Confession, which binds the priest not to reveal anything he has heard during the confession of sins.

St. John of Damascus

John of Damascus, or John Damascene, is normally considered the last writer of the Patristic age. Living between 650 and 750 (the exact dates of his birth and death are unknown), he did much of his writing in Jerusalem, which was then under Moslem control. His great treatise, *De Fide Orthodoxa,* is perhaps the third part of a single work, as the Eastern manuscripts seem to indicate.[109] In the fourth part into which the *De Fide Orthodoxa* is normally broken down, John Damascene deals with the Eucharistic Mystery.

> Since we humans are something twofold and compound, it is necessary that our birth be twofold, and likewise our food. Thus we were given a birth by water and the Holy Spirit; I speak of holy Baptism: and the food is the very Bread of life that has come down from heaven, Our Lord Jesus Christ. On the night on which he gave himself up, about to take on a voluntary death for our sakes, he established a New Covenant with his holy disciples and, through them, with all those who believe in him. Therefore, in the Upper Room of holy and illustrious Sion, after eating the old Passover with his disciples and having fulfilled the Old Covenant, he washed the feet of his disciples, thus providing a symbol [Gk. *symbolon*] of holy Baptism. Then, having broken the bread, he gave it to them, saying, "Take, eat, this is my Body which is broken for you for the remission of sins." Likewise, taking a cup of wine and water, he gave it to them, saying, "All of you, drink of this; this is my Blood of the New Covenant, poured out for you for the remission of sins. Do this in remembrance of me." For as

[109] The standard Greek text of the *De Fide Orthodoxa* is still that found in the *PG,* 94.

often as you eat this Bread and drink this Cup, you proclaim the death of the Son of Man, and you confess his Resurrection until he comes (cf. 1 Cor 11:26).

If the Word of God is living and powerful, and if the Lord does all things whatsoever he wills; if he said, "Let there be light", and it happened; if he said, "Let there be a firmament", and it happened; ... if finally the Word of God himself willingly became man and made Flesh for himself out of the most pure and undefiled blood of the holy and ever Virgin, why should he not be capable of making [Gk. *poiesai*] bread his Body and wine and water his Blood? ... God said, "This is my Body", and, "This is my Blood", and, "Do this in remembrance of me." And so it is done, by his all-powerful command, until he comes, for this is why he said, "until he comes". Through the invocation [Gk. *dia tes epikleseos*], it, namely, the overshadowing power of the Holy Spirit, becomes like rain to newly planted land. For just as all that God made he made through the power of the Holy Spirit, so now these things, which surpass nature and which cannot be taken in or understood except through faith, are made by the power of the Spirit. "How shall this happen to me", said the holy Virgin, "since I do not know man?" The Archangel Gabriel replied, "The Holy Spirit will come upon you, and the power of the Most High shall overshadow you." And now you also ask how the bread becomes the Body of Christ and the wine and water his Blood. I say to you: the Holy Spirit is present and does these things, which surpass reason and thought.

Bread and wine are used because God knows human weakness, which so often turns away from things little tried by use. Thus it happens according to his accustomed mercy to us that he effects the things that are higher than nature through those things that are naturally familiar to us. Just as in the case of Baptism—since it is customary for men to wash themselves with water and anoint themselves with oil—he has joined to the oil and water the grace of the Spirit and made them the bath of regeneration, so, since it is the custom of men to eat bread and drink wine and water, he has joined to them his divinity and made them his Body and Blood so that we might rise to what is above nature through things that are familiar and harmonious with nature. The Body that is from the holy Virgin is truly united to the Divinity—not that the Body taken into heaven comes down but rather that this bread and wine are changed [Gk. *metapoiountai*] into the Body and Blood of God. If you ask how this happens, it is sufficient for you to hear that it happens through the Holy Spirit, just as, through the Spirit, the Lord took on Flesh, which subsisted in him and was born of the holy Mother of God. And we know nothing more except that the Word of God is true and effective and all-powerful, although the manner [of his working] cannot be understood. However, it is not inaccurate to say that, just as in nature the bread and wine and water are changed [Gk. *metaballontai*] into the body and blood of the one who eats and drinks and are changed in such a way that they become no other body than that of the one who ate them, so the bread that has been set forth [lit., *ho tes protheseos artos*][110] and the wine and water, through the invocation [Gk. *epikleseos*] and coming of the Holy Spirit, are supernaturally transformed [Gk. *huperphuos metapoiountai*] into the Body and Blood of Christ and are not two things but one and the same.

Therefore, for those who receive worthily with faith, it is for the remission of sins, for everlasting life, and as a defense for body and soul; for those who receive unworthily without faith, it is received unto penalty and punishment. . . .

The bread and wine are not a type [Gk. *tupos*] of the Body and Blood of Christ (may no one say that!); rather it is the very deified Body of the Lord. He himself said, "This is my Body", not a type of my Body, and, "This is my Blood", not a type of my Blood, but "my Blood". . . .

. . . Let us approach with ardent desire and receive the Body of the Crucified with our hands held in the form of a cross; taking it to our eyes and lips and foreheads,[111] let us partake of the Divine

---

[110] *PG,* 94, 1145, n. 82, has a long note on the phrase, explaining that it refers to the bread set out on the *prothesis,* the small table to the right of the altar of sacrifice during the Mass. Cf. also Jurgens, 3, p. 343, where it is translated "bread on the credence table". Perhaps a more likely origin of the phrase can be found in the words of Jesus in Mt 12:4, where the Greek is identical with Theodore's: *kai tous artous tes protheseos.*

[111] Touching the forehead and eyes with the Host before receiving the Sacrament was apparently something common in some parts of the Eastern Church. It is also mentioned in the *Jerusalem Catechesis,* 21, op. cit., pp. 170–73.

Coal . . . in order that we may be inflamed and divinized by our share in the divine fire. Isaiah saw [this] coal. Now coal is not simple wood but rather wood united with fire. So also the Bread of Communion is not simple bread but bread united with the Divinity. And the Body joined to the Divinity is not one nature. Rather the nature of the Body is one, and another the nature of the Divinity joined to the Body. There is not one nature, but two.

. . .

But if some called the bread and the wine antitypes [Gk. *antitupa*] of the Body and Blood of the Lord — as did the Godbearing Basil — they said this referring to the offering [Gk. *prosphoran*] itself, not after but before it was sanctified.

. . .

With all our strength, therefore, let us be careful not to receive Communion from heretics or grant it to them; as the Lord says, "Do not give what is holy to dogs or cast your pearls before swine."[112]

Like St. Ambrose, John cites God's power in creation and at the Incarnation to demonstrate the possibility of the transformation of the elements that takes place in the celebration of the Eucharist. Indeed, following the Septuagint translation of Genesis 1:1, he, like other Fathers of the East, uses the same word (Gk. *poiein*) to speak of God's making the world and "making bread his Body". With the words "so also the Bread of Communion is not simple bread but bread united with the Divinity", etc., John could be understood as implying that the Eucharistic change follows the pattern of the Hypostatic Union, a pattern of thought already considered above in the case of Theodore of Mopsuestia. If this were so, the bread would remain truly bread, with the Body of Christ joined to or "added" to it. This, however, is not what Damascene is saying. He has already explicitly stated that the transformation caused by the Spirit makes the bread and wine and the Body and Blood of Christ "not two things, but one and the same". What he is saying subsequently in the passage in question is

[112] *PG*, 94, 1137–53.

that we must not think that the Eucharistic elements have become only the Lord's Body and Blood, separated in some way from his Divinity. Rather, his Body and Blood, his human nature, are united with his Divinity in One inseparable Person. Thus, when we receive his Body and Blood, we also receive his Divinity. As evidence for this understanding of what John is saying, the footnote in Migne[113] accurately refers one to Damascene's *Third Discourse on Images,* where we read:

> Men indeed become participants in and sharers of the Divine Nature, i.e., those men who receive the holy Body of Christ and drink his precious Blood. For his Body and Blood are joined to the Divinity hypostatically, and the two natures are joined inseparably in the unity of Person in the one Body of Christ that we receive. Therefore we are made sharers of both natures.[114]

John's remarks concerning the different effects produced by Eucharistic reception by the worthy and unworthy anticipate Aquinas' verse in the *Lauda Sion:*

Sumunt boni, sumunt mali:	*The good receive, the evil receive:*
Sorte tamen inaequali,	*But to an unequal fate,*
Vitae vel interitus.	*One of life or of damnation.*
Mors est malis, vita bonis:	*Death for the evil; life for the*
Vide, paris sumptionis	*good.*
Quam sit dispar exitus.	*See what disparate results*
	for what is equally received.

The writings of the Fathers of the Church reveal the wonderfully pluriform nature of their reflections on the Eucharist, a plurality of approaches that highlights the many aspects of the Sacrament itself. They all worked from two apparently fundamental data of faith: the Presence of Christ himself in the Sacrament and the sacrificial aspect of the Sacrament. The Presence was the Flesh born of Mary, and so the Eucharist was to be adored. With

---

[113] *PG,* 94, 1149, n. 85.
[114] *PG,* 94, 1348.

increasing perception they mentioned and reflected upon the change that takes place in the elements of bread and wine, although it is surely true that some of them realized the extent and profundity of that change and made more of it than did others. In none of them were the symbolic aspects of the Sacrament neglected. The very formation of the bread and wine mirrored the unity of the Church. The Reality that the bread and wine became in the Consecration created the unity of the Church and was the motive and cause for fraternal charity. For the Fathers the Eucharist was, as well, meal and nourishment, pledge of eternal life to all who received worthily, even while it brought condemnation to the unworthy communicant, an antidote to sin, the means by which our humanity is made sharer of the divine nature, thanksgiving to the Heavenly Father for his creation and for what he had done for us in Christ, our share in Christ's heavenly offering.

St. Thomas Aquinas wrote: "The common spiritual good of the whole Church is substantially contained in the Sacrament of the Eucharist."[115] The teaching of Aquinas can be considered a fair summation of the writings of the Church Fathers. The Eucharist is Christ who is himself our life and all our good. As Chrysostom preached: "Behold, you not only see him, you touch him, you eat him."

It would not be fair, however, to pretend that the Patristic age had settled all questions for subsequent Christian ages. Problems in interpreting their teaching would arise again and again. Moreover, they left some questions unconsidered or unanswered. New ones would arise. Some individual answers would be reconsidered and rejected. A more consistent terminology would have to be developed. New forms of Eucharistic practice and devotion would need to be judged by what was present or implied in their teaching. Patristic interpretation of the Scriptures would be challenged by newer methods of exegesis. In short, the Fathers were but the beginnings, and history would not stop where they left it.

[115] *S.Th.*, III, q. 65, a. 3, ad 1.

Indeed, the nature of the Mystery itself guaranteed that no age or group would exhaust the riches available there. Nonetheless the Fathers were privileged voices in a living Church and in a Church *in which they still live,* since the Eucharist itself gives them present communion with us. No Eucharist is ever celebrated except in union with the Blessed Ever-Virgin Mary and all the saints. The Eucharist itself keeps their witness alive, since he feeds them now in heaven who fed them here.

Reprise

The age of the Fathers passed, through the disintegration of the world as they knew it, into what we call the Middle Ages.

The early Middle Ages in Western Europe were, on the one hand, a period of preservation and reflection on the thought of the Patristic era, and, on the other hand, a time that witnessed the first major disagreements concerning the Mystery. Some have attempted to schematize the Eucharistic theology of the period by viewing it as a kind of parallel development of Ambrosian and Augustinian perspectives on the Sacrament, the former "realist" in its understanding of the Presence of Christ, the latter developing a more "spiritual" or mystical understanding.[116] One difficulty with such an approach is that it would seem to presuppose some (undemonstrated) difference between Augustine and his "father in the Faith". A greater difficulty is the fact that the early Medieval writers themselves were largely unaware of such a supposed diver-

---

[116] Thus, McCue writes: "There were, in the ninth, tenth, and eleventh centuries, a number of theologians, largely Augustinian in their inspiration, who seemed to some to be evacuating the Eucharist of its content and substance. Their opponents, deriving more from Ambrose, seemed to the 'Augustinians' to be guilty of theological crudity and of a grotesquely physical conception of the Eucharist" ("The Doctrine of Transubstantiation from Beraengar through Trent: The Point at Issue", *Harvard Theological Review* 61:385–430). This viewpoint is that which was set forth by Joseph Geiselmann in *Die Eucharistielehre der Vorscholastik,* pp. 4–7, 45–69. He recognized, however, that many "Augustinians" held a "realist" view (cf. pp. 97–104).

gence between Ambrose and Augustine. Even when disagreeing with one another, the Medieval writers cite both Fathers to substantiate their own views. Others see this period—and the preceding Patristic one—as a witness to a "theological pluralism" in respect to the Eucharist, one found quite tolerable at least until the controversy caused by Berengarius.[117] Still others view the period as a gradual solidification of the doctrines of Presence and change of the elements found in the Fathers until the point that the Church defines both at Lateran IV and Trent. In fact these last two positions need not—and should not—be taken as opposing alternatives. There was indeed a "plurality of theologies" in the Patristic approach to the Eucharist. The same was true in the early and later Medieval periods. Indeed, it is so today. The very wealth of the Eucharist with the manifold facets that belong to the Sacrament guarantees that there have been and always will be various legitimate ways in which to approach the consideration of the Sacrament. Only when the approaches are mutually contradictory has it been necessary for the Church, guided by the Spirit, to discern the truth in one way as opposed to others. Such an act of discernment will inevitably leave to one side or even reject certain "theologies" or explanations that are seen to be incompatible with the Faith that has been passed down. This process will also allow for a proper development of doctrine, a deepening of awareness in respect to the various aspects of the Mystery. Inevitably it will be seen that even some of the views and terminology of the Fathers of the Church—as well as those of later theologians—were inadequate. In respect to the nature of Christ's Presence in the

---

[117] Such is basically the thesis of Gary Macy, *The Theologies of the Eucharist in the Early Scholastic Period.* He concludes his work thus: "The purpose of this book has been to argue that the early Scholastic period, the first period in Christian history to discuss the Eucharist at length, was witness to a diversity of approaches to the Sacrament. Further, this diversity, with its tensions intact, continued into the high Scholastic period. The myth that the early Scholastic period presented a unified theology of the Sacrament . . . ought now be laid to rest" (p. 141). With this approach J. Pelikan would appear to be in agreement (cf. vol. 4, pp. 5, 10, 59).

Sacrament, the type of change that takes place in the elements, and the sacrificial aspect of the Eucharist, however, it is to be noticed that both Lateran IV and Trent will affirm what the majority of the Fathers and of the theologians previous to both those councils actually held and defended or, at least, can be defended as having held. Such an observation, moreover, can be recognized as a historical fact without interpreting it to mean that the Church will—or need—always follow the "majority view" of previous ages. Even the Fathers are witnesses to the Faith of the Church; they do not create it. In truth, the early Medieval period can best be viewed as a time of theological evaluation of the Patristic evidence. And, if one man can be claimed to be the father of this period of theological reflection in respect to the Eucharist, that man is Paschasius Radbertus.

Paschasius Radbertus

St. Paschasius was born near the end of the eighth century, was abbot of the monastery of Corbie from 842 to 847, and died in 859. He is most famous for his great work *De Corpore et Sanguine Domini,* which is Christianity's first complete theological monograph on the Eucharist, written probably between 831 and 833.[118] It is for that reason that his work is included in this chapter devoted to the Fathers, since, in a sense, he summarizes much of their thought on certain essential aspects of the Mystery. His treatise contains a prologue and twenty-two chapters. The very chapter headings are illustrative, because in a certain way they prefigure the agenda for much later Scholastic discussion of the Eucharist. Some of those headings are: "It Is Not to Be Doubted That the Eucharist Is the True Body and Blood of Christ" (1); "None of the Faithful Should Be Ignorant of This Mystery" (2);

---

[118] The critical edition for the *De Corpore et Sanguine Domini* is to be found in the *CCCM,* vol. 16. All references are to that edition. The *Cambridge Medieval History,* vol. 6, in a fine and faithful summary, calls Paschasius' work "an epoch in the history of the doctrine [of the Eucharist]" (p. 674).

"What Are Sacraments?" (3); "Whether This Mystery of the Chalice Becomes a Sacrament in Figure or in Reality" (4); "In What Ways the Body of Christ Is Spoken Of" (7); "That in This Communion Either Judgment or Reward Is Received" (8); "Why This Mystery Is Celebrated with Bread and Wine" (10); "Why Water Is Added to the Chalice" (11).

Paschasius began his treatment by reminding the reader of the creative power of God, to whom all natures are subject.

> Indeed, "all that the Lord wills he does in heaven and on earth" (Ps 135:6). And because he willed it this figure of bread and wine is permitted to be such that, after the Consecration, it must be believed to be none other than the Flesh and Blood of Christ. Therefore Truth himself said to his disciples, "This is my Flesh for the life of the world" (Jn 6:51). And—as I speak more wondrously —it is clearly no other Flesh than that which was born of Mary and suffered on the Cross and rose from the tomb.[119]

> . . .

> But truly, if anyone should not believe this, [then I ask] what if he should see Christ on the Cross in the appearance [Lat. *in speciem*] of a slave? How would he know him to be God unless he had first believed through faith? Likewise in respect to this Body, where another appearance presents itself. How will he see the Flesh of Christ unless he first believes more truly through faith?[120]

His doctrine on the identity of the Eucharistic Body with the Body born of Mary and the Body that suffered on the Cross and rose is a teaching repeated frequently throughout the work. When that teaching subsequently became a point of controversy, Fredugard of Saint-Riquier, a monk and friend of Paschasius, wrote to him and asked him how to reconcile this teaching with that of Augustine in the *De Doctrina Christiana* (3, 6). Radbertus responded by restating his position and citing Augustine's remarks from *Denis* 3 (19, 7, 9) on "recognize in the bread what hung on the wood", etc.[121]

---

[119] *De Corp.*, I, 45–52, pp. 14–15.
[120] *De Corp.*, I, p. 15, lines 61–65.
[121] Paschasius, *Epistola ad Fredugardum*, op. cit., pp. 146–47.

And, after citing other Fathers and further texts from Augustine, he concludes, "From all this one is able to see that not all who read Augustine understand him."[122]

Chapter 3 of the *De Corpore* teaches that the Eucharist, like Baptism and the Scriptures, is a sacrament, viz., "whatever is given to us in a sacred celebration as a pledge of salvation since the visible realities work invisibly within us".[123] For Paschasius, the very humanity of Christ is a sacrament.[124] It is that sacred Humanity that is present to us in the Sacrament of the Eucharist, in reality and not merely symbolically.

> No one who believes the divine words will doubt that this Sacrament becomes in truth the Body and Blood by the Consecration of the Mystery. For Truth says, "My Flesh is true food and my Blood is true drink" (Jn 5:55). . . . Therefore if it is truly food it is also true Flesh, and if it truly is drink it is also true Blood. . . .
>
> "But because it is not right that Christ be devoured by teeth, he willed that this bread and wine be truly and efficaciously created his Flesh and Blood in Mystery by the Consecration of the Holy Spirit, who creates it to be immolated mystically and daily for the life of the world, so that, just as true Flesh was created from the Virgin by the Holy Spirit and without intercourse, so the same Body and Blood of Christ might be mystically consecrated from the substance of bread and wine by the same Spirit.[125]

---

[122] *Epist. ad Fred.,* p. 151, line 203.

[123] *De Corp.,* 3, p. 23, lines 1–4. "Sacramentum igitur est quicquid in aliqua celebratione divina nobis quasi pignus salutis traditur, cum res gesta visibilis longe aliud invisibile intus operatur quod sancte accipiendum sit."

[124] *De Corp.,* 3, lines 24–30. "Fit ergo et Christi nativitas atque omnis illa humanitatis dispensatio magnum quoddam sacramentum, quia in homine visibili divina majestas intus ob consecrationem nostram ea quae fiebant secretius potestate sua invisibiliter operabatur. Unde mysterium vel sacramentum, quod Deus homo factus est, iure dicitur."

[125] *De Corp.* 4, pp. 27–28, lines 3–20. The Latin of the last part of the quotation reads: "Sed quia Christum vorari fas dentibus non est, voluit in misterio hunc panem et vinum vere carnem suam et sanguinem consecratione Spiritus Sancti potentialiter creari, creando vero cotidie pro mundi vita mystice immolari, ut sicut de virgine per Spiritum vera caro sine coitu creatur, ita per eundem ex substantia panis ac vini mystice idem Christi et sanguis consecretur."

The reference to the Flesh of Christ being immolated "mystically and daily for the life of the world" is just one of many references that Radbertus makes to the Eucharist as sacrifice.[126] To say that "the most important aspect of the Eucharist for Radbertus was the sacrifice" and that at his time "the sacrificial interpretation of the Eucharist was embedded much more firmly in the Church than was the idea of the Real Presence"[127] is probably to draw a distinction that Radbertus would not have made and surely to understate the Church's secure convictions—at that era and previously—concerning the reality of Christ's Eucharistic Presence. Nevertheless, as the conclusion of an eminent non-Catholic scholar, the statement regarding sacrifice is very significant in light of the disputes that would be raised about the Eucharist as sacrifice at the time of the Protestant Reformation. As was true throughout the Patristic period, so too throughout the early and later Medieval periods, the sacrificial aspect of the Eucharist was an undisputed datum. So, too, was the reality of the Presence. What was lacking in both cases was a profound reflection on the data and terminology suitable to make the necessary distinctions. It is to the great credit of Paschasius that his work sparked further considerations on the relationship between the Eucharistic Body and the natural Body of Christ—considerations that would be confirmed and deepened during the controversies aroused by Berengarius two centuries later. It did not, however, raise the parallel consideration touching upon the relationship between the Eucharistic sacrifice and the "once-and-for-all" sacrifice of Calvary.[128]

His emphasis on the reality of the Presence did not lead Paschasius to deny that there are symbolic elements in the Eucharistic Mystery. The mixing of the water with the wine is symbolic, as are the *fractio* and the symbolic manner in which the "Lamb is daily

---

[126] Cf., for example, *De Corp.,* 9, pp. 134–78, lines 4–19, op. cit., pp. 52–53, 57–59.

[127] Pelikan, 3, pp. 79, 80.

[128] Paschasius himself clearly taught the uniqueness or "once-and-for-all" nature of the sacrifice of Calvary. Cf. *De Corp.,* 9, lines 4–8; op. cit., p. 52.

immolated". Nor did his stress on the reality lead him to neglect the Augustinian distinction between a reception that is merely physical and a reception that is physical and spiritual. Doing an exegesis of St. Paul's words to the Corinthians (1 Cor 11:28–29), Paschasius states that by the sinner who fails to examine himself and who fails to discern the Body of the Lord,[129] judgment is received and not a fruitful reception of Christ.[130]

> What does the sinner eat and what does he drink? Not indeed the Flesh and Blood in a way that is for his profit, but rather judgment, even though it appears that he receives the Sacrament of the altar along with others.... For him the power of the Sacrament is withdrawn, and because of presumption his liability to judgment is doubled [Lat. *Propter quod illi virtus sacramenti subtrahitur et in eodem ob praesumptionem iudicium reatus duplicatur*].[131]

Paschasius distinguished a threefold usage of the term *Body of Christ.* It is the Church, the Sacrament, and the Body born of Mary "into which the Sacrament is transferred".[132] It is the sacramental reception of the Body born of Mary that makes Christians members of Christ, thereby making them members of the Church, the Body of Christ. Thus, it is fair to say that for Radbertus, the "primary analogue" is the risen Body of Christ, with which the sacramental Body is identical. The Church is called Body of Christ through relation to the risen-sacramental Body.

Chapter XV teaches that this Mystery is effected (*conficitur*) by the consecratory words of the Lord as he spoke them at the Last Supper. Chapter XVI says that after the Consecration, the Lord's

---

[129] Some have held in recent years that St. Paul's reference in 1 Cor. 11:29 to the person who "eats and drinks without recognizing the Body eats and drinks judgment on himself" is to be understood as a reference to a failure to recognize the Christian community as the ecclesial Body of Christ. Radbertus does not understand the text this way, nor, as far as I can discover, did any of the Fathers.

[130] *De Corp.,* 6, pp. 35–36, lines 30–50.

[131] *De Corp.,* 6, p. 35, lines 30–40.

[132] *De Corp.,* 7, p. 38, line 26.

Body can still rightly be called bread. "It is Flesh according to grace; it is bread according to its efficacy. Just as earthly bread ministers to temporal life, so this Bread offers eternal and heavenly life, because he is eternal life." The language is reminiscent of Augustine and should be sufficient to exonerate Paschasius from the charges of "excessive realism" that some have made against his Eucharistic doctrine.[133] In fact, his work is a faithful synopsis of much of the Patristic Tradition, a Tradition that was soon to be challenged and reexamined.

Rabanus Maurus

One important aspect of Paschasius' work was challenged during his lifetime by no less a figure than Rabanus Maurus (ca. 780–856), the Abbot of Fulda and later Archbishop of Mainz. While he was still a monk at Fulda, Maurus wrote to his abbot predecessor, Eigil, a letter that refers to the teaching repeated by Paschasius that the Eucharistic Flesh is the same Flesh born of Mary. Maurus says that Paschasius attributes this teaching to Ambrose. Maurus, however, says he never had heard of any such teaching as being put forth by Ambrose and denies that the Eucharist is the same Flesh.[134] In another letter, this one to Bishop Heribald of Auxerre, to accompany Maurus' work *Poenitentiale,* he repeated the same opinion, referring to his earlier letter to Eigil: "Recently, some who do not think correctly about the very Sacrament of the Body and Blood of the Lord have said that it [the Sacrament] is the Body and Blood of the Lord that were born from Mary and in which the Lord himself suffered on the Cross and that rose from the tomb. Writing to Abbot Eigil, I resisted this error

---

[133] Even Johann Auer (*Allgemeine Sakramentenlehre und Das Mysterium der Eucharistie*) speaks of the "extreme Capharnaitic realism" of Paschasius ("Es ging um die Auseinandersetzung mit dem extrem *kapharnaitischen historischen Realismus des Paschasius Radbertus . . .* ", p. 193).

[134] Rabanus Maurus, *Epistola III, ad Egilem; PL,* 112, 1513, 2.

as much as I could, and set forth that which should really be believed."[135] Since Maurus himself believed that the Lord's Body and Blood were truly present in the Eucharist, however, it may be that his difficulties involved not the identity of the Presence but the different manners or modes in which the identical Presence existed.

Ratramnus of Corbie

Another—and ultimately more influential—viewpoint came from within Paschasius' own monastery at Corbie. Ratramnus of Corbie (died 868), in his work *De Corpore et Sanguine Domini,* defended a Eucharistic doctrine quite different—at least in appearance—from that of the man who may have been his teacher as well as his abbot. It is still disputed whether Ratramnus was directly challenging the doctrine of Paschasius,[136] but, whatever the actual situation at Corbie, most subsequent theologians certainly viewed the differences between the ideas of two men as a conflict, even if they were not personally in conflict.

Ratramnus' thought lacks somewhat in clarity,[137] and there are several questions one would like to be able to ask him. Some

[135] Rabanus Maurus, *Epistola LVI,* in *Monumenta Germaniae Historica: Epistolae,* vol. 5, Berlin, 1899, p. 513. Also in *PL,* 110, 492–93.

[136] Gary Macy is one who thinks that the different approaches of the two men "existed in relative harmony at the monastery of Corbie" (p. 22). The *Cambridge Medieval History,* vol. 6, notes that "the use made of the book at a much later date by convinced opponents of the doctrine of transubstantiation is against the complete validity of this view" (p. 676). Pelikan, along with most writers since the tenth century, describes viewpoints of Paschasius and Ratramnus as a "conflict" (3, p. 74). Geiselmann, too, considers Ratramnus' doctrine heterodox (pp. 176–218).

[137] Stone comments: "It is tantalizing to be baffled by the problem of Ratramn's meaning. The present writer has read the book [the *De Corp.,* etc.] many times in the hope of being able to form some clear idea on this subject, and can only confess his failure to reach a conclusion which seems to him to satisfy all the elements in Ratramn's teaching" (1, p. 233). Geiselmann (pp. 176–218), on the other hand, judges Ratramnus' work to be heretical.

things, however, seem to be clear. Ratramnus drew a sharp distinction between truth (*veritas*) and figure (*figura*). Setting out to reply to the questions put to him by Emperor Charles the Bald, Ratramnus began his work by defining what he meant by the two terms.

> Figure is a kind of hiding . . . of what is meant to be shown. For example, . . . when Christ in the Gospel says, "I am the living Bread who have come down from heaven", or when he calls himself the vine and his disciples the branches . . . all these things say one thing but imply another.
>
> Truth is the manifest setting forth of a reality such that it is not hidden by any images or shadows, or, to speak more clearly, it is the setting forth of things in their pure, open, and natural signification, as is the case when one says that Christ was born of the Virgin, suffered, was crucified, died, and was buried. In these cases nothing is hidden by figures that are obscure; the truth of the reality is set forth by the significance of the natural words; nothing other than what is said is to be understood. But in the cases mentioned above [when speaking of "figure"] it is not thus. Substantially the bread is not Christ or the vine Christ or the branches Apostles. Therefore these are a figure.[138]

Ratramnus is not saying that things are simply what they appear to be; he is not what would later be called an empiricist. He admits that faith can discern a deeper reality than that which is presented "in figure".

> This bread which is made [*conficitur*] the Body of Christ through the ministry of the priest manifests itself externally to the human sense as one thing, but something else cries out internally to the minds of the faithful. Externally indeed the form of bread, which

[138] Ratramnus, *De Corpore,* 7–8, *PL,* 121, 130 (pp. 34–35). The newer edition of Ratramnus' work (*De Corpore et Sanguine domini. Texte Établi d'après les Manuscrits et Notice bibliographique*), edited by J. N. Bakhuizen van den Brink, differs in no substantial way from the *PL* in the texts cited here. Page references to the Bakhuizen edition are put in parentheses for reference convenience.

was present before, is set forth; its color is offered; its taste is
received. But internally something much more precious and far
more excellent is intimated because it is heavenly and divine. The
Body of Christ is shown forth, intuited, seen, received, eaten, not
by the senses of the flesh but by the mind of the faithful.[139]

Nevertheless, having defined truth and figure as he did, Ratramnus necessarily says that the Eucharist is not the Body and
Blood of Christ "in truth" but rather "in figure" or "in Sacrament".
The Eucharist is the "Sacrament of the Body of Christ"; it is not
the truth of the Body and Blood born of Mary but the figure or
Sacrament of that Body and Blood. Citing Ambrose (cf. p. 42
above), Ratramnus continued:

About the Flesh of Christ that was crucified and buried . . . he
says: Thus it is the true Flesh of Christ. But concerning that which
is received in the Sacrament, he says, "Therefore it is truly the
Sacrament of that Flesh", thereby distinguishing the Sacrament of
the Flesh from the truth of the Flesh. . . . That Flesh, according to
which Christ was crucified and buried, is not a Mystery but a truth
of nature. However, this Flesh, which contains in mystery the likeness of that other Flesh, is not Flesh in appearance but rather a
Sacrament. If in appearance [in specie] it is bread, in Sacrament
it is the true Body of Christ.[140]

All of the above can carry a meaning in harmony with what
Paschasius himself wrote. Indeed, it is at least a defensible thesis
that the difference between the two was one of terminology, not
of substance. Nevertheless, there are real differences. Ratramnus
paid but little attention to the change that takes place in the
elements of bread and wine, and what references he did make are
capable of various interpretations, although they tend to stress no
realistic change in the bread and wine (cf. chapters 12 and 13).
Furthermore, having defined truth as that which is clear and

[139] Ratramnus, *De Corpore,* 9; *PL,* 121, 131 (p. 35).

[140] Ratramnus, *De Corpore,* 57; *PL,* 121, 150–51 (pp. 48–49). There is one
insignificant verbal difference between the *PL* and the Bakhuizen edition.

evident and consequently having to say that the Eucharist was not Christ's Body "in truth" but only in "figure" or Sacrament, Ratramnus had "muddied the waters". For others who would follow him and who would equate "truth" with "reality", it would be easy enough to interpret him as saying that Christ was present not in the reality of his Body and Blood but *only* in figure or sign. Indeed, there are passages in Ratramnus that lend strong support to such an interpretation.

> Therefore it appears that there are many differences that separate [the real Body from the Eucharistic Body], as great as between a pledge and the reality for which the pledge is given, between an image and the reality whose image it is, between the appearance and the truth. Therefore we see that many differences separate the Mystery of the Blood and Body of Christ that is now received by the faithful in the Church and that Body that was born of the Virgin Mary and that suffered, was buried, rose, ascended above the heavens, and sits at the right hand of the Father.[141]

Rightly or wrongly, it is the symbolic interpretation of Ratramnus' work that prevailed. His book remained largely unknown through the tenth century and then, by some accident of history whose origins still remain unknown, reappeared in the eleventh century under the name of another man, John Scotus Erigena. As such it would be used by Berengarius and by many subsequent writers. "The treatise of Ratramnus was to come out of the shadows even later than that, when it became 'a sort of shibboleth on the subject of Eucharistic doctrine' during the controversies of the Reformation in the sixteenth century".[142]

---

[141] Ratramnus, *De Corpore*, 89; *PL*, 121, 165 (pp. 56–57). The initial "therefore" is not present in the newer edition of the work.

[142] Pelikan, 3, p. 80.

II

"This Is a Hard Teaching.
Who Can Accept It?"

"Then the Jews began to argue sharply among themselves, 'How can this man give us his flesh to eat?' " (Jn 6:52). And "on hearing it, many of his disciples said, 'This is a hard teaching. Who can accept it?' " (Jn 6:60).

The Eucharistic Mystery concerns the Word of life. Indeed, St. John records that, when Jesus had finished his discourse in the synagogue at Capernaum, he said to his astounded listeners, "The words I have spoken to you are spirit, and they are life." Such they were, but he had expressed them—perhaps intentionally so—in such a provocative way that they scandalized not only the Jews in general but the Jews who were his disciples as well. To a Jew the notion of eating flesh and drinking blood was a horror. Indeed, through the prophet Ezekiel, God had used the imagery of having their flesh and blood eaten as the ultimate disgrace to be visited upon sinners.

> Call out to every bird and all the wild animals: "Assemble and come together from all around to the sacrifice I am preparing for you, the great sacrifice on the mountains of Israel. There you will eat flesh and drink blood. You will eat the flesh of mighty men and drink the blood of the princes of the earth as if they were rams and lambs, goats and bulls.... At the sacrifice I am preparing for you, you will eat fat till you are glutted and drink blood till you are drunk" (Ezek 39:17–19).

Now at Capernaum the Eternal One who had inspired those words was telling them that, at his sacrifice, they and not animals would indeed eat the Flesh of the Mighty and drink the Blood of the Prince of the princes of the earth. Knowing the shock created by the very thought, Jesus added immediately, "Yet there are some of you who do not believe" (Jn 6:63–64).

The scandal of the Mystery has never gone away; it is for many just too much to accept. Flannery O'Connor, in one of her letters, recalls a visit she made to another well-known author and former Catholic. This latter "said that when she was a child and received the Host, she thought of it as the Holy Ghost, he being the 'most portable' Person of the Trinity; now she thought of it as a symbol and implied that it was a pretty good one. I then said, in a very shaky voice, 'Well, if it's a symbol, to hell with it.' That was all the defense I was capable of, but I realize now that this is all I will ever be able to say about it, outside of a story, except that it is the center of existence for me; all the rest of life is expendable."[1]

It is surely true that the Mystery of the Eucharist can be propounded in such a way that all of the "shock value" contained in the words of Jesus is removed by anticipation. Such a form of pedagogy or catechesis, however, departs from the approach taken by the Lord himself. It can happen that, by removing the shock, one will remove as well an accurate appreciation of the Eucharist, thereby obviating the response in faith that is necessary to accept Christ's words. Jesus may have intended to shock. Indeed, on the occasion of his synagogue talk at Capernaum, he let the words stand by themselves, refusing to give any explanation that would soften their impact. What he taught was beyond human nature's ability to comprehend. ("That is called Flesh which flesh does not understand, and because it is called Flesh, so much the more does flesh not understand", Augustine would say.) The Lord, however, was looking for faith, faith in himself and faith in his words, well aware, as he himself said, that no one could offer such faith "unless the Father draw him" (Jn 6:44). And so many found the saying too much to take. They went away.

Through the centuries the Church has consistently refused to mitigate the shock contained in the words of the Lord at Capernaum.

---

[1] Flannery O'Connor, *The Habit of Being*, p. 125.

Her pedagogy is like her Master's. Recognize in all its fullness what it is you are expected to believe and pray that the Father will lead you to accept. Let him accept it who can. Dissent to the Church's teaching is not only a phenomenon of the twentieth century; it has always existed. And this dissent has touched upon not merely secondary issues but frequently upon those most central to the Catholic understanding of Jesus' message. None more so than the Eucharist. Many have not been able to accept the Mystery as the Church meditated upon it and expounded it more adequately, but their very unwillingness or inability has been the occasion used by the Spirit to deepen the Church's appreciation for what Jesus meant. Since the lack of faith of some has, in its own way, stimulated the faith of others, this chapter is mainly given over to those who have stumbled on the "hard teaching".

Berengarius of Tours

It is with Berengarius of Tours that the Church began to witness the major periodic controversies provoked by the words of Jesus as recorded in John 6. Indeed, the Berengarian conflict could almost be called paradigmatic for the many disputes that would follow.

Berengarius was born in Tours, France, around the year 1010, and came from a well-to-do family. Indeed, the family riches came to play an important role in his later career since, as the major modern study on Berengarius and his work states, he would use that wealth to help the poor (his generosity was notable) and "to sustain his heterodox propaganda".[2] Around 1040 he was made Archdeacon of Angers, although he continued to reside and teach in Tours. Much influenced by the work of Ratramnus—which he, like all others in his day, attributed to John Scotus Erigena—Berengarius began the controversy by a letter he wrote to Lanfranc

---

[2] Jean de Montclos, *Lanfranc et Bérenger: la Controverse Eucharistique du XIe Siècle,* p. 30. Pelikan, 3, p. 316, says of Montclos' work that it will be "for some time to come, the definitive monograph".

(born in Pavia around 1010, Prior of the Monastery of Bec at the time of Berengarius' letter, and later Archbishop of Canterbury). Berengarius had heard that Lanfranc had attacked the Eucharistic teaching of Scotus Erigena (i.e., Ratramnus) while upholding that of St. Paschasius. "Berengarius saw in Paschasius the defender of that realistic conception of the Eucharist that had been adopted by the great mass of ignorant people. On the other hand, he believed that he found in the treatise of 'John Scotus' the justification for a pure symbolism, the only teaching conformable—so he thought— to the traditional data."[3] In his letter to Lanfranc, he asserted that if Scotus (Ratramnus) was heretical, so too were Augustine, Ambrose, and Jerome.

In 1050 at a synod in Rome, with Lanfranc present, Berengarius' defense of Ratramnus' opinions was considered before Pope Leo IX and other European bishops. The defense was rejected, and Berengarius was provisionally excommunicated until he should appear before a "follow-up" synod to be held in September of the same year at Vercelli. By mischance, Berengarius did not appear at Vercelli, while Lanfranc did. Parts of Ratramnus' work (at least Chapters 84–87) were read at Vercelli by the Pope and bishops. They were condemned as heretical. The condemnation of Berengarius was confirmed because of his defense of Scotus (Ratramnus) in the letter to Lanfranc.

Claiming that he had been condemned without a hearing, Berengarius wrote and circulated a pamphlet, now lost, in which, among other things, he accused Leo IX of a lack of judgment. His unwillingness to disavow his defense of Ratramnus led to a further condemnation at a synod in Paris in 1051. Still another synod was held at Tours in 1054. It was presided over by Hildebrand, later Pope Gregory VII. This time Berengarius was present to speak on his own behalf. According to his own account, as well as that of

---

[3] Montclos, p. 49: "Bérenger voyait en Paschase le défenseur de la conception réaliste de l'eucharistie adoptée par la grande masse ignare. Par contre, il
croyait trouver dans le traité de 'Jean Scot' la justification d'un pur symbolisme,
seul conforme, sensait-il, aux données traditionnelles."

Lanfranc, Berengarius, when questioned, assured the bishops that he believed that, after the Consecration, the Eucharist was really the Body and Blood of Christ.[4]

Differing evaluations have been made of what it was that Berengarius was actually holding concerning the Eucharist at this stage of the controversy. Stone writes:

> It is probable that Berengar in the earlier stages of his teaching was desirous of emphasizing the spiritual character of the Consecration of the elements and the Presence of Christ. From this he himself at times may have gone on to deny the traditional doctrine that the consecrated elements are the Body and Blood of Christ.[5]

The modern study done by Montclos is more severe in its judgment, claiming that Berengarius would use realistic formulations of the doctrine while giving them a meaning different from their traditional sense.[6] Indeed, says Montclos, Berengarius succeeded in using equivocal formulas for nearly thirty years in order to continue his "semiclandestine fight in favor of Eucharistic symbolism".[7] As the result of his study of the matter, Montclos concludes that, by 1059, the Eucharistic doctrine of Berengarius could be summarized in four points: (1) the bread and wine remain intact after the Consecration; (2) the Consecration does not change the nature of the bread and wine but adds to them a

---

[4] Lanfranc, *Liber de Corpore et Sanguine Domini; PL* 150, 413–14: "Denique in concilio Turonensi, cui ipsius interfuere ac praefuere legati, data est tibi optio defendendi partem tuam. Quam cum defendendam suscipere non auderes, confessus coram omnibus communem Ecclesiae fidem jurasti, ab illa hora te ita crediturum sicut in Romano concilio te jurasse est superius comprehensum."

Berengarius' own account is found in the *De Sacra Coena* (17/29–18/2). "Hic ego inquam: Certissimum habete dicere me panem atque vinum altaris post consecrationem Christi esse revera corpus et sanguinem."

[5] Stone, I, pp. 257–58.

[6] Montclos, p. 124: "Mais il utilisait les formules réalistes en leur donnant un sens différent de leur sens traditionnel."

[7] Montclos, p. 119: "Il réussit, néanmoins, en utilisant des formules équivoques, à prolonger pendant près de trente ans un combat semi-clandestin en faveur du symbolisme eucharistique."

value or power that makes them Sacraments or signs of the Body and Blood of Christ; (3) there must be a similitude between the Sacraments and the reality designated by the Sacraments, and (4) one can say that, after the Consecration, the bread and wine become the true Body and Blood of Christ, in the sense that, through our faith and understanding, the risen Body of Christ is spiritually offered to and received by the communicant.[8]

Montclos' evaluation can be substantiated by a letter written by Berengarius to Adelman, the Bishop of Brescia, shortly before 1059. Fragments of this letter survive. In it Berengarius writes:

> Since you say that you have heard that I have declared that the bread and wine of the altar are not, after the Consecration, the true Body and Blood of Christ, you should know that I have never admitted this Manichaean opinion. I have held and hold that Christ had a true and human Body; they held that it was a phantasm. Furthermore I am not unaware of the fact that the Body of Christ, after it had obediently experienced death, resides at the Father's right hand, having been raised to immortality and impassibility. I see most certainly . . . that it becomes the Body of Christ, and I must concede that it becomes the true Body of Christ since Christ only has a true Body. . . . And because of this I am able to concede that, after the Consecration, the bread and wine themselves have become, for faith and understanding, the Body and Blood of Christ.[9]
>
> I have never found that the Scriptures called the Body and Blood of Christ a figure [figuram] or a likeness [similitudinem], and I have never called them that—but I am speaking of the very realities of the Sacraments [res ipsas sacramentorum], not of the Sacraments themselves. The Sacraments themselves, as Sacraments, I have judged to be called signs, figure, likeness, and pledge. . . .
>
> My adversaries, the common mass [vulgus]—and with the com-

[8] Montclos, pp. 142–48.

[9] Berengarius, *Epistola contra Almannum,* pp. 531–32, lines 1–15. The final sentence reads in Latin: "Ac per hoc non concedere nullus possum post consecrationem ipsum panem et vinum factum esse fidei et intellectui verum Christi corpus et sanguinem."

mon mass, the raving Paschasius and Lanfranc and others—understood the question this way: bread and wine are present on the altar up to the Consecration. At the Consecration, the bread and wine, by their corruption or absorption, sensually pass over into [being] a piece of the Flesh and Blood of Christ.[10]

My case—or rather that of the Scriptures—is this: the bread and wine of the Lord's table are changed, according to the Scriptures, not into a piece but into the whole Body and Blood of Christ—not sensually but intellectually, not through an absorption but through an assumption.[11]

It is clear that Berengarius differentiates between the Sacrament and the reality (*res*) of the Sacrament. In this he appeals to Augustine, and does so, I think, with reason. But from this he concludes that we eat the Body of the Lord in sign, while Augustine clearly said that we, unlike the Jews with their sacraments, eat in truth. Berengarius, in short, *separates* the reality and the sign or Sacrament of the reality. From this follows his teaching on the nature of the change that takes place. Bread and wine are changed; they are "assumed" becoming sacred signs, Sacraments. As such the bread and wine themselves have become, *for faith and understanding,* the Body and Blood. And by contrasting his position with that of the common mass and Paschasius and Lanfranc (whose views are distorted by Berengarius), he makes it clear that he is not speaking about a change in the elements themselves. Thus, by 1059, the disagreement centered on what would continue to be the focal point: What kind of change takes place in the bread and wine?

By 1059, also, the dispute had moved far beyond the case of a

[10] Berengarius, *Epistola contra Almannum,* p. 534, lines 71–75. The Latin of the opinion he ascribes to Paschasius and Lanfranc reads: "Urgente consecratione panem et vinum per corruptionem vel absumptione sui in portiunculam carnis Christi sensualiter transire et sanguinis."

[11] Berengarius, *Epistola contra Almannum,* p. 534, lines 76–80. The Latin reads: "Panem et vinum mensae dominicae non sensualiter, sed intellectualiter, non per absumptionem, sed per assumptionem, non in portiunculam carnis, contra scripturas, sed, secundum scripturas, in totum converti Christi corpus et sanguinem."

few theologians disputing different theories. Berengarius had many partisans, clerical and lay. Taking into account the difficulties of communication and transportation of the times, the controversy and consequent confusion among the faithful was becoming relatively widespread.

In an effort to end the dispute, another synod was called and met in Rome under the presidency of Pope Nicholas II in 1059. Berengarius attended; Lanfranc did not. An account was made to the bishops by Cardinal Humbert concerning Berengarius' theology of the Eucharist. The teaching was found to be erroneous, and Berengarius was asked to and did subscribe to a profession of faith, after which his writings on the Eucharist were burned.[12]

Hardly had he returned to France, however, before he wrote a pamphlet attacking the Pope and the synod, while defending again his own equivocal positions. Lanfranc answered him, publishing around 1065 his work *De Corpore et Sanguine Domini.* To this Berengarius responded in 1067 with his *De Coena Domini Adversus Lanfrancum.* It is not properly speaking a book on the Eucharist but rather an extensive defense of his own teaching, containing strong criticism of Humbert, Paschasius, and Lanfranc. Nevertheless, it is in this work, long thought to have been destroyed but rediscovered in the eighteenth century, that we find the fullest extant description of Berengarius' opinions in his own words.

> It is said in the Scriptures that the bread of the altar becomes, from bread, the Body of Christ, just as the bad servant is said to become, from the bad servant, the good son, while not losing the nature of his own soul and body. Thus Ambrose in his book on the Sacraments, making a comparison between the change of the bread and wine into the Body and Blood of Christ and the change of the bad servant into the son of God, says, "You were the old man but, after you had been consecrated, you began to be a new creature." . . . Therefore the Flesh of Christ, which for a thousand years already has possessed immortality and is in no way able to begin to exist now, does not become present from the bread

---

[12] Berengarius' Profession of Faith of 1059 is found on p. 177.

through the generation of itself and the corruption of the subject of the bread. This is true because this Flesh is not able to be assumed in such a way that, having been destroyed and restored, it begins to exist again, since it is immortal and incorruptible. Rather the bread of the altar, which by no means was flesh before the Consecration, becomes the Flesh of Christ, not through corruption of itself but through Consecration. That which is consecrated is not able to cease existing materially.[13]

One who objects to the teaching will say: I do not see the appearance [*speciem*] of blood. And St. Ambrose agrees with the objection that in no way does one see blood in the chalice . . . ; the chalice does not contain the appearance of blood, but contains, says Ambrose, the likeness of blood. It is necessary to repeat this: the Blood as such is present. The chalice does not contain the appearance of blood, but it has the likeness of blood, namely, the wine which has been made the Sacrament of that Blood. It is as if one were to say: if the Author of salvation should indicate to you the use of human blood in a sensual fashion, you would properly shrink from it as something shameful or evil. You would shrink from it not only in respect to what the eye would behold — as Lanfranc and Paschasius, the monk of Corbie, foolishly say — but also in respect to every bodily sense, but above all in respect to what the intellect perceives, the intellect being the glory of the inner man, where the horror at such a thing would be the greatest. As the Blood of Christ is offered you so that you might be washed in it, although not in any carnal fashion, so it is offered to you in order that you may also drink it, although not in any carnal fashion. If the Lord God had instituted these things to be done by you in a sensual manner according to the exterior man, rightly would you shrink from it in accordance with the dignity of the intellect. But nothing has been offered to you which you should rightly shun. Christ the Lord demands from you that you believe that, in his mercy toward the human race, he has shed his Blood and that, by thus believing in his Blood, you may be washed from all sin; he demands that, always keeping that same Blood of Christ in remembrance, you may construct the life of your interior self on

[13] Berengarius, *De Coena,* pp. 90–91.

it as food for the journey of this life just as you construct the life of your exterior self on outward food and drink. There is nothing to shrink from except from the evil of Naaman who, at first, held in contempt the waters of the Jordan . . . for the Lord demands that, believing inwardly . . . , you may be outwardly immersed in the element of water and, by means of this element, represent to yourself the death of Christ so that you may be immersed in it as someone to be killed and drawn forth from it as one to be vivified . . . he demands that by means of bodily eating and drinking, which take place through outward things, namely, through bread and wine, you may remind yourself [*commonefacias*] of the spiritual eating and drinking of the Flesh and Blood of Christ, which takes place in the mind, thus refreshing yourself inwardly from the Incarnation and Passion of the Word. . . . There is no reason why you should shrink from eating the bread and drinking the wine because it is a holy and well-known part of creation, as Ambrose says in that same treatise on the Sacrament.[14]

From such texts it would appear that the Eucharistic elements play the same role as does the element of water in Baptism. And that, of course, is the central point of dispute in the entire controversy, namely, does anything more happen to the Eucharistic elements than happens to the material elements used in the other sacraments? It is not the case, says Berengarius, that nothing happens to the sacramental elements. The Consecration, according to Berengarius, does effect a change. He has affirmed and continues to affirm that the Consecration changes the elements into the true Body and Blood of Christ. In attempting to describe this change, however, he writes:

Some things are changed [*convertuntur*] through the corruption of the subject into something which it was not before. It is something completely different, however, to change something through the consecration of the subject. . . . All Scripture testifies to the fact that the bread and wine are changed, through consecration, into the Body and Blood of Christ. It is evident, therefore, that every-

[14] Berengarius, *De Coena,* pp. 221–23.

thing that is consecrated, everything that is blessed by God, is not assumed, not taken away, not destroyed, but rather remains and is necessarily advanced to something better than it was before.[15]

It is not easy to determine with precision what it was he actually held concerning the presence and the change that takes place in the elements. Even his contemporaries were not of one mind as to what he held. Thus, Guitmund, Bishop of Aversa, in his work *De Corporis et Sanguinis Christi Veritate in Eucharistia,* which he wrote between 1059 and 1070, says the following:

> All the Berengarians agree that the bread and wine are not essentially [*essentialiter*] changed, but, as I have been able to determine from some of them, there are differences among them. Some say that there is nothing at all of the Body and Blood of the Lord present in these Sacraments but that they are only shadows and figures [*umbras et figuras esse*]. Others, however, ceding to the right reason of the Church while not drawing away from folly—and so that they might seem to be with us in some manner—say that the Body and Blood of the Lord are truly there but are contained in a hidden way and are, if I may speak thus, impanated in a certain way [*impanari*]. And they say that this more subtle opinion is the opinion of Berengarius himself. Others indeed, who are not really Berengarians but actually strongly repudiating Berengarius . . . are accustomed to think that the bread and wine partly change and partly remain the same. Others . . . think that the bread and wine are completely changed but that when the unworthy approach to receive the Body and Blood of the Lord, the Sacraments revert to bread and wine.[16]

From the fact that the "Berengarians" differed among themselves, it is probably safe to infer that their leader, Berengarius himself, never explained himself with such clarity as to preclude various interpretations. Guitmund declares that, according to some interpreters, Berengarius may not have been a pure symbolist—as were

[15] Berengarius, *De Coena,* p. 248.

[16] Guitmund, *De Corporis et Sanguinis Christi Veritate in Eucharistia; PL,* 149, 1430–31.

some of his followers—but held for impanation, the view that would hold that Christ was truly physically present but that the full reality of the bread and wine remained as well.[17] Lanfranc and most other contemporaries—as well as Montclos' study—hold that Berengarius defended a purely symbolic Presence. In fact, if one may find a parallel in later history, it is possible that Berengarius' own thought fluctuated between the "Presence in symbol" of a Zwingli and the "Presence in power or virtue" of a Calvin. Since he was so consistent in declaring that the reality of the Sacrament was eaten in faith and understanding, and not in any way sensually, it does not seem accurate to attribute to him a theory of impanation. But his own studied ambiguities certainly left room for such an understanding. What all agree upon is that Berengarius taught the continued existence of the full reality of the bread and wine after the Consecration and denied that Christ was received bodily; he was rather received only according to faith and understanding.

The difficulty in determining Berengarius' precise thought on the Eucharist becomes apparent in the events of the Roman synods of 1078 and 1079. Before recording those events, however, some further consideration should be given to the work of Guitmund of Aversa. He is one of those "little ones" whose name often carries scant if any recognition and whose work, when referred to at all in the textbooks, usually manages to secure a footnote or two or serves as an appendix to the thought of Lanfranc, Berengarius' great protagonist.[18] Yet he clearly deserves more attention,

[17] Montclos says that Guitmund's view is not to be accepted and that the theory of impanation is "very far" from what was actually held by the deacon of Tours (p. 200 note, and p. 2).

[18] Geiselmann (pp. 375ff. and passim) and Stone treat of Guitmund extensively, but Stone writes: "His book on the Eucharist is longer and more systematic than either of those by Lanfranc and Durand of Troan; and it shows traces of a more careful study both of the opinions of Berengar and of other current views. Yet, in spite of his great reputation, he appears to have possessed

since his positive contribution to the Catholic theology of the Eucharist at least equals that of Lanfranc, may have contributed significantly to the dogmatic formulations of 1079, and anticipated some of the great synthesis of St. Thomas.

Guitmund was born in Normandy, became a Benedictine monk, and was made a cardinal of the Roman Church by Gregory VII and Bishop of Aversa near Naples by Urban II. He died around 1090.

In his already cited treatise, Guitmund's theology on the Eucharist can be summarized as follows:

1. The Eucharistic Body is the Body that was born of Mary, died on the Cross, and now reigns glorious and immutable in heaven.[19]

2. The change that takes place in the elements is the "Mystery of faith" and cannot be comprehended by the senses or the intelligence. "It must not be understood first so that it can afterward be believed; it must be believed first, so that it can afterward be understood."[20]

3. Of the four kinds of changes with which we are familiar (namely, [a] creation from nothing, [b] a change of "accidents", [c] a change of one "substance" into something else that did not previously exist, and [d] a change of a "substance" into something that previously existed), the Eucharist is the fourth kind. Further-

---

much less insight than either . . . ; and his theological statements differ in important respects from both earlier and later Western theology" (I, p. 253). Montclos admits that Guitmund's work corrects and perfects that of Lanfranc but is in some aspects deficient (pp. 460–62). A Lutheran theologian, on the other hand, has written: "The doctrine of transubstantiation grew slowly, but with logical consequence, out of the theological work of the adversaries of Berengar, the most important of whom seems to have been Guitmund of Aversa. Almost all elements of the later dogma except the word *transubstantiation* originated with him" (H. Sasse, *This Is My Body*, p. 38). In fact, of course, the elements of the doctrine long predate Guitmund.

[19] Guitmund, *De Corporis; PL*, 149, 1427–94 passim.

[20] Guitmund, *De Corporis; PL*, 149, 1439 and 1441.

more, it is unique in its kind since the bread and wine are changed into the already existing Body and Blood of Christ.[21]

4. The change that occurs in the elements is one whereby "the bread and wine of the altar are substantially converted into the Body and Blood of the Lord".[22] Indeed, "God has made a change [*mutationem*] of the bread and wine into the substance of the Body and Blood of Christ."[23] Guitmund also calls this change a "transmutation" [*transmutari*].[24]

5. In this change, Christ is not brought down from heaven.[25]

6. After the change, Christ's Body and Blood are "substantially" present, but not the "qualities" of that Body.[26] It is the same Body (see no. 1 above) but in a different form.[27] By "qualities" Guitmund means "sensual qualities" or "accidents".

7. The "accidents" of the bread and wine remain. "Indeed the sensual qualities that by the most high wisdom of God, he wishes to remain after the change of substance, show forth what is their own. Thus it happens that color and taste and smell and any other accidents of the first substance, i.e., of the bread, remain."[28]

8. The "accidents" of the bread and wine can corrupt, but nothing happens to the "substance of the Lord's Body".[29]

---

[21] Guitmund, *De Corporis; PL,* 149, 1443–44 and 1440.

[22] Guitmund, *De Corporis; PL,* 149, 1488.

[23] Guitmund, *De Corporis; PL,* 149, 1489.

[24] Guitmund, *De Corporis; PL,* 149, 1491. Cf. all of 1483–84.

[25] Guitmund, *De Corporis; PL,* 149, 1436 and 1466.

[26] Guitmund, *De Corporis; PL,* 149, 1463, 1469, 1476. This teaching is repeated in a summary fashion in his *Confessio; PL,* 149, 1500.

[27] Guitmund, *De Corporis; PL,* 149, 1462.

[28] Guitmund, *De Corporis; PL,* 149, 1450. The Latin reads: "Qualitates vero sensuales, quas ibidem post immutationem substantiae Dei remanere altissimo concilio voluit, ostendunt quod suum est. Unde fit ut color et sapor, odor quoque, et si qua huiusmodi accidentia prioris essentiae videlicet panis servata sunt." On the "accidents", cf. also 1443 and 1481.

[29] Guitmund, *De Corporis; PL,* 149, 1448–50. Note 10 in *PL* 149, 1448, as well as Stone, I, p. 254, indicate that Guitmund apparently teaches an immutability of the accidents of bread and wine after the Consecration. Such a view is not quite accurate. What Guitmund does say is that he thinks God will keep

9. In the Eucharist, the Body of Christ is truly touched by our hands and truly eaten, but in such cases he himself is in no way wounded or hurt.[30]

10. Like the eating, the *fractio,* the breaking of the Host at Mass, does not hurt the Lord, nor does it divide him, even though the Host is divided. This *fractio* is a symbolic expression [*similitudo*] of his Passion and death, whence the Mass gets its sacrificial aspect.[31]

11. The Body of Christ is present in each part of the Host as well as in the entire Host, but remains One Body; his Body is totally present in a "thousand Hosts at a thousand Masses" but remains only the One identical Body.[32]

Guitmund's achievement is truly quite an amazing one. If he is not the first,[33] he is among the first to use the "substance-accidents" distinction to help clarify the problem involved in a real change that leaves the appearances of the former elements intact. His notion of the "substantial" Presence of Christ's Body, whole in the entire Host, whole in all the parts of the Host, is another major advance and indicates that his notion of substance (which he never defines) cannot be one that merely sees it as a kind of "material substratum" of reality. His description of the change is, verbally at least, very close to that used later at the Council of Trent. Indeed, his doctrine is far removed from the "ultrarealism" charge that is often directed at him as well as at other early Medieval theologians.

---

the accidents of bread and wine immutable, such that they will not corrupt etc. However, he admits he can envision cases where the accidents will corrupt or suffer harm. Even in such cases, however, the substance of the Body and Blood of Christ remains unharmed.

[30] Guitmund, *De Corporis; PL,* 149, 1432–33.

[31] Guitmund, *De Corporis; PL,* 149, 1434.

[32] Guitmund, *De Corporis; PL,* 149, 1434–35, 1440.

[33] Geiselmann claims that it was Berengarius who first used the distinction: "Berengar ist demnach der erste, der die Begriffe forma und materia bzw subiectum und accidens in der Eucharistielehre anwendet" (p. 340).

There are defects, of course, as well as unanswered questions. The major defect would seem to be his notion that the "accidents" of Christ's Body are not present. However, he may mean by this what he teaches elsewhere when he says that the Lord's Body is present in "another form" in the Eucharist than it is in heaven, even though it is the identical Body. The major question is the relationship of his terminology and concepts to the categories of the philosophy of Aristotle. In his use of the words *substance* and *substantial change* he is following Paschasius. But his manner of explaining that change, his forceful rejection of any theory of impanation, and his use of the word *accidents* are terminologically very like those used by later writers who adapt the Aristotelian framework to defend and illuminate the revealed truth. Guitmund, however, does this at a time (ca. 1075) that predates the time usually fixed for the "Aristotelian revival" in Europe, although it is true that the works of Boethius in the sixth century had reintroduced much of the Aristotelian thought pattern. That problem, however, is one for the historians of philosophy. Guitmund wrote not as a philosopher but as a theologian striving to make a coherent presentation of what the Church believed and believes about the Eucharistic Mystery. He did this well, taking care at the same time to appeal to the traditional Faith as passed on by the Fathers, especially St. Augustine, whose "difficult texts" (particularly the ones seen in Section I above) Guitmund carefully analyzed. Whether Guitmund directly influenced the Church's final statement on Berengarius can only be conjectured, but there are noticeable similarities.

The Roman Synods of 1078 and 1079 were presided over by Hildebrand, now Pope Gregory VII. Since he had been his predecessor's legate at the Synod of Tours, the problem was not a new one to him. Nevertheless, the subtlety of Berengarius' thought apparently escaped the Pope initially. At the Synod in 1078, Berengarius submitted a profession of faith, composed by himself, that said that after the Consecration the bread is the true Body of Christ born of Mary and the wine is the true Blood of Christ that flowed from his side on the Cross. The confession was equivocal, since it would still allow him to maintain that the bread and wine also remained what they had been before the Consecration.

The Pope at first accepted the profession and declared Berengarius' doctrine to be in conformity with that of the Church. Further reflection, prompted by the advice of other bishops, helped him to see the ambiguity of the profession. Gregory then declared that the matter needed further consideration. This took place in Lent of 1079, where a confession that declared that the bread and wine were "substantially converted" into the Body and Blood of Christ was submitted to Berengarius. He signed it, promised to teach his own views no longer, and retired to an eremitical life on the island of St. Cosmé near Tours. There he wrote his *Memoir,* which apologizes for his errors but is in a certain sense an apologia for his own case. He died on the Feast of the Epiphany, 1088, one year before the death of Lanfranc at Canterbury.

Montclos closes his study on Berengarius noting that his case was a complex one: a man of intellectual pride with a myopic view of the Church's articles of faith, a man whose mental state was paranoid but whose thought was explainable in part because of "the grave insufficiencies of the Eucharistic theology of his time".[34] It is a harsh judgment, made only harsher perhaps by pointing out that, at least in some cases, the "theological insufficiencies" were not as great as one might think, although one can say on the other hand that the insights of a Guitmund might not have appeared but for the scandal given to the faith of the masses by a man who so disdained them. Speaking of such scandals, Jesus had said, "It is necessary that scandals come, but woe to the man by whom they come" (Mt 18:7). St. Paul, picking up the thought and applying it in the context of the Eucharist, wrote: "I hear that when you come together as a Church there are divisions among you, and to some extent I believe it. No doubt there have to be differences among you to show which of you have God's approval" (1 Cor 11:18–19). It is the recognition that scandals and dissension are not good in themselves but that, in a fallen world, they are

[34] Montclos, p. 244.

inevitable and that from them good can come. This was certainly true at the time of the furor raised by Berengarius. And of the man himself, it is well to remember his deserved reputation for almsgiving to the poor.

He has never been forgotten and has always had his defenders. Berengarius was considered a hero by many (Martin Luther being the notable exception) who, in subsequent ages, would dissent from the teaching of the Catholic Church concerning the Eucharist. Even in the nineteenth century, Samuel Taylor Coleridge, showing the same disdain for the faith of "uncongenial minds", could praise him thus in one of his deservedly less-remembered poems:

Lines: Suggested by the Last Words of Berengarius

No more 'twixt conscience staggering and the Pope
Soon shall I now before my God appear,
By him to be acquitted, as I hope;
By him to be condemned, as I fear.

Reflection on the Above

Lynx amid moles! had I stood by thy bed,
Be of good cheer, meek soul! I would have said:
I see a hope spring from that humble fear.
All are not strong alike through storms to steer
Right onward. What? though dread of threatened death
And dungeon torture made thy hand and breath
Inconstant to the truth within thy heart!
That truth, from which, through fear, thou twice didst start,
Fear haply told thee, was a learned strife,
Or not so vital as to claim thy life:
And myriads had reached Heaven who never knew
Where lay the difference 'twixt the false and true!

Ye, who secure 'mid trophies not your own,
Judge him who won them when he stood alone,
And proudly talk of recreant Beregare—
O first the age, and then the man compare!
That age how dark! congenial minds how rare!

No host of friends with kindred zeal did burn!
No throbbing hearts awaited his return!
Prostrate alike when prince and peasant fell,
He only disenchanted from the spell,
Like the weak worm that gems the starless night,
Moved in the scanty circlet of his light.[35]

The Cathari

The centuries immediately after the controversy over Berengarius'
thought witnessed other heresies that touched directly or indirectly
upon the Eucharist. The most widespread arose among those sects
of a Manichaean type whose members came to be called "Cathari"
(the "pure ones"). The origins of these groups are still obscure,
but there appears to be some connection between them and the
Gnosticlike group in the Byzantine Empire called Bogomils. Common to these various movements was a disdain for material reality
and a consequent shunning of the Catholic sacraments. In the
twelfth and thirteenth centuries they became fairly widespread in
the Rhineland, northern Italy, and in southern France. In France,
because of their prominence around the city of Albi, they came to
be called Albigenses or Albigensians. Their teaching in respect to
the Eucharist was described by a monk of the Empire, Eckbert of
Schonau, around 1165:

> They completely spurn and consider of no value Masses that are
> celebrated in the churches. If, by chance, they go to hear Mass
> with the people among whom they live, or even go to receive the
> Eucharist, they do so completely out of pretense in order that their
> lack of faith may not be known. They claim that the order of
> priests in the Roman Church and in all the Churches of the
> Catholic Faith has completely perished and that no true priests are
> found except in their own sect.

[35] *Coleridge: Poetical Works,* edited by Ernest Hartley Coleridge, London:
Oxford University Press, 1973, pp. 460–61. The poem first appeared in 1827.

They believe that in no way do the Body and Blood of the Lord come about by our Consecration and that we are not able to receive that Body and Blood through Communion; they say that they alone confect the Body of the Lord at their tables. But there is ingenuity in these words: they do not mean that true Body of Christ which we believe to have been born of the Virgin Mary and which suffered on the Cross, but rather call their own flesh the Body of the Lord and claim that the Body of the Lord is present inasmuch as they nourish their own bodies at their meals.[36]

Like all orthodox believers of the period, Eckbert applies the criterion of identity between the Body born of Mary and the Eucharist to determine what is actually being believed. The disdain for the priesthood that Eckbert mentioned appeared in other groups as well, notably among the Waldensians, followers of Peter Waldo (Valdo), who reacted against the worldly lives of many of the clergy of the period by claiming that any truly holy person could confect the Eucharist.[37]

Apart from such movements, the years after 1079 saw a general theological consensus develop concerning the Eucharist. There was, of course, much that remained to be examined in detail, and theologians explained the 1079 teaching on "substantially changed" in various ways. There had to be taken in account the "incon-

[36] Eckbert of Schonau, *Sermo I; PL,* 195, 15. Cf. also Radulphus Ardens' *Homily XIX (PL,* 155, 2011), where Radulphus says that the Cathari "say that the Sacrament of the altar is merely bread". Lambert, *Medieval Heresy,* treats well the rise of the differing heresies of the period, and Moore, *The Birth of Popular Heresy,* gives the translation of many other documents of the period that indicate positions like those mentioned by Eckbert on the part of the various groups of Cathari: no true Presence of Christ, and no priesthood in the Catholic Church.

[37] The denial of a true priesthood in the Catholic Church and the position that held that any truly good person could confect the Eucharist was an issue addressed by the Church in the *Profession of Faith Prescribed for the Waldensians,* who submitted to Church discipline, and in the Creed *Firmiter* of Lateran Council IV in 1215. For both of these cf. below, pp. 185–86. Cf. Gary Macy, pp. 56–57, for a treatment of the Waldensian view that a layperson could consecrate.

veniences" attendant upon the Church's firm defense of the truth
of Christ's physical Presence in the Eucharist. Matters that had
long been a problem were now examined by the practitioners in
this first age of "scientific theology". One of the questions was
that concerning the reception of the Eucharist by those who were
morally unworthy or lacking in faith, to which were added the
questions about what happened when the Eucharist suffered the
indignities of being lost, or of corrupting, or of being consumed
by rodents and the like. That last question may seem ridiculous,
but in fact it is evidence of the realistic views that Christians had
of the Eucharistic Presence. It was a question that served as a type
of "limit situation" for those who defended such a realistic
understanding. Even as late as the time of St. Bonaventure (1217–74)
there existed the opinion that, in such cases, the substance of the
Lord's Body and Blood departed the Sacrament and that the
Sacrament changed back into actual bread and wine. Although it
was a view that Guitmund had already considered and rejected,
Bonaventure held this opinion and said it was the more common
one.[38] Gradually abandoned, it reemerged in the fourteenth century under the auspices of Peter of Bonageta and John of Latone
and was condemned by Pope Gregory XI in 1371. Two of the
condemned propositions put forward by these men read:

> If the consecrated Host is defiled by a rodent or consumed by an
> animal it happens that . . . the Body of Christ ceases to exist under
> them and the substance of bread returns.
>
> If the consecrated Host is consumed by the just or by the sinner
> it happens that, while the species [Lat. *species*] is being consumed
> by the teeth, Christ himself is taken back to heaven and not taken
> into the stomach (DS 1103).

Since the opinion expressed in these statements is condemned, it
can be seen that the Church was reaffirming not only the reality
of the Lord's Presence but also the fact that the change in the

[38] Bonaventure, *Commentary on the Sentences,* IV, dist. 13, a. 2, q. 1, *Opera
Omnia,* vol. 4, Italy: Quaracchi, 1889, p. 308. Guitmund's rejection of the
opinion is found in *PL* 149, 1494.

elements was irreversible. And the Church was reaffirming its teaching in terms quite as realistic as those of Berengarius' confession in 1059.

Bandinelli and Alan of Lille

By the middle of the twelfth century, Roland Bandinelli (ca. 1105–81), who later became Pope Alexander III, and others used the term "transubstantiation" to describe the change, but this was merely a neologism, and no more was intended by it than was already included in the *substantialiter converti* of 1079. A precise explanation of what was intended by the word *transubstantiation* is to be found in the works of a contemporary of Brandinelli, the Cistercian monk-theologian Alan of Lille (born ca. 1116; died Cîteaux, 1202). Writing his *Four Books against the Heretics* around 1180 and directing it, at least in part, against the Albigensians, Alan gave the following presentation of the Eucharistic change:

> Transubstantiation is that type of change according to which both the matter and the substantial form are changed, while the accidents remain. Thus it is called transubstantiation because nothing of the substance remains, neither as regards matter nor substantial nature. This type of change occurs in the Consecration of the bread. For the bread is changed into the Body of Christ in such a way that nothing of the matter of bread remains; nor does the substance of bread remain. Rather, only certain accidental things remain, such as roundness, whiteness, taste. . . .
>
> According to this change of transubstantiation, it must be said that the bread is changed or converted into the Body of Christ. We admit that other words signify this change, such as the bread becomes the Body of Christ; not, however, that it begins to be the Body of Christ. For we say that the bread ceases to exist, but it is not corrupted. It does not cease to be through natural weakness but by means of a miracle. . . .
>
> We say also that, although the Body of Christ is eaten, it is always incorruptible and remains indivisible. When the Body of Christ is said to be divided or broken, we refer to the form of the bread rather than to the Body of Christ. The fraction or division

does not take place in the Body of Christ but rather in the form of the bread. And it is not to be wondered at that he, who made all things from nothing, makes it happen that the accidents exist without a material subject. . . . Moreover we are able to say that color and taste remain in the form of the bread and thus, miraculously, an accident remains in an accident. . . .

We say that, when this form of bread is divided into parts, just as the whole Body of Christ lay hidden whole and entire under the whole form so after the division the Body lies hidden whole and entire under each portion of the broken Host . . . we also say that under this meager form of bread the whole Body of Christ lies hidden because, since it is now glorified, it is of such subtlety . . . that it is able to lie hidden in a small space, even though his members are distinct. . . .

If a mouse approaches the pyx we say that it does not eat the Body of Christ but only the form of bread, which even miraculously works to the nourishment of the mouse as if the substance of bread were there.[39]

The language has become *in part* the terminology of Aristotle, but what is being asserted, although with more precision, are the same essentials of the Eucharistic Mystery seen earlier. Alan uses the Aristotelian *accident* and *accidents,* although he will at times still use the word *form* to signify what remains of the bread and wine. Thus he can write that the accidents of bread and wine remain—miraculously—without a subject in which they inhere and that the accidents of color and taste remain in the form of the bread, accidents remaining in an accident. Aquinas will defend the same view, clarifying it only by saying that the accidents of color, taste, etc. remain in the accident of dimensive quantity, which itself—miraculously—remains without a subject.[40] As far as Christ's Body is concerned, Alan is teaching that his Body is there dimensionally, i.e., with its physical members distinct. To explain this he appeals to the powers of the "glorified" Body. With this

---

[39] Alan of Lille, *Contra Haereticos Libri Quatuor,* I, chap. 68; *PL,* 210, 360–63.

[40] *S.T.,* III, q. 77, a. 1–2.

position too Aquinas will agree, using a language different from Alan's while not being much more illuminating in reality, since both of them are dealing with something unique and known only by a mind drawing inevitable consequences from a truth apprehended by faith in revelation.[41] In fact, Alan's views throughout are basically the same ones that will be later defended by Aquinas, and, given an advance in terminology, are also fundamentally the views defended by Guitmund.

Alan's explanation of the meaning of transubstantiation—and similar views of others like him—must be seen as the context in which the word was taken up and used in the great Creed proclaimed by the Fourth Lateran Council in 1215.[42]

By the time of Lateran IV's profession of faith, various possible explanations of the Eucharistic change had already made their appearance and can be summarized as follows:

1. The purely symbolic. This held that the elements of bread and wine remained exactly what they had been but that, in the sacramental context, they were signs or reminders of the heavenly Lord with whom the believer communicated spiritually.

2. Impanation. Strictly speaking, this would have been the view that modeled the Eucharistic change after the hypostatic union of the Son with his human nature in the Incarnation. In this view, the elements, while retaining the full reality that was theirs, would have been inseparably joined to the heavenly Body of Christ so as to be identified with that Body.

3. Companation—or what was later called consubstantiation. This view, very similar to the previous one and often not distin-

---

[41] S.T., III, q. 76, a. 4c and ad 1. "The whole dimensive quantity of the Body of Christ, and all its other accidents, is present by the force of real concomitance. . . . The dimensive quantity of the Body of Christ is present in this Sacrament, not according to its proper mode [of being], viz., the whole quantity in the whole of the Sacrament and each of the parts of the Body's quantity in parts of the Sacrament. Rather the dimensive quantity is present in a mode [of being] proper to a substance, i.e., the whole quantity in the whole Sacrament and the whole quantity in each part as well."

[42] See below, pp. 185ff., for the Creed *Firmiter* and its significance.

guished from it, would hold that the elements of bread and wine remained what they were but that the substance of the Body and Blood of Christ became present along with the substances of bread and wine. One may say that it was the *intimacy* of the union that distinguishes impanation and companation. Although both opinions held that the substance of bread and wine remained after the Consecration, companation tended to hold for a juxtaposition of the two substances (i.e., the bread and wine and the Body and Blood of Christ) while impanation tended toward an assumption by Christ of the elements that, while leaving them what they had been, identified them with him.

4. Transubstantiation. This involved a change from one substance to the other, leaving intact only the appearances of the previous substances of bread and wine. At the period of which we are speaking, there was no consensus among the theologians as to how this occurred. Some thought that the substances of bread and wine were annihilated and replaced by the substance of Christ's Body and Blood. Others held that the substance of bread and wine collapsed into or was reduced to a more elementary form of matter. A third view, which was espoused by Aquinas and became the prevailing understanding, held that the substance of bread and wine passed over into the substance of the Body and Blood of Christ.[43]

[43] *S.Th.*, III, q. 75, a. 4: "It must be said that in this Sacrament there is the true Body of Christ, and that it does not begin to be there by any local movement. Now since the Body of Christ is not present as in place it is necessary to say that it begins to be there through the conversion of the substance of bread into itself.

"This conversion is not like any natural conversion but is, rather, completely supernatural, brought about by the power of God alone. . . . Every conversion that occurs according to natural laws is a change of forms. But God is infinite Act. . . . Therefore his activity extends to the whole nature of being. He is able not only to effect a change of forms, as, for example, when different forms succeed one another in the same subject, but also to effect a conversion of the whole being so that the whole substance of one thing is changed into that of another.

"And by the divine power this is what happens in this Sacrament. The

Duns Scotus

In the period after Lateran IV, all theologians held that the first view, the purely symbolic, was heretical. The same cannot be said of impanation and companation. Although research has been unable to discover any theologian who defended those views, it would appear that not all theologians were willing to label them heretical.[44] Indeed, St. Thomas may have been the first to do

---

whole substance of bread is changed into the whole substance of the Body of Christ and the whole substance of wine into the whole substance of the Blood of Christ. Thus it is not a change of forms but a change of substance. It is not found among the various types of natural change but can be called by its own name, transubstantiation."

[44] James F. McCue, in his "The Doctrine of Transubstantiation from Berengar through Trent: The Point at Issue" (*Harvard Theological Review* 61:385–430), cites Peter Lombard, the *Glossa* on the Decretals of Gratian, William of Auxerre, Hugh of St. Cher, and others as examples of theologians who between 1215 and 1250 defended transubstantiation and repudiated consubstantiation without, however, listing it as heresy or invoking the Creed of Lateran IV against it.

McCue's thesis is that the failure of such theologians to condemn as heretical consubstantiation indicates that, at least initially, Lateran IV's *Firmiter* was not viewed as a final determination by the Church on this matter. The impression that it was such a final determination was a mistaken notion that grew gradually "through inadvertence and misunderstanding" (p. 430). The Council of Trent was in a sense a victim of this misunderstanding when it repeated a teaching that it thought had previously been definitively proclaimed.

McCue's evidence will not support the thesis for several reasons: (1) none of the post–Lateran IV sources cited actually defends consubstantiation; indeed, all reject it even though not claiming it to be heretical; (2) the appeal to the nonmention of Lateran IV by these same sources is an argument from silence that may have other explanations (it is quite possible, for example, that the *Firmiter* was unknown to some of these writers or that they presumed that their rejection of it was enough to indicate that it was heretical); (3) even Aquinas, who labels consubstantiation heretical, does not appeal to Lateran IV; (4) some period of reflection on the full significance of the Lateran decree is to be expected as part of the normal process of dogmatic maturation; (5) even dissent on the part of some theologians is never determinative of the Church's Faith. Cf. also n. 45 below.

so.[45] In this view he was followed by John Duns Scotus (1266–1308), who wrote:

> I say that it is quite possible for God to have brought it about that the Body of Christ be truly present even while the substance of bread remain . . . ; but this is not the whole truth concerning the Eucharist because God did not bring it about as this opinion holds. . . . We must say that the Church has declared this understanding [i.e., transubstantiation] to be a truth of the Faith in the Creed *Firmiter* published by the Lateran Council under Innocent III. . . . Whatever is said there as having to be believed must be held as of the substance of the Faith because it is a solemn declaration made by the Church.
>
> And if you ask why the Church chose so difficult an understanding of this Article of Faith when the words of Scripture can be satisfied by an understanding that would be easier and more true as far as appearances are concerned, I reply that the Scriptures are expounded by the same Spirit who established them. And so it must be supposed that the Catholic Church has expounded the Faith passed on to us by that same Spirit . . . and therefore has chosen this understanding because it is true. For it is not in the power of the Church to make something true or false; it is in the power of God who ordains [such things]. The Church has expounded the understanding handed on by God and has done so, we believe, under God's direction.[46]

Several things are of particular interest in Scotus' remarks:

1. He notes that God could have brought it about that the full reality of the bread and wine remain along with the true substance of Christ.

---

[45] *S.T.,* III, q. 75, a. 2. We say that St. Thomas *may* have been the first to label such views heretical because Alan of Lille had already answered the question "Whether it is an Article of Faith that the bread is transubstantiated into the Body of Christ" affirmatively (*Contra Haereticos Libri Quatuor,* I, chap. 59; *PL,* 210, 363).

[46] John Duns Scotus, *Quaestiones In Librum Sententiarum,* IV, dist. II, q. 3, in *Opera Omnia Joannis Duns Scoti,* 17, Paris: Vives, 1894, pp. 375–76.

2. At least as far as appearances go, transubstantiation is a more difficult doctrine to accept than consubstantiation.

3. Nonetheless, given the possible alternative(s), God chose that manner of change that we call transubstantiation and has revealed this to us.

4. At Lateran IV the Church, faithful to God's revelation, has determined that transubstantiation is of the substance of the Faith.

Thus, Scotus thought that consubstantiation was from an a priori point of view theoretically possible, even though de facto it was not so. This theoretical possibility may or may not be true in fact, but it does indicate that, at least for some great theologians, transubstantiation was not simply the only way in which the doctrine of the substantial Presence of Christ's Body and Blood could have been achieved. For them, it was not the *necessary* consequence of bodily Presence of Christ; indeed, it was *something more* than is necessitated by that bodily Presence. And this "something more" has been revealed as true by God.

The Early Reformation

It was the following century, the fourteenth, that witnessed the development of those tendencies that would culminate in the Reformation. In many ways it was a baneful era. The philosophical and theological synthesis of the thirteenth century spent itself and moved into varying and often contradictory currents. The work of the monasteries, which had come to flower in the thirteenth century, was increasingly overshadowed by clear signs of laxity, greed, and corruption in many areas of Europe. The reforming zeal of the mendicant orders, the Dominicans and the Franciscans, diminished as the friars staked out their own domains of privilege and power against the secular clergy. Midway through the century, Europe was afflicted with the scourge of the Black Death, which reduced the population in many places by as much as half (or even more according to some calculations), effectively destroying much of the social equilibrium of the Middle Ages.

The papacy, having guided the Church for almost seventy years from Avignon in France, finally returned to Rome before the end of this century, only to fall victim to the Great Western Schism, which saw three men claiming to be Pope. Saints and sinners, kings, bishops, and laity divided their loyalties among the three.

The theological synthesis of the previous century was threatened by evidences of a strange and dangerous dichotomy between faith and reason. Ockham defended transubstantiation but did so strictly because the Church had so determined, since he considered that it would be more reasonable to hold companation. There were others who questioned the binding nature of Lateran IV's teaching on transubstantiation. The Dominican John Quidort (John of Paris), who lived from 1250 to 1306 and was a staunch defender of Aquinas in the days when Thomas' philosophy and theology were the subject of much criticism, was one such. Even as a student, however, his thought on the Eucharist was suspect, and later he wrote to the effect that consubstantiation was an acceptable view since, as far as he could see, the Church had not excluded this opinion. His position was condemned by the Archbishop of Paris.

Wyclif

It was in England, where the War of the Roses was soon to erupt, that the remote beginnings of the Eucharistic controversies that would shake Christendom at the time of the Reformation first appeared. And they did so in the person of John Wyclif. Wyclif was born around 1330. Ordained a priest, he received his doctorate in theology at Oxford, where he stayed on to become Master of Balliol College. Although much about his life and personality remains obscure, he appears to have been a conscientious but opinionated man, convinced of the necessity for the reform of clerical life and for a withdrawal of the clergy from a direct participation in political affairs. He was, also, what has been called an "ultrarealist" in his philosophical thought, leading him to a tendency to equate a reality with its appearances. In respect to his thought on the Eucharist, a sympathetic modern biographer has written:

> While investigating the problem historically, Wyclif discovered Berengar, the bishop [*sic*] of Tours in the eleventh century who believed in logic with the same dedication as Wyclif himself. . . .
> Wyclif maintained that in its first thousand years, the church believed as Berengar did, but it changed its beliefs during the reign of Innocent III at the end of the twelfth century, only two hundred years before Wyclif's time. So for his explanation of the mystery of the Eucharist, Wyclif looked to an earlier, simpler age as he had for his vision of Christian poverty.[47]

Wyclif for a part of his life defended the doctrine of transubstantiation, but early in the 1380s came to reject it as heretical. His most comprehensive explanation of Eucharistic doctrine is found in his work *De Eucharistia Tractatus Major.* There he writes:

> And it is not unfitting that Christ is sacramentally in the water or some other thing mixed with wine, and even more so in the midst of the air, but preeminently in the soul, since the purpose of this Sacrament is that Christ inhabit the soul by means of virtues, so that the layman, remembering the Body of Christ in heaven, brings it about better and more effectively than the priest who consecrates, and equally really, though in a different manner, that the Body of Christ is with him. But the common man [Lat. *vulgus*] most faithlessly and blasphemously believes that this sacramental sign of the Body of Christ is really Christ himself. And in this heresy clergy and prelates are involved.[48]

> It remains that we consider further the matter of the multiplication of the Body.
> Concerning this matter there are two opinions: the first, which is ascribed to the Subtle Doctor [i.e., Scotus] and his followers, says that the same Body can be simultaneously multiplied in its own dimensions in various places. The second, which is ascribed to the Common Doctor [i.e., Aquinas] and his followers, says that

[47] Louis Brewer Hall, *The Perilous Vision of John Wyclif,* p. 154.
[48] Wyclif, *De Eucharistia,* cap. 4, pp. 111–12.

the same Body can be multiplied simultaneously in any place so that it is one place in its own dimensions and in other places virtually or sacramentally, so that the Body of Christ is in heaven in its own dimensions and sacramentally in all those distant places in which there is a consecrated Host.[49]

A long digression follows this presentation of the teaching of Scotus and Aquinas, at the end of which he concludes that the position of Aquinas (as he interprets it) is to be preferred, i.e., a body cannot exist locally in two different places at the same time. He then continues:

It is repugnant that the numerically identical Body be extended through many places; however, it can be extended in one place while having another form of spiritual existence—either in sign or power—in another place, as is the case with a king. And this is the way it is with the Body of Christ, which is dimensionally in heaven and virtually in the Host as in a sign.[50]

It seems that Christ is in the Host as in a sign because otherwise the Host would not be a sacrament. He is not there in the signs, however, without being really and truly there according to his entire humanity. Thus it is conceded that Christ is not there as being only in sign since he is there more efficaciously than in a sign.[51]

Wyclif explicitly rejects the view according to which Christ becomes present through impanation or companation, which latter term he describes as "identification" with the elements.[52] And he frequently states that the Eucharistic elements are not a mere or empty sign. But what kind of a Presence of Christ exists in the Eucharist according to Wyclif is something not easy to determine. At times, despite his explicit rejection of the same, he appears to hold a view similar to that described as companation or

[49] Wyclif, *De Eucharistia,* cap. 8, pp. 232–33.
[50] Wyclif, *De Eucharistia,* cap. 8, p. 271.
[51] Wyclif, *De Eucharistia,* cap. 4, p. 121.
[52] Wyclif, *De Eucharistia,* cap. 5, pp. 195–99; cap. 6, pp. 221–22.

consubstantiation. In comparing the eminent dignity of the Eucharist to the other sacraments of the Old and New Covenants he writes:

> Thus it is commonly said that this Sacrament excels the others in three ways. First, because the other sacraments are far distant in time and place from the sacramental reality. This Sacrament has its reality concomitant with it in time and place; ... this Sacrament has the whole humanity of Christ necessarily concomitant with it.[53]

In all likelihood, however, such passages as this last are to be interpreted in the sense of a virtual presence, since this is the type of presence most mentioned by Wyclif and the one he defends at the end of his work when explicitly treating of the types of presence.

What this virtual presence meant for Wyclif is a matter of interpretation. He calls it a vicarious presence of Christ in power.

> Infinite are the arguments according to which the Catholic can say that the Body of Christ is there virtually and in sign—not the Body of Christ as it is in heaven but rather with the sign as its vicar.[54]

Apart from the difficulty in determining precisely his teaching on the kind of presence of Christ in the Eucharist, it is clear that he rejected transubstantiation and vigorously defended the continuing existence of bread and wine in their full natural reality, repudiating any notion that claimed that only the accidents of bread and wine remained without any proper subject in which they inhered.

> Although I once labored to describe transubstantiation in a manner harmonious with the sense of the early Church, it now seems to me that it is contrary to the sense of the early Church, the latter Church erring in this matter. For if transubstantiation

---

[53] Wyclif, *De Eucharistia,* cap. 4, p. 87.
[54] Wyclif, *De Eucharistia,* cap. 9, p. 303.

is the cession of one substance to another in respect to place so that the transubstantiated substance remains in the same place as before and a more noble substance is present in that place sacramentally in a way that the previous substance is subordinated to it as signifying it, then it happens that the bread is transubstantiated in such a manner that it is not changed but remains, after the Consecration, as the subject for the accidents. But this is said to be contrary to the decrees of the Church. Thus, I now dismiss this attempt at reconciliation and call transubstantiation the conversion of one substance into another, as semen is converted into a living body, as man is changed into dust.[55]

But the Avignon Church is not able to establish said transubstantiation either by Scripture or reason or revelation. Therefore we are not held to believe more than the primitive Church believed.[56]

Natural reason teaches that it is not possible for accidents to exist without a subject. A subject cannot exist without its accidents, and therefore this is much more true the other way around.[57]

He explicitly rejects the *Firmiter* of Lateran IV if it is understood in the sense of a transubstantiation that means that bread and wine do not exist after the Consecration. He even claims that such an understanding is contrary not only to the Fathers, especially Augustine, but even to the confession that was made by Berengarius under Pope Nicholas II, since Wyclif read the *Ego Berengarius* of 1059 as declaring that bread and wine and Christ were present after the Consecration.[58] It is from this defense of the *Ego Berengarius* that his biographer cited above is able to say

---

[55] Wyclif, *De Eucharistia,* cap. 2, pp. 52–53.

[56] Wyclif, *De Eucharistia,* cap. 3, p. 61.

[57] Wyclif, *De Eucharistia,* cap. 5, p. 132.

[58] Wyclif, *De Eucharistia,* cap. 3, p. 62; cap. 4, pp. 107, 111. He is willing, however, to interpret the *Firmiter* in light of what he considers to be the true Faith of the Church, viz., as allowing for the remaining of the bread and wine after the Consecration (cap. 5, p. 141).

that Wyclif found in Berengarius the true Faith of the Church—
although Wyclif never considered himself to be defending what
had been condemned in Berengarius' teaching. As a consequence
of his views, Wyclif also attacked the adoration of the Host as a
form of idolatry.

> The Christian ought to be careful not to adore that which the
> moderns call accidents and which the early Church called bread
> and wine as if they were the true Body and Blood of Christ. . . .
> Although that sign has greater efficacy than the signs of the Old
> Law and of our statues . . . nevertheless it would be great infidelity
> to believe that this sign—so abject in its nature—is God.[59]

Odi profanum vulgus et arceo (I hate the common crowd and
shun it). The words of Horace in the third book of his *Odes*
capture some of the disdain of the Oxford theologian for his
fellowmen. "The *common people* believe most faithlessly and
blasphemously", etc. We have seen the same attitude earlier in
Berengarius, and it will appear again. The implication in all cases
is that the ordinary people are too uneducated (and, consequently
—by a common lapse of logic—too unintelligent) to grasp the
truth as the trained theologian can. It is an attitude, of course,
quite contrary to that of the God of revelation. "I will remove
from this city those who rejoice in their pride. Never again will
you be haughty on my holy hill. But I will leave within you the
meek and humble who trust in the name of the Lord" (Zeph
3:11–12). It is such contempt for the "simple" that strikes at the
faith of those to whom the Father has chosen to reveal the Mysteries while he hides the same Mysteries from the "wise and the
learned" (Mt 11:25). But, in testifying that his own teaching is
opposed to the "heresy" of the common people, the clergy and
even prelates—as well as to what had already been taught by the
Church in synods and councils—Wyclif was giving inadvertent
witness to the great truth of the *sensus fidelium,* that infallible

---

[59] Wyclif, *De Eucharistia,* cap. 3, pp. 62–63.

instinct for truth spoken of by Vatican Council II, quoting St. Augustine.[60]

For his teaching on the Eucharist, as well as for other opinions, John Wyclif was condemned during his lifetime at various local synods in England, although, because of his high political connections (John of Gaunt, virtual ruler of the kingdom, was for a long time his patron), the full consequences of the condemnations were never carried out. He was not excommunicated and died in his own parish in 1384.

Wyclif is defended at times on the grounds that his errors are due not so much to his theology as to his inadequate philosophy.[61] And in this there is some truth, although it must also be noted that he was at least equally influenced by his own exegesis of Sacred Scripture. In both fields, however, he was to a great extent "his own man", going his own way even when it departed from the context in which the Church read the Scriptures and from what the Tradition had passed down concerning the nature of the Eucharistic Mystery.

Although not himself the actual founder of the group, Wyclif's theories were the theological rationale for the Lollard movement in England. The word *Lollard* probably came from the Dutch and meant a "mumbler", i.e., a person who was constantly mumbling prayers of devotion. In 1395 the Lollards presented to Parliament a statement of their beliefs called the *Twelve Conclusions.* Conclusion number 4 attacked the "pretended miracle" of the altar and claimed that it led to idolatry, since in reality the Body of Christ remained in heaven. The Lollards formed a body that aimed not only at religious change but also at social change, and their agitation soon

[60] *Lumen Gentium* (*The Dogmatic Constitution on the Church*), 12.

[61] Schillebeeckx (*The Eucharist,* pp. 48–49) correctly sees Wyclif as being a prisoner of his rigid Aristotelian philosophy. "Faithful to the authentic, historical Aristotelianism, which could not admit any division between substance and accidents, he denied transubstantiation." Wyclif's dilemma is a good reminder of the fact that the doctrine of transubstantiation is *not* Aristotelian. St. Thomas had used Aristotelian categories to delineate the mystery, but only after *profoundly modifying* Aristotle's philosophy.

stirred many in England. To counter them, King and Parliament passed, in 1401, the first law for capital punishment of heretics in England. It mandated death by burning for heresy, a prelude to the terrible brutality of the following century.

Hus and the Utraquists

Even more significant than his influence on the Lollard movement was Wyclif's influence on the young students from Bohemia who studied under him at Oxford. They carried his thought and writings back with them to Prague, where they were taken up and defended by John Hus. Hus himself appears always to have accepted and taught the doctrines of the Presence of Christ's Body and Blood in the Eucharist and of transubstantiation, but his preaching on the Eucharist and the subsequent teaching of his disciples led to the Utraquist controversy. The word *Utraquist* refers to "both forms" of the Eucharist and came to signify the movement to restore reception of the Eucharistic cup to all the faithful, a practice that was carried out in various ways in the early Church but, by the fourteenth century, one that had fallen into general disuse for almost four centuries. The desire for reception in both kinds, undoubtedly good in itself, was unfortunately accompanied by other more problematic factors. In a somewhat excessive exaltation of the primitive, some of the Utraquists were also demanding that the Eucharist be celebrated after a common meal, as it was at the Last Supper and in the agape meal mentioned in 1 Corinthians 11. They held, too, that, in order to accomplish such a union between Eucharist and meal, the Church's rules concerning the Eucharistic fast should be abolished.

There was also a more substantial difficulty associated with the request for a return of the cup to all the faithful, and it involved the centuries-old problem concerning the real and the symbolic aspects of the Eucharist. The double Consecration of the bread and cup symbolized the separation of Christ's Body and Blood when he shed his Blood for us on Calvary. The risen Christ, however, was present whole and entire in both of the consecrated elements since he was understood to be incapable of undergoing in the Sacrament actual separation of his Body and Blood. Aquinas and other theologians explained this by the theory of *concomitance*.

> According to the Catholic Faith it is necessary to confess that the whole Christ is present in this Sacrament. Nevertheless it should be known that there are two ways in which Christ is present in the Sacrament: in one manner by the power of the sacramental sign; in another by natural concomitance. By the power of the sacramental sign, there is present under the species of this Sacrament that into which the formerly existing substances of bread and wine were directly changed. This is signified by the words of the formula that is effective in this Sacrament as in others, namely, "This is my Body", "This is my Blood." However, by natural concomitance there is present in the Sacrament all that is really joined to that in which the change terminates. If two things are really joined, one is present wherever the other is; only by an act of the mind are things that are really joined separated.[62]

By this distinction the differences between the symbolic and real aspects of the Sacrament were preserved. The One and Identical Lord was completely present under the appearances of each of the elements; his death was memorialized through the symbolic separation of Body and Blood. Some of the Utraquists tended to lose sight of this truth and claimed that the twofold reception was necessary not only for the symbolic completion of the Sacrament but also for its actual completion, as if the Lord were only imperfectly or incompletely received under one form.

In a decree subsequently approved by Pope Martin V, whose election by the bishops at Constance effectively ended the schism created by the different claimants to the papacy, the Council of Constance (1414–18) addressed the question posed by the Utraquists.

> Since in some parts of the world some people are temerariously asserting that the Christian people should receive the Sacred Sacra-

---

[62] *S. Th.*, III, q. 76, a. 1.

ment of the Eucharist under each species of bread and wine . . . and to do this not fasting, after a supper or otherwise . . . this present Council declares: although Christ instituted this venerable Sacrament after a supper and administered it to his disciples under the species of bread and wine, nevertheless the praiseworthy authority of the sacred canons and the approved custom of the Church have established and establish that this Sacrament should not be effected after a supper or received by the faithful who are not fasting except in the case of the sick or of some other necessity. . . .

And the custom has been reasonably introduced in order to avoid certain dangers and scandals . . . , namely, that it be received by the priests under both species and by the laity only under the species of bread, since it must be firmly believed and in no way doubted that the whole Body and Blood of Christ are truly contained both under the species of bread and under the species of wine. Therefore since this custom has been reasonably introduced by the Church and the holy Fathers and has been observed for a very long time, it must be held to be a law that it is not permitted to reject or to change at will without the authority of the Church (DS 1198–99).[63]

---

[63] The issue refused to go away, however, and until the Reformation and during it there were repeated requests from one or another province of the Church to permit the use of the cup. The Council of Trent took the matter under consideration at its twenty-first session in 1562 and issued a decree touching only on the principles of doctrine that were involved. It taught:

"Canon I. If anyone says that, by a precept of God or because it is necessary for salvation, that each and every one of the Christian faithful should receive each species of the most holy Sacrament of the Eucharist, let him be anathema (DS 1731).

Canon II. If anyone should say that the holy Catholic Church was not led by just and reasonable motives [to legislate] that laity and even priests who are not celebrating should communicate only under the species of bread, or that the Church has erred in doing this, let him be anathema (DS 1732).

Canon III. If anyone should deny that the whole and entire Christ, Font and Author of all graces, is not received under the one species of bread because—as some falsely assert—he is not received under both species as Christ himself instituted the Sacrament, let him be anathema (DS 1733).

The dogmatic truths were easier to determine, however, than was the practical question as to whether the Church should now permit, at least in some cases, a return to the older custom. There was much disagreement

Having spoken on the Utraquist controversy, the bishops at Constance then turned to the teaching of Wyclif and condemned the following five propositions:

> The substance of material bread and the substance of material wine remain in the Sacrament of the altar.
>
> The accidents of bread do not remain without a subject in the same Sacrament.
>
> In the same Sacrament Christ is not identically and really present in his proper corporeal Presence.
>
> If a bishop or priest is in mortal sin, he does not ordain or consecrate, or confect the Eucharist, or baptize.
>
> That Christ instituted the Mass is something not founded on Scripture (DS 1151–55).

Since the above propositions are condemned, the bishops at Constance were teaching the truths opposed to them, viz., that Christ in his proper and identical Body is present in the Eucharist; that Christ is present there in such a way that the substance of bread and wine no longer remains, and that only the accidents of bread and wine remain, existing miraculously since they have no proper subject in which to inhere. The use of the word *accidents* here is novel for a major document of the Church, since it is more directly Aristotelian than the language previously and subsequently

---

among the bishops on this point, and they solved their difficulties by a decree at the twenty-second session of the Council in 1562 leaving it for the Pope to decide when and under what circumstances the practice of receiving from the cup should be granted to those requesting it (DS 1760). In effect, however, the practice of the centuries immediately previous to the Reformation prevailed.

At the Second Vatican Council, in an atmosphere freed from the doctrinal dangers and from the polemics of earlier times, the Pope and bishops decided that, in specific cases to be determined by the Apostolic See, Communion under both kinds should be restored to all the faithful (*Sacrosanctum Concilium* [*Constitution on the Sacred Liturgy*], 55). The norms of this constitution were implemented and extended by subsequent documents: *Ecclesiae semper* of March 1965 (*AAS*, 57, pp. 411–12); *Eucharisticum Mysterium*, 32, of May 1967 (*AAS*, 59, pp. 558–59); and *Sacramentali Communione* of Jan. 1970 (*AAS*, 62, pp. 664–67).

used to describe what remains of the bread and wine. Perhaps it is to be understood not in the strict sense given to it in the philosophy of Aristotle but as an alternate expression for the usual words *species* or *appearances.*

The Protestant Reformation

Although John Wyclif can in all truth be called the Father of the Reformation, that storm that shook Western Christendom one hundred years after Wyclif's condemnation at Constance was of such magnitude that Wyclif's name is almost forgotten at times because of the more enduring effects of the work of Martin Luther, Ulrich Zwingli, and John Calvin.

Luther

As a reformer, Martin Luther (1483–1546) produced his major work on the Eucharist in the book *On the Babylonian Captivity of the Church.*[64] In this essay—which was to provoke Henry VIII of England to publish his *On the Seven Sacraments,* for which he received the title "Defender of the Faith"—Luther listed three "captivities" of the Sacrament of the Eucharist by the Roman Church:

1. The denial of both species to all the faithful
2. The doctrine of transubstantiation
3. The notion that the Mass is a sacrifice

Having appealed for the return of the Eucharistic cup to all the faithful (although "I do not urge that both kinds be seized upon by force, as if we were bound to this form by a rigorous command"),[65] Luther turned his attention to transubstantiation, viewing it as a "less grievous" evil than the former.

---

[64] Martin Luther, *On the Babylonian Captivity of the Church,* in vol. 36 of *Luther's Works.*

[65] Luther, *Babylonian Captivity,* p. 28.

Here I shall be called a Wycliffite and a heretic by six hundred names. But what of it? Since the Roman bishop has ceased to be a bishop and has become a tyrant, I fear none of his decrees; for I know that it is not within his power, or that of any general council, to make new Articles of Faith.

Some time ago, when I was drinking in Scholastic theology, the learned Cardinal of Cambrai gave me food for thought in his comments on the fourth book of the Sentences. He argues with great acumen that to hold that real bread and real wine, and not merely their accidents, are present on the altar, would be much more probable and require fewer superfluous miracles — if only the Church had not decreed otherwise.[66] When I learned later what church it was that had decreed this, namely, the Thomistic — that is, the Aristotelian church — I grew bolder, and after floating in a sea of doubt, I at last found rest for my conscience in the above view, namely, that it is real bread and real wine, in which Christ's real Flesh and real Blood are present in no other way and to no less a degree than the others assert them to be under their accidents.[67]

. . .

For my part, if I cannot fathom how the bread is the Body of Christ, yet I will take my reason captive to the obedience of Christ [1 Cor 10:5], and clinging simply to his words, firmly believe not only that the Body of Christ is in the bread but that the bread is the Body of Christ. . . . What does it matter if philosophy cannot fathom this? The Holy Spirit is greater than Aristotle.[68]

From this position adopted in 1520 Luther never afterward departed. Christ's Body and Blood are truly present in the Eucharistic elements. He frequently calls this Presence a "substantial" one, using the term substantial in its traditional sense. Nonetheless, the full reality of bread and wine also remains. In his 1528

[66] The "learned Cardinal of Cambrai" to whom Luther refers was Pierre d'Ailly (1350–1420), one of the judges of Hus at Constance. In his commentary on the *Sentences* of Lombard (IV, VI, 2), d'Ailly expressed the position mentioned by Luther, although because the Church favored transubstantiation d'Ailly accepted it.

[67] Luther, *Babylonian Captivity*, p. 29.

[68] Luther, *Babylonian Captivity*, p. 34.

Confession Concerning Christ's Supper, Luther, faced now not only with Roman Catholic opponents but also with the symbolic interpretation of the Eucharist propounded by Zwingli and Oecolampadius, again stated his faith. It has been called by an editor of his works "the most detailed and the most profound of Luther's treatises on the Lord's Supper."[69]

> It is not necessary . . . that one of the two disappear or be annihilated, but both the bread and the Body remain, and by virtue of the sacramental unity it is correct to say, "This is my Body", designating the bread with the word "this". For now it is no longer ordinary bread in the oven but a "Flesh-bread" or "Body-bread", i.e., a bread that has become one sacramental substance, one with the Body of Christ.[70]

> Therefore it is entirely correct to say, if one points to the bread, "This is Christ's Body", and whoever sees the bread sees Christ's Body. . . . Thus also it is correct to say, "He who takes hold of this bread, takes hold of Christ's Body; and he who eats this bread, eats Christ's Body; he who crushes this bread with teeth or tongue, crushes with teeth or tongue the Body of Christ." And yet it remains absolutely true that no one sees or grasps or eats or chews Christ's Body in the way he visibly sees and chews any other flesh. What one does to the bread is rightly and properly attributed to the Body of Christ by virtue of the sacramental union.[71]

In 1530 the *Augsburg Confession,* which stands today as the common profession among Lutherans, declared:

> Our churches teach that the Body and Blood of Christ are truly present and are distributed to those who eat in the Supper of the Lord. They disapprove of those who teach otherwise.[72]

---

[69] Robert H. Fischer, in *Luther's Works,* vol. 37, p. 158.

[70] Luther, *Confession concerning Christ's Supper,* in *Luther's Works,* vol. 37, p. 303.

[71] Luther, *Confession,* p. 300.

[72] *Augsburg Confession,* 10, in Joseph A. Burgess, ed., *The Role of the Augsburg Confession,* p. 173.

It can readily be seen how far removed from the positions of a Berengarius or a Wyclif were Luther's views on the Presence of Christ in the Sacrament. Nevertheless he drew back from some of the practices that the Church had come to see as a consequence of this great truth. Adhering to the correct view that the Sacrament had been instituted by Christ as nourishment for the faithful but interpreting that truth in an exclusionary fashion, he rejected the practice by which the Sacrament was reserved in the tabernacle for adoration and to be brought to the sick. For Luther the sacramental elements that remained after the celebration of the liturgy were to be consumed immediately.[73]

His rejection of transubstantiation left him open to the charge of Zwingli and others that he was teaching a doctrine that necessitated a multiplication of Christ's Body such that it would be *locally* present wherever the Sacrament was present. To answer this difficulty, he somewhat reluctantly advanced what has been called—by others, not by Luther—the theory of "ubiquity", a view that he defended but never intended to be taken as a matter of faith.

> If God and man are one person [in Christ] and the two natures are so united that they belong together more intimately than body and soul, then Christ must also be man wherever he is God.... It was on this point that I insisted when I showed that God and man were one Person, and that Christ thereby had acquired a supernatural existence or mode of being whereby he can be everywhere.[74]

---

[73] In his letter of July 20, 1543, (text in Stone, II, p. 24) he gives specific instructions on disposition of the consecrated elements at the end of the liturgy so that there would be no "bad example" or "irreverence". Whether he believed that the change in the elements was permanent, i.e., such that Christ's Body would remain in them even should they not be consumed at the end of the liturgical action, is disputed.

[74] Luther, *Confession,* p. 229. Cf. also his *This Is My Body,* written in 1527 (*Luther's Works,* vol. 37), pp. 61ff. Luther's theory was not novel in all respects. It is possible that some of the Fathers held views like it, and some of the twelfth-century theologians were expressing *similar* views. Thus Hugh of Metellus (ca. 1157) held that Christ's Body was not subject to the ordinary laws

In essence the theory held that wherever the Person of the Son was, his human nature (inseparable from the divinity of the Second Person since the Incarnation) was—or at least could be—present. Nevertheless, the Eucharistic Presence is unique since there Christ has bound himself to the bread and wine so that he can be eaten. The theory had confused the inseparability of the two natures with coextension. The Church had never passed a definitive judgment on the question of a local Presence of the Lord in the Eucharist, but most theologians[75] held that Christ's risen Body —like his Body before his Passion and Resurrection—could only be

---

of human nature, as was evident in the case of the Virgin Birth and in his appearing, after the Resurrection, in the Upper Room even though the doors were closed (*Epistola IV; PL*, 188, 1274). Like thoughts were expressed by William of St. Thierry (died 1148) in his *De Sacramento Altaris* (*PL*, 180, 347), Hugh of St. Victor (died 1141) in his *De Sacramentis Christianae Fidei* (*PL*, 176, 469), Hildebert of Lavardin (died 1133) in his *De Sacramento Altaris* (*PL*, 171, 1149–54), and by Alger of Liège (died ca. 1132) in his *De Sacramentis Corporis et Sanguinis Dominici* (*PL*, 180, 782). In all of them, however, it is not actual ubiquity that is being taught, rather, an appeal is made to the power of God and the glorified humanity of Christ in order to explain how the Lord's Body can be present in heaven and also in the Eucharist. Pelikan (3, p. 194) quotes Alger as writing: "the flesh of Christ, which has been exalted by God above all creatures . . . is present everywhere, wherever it pleases through the omnipotence that has been given to it in heaven and on earth." The full quotation reads: "Only the flesh of Christ, which has been exalted by God above every creature, has been given this power that is above and beyond all nature, namely, that through the omnipotence that has been given to it in heaven and on earth, it may be everywhere as it pleases, not by passing from place to place, but rather, remaining there where it is and existing in other places where it wills, it may be whole and entire and substantially present in heaven and on earth" (*Quo privilegio sola caro Christi, quae super omnem creaturam a Deo exaltata est, super omnem et praeter omnem naturam insignita est, ut per omnipotentiam, quae ei data est in coelo et in terra, quicumque, quomodocunque sibi placuerit, non de loco ad locum transeundo, sed ibi, ubi est, remanendo, et alibi ubicunque voluerit existendo, tota et integra et substantialiter sit et in coelo et in terra*).

[75] John Duns Scotus was a major exception. He held that Christ's Body could be locally present in different places at the same time. Cf. *In Sent.*, 17, dist. X, q. II and III, pp. 190–228.

dimensionally or locally present in one place at a time. To hold the opposite would appear—logically, at least—to deny the true (and therefore limited) materiality of his risen Body while simultaneously falling into various philosophical difficulties. Zwingli, Oecolampadius, and others made the most of Luther's difficulties in order to buttress their own symbolic understanding of the Eucharistic Presence of Christ.

Luther's defense of the Real Presence (a term that at this period had became generally current, previous terminology speaking usually[76] of the "truth" of Christ's Presence or of his true Presence in the Eucharist), coupled with his rejection of transubstantiation, was, in a sense, a throwback to a view that was held by a few writers in the Patristic era. Fully Catholic in his defense of the corporeal reality of the Eucharistic Presence, he had rejected the Church's more developed awareness of the nature of the change that takes place in the elements of the bread and wine, an awareness that adopted the more widespread Patristic evidence for such change as a deeper insight into the full truth of the Mystery of Faith.

More radical was Luther's rejection of the sacrificial aspects of the Eucharist. The language of sacrifice was widely applied to the Eucharist in Patristic times—as Luther admitted—and was a datum of belief practically unquestioned until his own writings on the matter. Apparently Luther was moved to his rejection of the Mass as a sacrifice by his views on the nature of faith and good works. For him, a man was justified by faith; human works are incapable of "exacting" anything from God. He considered Catholic theology to be teaching that the Mass as a sacrifice was a "good work" offered to God to propitiate him and win favors from him. It could not be Christ's sacrifice, since that had been offered "once and for all" (Heb 10:12) on Calvary. Therefore it was the sacrifice of the Church or the priest offering Christ to the Father—a "good

---

[76] Cf., however, below, p. 196, for its earlier usage.

work" on the part of the Church or priest, something Luther found unnecessary and even, in his words, "an abomination".

> This has been the fate of the mass; it has been converted by the teaching of godless men into a good work. They themselves call it an *opus operatum,* and by it they presume themselves to be all-powerful with God. Next they proceed to the very height of madness, and after inventing the lie that the mass is effective simply by virtue of the act having been performed, they add another one to the effect that the mass is nonetheless profitable to others.... On such a foundation of sand they base their applications, participations, brotherhoods, anniversaries, and numberless other lucrative and profitable schemes of that kind.[77]

> If, however, you recognize that this Sacrament is a promise and not a sacrifice, you are not uncertain and are aware of no anger [on the part of God].... And as he promises and shows himself to be gracious and merciful, so you will find him to be, if you hold and believe him to be thus. And if you notice that he promises you nothing but grace, then you will understand with a light and joyous conscience that he demands nothing from you in the way of gift or sacrifice but that he lovingly entreats and encourages you to accept his gift.[78]

> The priest offers up once again the Lord Christ, who offered himself only once (Heb 9:25–26), just as he died only once and cannot die again or be offered up again (Rom 6:9–10). For through his one death and sacrifice he has taken away and swallowed up all sins. Yet they go ahead and every day offer him up more than a hundred thousand times throughout the world. They thereby deny, both with their deeds and in their hearts, that Christ has washed sin away and has died and risen again. This is such an abomination that I don't believe it could be sufficiently punished on earth if it rained pure fire from heaven.

---

[77] Luther, *Babylonian Captivity,* p. 47. His reference to "applications, participations, etc." is to the custom whereby the faithful offered stipends to have Masses said for them, or to be able to share in the Masses offered in various places.

[78] Luther, *The Misuse of the Mass,* in *Luther's Works,* vol. 36, p. 176.

The blasphemy is so great that it must simply wait for eternal hell fire.[79]

The *Augsburg Confession* repeated the essential elements of Luther's position on the Mass as sacrifice.

> To all this was added an opinion which infinitely increased private Masses, namely, that Christ had by his Passion made satisfaction for original sin and had instituted the Mass in which an oblation should be made for daily sins, mortal and venial. From this has come the common opinion that the Mass is a work which by its performance takes away the sins of the living and the dead. Thus was introduced a debate on whether one Mass said for many people is worth as much as special Masses said for individuals. . . .
>
> Concerning these opinions, our teachers have warned that they depart from the Holy Scriptures and diminish the glory of Christ's Passion, for the Passion of Christ was an oblation and satisfaction not only for original guilt but also for other sins. . . .
>
> The Scriptures also teach that we are justified before God through faith in Christ. Now, if the Mass takes away the sins of the living and the dead by a performance of the outward act, justification comes from the work of the Mass and not from faith. But the Scriptures do not allow this.[80]

For Luther, then, the Eucharistic celebration, in which Christ becomes corporeally and substantially present, is a "promise" or a "pledge" of grace and favor. It is the New Testament offered to us —but it is not propitiatory.

> See, then, what a beautiful, great, marvelous thing this is, how everything meshes together in one sacramental reality. The words are the first thing, for without the words the cup and the bread would be nothing. Further, without bread and cup, the Body and Blood of Christ would not be there. Without the Body and Blood of Christ, the New Testament would not be there. Without the

[79] Luther, *The Abomination of the Secret Mass,* in *Luther's Works,* vol. 36, p. 320.

[80] *Augsburg Confession,* 24, in Joseph A. Burgess, pp. 184–85.

New Testament, forgiveness of sins would not be there. Thus the words first connect the bread and cup to the Sacrament; bread and cup embrace the Body and Blood of Christ; Body and Blood of Christ embrace the New Testament; the New Testament embraces the forgiveness of sins; forgiveness of sins embraces eternal life and salvation. See, all this the words of the Supper offer and give us, and we embrace it by faith. Ought not the devil, then, hate such a Supper and rouse fanatics against it?[81]

Beautiful words, and, as far as they go, a wonderful summary of Eucharistic faith! For Catholics, however, it is an incomplete faith. For his fellow reformers, on the other hand, it was a faith all too Catholic.

Zwingli

In respect to Eucharistic doctrine, Luther's chief adversary among the reformers was Ulrich Zwingli. Zwingli was Swiss, born in 1484, became a priest, and in 1519 was assigned to Zurich, already a reformer at heart. By 1523 he was writing on the Eucharist and propounding a teaching markedly different from that of the Church and of Luther. Like Luther, Zwingli rejected the sacrificial nature of the Mass; unlike Luther, he also rejected the Real Presence, opting instead for a Presence that was purely symbolic. In this position he was strongly supported by his friend Johannes Oecolampadius (1482–1531). It was a position repudiated by Erasmus (1466–1536), whose exegesis of the sixth chapter of St. John's Gospel in a non-Eucharistic sense had much influenced Zwingli. Zwingli's rejection of Luther's views on the Eucharist led to intense polemic and threatened to split the camp of the reformers. In an effort to bridge the difficulties, a conference was held at Marburg in October of 1529, at which Luther, Melancthon, Zwingli, and Oecolampadius participated. Although agreement was reached

[81] Luther, *Confession,* p. 338. The "fanatics" referred to are Zwingli, Oecolampadius, and their followers.

on many issues, the differences on the Presence of Christ led only to an agreement to disagree. Luther clung firmly to the literal truth of the words "This is my Body", while Zwingli countered with John 6:63 ("The Spirit gives life; the Flesh counts for nothing") as proving that the "is" meant "signifies".

Zwingli's fullest treatment of the Eucharist is found in his *Commentary on True and False Religion,* published in 1525. In it he writes:

> The "Eucharist", then, or "Synaxis", or Lord's Supper, is nothing but the commemoration by which those who firmly believe that by Christ's death and blood they have become reconciled with the Father proclaim this life-bringing death, that is, preach it with praise and thanksgiving.[82]

> We, therefore, now understand from the very name what the Eucharist, that is, the Lord's Supper, is: namely, the thanksgiving and common rejoicing of those who declare the death of Christ, that is, trumpet, praise, confess, and exalt his name above all others. But since that most significant discourse of Christ's which is embraced in the sixth chapter of John is not correctly understood by the great majority, though they boldly distort it into other meanings, I have determined above all things to declare the primary sense of this passage, that those who force all Scripture willy-nilly to serve their own view may not be able to get here weapons to defend their error.[83]

> Now I want no one to suffer himself to be offended by this painstaking examination of words; for it is not upon them that I rely, but upon the one expression "The flesh profiteth nothing" (Jn 6:63). This expression is strong enough to prove that "is" in this passage [viz., the consecratory words] is used for "signifies" or "is a symbol of", even if the discourse itself con-

---

[82] Zwingli, *Commentary,* p. 237.
[83] Zwingli, *Commentary,* p. 200.

tained absolutely nothing by which the meaning here could be detected.[84]

I have now refuted, I hope, this senseless notion about bodily flesh. In doing that my only object was to prove that to teach that the bodily and sensible Flesh of Christ is eaten when we give thanks to God is not only impious but also foolish and monstrous, unless perhaps one is living among the Anthropophagi.[85]

In another work, Zwingli set forth his famous comparison of the Eucharist to the ring that a husband gives his wife.

Thus, I say, we have the Lord's Supper distinguished by the presence of Christ. But in all this is not the presence of the body of Christ sacramentally to the eye of faith, as I have always said, the gist of the whole matter? For as a husband's ring is no common gold to the wife but more than all the gems of the Indies, so to us is this sacrament, the food and drink of the Lord's Supper, sweeter than the flavor of the finest viands. And as the ring, though not itself the husband, has a touch of the husband's value because it was given by him as a sign of undying love, and because it recalls his form whenever it is looked upon, so the repast of the Supper, though not Christ's material body, rises to high value because it was given and instituted as an everlasting sign of the love of Christ. . . .[86]

It should be noted that, in the above citation—and in many other places—Zwingli can speak of a Presence of Christ in the Eucharist, but it is clearly a symbolic one.

---

[84] Zwingli, *Commentary*, p. 231. He writes elsewhere: "We are compelled to confess that the words 'this is my body', should not be understood naturally but figuratively, just as the words 'this is Jehovah's Passover' (Ex 12:11)" (*An Account of the Faith*, in *On Providence*, p. 52). The *An Account of the Faith* was presented to Charles V at the Diet of Augsburg in 1530.

[85] Zwingli, *Commentary*, p. 216. The reference to "Anthropophagi" (cannibals) is an interesting revival of the ancient pagan charge against the Christians.

[86] Zwingli, *Letter to the Princes of Germany*, in *On Providence*, p. 123. The letter was written in 1530.

His writings on the sacrificial nature of the Eucharist are less frequent, because the question of the Presence came to dominate the discussions. On the Mass as sacrifice, his clearest statement is found in his *Reply to Emser.* There he declares that the Mass cannot be an offering or sacrifice because (1) only the Blood of Christ takes away sin, (2) that Blood was shed only once, (3) Christ was offered only when he suffered, and (4) he can neither suffer nor be offered any more.[87]

Ulrich Zwingli died on the battlefield in 1531 in the Swiss civil war between the Catholic and Protestant cantons. The Introduction to the English edition of Zwingli's *Commentary on True and False Religion* has the following evaluation of his Eucharistic doctrine.

> It is now generally conceded that in the celebration of the Eucharist by the early Christians, those who took part in it found elements more realistic and with deeper religious values than are contained in Zwingli's theory of it. He finds no place for the central idea of a living personal fellowship between the glorified Christ and his disciples upon earth. He resolves it wholly into a solemn service commemorating a historical redemptive act that of course has significance for believers to the end of time. The distant historical fact is central, not the present living fellowship of the Lord and his people.
> ... The fact, also, that in the course of a generation Calvin's view of the Lord's Supper prevailed even in German Switzerland seems to indicate that Zwingli's theory came to be regarded as one-sided and unsatisfactory.[88]

---

[87] Zwingli, *Reply to Emser,* in *Commentary,* p. 393. Cf. also his *Exposition of the Christian Faith,* in *On Providence,* pp. 276–87.

[88] George Waarren Richards, "Introduction" to Zwingli, *Commentary,* p. 29. The most recent English study of his theology says: "Zwingli had greater difficulty in expressing the initiative of God in the Sacrament, in part because of the strong opposition of body and Spirit and the sharp distinction of a sign from what it signifies. He did not develop the positive elements in his theology ... he could equally have developed the few references to Christ or the Holy Spirit as feeding us in the Eucharist. This would have enabled him within the constraints of his own theology to speak of the sacraments as presenting, and

Calvin

John Calvin (1509–64), the Frenchman who became the guiding light of the Reform in Geneva, made the effort to bridge the difference between the Eucharistic doctrine of Luther and Zwingli, and his writings on the Eucharist are the most systematic and comprehensive among the works of the founding reformers. All the developed essentials of his Eucharistic teaching are set forth in the final edition of his *summa* of Reform theology, *Institutes of the Christian Religion,* published in 1559. In Book IV, chapters 17 and 18, he presents his doctrine, touching upon almost every Eucharistic question. He draws heavily from the Fathers, especially St. Augustine, whose writings he frequently interprets with great insight, although he never cites the more "realistic" Eucharistic texts of the great saint.

Like Luther and Zwingli, Calvin rejects the Catholic doctrine of the Mass as sacrifice, although he admits that the Fathers frequently called it such. He rejects Zwingli's symbolic understanding of the Sacrament. With Luther he rejects transubstantiation and teaches that bread and wine remain after the consecratory words. He rejects, also, the Catholic and Lutheran understanding of the Real Presence and repudiates Luther's notion of the "ubiquity" of Christ's human nature. He denounces adoration of the Sacrament as something leading to superstition and idolatry. Positively, Calvin evidences great respect for the Sacrament and advocates frequent and worthy reception of Communion in both kinds. While teaching that "Christ's Flesh itself does not enter into us",[89] and that "we maintain no other Presence than that of a relationship [between the elements and the Lord's Body and Blood],"[90] Calvin can and does speak of the faithful being "substantially" united to Christ. For Calvin it is the Holy Spirit "that bridges over the

---

not simply representing, Christ" (W. P. Stephens, *The Theology of Huldrych Zwingli,* p. 255).

[89] Calvin, *Institutes,* bk. IV, chap. 17, 32, p. 1404.

[90] Calvin, *Institutes,* bk. IV, chap. 17, p. 1374.

immense gap between the Sacrament on earth and the Body of Christ in heaven which is, as it was for Zwingli, a local distance that cannot be understood as a metaphysical distance between our world and the world of God".[91] The elements of bread and wine are not mere common bread and wine but rather, having received the consecratory word, the Sacrament of the Lord's Body and Blood, which brings to the Christian who receives worthily the forgiveness of sins, spiritual nourishment, the remembrance of his Passion, and a pledge of heavenly glory. The Supper is, in short, a powerful and effective sign, on the occasion of whose reception the Holy Spirit unites the heavenly Lord to us as our food, which we eat spiritually.

> They could never have been so foully deluded by Satan's tricks unless they had already been bewitched by this error [i.e., transubstantiation], that Christ's body, enclosed in bread, is transmitted by the mouth of the body into the stomach. The cause of such crude imagination was that among them consecration was virtually equivalent to magic incantation. But this principle was hidden from them, that the bread is a sacrament only to those persons to whom the word is directed; just as the water of baptism is not changed in itself, but as soon as the promise has been attached it begins to be for us what it was not before.[92]

> And surely certain men would rather manifest their ignorance to their great shame than yield even the least particle of their error. I am not speaking of the papists, whose doctrine is more tolerable or at least more modest. But some are carried away with such contentiousness as to say that because of the natures joined in Christ, wherever Christ's divinity is, there also is his flesh, which cannot be separated from it. As if that union had compounded from two natures some sort of intermediate being which was neither God nor man!
> ... Away with that calumny that Christ is removed from his Supper unless he lies hidden under the covering of bread! For since

[91] Sasse, p. 323. Cf. G. C. Berkouwer, *The Sacraments,* chaps. 10 and 11.
[92] Calvin, *Institutes,* bk. IV, chap. 17, 14, p. 1376.

this mystery is heavenly, there is no need to draw Christ to earth that he may be joined to us.[93]

Even though it seems unbelievable that Christ's Flesh, separated from us by such great distance, penetrates to us, so that it becomes our food, let us remember how far the secret power of the Holy Spirit towers above all our senses. . . . The Spirit truly unites things separated in space.[94]

On this account, Scripture, in speaking of our participation with Christ, relates its whole power to the Spirit. . . . For Paul, in the eighth chapter of Romans, states that Christ dwells in us only through his Spirit (Rom 8:9). Yet he does not take away that communion of his flesh and blood which we are now discussing but teaches that the Spirit alone causes us to possess Christ completely and have him dwelling in us.[95]

But if the function of the Sacrament is to help the otherwise weak mind of man so that it may rise up to look upon the sight of spiritual mysteries, then those who are halted at the outward sign wander from the right way of seeking Christ. What then? Shall we deny that this is superstitious worship when men prostrate themselves before bread to worship Christ there? Doubtless the Council of Nicaea meant to forestall this evil when it forbade us to fix our humble attention upon the symbols set before us.[96]

But the height of frightful abomination was when the devil raised up a sign by which it [i.e., the Lord's Supper] was not only to be obscured and perverted, but . . . to vanish and pass out of human memory. This happened when he blinded nearly the whole world with a most pestilential error—the belief that the Mass is a sacrifice and offering to obtain forgiveness of sins.

---

[93] Calvin, *Institutes,* bk. IV, chap. 17, 30–31, pp. 1402–3.

[94] Calvin, *Institutes,* bk. IV, chap. 17, 10, p. 1370.

[95] Calvin, *Institutes,* bk. IV, chap. 17, 12, p. 1373.

[96] Calvin, *Institutes,* bk. IV, chap. 17, 36, p. 1412. The reference to Nicaea is to Nicaea II (787) and its decree on the veneration of images against the Iconoclasts. Calvin is attempting to make what is said there about images apply to the Eucharist.

. . .

And this has not been accepted only as a popular notion, but the very action itself has been so framed as to be a kind of appeasement to make satisfaction to God for the expiation of the living and the dead.[97]

Calvin then proceeds to give the standard arguments against the Mass as sacrifice. It would take away from the unique sacrifice of Calvary; it would rob Christ of his unique priesthood by installing other "priestlings"; it would rob us of the Supper as a bestowal of grace by making it an offering of expiation. Even the Fathers are not to be excused in this regard. "I think they cannot be excused for having sinned somewhat in acting as they did. For they have followed the Jewish manner of sacrificing more closely than either Christ had ordained or the nature of the gospel allowed."[98] Malachi 1:11 was not talking of such sacrifice of expiation and propitiation when he spoke of pure sacrifices being offered everywhere but rather of the sacrifices of thanksgiving and praise offered by Christians.

In speaking of the worthiness with which the Supper is to be partaken, however, Calvin reveals both the value he attributes to the Sacrament and the effects it is meant to produce.

Since he is given us unto life, we understand that without him in us we would plainly be dead. Therefore, this is the worthiness — the best and only kind we can bring to God — to offer our vileness and (so to speak) our unworthiness to him so that his mercy may make us worthy of him; to despair in ourselves so that we may be comforted in him; to abase ourselves so that we may be lifted up by him; to accuse ourselves so that we may be justified by him; moreover, to aspire to that unity that he commends to us in his Supper; and, as he makes all of us one in himself, to desire one soul,

---

[97] Calvin, *Institutes,* bk. IV, chap. 18, 1, p. 1429.
[98] Calvin, *Institutes,* bk. IV, chap. 18, 11, p. 1440.

one heart, one tongue for us all. . . . We shall think that we, as being poor, come to a kindly giver; as sick, to a physician; as sinner, to the Author of righteousness; finally, as dead, to him who gives us life.[99]

Cranmer and the Thirty-Nine Articles of Anglicanism

The differences between Luther on the one hand and Zwingli and Calvin on the other in respect to the Eucharist and other doctrinal and disciplinary issues ultimately led to that division within Protestantism that has been designated by the terms *Evangelical* (Lutheran) and *Reformed* (Calvinism, Presbyterianism). Reformed is a designation that, with varying degrees of accuracy, can be applied to a far wider and more international community of churches than the largely (though never quite exclusively) Germanic ones that identified themselves as Lutheran. "Even the Church of England, which defied all efforts to categorize it confessionally, was in some sense a "Reformed" communion, as its *Thirty-Nine Articles of Religion* and its delegation at the Synod of Dort attest."[100]

The *Thirty-Nine Articles of Religion* of the Church of England first appeared in 1553 in the reign of Edward VI, son of Henry VIII. They were largely the work of Thomas Cranmer (1489–1556), the Archbishop of Canterbury, and accompanied his second *Book of Common Prayer,* which regularized the liturgical worship of the Church of England. Published in that year as *The Forty-Two Articles of Religion,* they were modified during the reign of Queen Elizabeth I in 1562 and again in 1571 to become the present

---

[99] Calvin, *Institutes,* bk. IV, chap. 17, 42, pp. 1419–20.
[100] Pelikan, 4, p. 184. Kurt Aland makes much the same judgment: "The confession of faith in the Forty-Two Articles indicates a stronger and stronger Calvinistic influence in the Reformation's development" (*Four Reformers,* p. 124).

thirty-nine. Even with this revision they remain largely the work of Cranmer.

Cranmer's own doctrine on the Eucharist appears to have gone through three stages: a Catholic period; a period in which his doctrine was similar to that of Luther; and a final period in which his Eucharistic doctrine was, depending on how one interprets it, Zwinglian or Calvinistic.[101] It is this final stage that is reflected in the *Articles.* Article XXVIII reads:

> The Lord's Supper is not only a sign of the mutual love of Christians among themselves but rather the Sacrament of our redemption through the death of Christ. And so, for those who receive properly, worthily, and with faith, the bread that we break is a communication of the Body of Christ; likewise the cup of blessing is a communication of the Blood of Christ.
>
> The transubstantiation of the bread and wine in the Eucharist cannot be proved from Sacred Scripture; it is contrary to the clear words of Scripture, overthrows the nature of a sacrament, and has been the occasion of many superstitions.
>
> The Body of Christ is given, received, and eaten in the Supper only in a heavenly and spiritual sense. Moreover the medium by which the Body of Christ is received and eaten in the Supper is faith.
>
> The Sacrament of the Eucharist by the institution of Christ is not reserved, carried about, elevated, or adored.[102]
>
> Article XXXI: The offering of Christ, made once, is the

[101] On the variations in Cranmer's thought on the Eucharist, cf. Peter Brooks, *Thomas Cranmer's Doctrine of the Eucharist,* Horton Davies' *Worship and Theology in England,* I, pp. 178–94, and Bouyer, *Eucharist,* pp. 407–19.

[102] Article XXVIII. Latin text in Browne, *An Exposition of the Thirty-Nine Articles,* p. 677. The remarks about not adoring the Eucharist were supplemented by the so-called Black Rubric in the *Book of Common Prayer* of 1552–53, which stated that any kneeling during the Eucharist was not to be interpreted as meaning that adoration was being given to the sacramental bread and wine or to any Real and essential Presence of Christ's natural Body and Blood. The Black Rubric was removed in the edition of the work done under Elizabeth, but Article XXVIII remained.

perfect redemption, propitiation, and satisfaction for the sins of the whole world, both original and actual; apart from that unique offering there is no other satisfaction for sins: therefore the sacrifices of the Mass, in which it was commonly said that the priest offers Christ for the remission of punishment or faults for the living and the dead, are blasphemous imaginings and pernicious deceits.[103]

Modern Disputes and Efforts toward Consensus

In response to the Eucharistic teaching of the reformers, the Council of Trent reaffirmed and defined previous positions on the major points of Catholic doctrine: the Real Presence of Christ in the Sacrament, Body, Blood, Soul, and Divinity; the fact that only the appearances and not the reality of the bread and wine remain after the Consecration, a Mystery fittingly called transubstantiation; the Mass as a sacrifice, truly propitiatory for the living and the dead; the Sacrament, to be offered the adoration or worship due to God alone.[104] With the consolidation of the Reformed theology in the Church of England, the fundamental Eucharistic positions of the Reformation were fixed in place, at least for a time. Calvin's doctrine on the Eucharist was dominant and came to the American continent with the Puritans, manifesting itself in varying degrees in almost all the Protestant communities that took root there. Even in the Lutheran communities in Germany, Calvin's theology made great inroads during the seventeenth and eighteenth centuries. In the nineteenth and twentieth centuries, however, many influences combined to produce a liturgical renewal in the various Christian bodies, moving many of them to a theology, at least in respect to the nature of Lord's Presence in the Eucharist, closer to that of Luther himself or even to that of the Catholic and Orthodox Churches.

[103] Article XXXI, in Browne, p. 737.
[104] Cf. pp. 212ff. below for the teaching and meaning of the Tridentine decrees.

Leenhardt

The liturgical revival and the consequent reexamination of the various aspects of the Eucharistic Mystery led to the publication in 1955 of a significant theological essay by Franz Leenhardt.[105] Aware that because of his work the author "in certain Protestant churches . . . would perhaps be called to account for heresy, with an anathema thrown in",[106] Leenhardt defended himself by writing:

> If the recent past is considered, it will be thought that the thesis presented here is quite new. But the foundation of the thesis is not in fact so. Not only did the Christian Church profess a similar faith for many centuries before the Reformation, but even after the Reformation the faith of the Protestants lived by the same certainties that I am expounding here. . . . The authentic Protestant theology was not, as far as the subject treated here is concerned, as far distant as many imagine from the Roman theology, at least in certain of its manifestations.[107]

What is most immediately striking about the Leenhardt's work is a return to and even a defense of the Catholic terminology of transubstantiation and sacrifice. Chapter 3 of the work is entitled "Transubstantiation", and Leenhardt writes:

> The word *transubstantiation* expresses this transformation [which takes place in the celebration of the Eucharist] without attempting to provide an explanation of it. . . . It is useful because it preserves two affirmations which are essential to faith, in which everything can be summed up: (1) the substance of things is not in their empirical data, but in the will of God who upholds them. And (2) Jesus Christ declares in the Upper Room, in a sovereign manner, his will that the bread should be his Body; he transforms the substance of this bread. Substance does not mean, for Christians,

---

[105] Leenhardt, "This Is My Body", in *Essays on the Lord's Supper*, pp. 24–85.
[106] Leenhardt, "This Is My Body", p. 24.
[107] Leenhardt, "This Is My Body", pp. 25–26.

the matter behind the form, the substratum of the accidents. Let me repeat, substance is the final reality of things as faith recognizes it in God's creation and in his ordinance to his creatures.... Only the believer knows the substance of things and of man. Only he can recognize in the bread of the last Passover this new substance which is given to him by the word of Jesus Christ.[108]

Drawing a distinction between the outlook of Hebrew thought and what he terms the "static substantialism" of Greek philosophical categories, however, Leenhardt denies any permanent change in the bread and wine considered in themselves.

The affirmation that this is the Body of Christ is not made of an inert thing taken by itself; it can be made only of a thing which serves as a means of communication between Jesus and the believer, at the moment when he offers it to the believer and presents it to his faith. The object of this affirmation is not the thing in itself, but the thing as chosen and assumed by the will of Christ to serve as the organ of his Presence. This bread is truly the Body of Christ in the celebration of the rite, because it is as such that Christ presents it at that moment; it does not remain such outside this active presentation.

. . .

This object is sacred only in and through the action of Christ by which he assigns it a new end. Nothing of this sacred character can remain outside of Christ's action in giving the bread. Indeed this bread is the Body of Christ because Christ makes use of this bread. Outside this action it is only bread.[109]

It may be said that, for Leenhardt, the bread has a "contextual sacredness". In the Eucharistic rite Christ, Lord of all creation, is able to and does give the bread a new finality, "assigns it a new end" by and through which he gives himself, in his total reality, to

[108] Leenhardt, "This Is My Body", p. 50.
[109] Leenhardt, "This Is My Body", pp. 53–54.

the believing recipient. Apart from the ritual context of bestowal, the bread remains what it was. This becomes very clear in what Leenhardt writes concerning reservation of the Sacrament.

> The reservation of the bread after a service of the Lord's Supper can recall the promise of Christ and efficaciously invite the believers to benefit from the offering made by Christ to make himself present in the celebration of the Paschal meal. But the menace of idolatry is too close to run the risk. Outside the actual dialogue of Christ with believers the bread is not the sacramental sign of Christ's Presence in the Church.[110]

Thus, Leenhardt remains fundamentally within the Tradition of the Reform since, for Catholic Faith, Christ's bestowal of himself through the elements so affects them that their very reality is changed into his reality and remains changed as long as the appearances of the bread and wine remain intact.

In his treatment of the Lord's Supper as a sacrifice, Leenhardt continues in the same ecumenical vein evident in his treatment of transubstantiation. He is critical of what he considers both Catholic and Protestant excesses in considering the sacrificial aspects of the Eucharist. Of the Catholic excesses he writes:

> The whole theological and devotional literature clearly indicates that the believers expect the Mass to provide them with divine graces which the Cross did not have as its object. The Mass is a sacrifice which *disposes* God and even *obliges* him to bestow the pledges of his mercy:[111] ... God, says the Council of Trent, is

[110] Leenhardt, "This Is My Body", p. 76.

[111] Leenhardt rightly attributes the italicized words to Maurice de la Taille, S.J., author of *The Mystery of Faith,* one of the most distinguished Catholic works on the Eucharist in the twentieth century. De la Taille wrote: "In a word, whatever fruit there be of the sacrifice itself, or *ex opere operato,* can only consist in this: that in view of our sacrifice, over and above the mere consideration of the intensity of our devotion, God is *prepared* and in a manner *bound* to bestow his mercy on us in a way suitable to our own individual state and condition. Hence the Apostle wrote: he died for our sins (to make propitiation for them), and he arose for our justification (to effect it)" (*The Mystery of Faith,* 2, Thesis XXV, 1, p. 226).

appeased by this oblation of the Mass and he accords, thanks to it, the gift of penitence, and he forgives sins, even the most serious crimes. Whether one wishes it or not, the sacrifice of the altar, thus envisaged, obtains from the divine mercy what the Cross was insufficient to secure. The difficulty can be made a little less by saying that this oblation only "recalls" before God the unique Victim of the one sacrifice of the Cross. It still remains true that, if the Godhead needs to have something recalled, that is a sign of an insufficiency which is entirely incompatible both with the dignity of the Victim on the Cross and the love of God himself.[112]

Of Protestant excesses:

The reaction against the sacrificial interpretation of the Lord's Supper . . . issues in a refusal to see in it anything but a commemoration, a recalling, an evocation, an acted preaching. The unique character and the unique efficacy of the sacrifice of the Cross are thus perfectly safeguarded, but at the price of a remoteness of the Cross in time; the sacrifice loses all its contemporaneity by dint of our concentration on its beneficial effect.[113]

For Leenhardt, the sacrificial aspect of the Mass means that it is, like the Hebrew notion of memorial, an effective recalling. It is, therefore, a truly efficient rite, through which God makes present here and now that which was accomplished in the once-and-for-all sacrifice of Christ, which was of itself totally sufficient.

The Sacrament of the Lord's Supper derives its meaning from the conditions of the redemptive action of God in Christ. God has accomplished everything, and this objective and perfect action must be placed within the reach of the individual. Inserted into the history of mankind, it must be inserted into the history of each individual man. The grace offered to all by the proclamation must

---

[112] Leenhardt, "This Is My Body", p. 57.
[113] Leenhardt, "This Is My Body", p. 58.

be conveyed to those who respond by faith to the divine summons addressed to them by means of the proclamation.[114]

The efficacy is such that it can be truly described as happening *ex opere operato:*

> The efficacy *ex opere operato* means that God *makes use of* the things and the actions to manifest and to realize his will; it means that these actions and these things have consequently a supernatural capacity which is given them by the divine will which they embody.[115]
>
> . . .
>
> This doctrine is concerned only with that aspect of the Sacrament which derives from the action of Christ, that which the Sacrament objectively is. It is not concerned with the subjective aspect of the sacramental event, that which concerns the believer. The Sacrament, if it conveys its fruit of grace, acts *ex opere operato,* but unbelief can establish an obstacle to its efficacy.[116]

Although it can be claimed—rightly, we think—that Leenhardt misunderstood the Catholic theologian he cited, the basic elements of his positive presentation are quite acceptable to Catholic theology. His explanation of *ex opere operato* captures the essence—here at least—of what the Church actually teaches. There is, however, no treatment of the propitiatory value of the Mass for the living and the dead, or any treatment of the sense in which the Church offers the Mass as a sacrifice in and with Christ. Nevertheless, Leenhardt's treatment of the Eucharistic Mystery was undoubtedly a work of ecumenical charity and served as a notable advance toward the dialogue that would grow after the Second Vatican Council. Before then, however, the influence of his views on transubstantiation would, along with parallel rethinking of that

---

[114] Leenhardt, "This Is My Body", p. 66.
[115] Leenhardt, "This Is My Body", p. 68.
[116] Leenhardt, "This Is My Body", p. 70.

doctrine by some Catholics, occasion yet another reaffirmation of the Church's doctrine on that matter.

Modern science, with its views of an atomic and subatomic structuring of material reality, had long posed questions for the meaning of "substance" and "change of substance" as used in the Church's dogmatic formulations of the Eucharistic Mystery. According to empirical science, nothing changed in the elements of bread and wine; they remained what they had been. Furthermore, bread and wine were not "natural" substances but rather a conglomerate or amalgamation of "substances" shaped not by nature itself but by man's industry. It was their relation to man's industry that determined their "being" and "meaning". Such being the case, what was it then that was actually being said when a change of "substance" was spoken of? For many, such considerations posed insurmountable difficulties for the Aristotelian and Thomistic philosophical categories in which the dogmatic definitions of Lateran IV and Trent had very frequently been explained. In addition to such considerations, it was also suggested that the usual explanations put forth to illuminate and defend the doctrine of transubstantiation resulted in an approach to the Mystery that was fundamentally "static", incapable of capturing the dynamic and personalistic sense of self-bestowal that marks Christ's action in communicating himself to the believer.

De Baciocchi and Transfinalization-Transignification

Already discussed in the 1940s, the considerations just mentioned led to a discussion in the 1950s and 1960s that ultimately centered on the meaning and value of the words *transignification* and *transfinalization* as suitable complements or alternatives to the term *transubstantiation*.[117] In a view that closely paralleled certain aspects

---

[117] A full history of the discussion—much of it in its more theoretical aspects carried on in Dutch—can be found in Powers (*Eucharistic Theology*) and Schillebeeckx ("Transubstantiation, Transfinalization, Transfiguration", *Worship* 40) and in the bibliographies they give.

of that of Leenhardt, the French theologian J. de Baciocchi appealed to the sovereignty that the resurrected Christ has over all creation to help understand the profundity of the Eucharistic change. If Christ is sovereign and all-powerful over created realities, the only definitive point of view concerning things is that which is held and willed by Christ. "Things are purely and simply that which they are for Christ, since the understanding of Christ is absolute norm for our understanding. . . . The sensible and physical-chemical properties [of things] have only a relative significance."[118] In the Eucharist, "the word of Christ, without altering the gifts in their empirical context, totally changes their social and religious finality".[119] For de Baciocchi this type of change is truly objective because of Christ's dominion over reality.

This notion of a change of finality or significance was developed by others within a "personalist" context in which the Eucharistic elements were presented as the effective signs of an interpersonal relationship with the risen Lord. He gives the elements a new finality or purpose, that, namely, of effecting his total and personal offer of himself to the Church and to the individual believer. Being "present" to another is essentially a matter of interpersonal communication, not a matter of bodily contiguity or closeness.

> Personal presence is the presence of person to person or . . . the presence of a person as a person to another person as a person. This personal presence is constituted essentially by mutual knowledge and love.
>
> A person becomes present to another person when, in what he is, he enters into the other person's knowledge and love, in what he is. He must reveal himself. He must make himself known as a subject. . . . His self-communication must be recognized and accepted, so that he is known as another subject or self.
>
> . . .

---

[118] J. de Baciocchi, "Présence Eucharistique et Transsubstantiation", p. 151.
[119] De Baciocchi, "Présence Eucharistique et Transsubstantiation", p. 150.

The word "presence" needs careful handling when it is used in a limited sense to designate the relation of Christ to the sacrament while prescinding from the interpersonal presence achieved in the sacrament as its effect. The image of the local presence of a body dominates the mind of many people. They cannot rise above the concept of presence as bodily juxtaposition. In fact, Christ is present in the sacraments because they are his actions.[120]

The various approaches had much to recommend them, at least insofar as they stressed elements sometimes left only implicit in the older theological presentations of Catholic doctrine. Nonetheless there were difficulties both in the general idea of reality conveyed and in the language and examples used to express it.[121] Accepting as truth the Lordship of Christ over creation, does it follow that reality is only that which he determines it to be or understands it to be? And, on a lower plane, is the same to be said for the things (e.g., bread and wine) produced by man? Do not things rather have a "consistency" and meaning in themselves—an existence in themselves that he, as Creator, gives them and that is subject to him, but that, nonetheless, as a real gift from him, enables them to have a stability and intelligibility that are their own? And is not the same to be said for what we as humans "create" or produce? According to the teaching of the Second Vatican Council: "By the very condition of creation all things are constituted with their own stability, truth, goodness, and proper laws and order, which man ought to reverence as he comes to know them by the methods proper to each of the sciences and the arts."[122] A view of reality

[120] Charles Davis, "Understanding the Real Presence", in *The Word in History*, pp. 160, 168. Cf. Schillebeeckx, "Transubstantiation, Transfinalization, Transfiguration", pp. 336ff., for a development of the same line of thought.

[121] Some of the examples used to illustrate the new viewpoints were very like Zwingli's example of the "ring" quoted above. For comments on such examples, cf. Schillebeeckx, "Transubstantiation, Transfinalization, Transfiguration", pp. 336–37.

[122] *Gaudium et Spes*, 36.

that would reduce the reality of a thing to *only* what it means for man or for Christ ultimately robs it of the very being that one claims it had been given. Once produced, bread and wine do have being, consistency, and meaning in themselves. Bread is not a newspaper, yet both were produced by man. They have a "for themselves" to which man, their producer, must relate. He is not capable of using the one for the other indifferently. It is this "for themselves" that approximates the notion of substance as used in the dogmatic definitions on the Eucharist. In the Eucharistic conversion, that which is intrinsic and proper to bread and wine, that which gives them stability and truth-intelligibility as real things, is totally changed by the power of Christ through his Spirit. He does this not by twisting their own reality to a meaning or finality other than what is proper to that reality but by changing totally what they were. The new significance or finality follows the change in being.

> One must say that bread and wine share above all in that autonomy that is common to every creaturely being, that is, that they share in that fundamental "substantiality" that is proper to what is created inasmuch as it is autonomous alongside of the divine being. Transubstantiation signifies that these things lose this type of creaturely autonomy, that they cease to consist simply in themselves in the manner that corresponds to being a creature, and become instead *pure* signs of his Presence among us.... Losing their creaturely independence, they no longer exist of themselves but only "for him, with him, and in him."[123]

The explanations given for transfinalization and transignification ran the risk of losing this awareness of the autonomy of created reality and, as a consequence, depicting the Eucharistic change as

---

[123] J. Ratzinger, "El problema de la transustanciación y la cuestión sobre el sentido de la Eucaristía", pp. 31–32. Piet Schoonenberg, S.J., in his article "Transubstantiation", published after *Mysterium Fidei,* still manifests an unawareness of what something is "for itself" and what it is "for us".

no more than a change of meaning or purpose, leaving them in themselves that which they had been. Implicit in all the discussion, but not raised explicitly, was the perennial question about what remains of the bread and wine after the Consecration. Since Berengarius this had been the neuralgic point of all the discussions of the Lord's Presence in the Sacrament. Only Luther had managed to maintain a realistic understanding of the Presence while affirming that the elements also remained true bread and wine. And those who disagreed with him labeled his position contradictory. The approaches that maintained that bread and wine remained in their full reality had, despite sometimes firm language about Christ being really and even substantially present, ultimately recoiled from saying that the Lord's actual Body was there to be eaten. For some the theologians who spoke of a new finality or significance for the elements of bread and wine appeared to be moving or had arrived at conclusions like those of Leenhardt. Christ truly and substantially bestowed himself in the Eucharistic action, but, apart from the action, the elements remained bread and wine. Such a position would indeed respect the autonomy of bread and wine but would locate that autonomy in their *meaning,* not in their being. By paradox, the Catholic view of transubstantiation, which denies the continued existence of bread and wine after the Consecration, actually defends the previous autonomous being — not merely meaning — of those elements.

Even the stress on the interpersonal nature of Presence ran the risk of devaluing the autonomy of one partner in the relationship by its sometimes slighting references to the value of physical or local Presence. In fact, normally speaking, local or physical presence of one person to another is a requisite for the establishment and even maintenance of truly interpersonal presence. Although not locally present in the Eucharist in the sense of being circumscribed by the Host or drawn out of heaven, Christ is truly physically present, and it is precisely that physical proximity that establishes and nourishes interpersonal Presence.

By 1965, intrinsic inadequacies in some of the newer explanations of the Eucharistic Presence had been aggravated by a wide circulation of such views in the media[124] and by consequent or concurrent abberations in Eucharistic belief and practice among some Catholics. In a homily on Holy Thursday of that year, Paul VI saw need to refer to those who viewed the Eucharist as "just a ritual meal or a case of a symbolic, not a real, Presence, or even the elevation of familiar things to a higher significance".[125] In June of the same year, at a Eucharistic Congress in Pisa, he spoke of "elusive interpretations of the traditional and authoritative doctrine of the Church". Finally, on September 2, 1965, he published the encyclical letter *Mysterium Fidei,* reaffirming the teaching of the Council of Trent on the Eucharist.[126]

In many ways the theological controversies that resulted in the issuance of the encyclical were the legacy of previous differences among Christians, many, but not all, stemming from the sixteenth-century reformers.

For a Catholic it is both sad and instructive to note that most of the leaders of those who dissented from Catholic doctrine on the Eucharist belonged to the Catholic clergy in all ranks. Berengarius was a deacon, Wyclif and Zwingli priests, Luther a monk, Cranmer a bishop. Those who by vocation were closest to the Lord in the Sacrament of his Body and Blood, those who would appear most likely to appreciate and defend the Sacrament, those best trained to understand the Mystery entrusted to the Church, were chief among those who found the teaching on the Eucharist a "hard saying" and were or became unwilling or unable to listen to it. St. John ended his account of the discourse at Capernaum by noting a similar fact: "Jesus replied, 'Have I not chosen you, the Twelve? Yet one of you is a devil.' He meant Judas, the son of Simon Iscariot, who, though one of the Twelve, was later to betray him"

---

[124] Schillebeeckx refers to the "completely inadequate" reporting of some of the media ("Transubstantiation, Transfinalization, Transfiguration", p. 333, n. 22). The media reports may indeed have not been an accurate presentation of what was actually being proposed by the theologians, but they give a fair presentation of how what was being said was *perceived.*

[125] Paul VI, "Homily for Holy Thursday, 1965"; *TPS,* vol. 10, no. 4, p. 310 n.

[126] For *Mysterium Fidei,* see below, pp. 261ff.

(Jn 6:70–71). That betrayal of Judas reached its "point of no return" at the Last Supper, when Christ entrusted to his followers the Sacrament of his Body and Blood. A moving and disturbing commentary on those events was given by Pope Paul VI in a homily for Holy Thursday 1971:

> Among the personages at the Last Supper there is another one we cannot forget, Judas. It is with a heavy heart that we see him sitting at the Paschal feast, and we cannot help being moved in rereading the Gospel narrative and seeing how the presence of the traitor weighs on the heart of the Teacher who, "troubled in spirit" (Jn 13:21), could no longer keep the oppressive secret.
>
> "Amen, amen, I say to you, one of you will betray me" (Jn 13:21). You know the rest: how the identification of the traitor was discreetly done, and how he, when discovered, furtively left the upper room. "Now it was night", says the Evangelist in conclusion (Jn 13:30). "And he who went out was night himself", remarked St. Augustine. Who does not feel a shudder in his heart at hearing the even graver and more terrible comment of Jesus: "It were better for that man if he had not been born" (Mk 14:21)?[127]

Every account of the Eucharist given in the New Testament contains the theme of betrayal: the sixth chapter of John, the Synoptic accounts of the Institution with their references to Judas' deed; the words of Paul in 1 Corinthians 11 about those who eat and drink unworthily. The Sacrament of his Presence continues the Mystery of his Person: a sign of contradiction (cf. Lk 2:34).

Closely aligned with the various dissenting views on the Eucharist, there have appeared historically dissenting positions on the ministry that serves the Sacrament. It must be noted, at least in passing, that in addition to the differences on Eucharistic doctrine itself, the reformers had distanced themselves from Catholic doctrine in respect to the sacramentality of the Christian ministry, its meaning, and the necessity of a valid ordination by a direct successor of the Apostles. As a result, defects entered in that led the Catholic Church to conclude that the necessary requirements

---

[127] Paul VI, "Homily on Holy Thursday, 1971", *TPS,* 16, no. 1, p. 11.

for true and valid Orders were not present, with the result that their celebrations of the Lord's Supper did not effect the Real Presence of Christ in the Eucharistic elements or render present sacramentally Christ's sacrifice. With sadness the Second Vatican Council noted this consequence of the division of the sixteenth century when it taught:

> The ecclesial communities separated from us, although they lack the full union with us that flows from Baptism and although we believe that they have not preserved the genuine and integral substance of the Eucharistic Mystery, especially because of the defect of the Sacrament of Orders, do profess, nevertheless— when they celebrate the memory of the Lord's death and Resurrection in the Holy Supper—that it signifies life in communion with Christ and they await his glorious coming. Therefore the doctrine about the Lord's Supper, the other sacraments, and the cult and ministries of the Church should constitute an object of dialogue.[128]

The council, in the above passage, was clearly attempting to emphasize the salutary significance of the celebrations of the Lord's Supper in the Christian bodies that are the descendants of the Reformation. Such celebrations are certainly opportunities and occasions for receiving divine grace, even though they are not the effective and efficient causes of such grace as is the case when a valid sacrament is celebrated. Although the Catholic Church believes that the Lord is not corporally present in such celebrations, he is surely spiritually present and prepared to bestow upon those who participate worthily and with faith a share in the immeasurable abundance of blessings that his Passion and Resurrection won for the human race. In their own way—comparable to a paraliturgical action within the Catholic Church—such celebrations may even be said to participate in the efficacy of the Eucharistic Mystery and are surely a means that mysteriously and gently orients the participant toward full union with the Catholic Church

---

[128] *Unitatis Redintegratio* (*Decree on Ecumenism*), 22.

and the Sacrament that creates the Church and that she daily celebrates.

Because the Lord's Body and Blood are not substantially present, a Catholic is never permitted to partake of the Communion services in such celebrations of the Lord's Supper. On the other hand, like the Lord himself when he marveled at the faith of the Syro-Phoenician woman, the Church does not refuse to take from her table that by which she lives and feed those who stand outside. In specific circumstances individual baptized Christians who are not Catholic may be permitted to receive the Eucharist in the Catholic Church. According to the norms of the Church, the conditions for such an occurrence are:

1. There must exist a danger of death or some grave and urgent need.

2. A spontaneous request must be made by the baptized non-Catholic.

3. The non-Catholic Christian must be unable to approach a minister of his own Christian community.

4. The person must be suitably disposed spiritually and have shown that he shares the Faith of the Catholic Church in respect to the Eucharist.

All the conditions must be simultaneously fulfilled. The judgment as to whether the conditions are met is left to the diocesan bishop or the Episcopal Conference, and consultation, at least on the local level, should be had with the non-Catholic churches or communities before general norms are issued by the Episcopal Conference or diocesan bishop.[129]

The preceding remarks and norms for Eucharistic reception apply to the churches and communities that are descendants of the

---

[129] The norms governing the admission of baptized non-Catholics to Catholic Eucharist are set forth in the *Instruction* issued by the Secretariat for Christian unity (*AAS,* 64 (1972), pp. 518–25; *TPS,* 17, no. 2, pp. 173–79), the subsequent notification by the same Secretariat (*AAS,* 65 (1973), pp. 616–19), and the 1983 Code of Canon Law, canon 844, sec. 4.

Reformation. The situation is different when one is treating of the Orthodox Churches of the East that are separated from Rome. In the seventeenth century these churches reaffirmed the traditional Faith in the Eucharist in their *Orthodox Confession of the Catholic Apostolic Eastern Church,* accepted at Jerusalem in 1672. This confession included "transubstantiation" among the concepts used to indicate the change in the elements of bread and wine.[130] These churches also preserved the apostolic succession in the Sacrament of Orders. Thus, in speaking of them, Vatican Council II stated:

> Moreover, since these churches, although separated, have true sacraments, especially — by the power of apostolic succession — the priesthood and the Eucharist, they are still joined to us by a tight necessity. Therefore, a certain sharing in the Holy Things, given opportune circumstances and the approval of ecclesiastic authority, is not only possible but even suggested.[131]

As a result of the existence of the true Sacraments of Orders and Eucharist in the separated churches of the East, the norms that govern the practice of "intercommunion" are different. As often as necessity or true spiritual usefulness urges it, a Catholic may lawfully receive the Sacraments of Penance, Anointing, and Eucharist from non-Catholic ministers in whose churches these sacraments are recognized as valid by the Catholic Church. This can be done on the condition that some physical or moral impossibility prevents them from approaching a Catholic minister and as long as they avoid the danger of the sin of thinking that it makes no difference as to what religion or church one belongs to or worships in. Likewise, members of such churches may receive the Sacraments of Penance, Eucharist, and Anointing from a Catholic minister as long as they spontaneously ask for them and are properly disposed.[132]

---

[130] For a recent presentation of the Eucharistic doctrine of the Eastern Orthodox churches, cf. Alexander Schmemann, *The Eucharist,* pp. 162ff., in particular, reference to transubstantiation.

[131] *Unitatis Redintegratio,* 15.

[132] Cf. 1983 Code of Canon Law, Canon 844, nos. 2 and 3.

Anglican–Roman Catholic International Commission's *Final Report*

The period following the Second Vatican Council has witnessed major advances in the ecumenical dialogue among the Christian churches and communities. In almost all of these discussions, the questions concerning the Eucharist and the Sacrament of Orders have received considerable attention by the participants in the dialogue, and in several cases statements of consensus have been issued. Most such statements, the work of individual bishops, ministers, and theologians, await official reactions by the leaders of the various communities. The Catholic Church, however, has made the *Final Report* of the Anglican–Roman Catholic International Commission (ARCIC) the subject of an official declaration. This declaration has come from the Catholic Congregation for the Doctrine of the Faith in 1982, and it hailed the *Final Report* as "a singular event in the history of the relations between the two communions and is, at the same time, a notable effort toward reconciliation".[133] In respect to the *Final Report*'s statement on the Eucharist, the Congregation notes, however, that there is work still to be done on areas that were either not touched upon or that were lacking in clarity or that failed to take into account adequately Roman Catholic teaching on the matters in question. In respect to the sacrificial aspect of the Eucharist, the Congregation noted that "the propitiatory value that Catholic dogma attributes to the Eucharist" is not mentioned and that greater clarity is needed in expressing the truth that the Church, through the ministry of the priest, offers the sacrifice of Christ in him and with him.[134] In respect to the Real Presence, it is noted that "several formulations [of the *Final Report*] clearly affirm the Real Presence of the Body and Blood of Christ in the Sacrament", but

---

[133] Congregation for the Doctrine of the Faith, *Some Observations on the Final Report of the Anglican-Roman Catholic International Commission,* in *TPS,* 27, no. 3, p. 257. The official text is found in *AAS,* 74, pp. 1060–74.

[134] Idem, p. 260.

that others "do not seem to indicate adequately what the Church understands by 'transubstantiation'". The Congregation notes that these latter formulations "can be read with the understanding that, after the Eucharistic prayer, the bread and wine remain such in their ontological substance, even while becoming the sacramental mediation in the Body and Blood of Christ".[135] Such an understanding, of course, would be contrary to Catholic Faith, which teaches that bread and wine in their ontological reality do not remain after the Consecration. Finally, in respect to adoration of the Sacrament, the Congregation notes that a "divergence in theological judgments" cannot be admitted in this matter since "the adoration rendered to the Blessed Sacrament is the object of a dogmatic definition in the Catholic Church". The Congregation notes, as well, that "a question could arise here about the current status in the Anglican Communion of the . . . 'Black Rubric'".[136] Thus, despite an increasing convergence in regard to expressing Eucharistic faith, work remains to be done. What is remarkable, however, is how much has already been achieved.

The *Lima Text (BEM)*

Another major fruit of ecumenical dialogue is the so-called *Lima Text* on Baptism, Eucharist, and Ministry (referred to as the *BEM* document) produced by the Faith and Order Commission of the World Council of Churches in 1982.[137] The document is not an accepted statement of belief of the member communities of the World Council, but it is a proposal submitted to the member communities and to the Roman Catholic Church for study and comment in the hopes that an agreed statement of faith can be reached. The *Lima Text* refers to the Eucharist as "the great sacrifice of praise by which the Church speaks on behalf of the

[135] Idem, p. 260, no. 2.
[136] Idem, p. 261.
[137] Faith and Order Paper no. III, *Baptism, Eucharist, and Ministry* (*Lima Text*), Geneva: World Council of Churches, 1982.

whole creation"[138] and as "the Sacrament of the unique sacrifice of Christ, who ever lives to make intercession for us".[139] Of Christ's Presence, the document says:

> The eucharistic meal is the sacrament of the Body and Blood of Christ, the sacrament of his Real Presence. . . . Christ's mode of presence in the eucharist is unique. . . . The Church confesses Christ's real, living, and active presence in the Eucharist. While Christ's real presence in the eucharist does not depend on the faith of the individual, all agree that to discern the body and blood of Christ, faith is required.[140]

The reintroduction of the language of sacrifice is a noteworthy advance in the ecumenical dialogue, as is the emphasis on the uniqueness of the Lord's "Real" Presence and its objective nature (i.e., his Presence does not depend on the faith of the individual). As the commentary that accompanies these affirmations notes, however, the formulations are capable of varying interpretations.[141]

On behalf of the Catholic Church, the Secretariat for Promoting Christian Unity, in consultation with the Congregation for the Doctrine of the Faith, issued a formal response, which was made public in November 1987. They hailed the *BEM* document as a "significant result of the ecumenical movement" and stated that "we believe that if it were accepted by the various churches and ecclesial communities, it would bring the churches to an important step forward in the ecumenical dialogue".[142] On the Eucharist, the Catholic response noted that "Catholics can recognize in the statement . . . much that corresponds to the understand-

---

[138] *Lima Text,* "Eucharist", II, 4, p. 10.

[139] *Lima Text,* "Eucharist", II, 8, p. 11.

[140] *Lima Text,* "Eucharist", II, 13, p. 12.

[141] The commentary on nos. 13, 14, and 15 indicates that there are differences touching upon the relation of the Lord's Presence to the elements as well as to the nature of the change that takes place in the elements. Cf. *Lima Text,* pp. 12–13.

[142] *Vatican Response to WCC Document: Baptism, Eucharist, and Ministry. An Appraisal.* Text in *Origins,* 17, no. 23 (Nov. 1987), p. 403.

ing and practice of the apostolic Faith"[143] and that "the connection established between the sacrifice of the Cross and the Eucharist correspond to Catholic understanding".[144] On the *BEM*'s statements on the Real Presence, the Catholic reply states that "we appreciate the presentation in the text of the Real Presence of Christ" and that "the statement about the fact and the mode of Christ's 'unique' Presence, which 'does not depend on the faith of the individual', is adequate".[145] Many other positive remarks are made as well. There are, however, instances where the Catholic response finds the document an inadequate presentation of the full Catholic Faith.

> From our view, although the text speaks of the "present efficacy" (no. 5) "of the sacrifice of Christ" and "the living and effective sign of his sacrifice" and the eucharist as the "sacrament of the unique sacrifice of Christ" (no. 8), it does not say unambiguously that the eucharist is in itself a real sacrifice, the memorial of the sacrifice of Christ on the Cross.[146]

> A distinction is made in Commentary 13 between churches that "believe" in the change of the elements and those which do not link Christ's presence "so definitively to the signs of bread and wine". But the final sentence seems to relativize the word *believe*. It asks whether the "difference can be accommodated with the convergence formulated in the text itself". On the one hand, we welcome the convergence that is taking place. On the other hand, we must note that for Catholic doctrine the conversion of the elements is a matter of faith and is only open to possible new theological explanations as to the how of the intrinsic change. The content of the word *transubstantiation* ought to be expressed without ambiguity. For Catholics this is a central mystery of faith, and they cannot accept expressions that are ambiguous.[147]

---

[143] *Origins*, p. 408.

[144] *Origins*, p. 409.

[145] *Origins*, p. 410.

[146] *Origins*, p. 410.

[147] *Origins*, p. 410. The response of the Russian Orthodox Church to the *BEM* document on this point is quite as explicit as that of the Catholic Church. It reads: "The document recognizes *anamnesis* as the essence of the

Other reservations are expressed in respect to the *BEM*'s statements on the perduring Presence of Christ in the Sacred Species after the celebration. Recognition is asked for the "legitimate and praiseworthy" forms of Eucharistic worship outside the celebration. And, finally, it is noted that even the acceptance of the *BEM* statement by a member community of the World Council of Churches "would not have the immediate result of allowing reciprocal Eucharistic sharing" with the Catholic Church, not only because of the specific reservations expressed but also because "Eucharistic sharing for the Catholic Church is intimately related to other basic factors such as unity in the whole Faith of the Church and particularly in regard to the Church and the ministry".[148] Undoubtedly this is so and indicates that further dialogue is necessary. Nevertheless, the length and specificity of detail in the Catholic response indicate that the Church considers the *BEM* statement to be of great importance.[149] It is a sign that, at least in the area of Eucharistic theology, some of the past divisions are being gradually overcome.

Unfortunately, but surely, the Mystery of the Eucharist in its full significance will always be "a hard saying" for some, but one can hope that for the majority of Christians—and then for the world—it will again become that "sign of unity and bond of charity" that Augustine knew the Sacrament to be.

---

eucharistic meal, whereas the Orthodox Church confesses as the essence of the Eucharist the transubstantiation of the holy gifts. The bread and wine are declared to be only 'the sacramental signs of Christ's body and blood'; whereas the Orthodox Church believes that the bread is really and truly and essentially itself the body of the Lord and the wine is itself the blood of the Lord. According to St. John of Damascus, 'the body is truly united with the Godhead; themselves the bread and wine are transubstantiated into the body and blood of God'—which means that they remain as such also outside the usage" (*Churches Respond to BEM,* vol. II, p. 8).

[148] *Origins,* p. 416.

[149] Reactions of other Christian communities to the *BEM* document can be found in *Churches Respond to BEM: Official Responses to the "Baptism, Eucharist and Ministry" Text* 2–3, edited by Max Thurian.

III

Peter and the Eucharist

When Jesus had finished his discourse in the synagogue at Capharnaum, "many of his disciples turned back and no longer followed him" (Jn 6:66). He then turned to the Twelve and asked, "You do not want to leave me too, do you? Simon Peter answered him, 'Lord, to whom shall we go? You have the words of eternal life. We believe and know that you are the Holy One of God,' " (Jn 6:67–69). Peter, through faith in the Lord, had overcome the difficulty of the "hard teaching". Trusting Christ, he became the first to put his faith in the Bread of life.

It has been observed that "from the time of Pius IX ... the popes have promoted Marian devotion by every means. From the nineteenth century Marianism and papalism have gone hand in hand and given each other mutual support."[1] There is insight in that statement, although not in the negative and polemical sense intended by its author. It is a perception of an intimate connection between two of the doctrines most difficult for many non-Catholic Christians to understand: the salvific role of Mary and the role of the papacy. Striking is the statement of the Pope who, having proclaimed Mary "Mother of the Church" during the Second Vatican Council, declared during the first meeting between a Pope and the leaders of the World Council of Churches on June 10, 1969, "We are here among you. Our name is Peter. Scripture tells what meaning Christ wanted to attribute to this name, what duties he imposes upon us. . . . The Lord has given us a ministry of

---

[1] Hans Küng, *On Being a Christian*, p. 461.

communion."[2] We are Peter, sent for a ministry of communion. Necessarily more intimate than the connection of the papacy with promoting devotion to the Mother of God has been the historical connection between the papacy and its defense and promotion of the Church's doctrine concerning the Eucharist. It is not a connection of recent centuries; it stretches back to that synagogue in Capernaum where Peter stood first among those who accepted the "hard teaching". "We believe and know", said Peter: faith preceding and seeking understanding. Commenting on the text in John, Augustine wrote:

> Peter replied on behalf of all, the one for the many, unity for the universal, . . . "If we depart from you, to whom will we go? You have the words of eternal life." See how Peter, by a gift of God and the grace of the Holy Spirit, understood. How was he able to understand, except for the fact that he believed? "You have the words of eternal life." You have eternal life in the ministering of your Body and Blood. "And we have believed and have known." We have believed so that we might know because, if we wanted first to know and then to believe, we would be able neither to know nor to believe. What have we believed and known? That you are the Christ, the Son of God, that is, that you are life eternal itself and that in your Flesh and Blood you give us nothing except what you are.[3]

The role of Mary, and Peter's faith. Each is a stumbling block in its own way, and both of them historically connected with the Church's faith in the Eucharist.

It would not be true to pretend, however, that, through the centuries, the faith of Peter's successors has always been foremost in the Church's defense of Eucharistic doctrine and piety. The Church is more than Peter; the Popes drink from the same fountain of truth as do all the faithful. With the exception of Clement

[2] Paul VI, "Address to the World Council of Churches", TPS, 14, no. 2, p. 150.

[3] Augustine, In Iohannis Evangelium, 27, 9; CCSL, 36, p. 274.

of Rome and the liturgical contributions of some of his successors, none of the Bishops of Rome during the Patristic era has left us a major contribution to Eucharistic doctrine. Perhaps such contributions existed; if so, they have been lost to us. Indeed, the personal understanding of one of Peter's successors may have been inadequate in respect to the Eucharist.[4] The laurels for outstanding expression of Eucharistic doctrine among the Fathers go not to the Bishops of Rome but to other bishops and churchmen. And much the same can be said of some subsequent ages. The faith of that "common herd"—so derided by Berengarius and others—has always been true to Peter's original confession. They are the ones who attended Mass, built the cathedrals in which it was offered, marched in the processions of Corpus Christi, spent nights of vigil in adoration and prayer, supported a sometimes decadent clergy so that they might not be deprived of the Eucharist, held firm when others doubted, and even gave their lives as martyrs for the truth of the Sacrament. With them were joined untold numbers of bishops, alone and in councils, priests, religious, catechists, and theologians who drew strength from the common faith and in turn nourished it. Increasingly, however, and especially in times of theological contestation, the "one spoke for the many, unity for the universal". Speaking with the voice of Peter and representing in their office the unity of the whole Church, the Bishops of Rome, from Silvester II to our own day, have repeated the "we believe and we know" of Peter. Peter's charism is unique. He is not simply the spokesman for the entire body, the expounder of the consensus of others, since, when he teaches definitively, his faith is normative and guaranteed as free from error. This chapter looks at the Church's repeated profession of faith in the Eucharist, especially as developed under the leadership of the Popes. Other voices will be heard as well, however, since—as will be obvious—in Peter, the multitude speaks.

---

[4] Cf. above, pp. 71–72.

The Early Centuries

Of particular importance for the life of the Church in the West was the development in Rome of the Eucharistic Prayer, which we today call the Roman Canon or Eucharistic Prayer I. Its origins, however, are clouded in obscurity. An early Eucharistic Prayer (previous to or concomitant with the development of the Roman Canon) is given to us by St. Hippolytus (died 235) in his work *Apostolic Tradition.*[5] Following the liturgical reforms of the Second Vatican Council, Eucharistic Prayer II of the current *Sacramentary* is substantially that given us by Hippolytus. The Roman Canon itself, with much of its wording and content, is known to have been in existence in the fourth century, a fact made evident in the writings of St. Ambrose.[6]

Apart from their sermons and their role in the dispute with the Eastern churches over the date for the celebration of Easter,[7] evidence of papal activity in respect to the Eucharist in these early centuries is mainly confined to liturgical matters. Although they themselves may not be the authors, the names of Leo the Great (440–61), Gelasius (492–96), and Gregory the Great (590–604) are associated with the compilation of the liturgical books, or sacramentaries, that bear their names.

In the disputes in France at the time of Paschasius and Ratramnus, there is no record of papal intervention. The papacy at the time was mainly concerned with continuing and preserving the much-needed reforms with which the name of Gregory the Great is so intimately linked. It is only toward the end of the first millennium of Christian history that necessity and opportunity occasioned the interventions of Peter's successors in the

[5] Cf. Quasten, *Patrology* 2, pp. 188–89, for the text of the Eucharistic Prayer of Hippolytus.

[6] Cf. Jungmann, *The Mass of the Roman Rite,* I, pp. 47–53.

[7] On the dispute over the celebration of Easter (the "Quartodeciman controversy") cf. Quasten, I, pp. 77, 243, 246, and Kelly, *The Oxford Dictionary of Popes,* pp. 10, 11, 12, as well as the standard Patristic histories.

Eucharistic controversies that would occur so frequently during the second millennium.

Silvester II (999–1003)

Gerbert of Auvergne, who as priest, theologian, and Archbishop of Ravenna was—like other men before and since—no great supporter of papal prerogatives, became, as Silvester II, the first French Pope, a forceful leader of Church reform, as well as the man who gave the famous crown to Stephen of Hungary. As Gerbert he wrote a very short treatise on the Eucharist, the *Libellus de Corpore et Sanguine Domini*.[8] Living a century after Paschasius and Ratramnus, it is evident from his work that there were some who denied the truth of Christ's bodily Presence in the Sacrament, interpreting the Mystery in a merely symbolic sense. Against them Gerbert quoted the Fathers, particularly Ambrose and Augustine. He himself, like Paschasius, maintains that the Sacrament is the same Body born of Mary.[9] Like some of the early Fathers, he puts great emphasis on the fact that "not only our souls but also our flesh is recreated through the Sacrament"[10] and that, through the Eucharist, we are intimately joined not only to Christ but also to God the Father.[11]

The Church's Response to Berengarius and Its Aftermath

Leo IX (1049–54) and Nicholas II (1058–61)

Leo and Nicholas were Popes during the beginnings of the Berengarian crisis. Under Leo, the teachings of Berengarius were

[8] Silvester II, *Libellus de Corpore et Sanguine Domini, PL,* 139.

[9] Silvester II, op. cit., *PL,* 139, 179.

[10] Silvester II, op. cit.; *PL,* 139, 188.

[11] Silvester II, op. cit.; *PL,* 139, 184.

condemned at the Synods of Rome and Vercelli. At the Lateran Synod, in 1059, under Nicholas, Berengarius was required to subscribe to the following profession of faith, probably drawn up by Cardinal Humbert.

> I, Berengarius, unworthy deacon of the Church of St. Maurice at Angers, knowing the true, Catholic, and apostolic Faith, condemn all heresy, especially that of which I have hitherto been guilty and that attempts to assert that the bread and wine that are placed on the altar are, after the Consecration, only a Sacrament [*solummodo sacramentum*] and not the true Body and Blood of Our Lord Jesus Christ and that they are not able to be touched or broken by the hands of the priests or chewed by the teeth of the faithful sensibly, but rather only sacramentally [*sensualiter nisi solo in sacramento*]. Moreover, I assent to the holy Roman and apostolic See and, concerning the Sacraments of the Lord's table, I profess with mouth and heart that I hold that Faith that the lord and venerable Pope Nicholas and this holy Synod, resting on the authority of the Gospels and the Apostles, have handed on to be held and have confirmed for me: namely, that the bread and wine that are placed on the altar are, after the Consecration, not only the Sacrament but the true Body and Blood of Our Lord Jesus Christ, and that they are in truth sensibly and not only sacramentally touched by the hands of the priests and are broken and chewed by the teeth of the faithful. I swear this by the holy and consubstantial Trinity and by these holy Gospels. I pronounce that those who will come forward against this Faith with their own doctrines and followers are worthy of eternal damnation. But if I myself should at some point presume to think or preach anything against these things, I submit myself to the severity of canon law. I have read and reread this and sign it willingly.[12]

What Pope Nicholas II had demanded and obtained from Berengarius was clearly a very forceful confession of the true Presence of the Lord in the Sacrament. Indeed, the words are often labeled "ultrarealistic", since they speak of the Lord's Body being *sensibly* touched, broken, and eaten. Understood in their

---

[12] Text in Montclos, pp. 171–72; also DS 690.

context, however, they are no more or less than the Church's way of denying any theory that says that the Lord is present in a merely symbolic fashion. No orthodox Christian had ever believed that his Body was touched, broken, and eaten according to its natural mode or form of being. This would be the position of those Augustine called "Capharnaites" and what the pagans called cannibalism. Such an understanding had always been rejected by the Fathers and the Church. No more than any of the Fathers did Nicholas II or the bishops with him accept so gross an understanding of the Lord's works. But they were unwilling, in the face of Berengarius' errors, to mitigate the "shock" contained in the words of Christ: he was giving us his very Flesh to be eaten. Nonetheless, the graphic nature of the words have required that they be put in their sacramental context by later theologians. When once the word *sacrament* was taken to mean more than the simple sign, St. Thomas was able to make a distinction not made in the confession of 1059. He wrote:

> Whatever is eaten in its proper form is also broken and chewed in its proper form. But the Body of Christ is not eaten in its proper form but rather in the form of the Sacrament. This is what Augustine means when he comments on John 6:64, saying, "This is to be understood of those who think in a carnal fashion. For they understood him to mean that flesh that is torn from a cadaver and sold in a meat market." And therefore the very Body of Christ is not broken except in its sacramental form. And that is the way the confession of Berengarius is to be understood: the breaking and chewing refer to the sacramental species or form under which the Body of Christ is really present.[13]

Guitmund, as seen above, had already given a similar interpretation, one perhaps even clearer than that of St. Thomas inasmuch as it better preserves the "hard saying" of the Lord without letting it appear to be cannibalism. The Lord's Flesh, he wrote, was truly eaten but did not suffer in the eating. Luther, too, found no cause

[13] *S. Th.,* III, q. 77, a. 7, ad 3. For the context of the citation from Augustine, cf. above, p. 67.

for embarrassment in the confession of 1059. Defending the reality of the Lord's Presence against Zwingli and Wyclif, he wrote:

> Therefore the fanatics are wrong, as well as the gloss in canon law, if they criticize Pope Nicholas for having forced Berengar to confess that the true Body of Christ is crushed and ground with the teeth. Would to God that all Popes had acted in so Christian a fashion in all other matters as this Pope did with Berengar in forcing this confession.[14]

Gregory VII (1073–85)

As seen above,[15] Hildebrand was long familiar with Berengarius and his views, although initially he appears to have understood inadequately the subtleties involved in the question.

At the Roman Synod of 1079, held under Gregory, Berengarius made the following profession of faith.

> I, Berengarius, believe in my heart and confess with my mouth that the bread and wine that are placed on the altar are, through the Mystery of the sacred prayer and the words of Our Redeemer, substantially changed [*substantialiter converti*] into the true and proper and life-giving Flesh and Blood of Our Lord Jesus Christ. And I believe that after the Consecration they are the true Body of Christ, which was born of the Virgin and which hung on the Cross as an oblation for the salvation of the world and which sits at the right hand of the Father, and the true Blood of Christ, which flowed from his side. They are such not only through the sign and power of the Sacrament [*per signum et virtutem sacramenti*] but in their proper nature and true substance [lit., *in proprietate naturae et veritate substantiae*].[16]

More technical in formulation than the confession of 1059 — and therefore less open to the unwarranted charge of "ultrarealism"

[14] Luther, *Confession,* pp. 300–301.
[15] Cf. pp. 97, 109–10.
[16] DS 700.

made against the earlier confession—there is, nonetheless, nothing really new in the terminology. Paschasius' "substantially created" (*substantialiter creari*) has become "substantially converted" so as to avoid the idea that the Eucharistic change is a creation in the strict sense (i.e., out of nothing). The expressions referring to a substantial change in this confession of 1059 are found in Guitmund and are the equivalent to Ambrose's speaking of "a change in nature" and to the thought of the Greek Fathers in the use of the words *transform* and *transelement.* Likewise the identification of the Eucharistic Body and the Body born of Mary and now glorified and seated at the right hand of the Father is merely a repetition of a theme that ultimately goes back to Ignatius of Antioch. What is "new" is that the Magisterium of the Church has here begun to use a language more technically suited to express its perennial belief.

This more precise use of terminology led, shortly after this time, to a clarification in the use of the words *Body of Christ.* Although there appear to have been a couple of early references to the Church as the "*Mystical* Body of Christ", the Church herself during the first millennium was normally called simply the Body of Christ. The controversies over the Eucharist and the consequent need to defend the identity between the historical-risen Body and the Eucharistic Body saw a shift in the nomenclature. Although not used by him, this change was already prepared by Paschasius. By the twelfth century, finally, it began to be more common to refer to the Church as the Mystical Body, thus distinguishing the Church from the historical-Eucharistic Body of the Lord.[17] The distinction, however, was not intended to lessen the "reality" of the Church as Body of Christ. Far from it. Rather it was intended to ground the Church's identity in the very mystery of Christ's proper flesh. As Henri de Lubac writes:

> St. Paul, as it happens, formulates in theory what emerges clearly from primitive Christian practice, and he does so by unit-

[17] Cf. de Lubac, *Corpus Mysticum,* esp. Chaps. 4 and 5.

ing in one the Eucharistic Mystery and that of the Christian community: "Is not the bread we break a participation in Christ's Body? The one bread makes us one body, though we are many in number; . . . " All the voices of Tradition vie with one another in commentary on this text, and the first theologians to speak of the Church as the *Mystical* Body of Christ are aiming at giving an exact commentary upon it. And they speak of it in a eucharistic context. By "the Mystical Body" they mean . . . the *corpus in mysterio,* the body mystically signified and realized by the Eucharist — in other words, the unity of the Christian community which is made real by the "holy mysteries" in an effective symbol (in the strict sense of the word "effective").[18]

Hadrian IV (1154-59)

During the reign of Hadrian, a relatively unknown theologian named Hugh Metellus wrote a letter to a certain Gerlandus, who apparently held a symbolic view of the Eucharist based on his understanding of Augustine. Hugh's letter of response (ca. 1157) is a good example of the standard orthodox Eucharistic theologian during the twelfth century. Against Gerlandus, Hugh defends Augustine: "You rely on the words of Augustine. You should not so rely because he is not of your opinion in this matter. . . . You say what Augustine says, but you do not understand what he means."[19] Hugh then proceeds to defend the reality of Christ's Presence in the Eucharist using texts from St. Paul and Augustine

---

[18] De Lubac, *The Splendor of the Church,* pp. 133. It is this intimate connection between the Eucharistic and ecclesial body which, says de Lubac, helps us understand those apparently ambiguous statements in Augustine. Thus, de Lubac writes: "Ainsi se renouvelle l'ambiguïté de certaines formules augustiniennes. . . . Ambiguïté voulue et significative, d'une grande portée doctrinale. C'est l'idée de la continuité réelle qui existe entre la Tête et les membres de l'unique Corps: 'Ecclesiae ut corpori suo corpus suum incorporat' (Alger of Liège) etc." (*Corpus Mysticum,* pp. 96-97).

[19] Hugh Metellus, *Epistola IV; PL,* 188, 1273.

and citing the teaching of the Roman Church. The word *transubstantiation*, which was about to appear in literature contemporaneous with Hugh, does not appear. Hugh has, however, some very clear words on the identity between the Victim on Calvary and the Victim of the Mass, the Priest of Calvary and the Priest of the Mass.

> On the altar he who sanctifies and he who is sanctified are the Same. The same One is Priest and Oblation, the same who immolates and who is immolated, the same who is God and Man.[20]

Alexander III (1159–81)

Alexander is remembered as the man who defended St. Thomas à Becket and then imposed the penalties of the Church upon the Archbishop of Canterbury's murderer, Henry II. He is also the Pope of the Third Lateran Council (1179), which began the Church's campaign against the Albigensian movement. Before he became Pope, moreover, it was he, as Rolando Bandinelli, who was among the first to use the word *transubstantiation* in a theological treatise, the *De Sententiis Rolandi,* published around 1140. The word appears as well in works of the same period whose authorship is questioned, among them a sermon of Hildebert of Lavardin, archbishop of Tours (1057–1134)[21] and a treatise of Stephen, Bishop of Autun (died ca. 1139) which states:

> We pray that the bread of men may become the bread of angels, that is, that the offering of bread and wine may be transubstantiated

---

[20] Hugh Metellus, *Epistola IV; PL,* 188, 1275.

[21] Hildebert, *Sermon 93; PL* 171, 776. The sermon may actually belong to Peter Comestor (died ca. 1180). Cf. L. Hödl, "Der Transsubstantiationsbegriff in der scholastischen Theologie des 12. Jahrhunderts", *Recherches de Théologie Ancienne et Médiévale,* 21 (1964), pp. 230–59, esp., p. 235. Also, A. Wilmart, "Les Sermons d'Hildebert", *Revue Bénédictine,* 47 (1935), pp. 12–51. Cf. also J. de Ghellinck, DTC, vol. V, col. 1234–1302, especially 1288 and 1290.

into the Body and Blood of Jesus Christ who is himself the blessed offering. . . . [22]

O outstanding miracle! O marvelous and most divine Sacrament! . . . What the priest takes up is not what he replaces on the altar. That which is taken up and placed down seem to be the same in appearance [Lat. *species*], color, and taste. Completely different, however, is that which appears from that which lies hidden within. Common bread is lifted up from the altar; the immortal Flesh of Christ is set down upon it. What was natural food has become spiritual food. What was the momentary refreshment of man has been made the eternal and unfailing nourishment of the angels.[23]

Innocent III (1198–1216) and the *Firmiter* of Lateran Council IV

Before he became Pope, Lothar of Segni had written a book on the Eucharist, *De Sacro Altaris Mysterio*,[24] a full theological treatise dealing with the Mass, its prayers, the sacrifice, and the Presence of the Body and Blood born of Mary and now reigning in heaven through transubstantiation.[25] Lothar made the distinction between the Body that is received sacramentally (viz., the Body born of Mary) and that which is received spiritually (viz., union with the Church, the ecclesial Body of Christ). He notes that the good and the evil receive the same Body of Christ in the Sacrament, but one does it worthily, the other to judgment. The future Pope was a

---

[22] Stephen, *Tractatus de Sacramento Altaris*, PL 172, 1291. It is possible that his work is to be attributed to a second bishop Stephen of Autun (c. 1170–89). Cf. D. van den Eynde, O.F.M., "Le tractatus 'De sacramento altaris' faussement attribué à Etienne de Beauge", *Recherches de Théologie Ancienne et Médiévale* 19 (1952), pp. 225–53.

[23] Stephen, *Tractatus de Sacramento Altaris*, PL 172, 1293.

[24] Innocent III, *De Sacro Altaris Mysterio; PL*, 217. It may be noted, parenthetically, that it is in this work that we appear to find our first references to the colors (white, red, green, and black) of the liturgical vestments used at Mass (*PL*, 217, 799–802).

[25] Innocent III, *De Sacro Altaris Mysterio; PL*, 217, 860–61. The use of the word had become common by the time Lothar of Segni wrote his work.

solid theologian in matters of the Eucharist, although there are some minor matters upon which he refuses to pass judgment (e.g., whether and how Christ is *locally* present in the Sacrament) and others where his teaching will not be in agreement with subsequent teaching (e.g., he thought that in the case of a desecration of the Sacrament or its being eaten by an animal, the substance of the Body and Blood of Christ miraculously departs, leaving present only the accidents of bread and wine, since the former substance of the bread and wine does not return).[26]

As Pope, Innocent III used the word *transubstantiation* in a letter of November 29, 1202, to the Archbishop of Paris.

> You have asked what was the form of the words used by Christ himself when he transubstantiated bread and wine into his Body and Blood, since in the Canon of the Mass . . . the words *Mysterium Fidei* are found interspersed with those of the Lord. . . . *"Mysterium Fidei"* is said because something other is believed than is seen, something different is seen than believed. For the appearance [Lat. *species*] of bread and wine is seen and the truth of the Flesh and Blood of Christ is believed, along with the grace [Lat. *virtus*] of unity and charity.
>
> . . .
>
> You have also asked whether the water mixed with the wine is changed into the Blood. About this the opinions of the scholars vary. . . . Some indeed hold that the water mixed with the wine is transubstantiated into the Blood. . . . Among the opinions that is judged more probable that asserts that the water, together with the wine, is changed [Lat. *transmutari*] into the Blood.[27]

[26] Innocent III, *De Sacro Altaris Mysterio; PL* 217, 863. It is interesting to note that Aquinas did not hesitate to disagree with Lothar. Apparently attributing papal authority to the *De Sacro Altaris Mysterio,* St. Thomas rejected the opinion put forth by Lothar that would allow for the fact that Christ at the Last Supper consecrated the Sacrament without using any words and that he only later gave the form of the words. Thomas says such an opinion is to be rejected as contrary to Scripture and that the "words of Innocent were expressing an opinion, not determinative teaching" (*S. Th.,* III, q. 78, a. 1, ad 1).

[27] Innocent III, *Epistola "Cum Marthae"; DS* 782–84.

With the reforms in the liturgy inaugurated by the Second Vatican Council, of course, the reason for Archbishop John's first question has disappeared. The words *Mysterium Fidei* have been removed from their former place in the midst of the words of Consecration of the wine and become the formula ("Let us proclaim the Mystery of Faith") for the acclamation of the people, which follows the Consecration.

The letter of Innocent to Archbishop John makes quite clear that the neologism *transubstantiation* is simply that: a new word to express the traditional Faith. It means no more and no less than what is expressed by its equivalent *transmutari*. The word is subsequently taken up into the Creed *Firmiter* of the great Medieval Council Lateran IV (1215). The section of the Creed pertinent to the Eucharist reads:

> There is one universal Church of the faithful, outside of which no one at all is saved. In this Church Jesus Christ is both priest and sacrifice. In the Sacrament of the Altar, under the species of bread and wine, his Body and Blood are truly contained, the bread having been transubstantiated into his Body and the wine into his Blood by the divine power. In order to complete the Mystery of unity, we receive from him what he received from us. And no one is able to confect this Sacrament except the priest who is properly ordained according to the keys of the Church, which Jesus Christ himself gave to the Apostles and their successors (DS 802).

As seen above, the teaching that only a validly ordained priest has the power to confect the Eucharist—as well as the fact that a real change took place in the elements—was a response to the position of the Waldensians and the Cathari.[28]

---

[28] Cf. above, p. 113. The teaching had already been set forth by Innocent III in the *Profession of Faith Prescribed for the Waldensians* in 1208 and repeated in 1210. The Waldensians returning to full union with the Church were to confess: "We firmly believe and confess that no one, no matter how upright, religious, holy, and prudent he may be, can or should consecrate the Eucharist or confect the Sacrifice of the Altar. This can and should be done only by a

The Middle Ages

The controversies over the Eucharist in the ninth and eleventh centuries had culminated, thanks in part to the heretical positions of the Cathari in the twelfth and thirteenth centuries, in a fixed doctrinal position at Lateran IV. Hand in hand, however, with this clarification of the doctrinal issues there had developed particular aspects of Eucharistic devotion that were to continue through the fourteenth and fifteenth centuries and that, even today, have a profound impact on Catholic devotion and piety. The elevation of the Host and the Precious Blood after the Consecration was introduced into the ritual of the Mass during the thirteenth century so that the faithful might look at and adore the Lord present in the Sacrament. Periods of Eucharistic adoration in which the Sacrament was set forth on the altar became common, only to become yet more common once the Sacrament was able to be set visibly before the eyes of faith through the use of the monstrance. The Grail (the cup of the Last Supper that had held the Precious

---

priest who has been properly ordained by a visible and tangible bishop" (DS 794).

The view that someone other than a properly ordained priest or bishop may be able to consecrate the Eucharist—at least in extraordinary situations—has reappeared in our day in the writings of Hans Küng (*The Church*, p. 443), E. Schillebeeckx (*Ministry*, pp. 80–85, 138–42), Leonardo Boff (*Ecclesiogenesis*, pp. 61–75), and others. To such assertions the Congregation for the Doctrine of the Faith, in the document of Aug. 6, 1983, entitled *Sacerdotium Ministeriale*, has replied by repeating the pertinent section of the *Firmiter*. It reads in part: "Although they may be expressed in various ways with different nuances, all these opinions lead to the same conclusion: that the power to confect the Sacrament of the Eucharist is not necessarily connected with sacramental ordination. It is evident that such a conclusion is absolutely incompatible with the Faith as it has been handed down ... since it is of the very nature of the Church that the power to consecrate the Eucharist is imparted only to the bishops and priests who are constituted its ministers by the reception of Holy Orders, the Church holds that the Eucharistic Mystery cannot be celebrated in any community except by an ordained priest, as expressly taught by the Fourth Lateran Council" (*TPS*, 28, no. 4, pp. 352, 354; *AAS*, 75, pp. 1004 and 1006).

Blood) became a theme of legend and literature, along with the stories of various quests to discover it. Accompanying these developments, however, there occurred others less positive and sometimes ultimately harmful. The Eucharist was received less frequently. As we know from Patristic writings, there had never been a time when all the faithful present at Mass communicated. The very penitential practice of the Early Church testifies to that fact. However, during the Middle Ages, the danger of unworthy or sacrilegious receptions of the Sacrament—so frequently warned against in the writings of the Fathers—diminished simply because more and more of the faithful received the Eucharist so infrequently. Whether this happened due to an exaggerated sense of devotion or simply to inertia and sin is not clear. Likely it was a combination of these and other factors. At any rate, so much a cause for concern did this infrequency of Eucharistic reception become that Lateran IV was obliged to enact the famous decree *Unius utriusque sexus* on the necessity of annual Confession and Communion.

> Each one of the faithful, of both sexes, having arrived at the age of discretion, shall faithfully confess all his sins at least once a year to his proper priest, shall strive with all his might to complete the penance imposed on him, and reverently receive the Sacrament of the Eucharist at least during Paschal time. He shall do this unless, at the advice of his proper priest, he is led to abstain for a time set by him, and because of some reasonable cause. If this law is not observed, such a person while living is to be barred entrance to the church and to be denied Christian burial when dead (DS 812).

Another unhappy development was the gradual multiplication of the number of Masses in order to satisfy the demands of the faithful.

> There arose during the last centuries of the Middle Ages an unnatural multiplication of Masses and, along with it, an unnatural increase in clergy of whom a part, at least, derived their entire

income from Masses either through endowments (foundations or chantries) or by way of Mass stipends.[29]

Jungmann traces the origin of such a development to an "unenlightened and isolated popularizing of another phase in the teaching of the Mass, the phase of the effects of the Mass".[30]

These last-mentioned developments were to have serious consequences, chief among them the greed of a clergy educated only to offer Mass. In this—along with stipend abuses and the inaccurate preaching of the doctrine on indulgences—fuel was prepared for what became the fire of the Reformation.

Nevertheless, one must be careful not to view all the developments through the prism of the ultimate abuses or the Reformation. Even fine scholars have at times presented the developments—and not only the abuses—in Eucharistic practice and devotion of the Middle Ages as a "falling away" from the pristine Faith of the early Church.[31] Such a tendency, however, misses the riches that came to the Church from the development of Eucharistic devotion during the Middle Ages. This development came, in turn, from true theological development and a more profound appreciation of the Mystery of the Eucharist. The literature of those ages reflects such insight and devotion. We have, for example, the anonymous early thirteenth-century work *The Quest of the Holy Grail,* which, at its ending, describes Galahad's discovery of the Grail and the Communion that follows the discovery.

Next Josephus acted as though he were entering on the Consecration of the Mass. After pausing a moment quietly, he took from

---

[29] Jungmann, *The Mass of the Roman Rite,* I, p. 130.

[30] Jungmann, *The Mass of the Roman Rite,* I, p. 129.

[31] Theodor Klauser, for example, in his *A Short History of the Western Liturgy,* entitles his study of the period from 1073 to Trent as the period of "Dissolution, Elaboration, Reinterpretation and Misinterpretation" (pp. 94–116). Even Jungmann, in my estimation, does not completely escape this tendency, at least in the *tone* of his remarks. Cf., for example, his treatment of these developments in *The Mass of the Roman Rite,* I, pp. 119–22, 130–32.

the Vessel a Host made in the likeness of bread. As he raised it aloft, there descended from above a figure like to a child, whose countenance glowed and blazed as being on fire; and he entered into the bread, which quite distinctly took on human form before the eyes of those assembled there. When Josephus had stood for some while holding his burden up to view, he replaced it in the Holy Vessel.

. . .

Then he took the Holy Vessel in his hands, and going to Galahad, who knelt at his approach, he gave his Savior to him. And Galahad, with both hands joined in homage, received with an overflowing heart. So too did the others, and to every one it seemed that the Host placed on his tongue was made of bread. When they had all received the holy food, which they found so honeyed and delectable that it seemed as though the essence of all sweetness was housed within their bodies . . . [32]

The description of the figure *"like* a child" entering the bread is—as is evident in subsequent parts of the work—a symbolic account of what takes place at the Consecration, not a vision of the child Christ in the Host. Note, too, the orthodoxy of the doctrine. It only *"seemed* the Host was made of bread". It is the holy food of all delights, "honeyed and delectable" so that one could indeed "taste and see how good the Lord is". The entire description breathes with Galahad's—as well as the author's—respect for the Eucharist. That same respect and awe are found in a novel about that period written in our own time—a novel hailed and awarded the Nobel Prize not only for its literary qualities but also for its accurate historical evocation of fourteenth-century Norway.

---

[32] *The Quest of the Holy Grail,* P. M. Matarasso, trans., Harmondsworth, England: Penguin Books, 1981, pp. 275–76. Tennyson captures the quoted section of *The Quest* faithfully in his *Idylls of the King: The Holy Grail:*

"And at the sacring of the mass I saw
The holy elements alone; bid he,
'Saw ye no more? I, Galahad, saw the Grail,
The Holy Grail, descend upon the shrine.
I saw the fiery face as of a child
That smote itself into the bread and went' " (p. 596).

Lavrans went by the well-trodden path over the fields to Rommundgaard. The moon was dipping behind the hills now—but thousands of stars glittered above the white mountains.... He hoped that the priest might be at home....

But when he was come in between the fences near the farm, he saw a little taper coming towards him. Old Audun was bearing it—when he marked that there was someone on his path, he rang his little silver bell. Lavrans Bjorgulfson threw himself on his knees in the snow-drift by the path.

Augun went by bearing the taper, and the bell that still tinkled gently. Behind him came Sira Eirik a-horseback. He lifted the pyx high in his hands when he came by the kneeling man—looked not to right or left but rode calmly past, while Lavrans bowed himself down and stretched his two hands up in greeting towards his Saviour.

... Lavrans said the prayers for the dying before he rose from the snow and went homewards. Even so, this meeting with God in the night had strengthened and comforted him much. [33]

The beginning of the following century, the fifteenth, saw the production of that classic *The Imitation of Christ,* the fourth book of which is filled with profound and tender Eucharistic devotion.

How great and honorable is the office of priests, who have been empowered to consecrate with sacred words the Lord of all majesty, to bless him with their lips, to hold him in their hand, to receive him with their mouth, and to administer him to others.

How clean should be the hands, how pure the mouth, how holy the body, and how undefiled the heart of the priest, into whom the Author of all purity so often enters.

What other people is so fortunate as the Christian people? What creature under heaven is so beloved as a devout soul into whom God comes, in order to feed him with his own glorious Body and Blood? O grace unspeakable, O marvelous condescension, O love without measure, bestowed only on man.

[33] Sigrid Undset, *Kristin Lavransdatter,* vol. 2, New York: Bantam Books, 1978, pp. 82–83.

It is not enough to prepare yourself by devotion before Communion; also you should keep yourself in a devout frame of mind after receiving this Sacrament. It is just as necessary to be watchful after as is the devout preparation beforehand; for careful guarding of devotion afterward is the best preparation for obtaining new grace.[34]

Finally, it must be noted that it was during this period that, among other masterpieces, the *Ave verum,* so rich in doctrine and art, was composed. Often attributed to Pope Innocent VI (1352–62) but probably predating him by some fifty years, the *Ave verum* is a hymn to the Eucharist that makes a confession of faith in terms that go back to Ignatius of Antioch, Ambrose, Augustine, Paschasius, and their followers. The Eucharist is the Body born of Mary.

Ave verum corpus, natum de Maria Virgine; vere passum, immolatum in cruce pro homine. Cuius latus perforatum unda fluxit et sanguine. Esto nobis praegustatum mortis in examine. O clemens, O pie, O dulcis Jesu, fili Mariae.

Hail true Body, born of Mary Virgin; which truly suffered and was immolated on the Cross for mankind. Whose side, pierced, poured forth water and Blood. Be for us a foretaste [of glory] at the moment of death. O clement, O holy, O sweet Jesus, Son of Mary.

With its doctrine so firmly grounded in the Faith of the early Church, the hymn has always been a great favorite of those who acknowledge the truth of Christ's bodily Presence in the Sacrament. Luther so admired it that he not only used it but added to it verses of his own.[35] Set to music many times and by many masters, its most beautiful setting is perhaps that done, just before his death, by Mozart in a piece (K. 618) that many consider among his most perfect.

[34] Thomas à Kempis, *The Imitation of Christ,* pp. 267–68, 272, 270.
[35] Pelikan, 4, p. 177.

Other examples could be given of the depth and abundance of proper Eucharistic doctrine in those ages, but one more may suffice, for it is in itself both a culminating point and a new starting point. It was the work of a Pope responding to the desires of the Christian people.

Urban IV (1261–64) and the *Transiturus*

Urban IV is responsible for decreeing the celebration of the Feast of Corpus Christi throughout the entire Church and for commissioning St. Thomas Aquinas to write the liturgical office for the same feast. The extension of the feast, which had originated in Belgium in the diocese of Liège in the 1240s, was accomplished by the publication of Urban's bull *Transiturus,* arguably the most beautiful document on the Eucharist ever composed by a successor of Peter. Although Stone translated large segments of the document,[36] apparently no full translation has ever been made into English. It reads as follows:

Transiturus — 1264

Bishop Urban, servant of the servants of God, to the venerable brothers, patriarchs, archbishops, bishops, and other prelates of the Church, health and the apostolic blessing.

About to pass from this world to the Father, Our Savior the Lord Jesus Christ, since the time of his Passion was at hand, having partaken of a meal in memory of his death, instituted the great and wonderful Sacrament of his Body and Blood, bestowing his Body as food and his Blood as drink. For, as often as we eat this bread and drink this cup, we announce the death of the Lord. Indeed, at the institution of this Sacrament, he himself said to the Apostles: "Do this in memory of me": so that for us the special and outstanding memorial of the extraordinary love with which he loved us

[36] Stone, I, pp. 344–46.

would be this lofty and venerable Sacrament; a memorial, I say, marvelous and stupendous, delectable, pleasant, most salutary, and priceless above all things—a memorial in which signs have been innovated and marvels altered; a memorial in which there is all delight [*in quo habetur omne delectamentum*] and sweetness to the taste, and in which the very sweetness of the Lord is tasted; a memorial indeed in which we attain support for our life and our salvation. This is the memorial most sweet and salvific in which we gratefully recall the memory of our redemption, in which we are drawn from evil, strengthened in good, and secure an increase in virtues and graces, the memorial in which we attain the corporeal Presence of the Savior himself.

Other things whose memory we keep we embrace spiritually and mentally: we do not thereby obtain their real presence. However, in this sacramental commemoration of Christ, Jesus Christ is present with us in his proper substance, although under another form. As he was about to ascend into heaven, he said to the Apostles and their helpers, "I will be with you all days even unto the consummation of the world." He comforted them with the gracious promise that he would remain and would be with them even by his corporeal presence. O worthy and uninterrupted memory, in which we recall that our death is dead, that our destruction has perished, and that the fruit affixed to the tree of the Cross has made it a life-giving tree for us. This is the glorious commemoration that fills the souls of the faithful with saving joy and supplies tears of devotion with an infusion of gladness. We exult remembering our wondrous liberation, and, remembering the Lord's Passion by which we have been liberated, we can scarcely contain our tears. Therefore in this most holy commemoration there is present to us simultaneously the joy of sweetness and tears, because in it we rejoice while crying and we cry while rejoicing devoutly. Ours are joyful tears and tear-filled joy, for the heart, filled with a powerful joy, spills forth sweet tears. O the immensity of divine love, the excess of divine piety, the abundance of divine generosity! For the Lord has given us all the things that lie beneath our feet and has given us dominion over all creatures on the earth. He has ennobled and raised up the dignity of man above the ministries of the angelic spirits. For they are administrators destined to minister unto those who have inherited salvation. And since his munificence toward us was so great, still willing to demonstrate with particular liberality his exuberant love for us, he revealed himself to us. Then, transcending even the fullness of generosity, he gave himself as our food. O singular and admirable liberality, when the Giver comes as the gift and is himself completely given with the gift! What great—even prodigal—generosity when anyone gives himself. Therefore he gave himself as nourishment, so that, since man had fallen through death, he might be lifted to life through food. Man fell by means of the food of the death-giving tree; man is raised up by means of the food of the life-giving tree. On the former hung the food of death, on the latter the nourishment of life. Eating of the former earned a wound; the taste of this later restored health. Eating wounded us, and eating healed us. See how the cure has come forth whence the wound arose, and life has come forth whence death entered in. Indeed about that eating it was said: "On whatever day you eat it, you shall die"; about this eating, he has spoken: "If anyone eats this bread, he shall live forever." This is the food that fully restores, truly nourishes, completely satisfies—not the body but the heart, not the flesh but the [soul], not the stomach but the mind. Therefore to man who needed spiritual nourishment the merciful Savior himself provided, by a holy ordinance, a food to feed the soul, a food that is more powerful and more noble than any food of this world. There is manifested a liberality worthy of him and a work of kindness suitable to him, and the eternal Word of God, which is spiritual food and refreshment to his creatures, became Flesh and gave himself as food [*in edulium*] to a spiritual creature of flesh and body, namely, mankind. Mankind has eaten the bread of angels. Thus the Savior says, "My Flesh is real food." This bread is taken but truly not consumed, is eaten but not digested, because by no means is it transformed into the eater. Rather, if it is worthily received, the recipient is conformed to it. O most excellent Sacrament! O Sacrament to be adored, venerated, worshiped, glorified, magnified with special praise, extolled with worthy hymns, honored by all kinds of study, accompanied by devout offerings, and guarded by sincere souls. O most noble memorial, to be entrusted to the innermost heart, firmly embraced by the soul, diligently reserved in the womb of the heart and in meditation, and sedulously examined by multitudes! We should celebrate continuously the memory of this memorial so that we may always be mindful of him whose memorial we know it to be, because the more frequently his gift and favor are looked upon, so much the more firmly are they kept in memory. Therefore, although this memorial Sacrament is frequented in the daily solemnities of the Mass, we nevertheless think it suitable and worthy that, at least once a year—especially to confound the lack of faith and the infamy of heretics—a more solemn and honorable memory of this Sacrament be held. This is so because on Holy Thursday, the day on which the Lord himself instituted this Sacrament, the universal Church, occupied with the reconciliation of penitents, blessing the chrism, fulfilling the Commandment about the washing of the feet and many other such things, is not sufficiently free to celebrate so great a Sacrament.

The Church herself does this same thing in respect to the saints, whom we venerate yearly. Although we frequently renew their memory in litanies and Masses and other ways, nevertheless she more solemnly recalls their birthdays on certain days throughout the year, celebrating special feasts on those days. And because something of the due solemnity may be omitted on these feasts—because of negligence, or some family concern, or out of human weakness—holy Mother Church has determined that on a certain day a commemoration of all the saints in general be made so that in this common celebration there might be supplied whatever is omitted on their proper festivals. Therefore, most especially must this be done in respect to the vivifying Sacrament of the Body and Blood of Jesus Christ, who is the crown and glory of all the saints. This feast must shine with a special festivity and honor so that whatever of solemnity is perhaps omitted in other Masses might be supplied in this feast with diligent devotion. The faithful, during this feast, mindful of not having fully performed the solemnities of the Mass because they were involved in necessary worldly pursuits or perhaps from negligence or human frailty, will then attentively restore what was lacking and do so in humility of spirit and purity of heart. Moreover we know that, while we were constituted in a lesser office, it was divinely revealed to certain Catholics that a feast of this kind should be celebrated generally throughout the Church. Therefore, to strengthen and exalt the Catholic Faith, we decree that, besides the daily memory that the Church makes of this Sacrament, there be celebrated a more solemn and special annual memorial, and we designate the Thursday after the octave of Pentecost, so that, on that Thursday, devout throngs of the faithful might gather lovingly for this purpose at the churches in order that both clergy and people might rise up and rejoice in songs of praise. Then let the hearts and votive offerings of all mouths and lips break forth in hymns of saving joy; then let faith sing, hope dance, charity exult, devotion applaud, the choir be jubilant, and purity delight. Then let each one with willing spirit and prompt will come together, laudably fulfilling his duties, celebrating the solemnity of so great a feast. And may it happen that ardor so inflame his faithful to the service of Christ that, through this and other merits accumulated with him, he, who gave himself as ransom for them, and gave himself as food to them, may, at the end of their lives, give them himself as their reward.

[There follows a short injunction to the bishops to see that the decree for the feast is carried out, and a listing of indulgences to be obtained by those who participate at the various aspects of the feast's celebration.] [37]

In addition to its lyrical exuberance, the document is filled with fine theology, more Patristic than Scholastic in its approach. It also contains what may be the first use of the term *Real Presence* in respect to the Eucharist, a term that became common thereafter.[38]

St. Thomas Aquinas

In faithfulness to Urban's commission, Aquinas composed the *Lauda Sion, Pange Lingua, Sacris sollemniis,* and *Verbum supernum,* those hymns that still comprise the Sequence of the Mass, and the hymns at Morning, Evening Prayer, and the Office of Readings respectively for the Feast. Each of them is a masterful theological

[37] Urban IV, *Transiturus,* Mansi, 28, pp. 484–89.
[38] Cf. above, p. 138.

compendium of Eucharistic doctrine, and parts of them (as, for example, the last verses of the *Sacris sollemniis,* which are generally known as the *Panis angelicus*) are still pieces familiar to and loved even by those not versed in Latin.

St. Thomas' theology of the Eucharist appears so frequently in this work that it would be superfluous to review it here. Something, however, must be said about his treatment of the Eucharist as sacrifice.

Aquinas clearly held that the Eucharist was a sacrifice and refers to it as such many times. Nonetheless, he devoted not one question and only one article (*S. Th.,* III, q. 83, a. 1) to that aspect of the Eucharist in his entire treatment of the Sacrament in his *Summa Theologiae.* For this omission, theologians in later centuries were to criticize him frequently, many of them stating that he was so preoccupied with the Medieval approach to the Eucharistic Presence that he neglected to appreciate it as sacrifice of Christ and of the Church. The criticism fails to understand his profound approach to the Sacrament. For St. Thomas the sacrificial aspect of the Eucharist is sacramental and largely depends upon the Presence. The sacrifice of Christ is present symbolically, its efficacy made present in and through the true Presence of the Priest and Victim who had undergone the sacrifice once and for all. He wrote:

It must be said that the celebration of this Sacrament is said to be the sacrifice [Lat. *immolatio*] of Christ in two ways. First, as St. Augustine says in his letter to Simplicianus: "It is customary for the symbols of things to be called by the name of the things for which they are symbols, as when looking at a picture on a table or a wall we say, 'It is Cicero', or, 'It is Sallust'." The celebration of this Sacrament, as we have already said (cf. III, q. 76, a. 2, ad 1, and q. 79, a. 1) is a kind of representative symbol [Lat. *imago repraesentativa*] of the Passion of Christ, which is a true sacrifice. . . .

In a second way Christ is said to be sacrificed in this celebration in respect to the effect of his Passion. Through this Sacrament we are made sharers of the fruits of the Lord's Passion. Therefore in one of the Sunday orations over the offerings it is said: "As often as the commemoration of this Victim is celebrated, the work of our redemption is effected."[39]

Therefore, as far as the first way is concerned, Christ can be said to be sacrificed even in the types of the Old Testament, just as it says in the Book of Revelation, "Their names are not written in the book of life of the Lamb who has been slain from the beginning of the world" (Rev 13:8). As far as the second way is concerned [viz., receiving the effects of his Passion], it is proper to this Sacrament that in its celebration Christ is sacrificed.[40]

When St. Thomas, following Augustine, calls the Mass a sacrifice in the sense that it is a representative symbol of Christ's Passion, it must not be thought that he is saying it is a mere commemoration or even a mere symbolic sacrifice. Although the "Sacrament is the sign of Christ's Passion, and not the Passion itself",[41] the Sacrament truly contains the "Christ *who has suffered*".

This Sacrament is said to be a sacrifice inasmuch as it represents the very Passion of Christ. Moreover, it is a Victim [Lat. *hostia*] inasmuch as it contains Christ himself who is, as Ephesians 5:2 tells us, a "fragrant sacrifice".[42]

[It is appropriate that the Body and Blood of Christ be truly present in this Sacrament] because of the perfection of the New Covenant. The sacrifices of the Old Covenant contained the true sacrifice of Christ's Passion only in symbol.
... Therefore it was necessary that the sacrifice of the New Covenant, instituted by Christ, have something more, namely, that it contain Christ himself who has suffered and contain him not only in symbol but in reality.[43]

[39] The oration cited by Aquinas was the Secret Prayer for the Ninth Sunday after Pentecost; it is now found, for example, as the Prayer over the Gifts for Votive Mass B of the Holy Eucharist.

[40] *S. Th.,* III, q. 83, a. 1.

[41] Aquinas, *In Quatuor Libros Sententiarum,* bk. IV, dist. XII, q. I, a. 3, quaest. III.

[42] *S. Th.,* III, q. 73, a. 4, ad 3.

[43] *S. Th.,* III, q. 75, a. 1.

By emphasizing that the Sacrament contains the "Christ *who has suffered*" (and not simply the Christ now glorified in heaven), Thomas highlights an important truth. Suffering changes a person. The risen Christ, truly glorified, is nonetheless always the Victim, the One who has gone through and endured and been permanently marked by his Passion. It is as such that he is present to us in the Eucharist, extending to us the effects or fruits of his victimhood. In this way the Common Doctor is repeating in his own way the vision of St. John in the Apocalypse: "Then I saw a Lamb, looking as if it had been slain, standing in the center of the throne" (Rev 5:6). The sacrificial state of Christ perdures even in his glorification. And that Victim, who is also Priest, is the same Priest and Victim in the sacramental sacrifice of the altar, even though he exercises his priesthood through his minister, who consecrates in Christ's person and through Christ's words.[44]

Thus, for Thomas, this Sacrament is a real sacrifice, because of the Victim-Priest who is truly present and acting and because it applies the value and fruits of the Passion. The Sacrament is also a sacrifice, because the once-and-for-all sacrifice is symbolically represented. This symbolic representation occurs, says Thomas, through the twofold Consecration (*S.Th.*, III, q. 76, a. 2, ad 1) in which this Sacrament is completed (*S.Th.*, III, q. 78, a. 1), as well as through other symbolic gestures, especially the breaking of the Host (*S.Th.*, III, q. 77, a. 7).

Concerning the effects of the Eucharist, Thomas is careful to draw a distinction between the effects of the Eucharist as Sacrament and as sacrifice.

> This Sacrament is simultaneously a sacrifice and a sacrament. It has the nature of sacrifice inasmuch as it is offered, the nature of a sacrament inasmuch as it is received. Therefore its sacramental effects are had by the one who receives; its sacrificial effects are had by the one who offers it or by those for whom it is offered.[45]

---

[44] Cf. *S.Th.*, III, q. 83, a. 1, ad 3, and 82, arts. 1 and 3.
[45] *S.Th.*, III, q. 79, a. 5.

The last lines of the above quotation are significant. Thomas is recognizing the fact that the effects of the Mass are shared in different degrees.[46] He mentions here the two principal degrees of sharing the effects or fruits of the Mass, viz., by the priest who offers and by the one or ones for whom the sacrifice is offered. Of course, the entire Church shares in various ways in the effects of the Mass—as do even those outside the Church who are in good faith and are united to Christ by grace and charity. Nonetheless, the Church has always recognized an *intrinsically* gradated level of sharing in the effects of the Eucharist. That truth is implied by the early custom of offering Masses for specific deceased persons as well as for the dead in general and by the insertions of specific names into the mementoes for the living and dead in the Roman Canon. It is the basis as well for the accepting of a monetary offering (stipend) by the priest with the consequent obligation of offering the Mass for the person giving the stipend or for that person's intention. Indeed, the stipend is only a specification of the prayers in the Memento for the Living where the priest prays: "For them we offer you or they themselves offer you this sacrifice of praise—for them and all their own" (or, as our present English translation beautifully reads: "For ourselves and those who are dear to us").[47]

This notion of a gradated level of sharing in the effects of the Mass has always been a difficulty for some—a difficulty increased at times because of the abuses, caused by greed, involving the stipend. The entire concept was attacked by the reformers and later by the Synod of Pistoia in 1786. This latter gathering of clerics taught that it was a false opinion "that those who assist the priest by an offering on the condition that he celebrate a Mass,

[46] St. Thomas' teaching on this matter is also found in his writings on the *Sentences* of Peter Lombard (*In Quatuor Libros Sent.,* IV, dist. XLV, q. II, a. IV, 3rd solution), where he teaches the gradated notion of suffrages, including those of the Mass.

[47] The *Sacramentary,* Eucharistic Prayer I. On the significance of remembrance of specific persons, as well as the stipend, cf. Jungmann, *The Mass of the Roman Rite,* 2, pp. 159–70, esp. pp. 165–66.

receive a special fruit from that Mass". Pope Pius VI condemned that assertion, declaring it "false, temerarious, pernicious, and injurious to the Church" (DS 2630).

As Aquinas notes, however, in the article cited above, the effects of both the Sacrament and the sacrifice can be impeded, as far as the individual is concerned, by a lack of devotion and fervor.

> Therefore, although the oblation of the Eucharist is sufficient of its own quantity for the satisfaction of all punishment due to sin, nevertheless it is satisfactory for those who offer it or for whom it is offered according to the amount of their devotion.[48]

Nonetheless, even though the effects may be individually impeded by a lack of devotion and fervor or "by a mind distracted by venial sin" (S. Th., III, q. 79, a. 8), the intrinsic value of the Sacrament and sacrifice is not impeded.

> Indeed, the offering of the sacrifice is multiplied in the many Masses, and, as a result, the effects of the sacrifice and the Sacrament are multiplied.[49]

Indeed, for Aquinas, the intrinsic effects of the Mass are unlimited.

> The effects of this Sacrament should be considered first of all and principally according to what the Sacrament contains, namely, Christ. . . . Secondly, one must consider what is represented through this Sacrament, namely, the Passion of Christ. Therefore, the effects that the Passion of Christ achieved for the world in general this Sacrament does for the individual.[50]

All in all, when seen in context, St. Thomas' theology of the sacrificial aspects of the Mass are both simple and profound. His antiphon for the *Magnificat,* also set to music many times, is a beautiful and concise summary of much Eucharistic doctrine.

---

[48] S. Th., III, q. 79, a. 5.
[49] S. Th., III, q. 79, a. 7, ad 3.
[50] S. Th., III, q. 79, a. 1.

O sacrum convivium, in quo Christus sumitur: recolitur memoria passionis eius, mens impletur gratia et futurae gloriae nobis pignus datur.	O sacred Banquet in which Christ is received: the memory of his Passion is recalled, the soul is filled with grace, and a pledge of future glory is given.

Clement IV (1265–68)

In a letter to the Archbishop of Narbonne, France (where he himself had previously been Archbishop), Clement IV responded to what were apparently some of the consequences of the Eucharistic opinions of John of Paris. The Pope wrote:

> We hear that you have said that the most holy Body of Our Lord Jesus Christ is not essentially present on the altar but is there as that which is signified under the sign. You have added that this is the celebrated opinion of [John of] Paris. . . . You should believe firmly what the Church universal holds, namely, that under the appearances of bread and wine, after the sacred words have been pronounced by the priest, there exist truly, really, and essentially the Body and Blood of Our Lord Jesus Christ, although locally [Lat. *localiter*] it is in heaven (DS 849).

This is one of the rare times in a Magisterial document that there is found mention of the nonlocal Presence of the Lord in the Eucharist. Paul VI refers to it again in *Mysterium Fidei* and the *Creed of the People of God*.

Clement V (1305–14)

So famous did the *Transiturus* become that it was fully repeated by this Pope, who inaugurated the so-called Babylonian captivity of the Church by moving the papacy to Avignon, France. The period that followed the move to France was a most troubled one for the Church, climaxed by the Great Western Schism and the efforts of the bishops at Constance to resolve it. The Eucharistic controversies dealt with at that Council, as confirmed by Pope Martin V, have been set forth in the previous chapter.

Eugene IV (1431–47) and the Council of Florence

The successor of Martin V, still beset by the aftermath of the Great Western Schism and the theories concerning the superiority of a General Council over the Pope, was instrumental in convoking a council that achieved ecclesial union with the separated churches of the East. The great Council, held at Florence (1439–45), produced a significant statement on the Eucharist and the other sacraments in the bull *Exsultate Deo* of November 22, 1439. The work is not an infallible document and is one of the rare examples of an authoritative conciliar teaching that was subsequently modified. Relying heavily on the small work of Aquinas *Concerning the Articles of Faith and the Sacraments of the Church,* the document gave a brief resume of each of the seven sacraments. For the Sacrament of Orders it held, along with almost all Medieval Western theology, that the matter for conferring orders was the *traditio instrumentorum,* the handing over of the vessels used to celebrate the Eucharist. Within a century the bishops of Rome were noting, in their own teaching, that historically the imposition of hands had, from time immemorial, constituted the matter of the Sacrament. In 1947, Pius XII determined that henceforward such would be the case for the Western Church. On the Eucharist, the decree of Florence said in part:

> The form of this Sacrament is the words of the Lord by which the Sacrament is effected. The priest, speaking in the person of Christ, confects this Sacrament. By the power of the words themselves the substance of bread is changed into the Body of Christ, and the substance of wine into his Blood in such a way that the whole Christ is contained under the appearance [Lat. *specie*] of bread and the whole Christ is contained under the appearance of

wine. Under each part of the consecrated Host and consecrated wine, the whole Christ is contained even when a separation has been made (DS 1321).

The effect of this Sacrament, which comes about in the soul of the person who receives worthily, is union of the person with Christ. And, because through grace the person is incorporated into Christ and united with his members, it follows that, through this Sacrament, grace is increased in the person who receives worthily. Every effect that material food and drink effect vis-à-vis our bodily life, viz., sustaining, giving growth, healing, and giving delight, the Sacrament effects vis-à-vis our spiritual life. As Pope Urban IV said, in this Sacrament we gratefully recall the memory of the Savior, are drawn back from evil, are strengthened in good, and advance in the growth of virtues and graces (DS 1322).

The first sentence of the above citation ("The form of this Sacrament is the words of the Lord by which the Sacrament is effected") is an indirect reference to the dispute between the Latin Church and some of the theologians of the Eastern churches concerning the meaning of the *epiclesis,* the invocation of the Holy Spirit. We have already seen indications from the Fathers[51] that the power of the Holy Spirit was invoked upon the gifts. Some of the ancient Eucharistic Prayers contained a special formulary for such an invocation. The Eastern liturgies have such a prayer, as did the Eucharistic Prayer of Hippolytus (Eucharistic Prayer II of the present *Sacramentary*). In the twelfth and thirteenth centuries, however, some theologians of the Orthodox churches began to intimate that this invocation was necessary to effect the Consecration of the elements, a position that found more favor in the fourteenth century. Under Benedict XII in 1341, this opinion was cited as erroneous (DS 1017). Originally it was the intention at Florence to define solemnly that the words of

[51] Cf. above, pp. 26, 30, 32, 69, etc. For indications in Augustine, cf. pp. 57 and 209.

Consecration effected the Eucharistic change. Not to offend the Eastern churches, however, such a definition was not made, but the efficacy of the consecratory words was taught as cited above. Later the Council of Trent (DS 1640) and Pope Pius X (DS 3556) would repeat the same teaching.[52]

For a Catholic there can be no doubt that the words of the Lord effect the Consecration, but it is also true that, for the Catholic, there can be no doubt that the words achieve their effect through the action of the Spirit of God. Even where there is no explicit prayer of *epiclesis* (as is the case in the Roman Canon), the action of the Holy Spirit is implicit from the whole context of the Church's Faith. In our own time, moreover, what was always implicit has been made explicit. In the Eucharistic Prayers published by the Church for liturgical use after the Second Vatican Council, the invocation of the Spirit finds its proper place in an unambiguous form.

The unity achieved with the East at Florence, allowing the churches of the East and West to share one Eucharistic table, did not endure. Some of the bishops of the East were never reconciled to it and continued to work against the union that had been achieved. Their efforts were aided by the fall of Constantinople to the Turks in 1452 and the consequent difficulty in communication between the churches of East and West. Within the century, moreover, the Western churches were racked by

---

[52] Johannes Emminghaus, *The Eucharist,* writes: "The Eastern and Western churches still disagree on the answer to the . . . question . . . : 'Does the Consecration take place through the *epiclesis,* or does it take place through the 'words of Consecration', which are spoken as a declaration rather than as a simple narration of a past event?' The Eastern Church maintains the first of these two views, while Latin theologians maintain the second, although the Church has never issued a dogmatic declaration on the point" (p. 80). The summation is not quite accurate. It would be fairer to say that many, even most, Eastern theologians hold the view ascribed to the East, and that, although the Western Church has never *defined* the matter, the effective nature of the consecratory words has been taught by two Councils of the Church as well as by the papal Magisterium.

major problems of their own as the Reformation split Western Christianity.

The Council of Trent

To reform Christian life in the Western churches and to combat the errors of the reformers, the Council of Trent was convoked in 1545. Its work was protracted and interrupted several times due to various religious and political disagreements. Eight sessions were held at Trent between 1545 and 1547. The meetings were then transferred to Bologna, where two sessions were held between 1547 and 1549. At that point the Council was suspended but later reconvened at Trent between 1551 and 1552 (sessions XI–XVI). The final period took place at Trent, sessions XVII–XXV being held between January 1562 and December 1563. Paul III (1534–49) convoked the Council; Julius III (1550–55), Marcellus II (1555), and Paul IV (1555–59) reconvoked and continued its work; and Pius IV (1559–65) closed it and confirmed all its decrees by the papal bull *Benedictus Deus* of January 26, 1564. Trent's major teachings on the Eucharist occurred during the pontificates of Julius III and Pius IV.

Julius III (1550–55)

A list of articles or propositions, previously examined in 1547, claiming to represent prevalent erroneous statements concerning the Eucharist was submitted to the consideration of the theologians and bishops at Trent in 1551, their judgment being asked concerning the orthodoxy or heterodoxy of the propositions. The articles read:

> I. In the Eucharist there are not truly present the Body and Blood or the divinity of Our Lord Jesus Christ. Rather these are there only in sign. This is the error of Zwingli, Oecolampadius, and the Sacramentarians.

There was unanimous agreement by the theologians and bishops at Trent that this article is heretical. Some raised the objection, however, that it was not certain that the attribution of the position to the persons mentioned was factually correct. This objection came up in the discussion of several of the articles and probably explains why, when the canons condemning the various errors were finally drawn up, no attribution was made as to who held the condemned positions.

II. Christ is set forth in the Eucharist to be eaten, but only spiritually through faith, not sacramentally. This proposition is held by the above-mentioned heretics, especially Oecolampadius.

This article, too, was unanimously agreed to be heretical, but many thought that what was expressed in it was already implied in Article I and would be condemned by the condemnation of Article I.

III. In the Eucharist there are indeed the Body and Blood of Our Lord Jesus Christ, but together with the substance of bread and wine, so that there is no transubstantiation but rather a hypostatic union of the humanity and the substance of bread and wine, such that it is true to say, "This bread is my Body", and "This wine is my Blood."
This opinion is attributed to Luther.

The history of the discussion on Article III is informative. The theologians and bishops were here discussing the question of the change in the elements of bread and wine. Although Luther probably would not have recognized as his own the notion of a "hypostatic union" between the bread and wine and the Body and Blood of the risen Lord (such a way of expressing the matter is closer to the position attributed to Pope Gelasius),[53] his manner of explaining the relationship between Christ's Body and the Eucharistic elements was certainly similar to the position here attributed to him.

[53] For Pope Gelasius, see above, pp. 71–72.

The discussion on Article III produced unanimity among the theologians and bishops at Trent. There were certain voices, however, who wanted some distinctions to be made. The theologian Melchior Cano considered Article III heretical. A Catholic, he said, had to accept as true the teaching that said there was a change in the elements. However, as far as transubstantiation was concerned, Cano thought that Lateran IV had not defined the matter, since he did not think that the *Firmiter* was a definitive decree.[54] What Cano was questioning was the term transubstantiation, not the reality of the substantial change.[55] His position vis-à-vis the definitive nature of Lateran IV's *Firmiter* was far from the majority opinion. Indeed, it was almost, but not quite, singular. In light of Cano's observations, however, and the subsequent ones of the Archbishop of Vienna, the ultimate decree of Trent was careful to define the truth of the substantial change, while teaching that the term transubstantiation was most fittingly used by the Church to describe that substantial change.

Archbishop Thomas Campeggio of Feltre thought that Article III was heretical but that its errors would be condemned by the condemnation of Article I, and need not be repeated.[56]

Christopher Patavinus, Master General of the Hermits of St. Augustine, in a written response, said Article III was heretical. He repeated, however, the opinion of Duns Scotus, saying that Christ could have willed it such that there be a hypostatic union with the bread and wine, but that, in fact, Christ had not willed it to be such.[57]

---

[54] *Concilium Tridentinum*, tome 7, pt. 4, vol. I, pp. 124–25.

[55] Pelikan, 4, p. 299, refers to Cano without naming him and calls him a "colleague" of the Archbishop of Vienna, thus allowing the inaccurate inference that two *bishops* at Trent expressed difficulties about the word *transubstantiation*. In fact, the opinions of Cano, the theologian, and the Archbishop of Vienna as well as those of Thomas Campeggio were of a different nature.

[56] *Concilium Tridentinum*, tome 7, pt. 4, vol. I, p. 149.

[57] *Concilium Tridentinum*, tome 7, pt. 4, vol. I, p. 169.

To Patavinus goes the honor of citing St. Augustine in defense of the Catholic doctrine on the Eucharist, using two very infrequently cited texts of the Doctor from Hippo. The texts are taken from Book III of Augustine's *De Trinitate* and read:

> [St. Paul] was able to preach the Lord Jesus Christ through signs, in one way by his tongue, another through his epistles, and another through the Sacrament of his Body and Blood. And we do not speak of the Body and Blood of Christ, meaning by that Paul's tongue, or the parchment and ink or the words made by his tongue or the signs written with letters. Rather we mean only that which has been taken from the fruit of the earth and properly consecrated by the mystical prayer [Lat. *ex fructibus terrae acceptum et prece mystica consecratum rite sumimus*] unto spiritual salvation and in memory of what the Lord suffered for us. Although it is brought to that visible form [Lat. *species*] by the hands of men, it is not made holy such as to be so great a Sacrament except by the Spirit of God working invisibly.[58]

The above is one of the rare cases when Augustine speaks of a consecratory prayer transforming the elements through the power of the Spirit. The second text of Augustine cited by Patavinus reads:

> It is like infants who have no knowledge of what is placed on the altar and of what is consumed when the holy celebration is completed or whence or how it is confected [Lat. *conficiatur*], or whence it is assumed for a religious use. If they never learn through their own experience or that of others and never see that form [Lat. *speciem*] except when it is offered and given during the celebration of the Sacraments, and it is told to them by very great authority whose Body and Blood it is, they will believe nothing other than that the Lord has appeared to the eyes of men in that form and that the liquid has certainly flowed from the side pierced in such a way.[59]

---

[58] Augustine, *De Trinitate*, bk. III, chap. 4; *CCSL*, 50, p. 136.

[59] Augustine, *De Trinitate*, bk. III, chap. 9; *CCSL*, 50, p. 149. The written intervention by Patavinus in which he cites the Augustinian texts is found in *Concilium Tridentinum*, tome 13, vol. I, p. 132.

This passage, in its context, is not free of all obscurity. Augustine is speaking here of how God manifests himself through the angels, and men, and things. He calls such manifestations "miracles and signs" and notes how God sometimes uses preexisting things to manifest himself by changing them in some way. If someone never saw the things so used outside of the context in which God employs them, the person could conclude that such things serve only the purpose God makes of them in special contexts. Thus, someone who never saw bread and wine except at Mass and had been told and believed that the forms were actually not bread and wine but the Body and Blood of Christ could form the conviction that such was the actual form in which Christ came and suffered. What is significant for Eucharistic theology is the implicit identification of the Eucharistic Blood with the Blood that flowed from Christ's side on the Cross, even though the form (species) be different.

Further discussion on Article III added nothing of substance. Nonetheless, what had been said was significant. There are those who at times imply that Trent, in its teaching on transubstantiation, rather blindly followed Lateran IV. A careful reading of the deliberations at Trent, however, reveals that such was not the case. The decision of Lateran IV was certainly viewed as normative by the vast majority, but it was seen for what it was, not an innovation but a clear presentation of the immemorial Faith of the Church.

The articles under consideration at Trent continue as follows:

IV. The Eucharist was instituted only for the remission of sins. This statement, as the Bishop of Rochester [John Fisher] says, is that of Luther.

This article, also, was judged heretical by all, although many noted that, if one omitted the "only", it could be held in some fashion. Others doubted that it was actually Luther's teaching.

V. Christ in the Eucharist is not to be adored, or venerated on feast days, or carried in processions, or brought to the sick, and adorers of the Eucharist are true idolaters.

This opinion is attributed to Luther.

All agreed that this article represented a heretical opinion.

VI. The Eucharist is not to be reserved in the tabernacle, but is to be immediately consumed and given to those present. . . . Nor is it lawful for anyone to communicate himself.

This opinion is attributed to Martin Bucer and Philip Melancthon.

VII. The Body of Christ does not remain in the consecrated Hosts or particles remaining after Communion. The Body of Christ is only there when the Sacrament is received, not before and not after reception.

This opinion is attributed to Luther.

All agreed that Articles VI and VII were heretical, but again some doubted the validity of the attributions.

VIII. It is of divine law that the people and children communicate under both species, and therefore they sin who force the people to use only one species.

This opinion is attributed to Luther.

IX. There is not contained under each species what is contained under both, nor does the communicant receive as much under one as he receives under both.

This opinion is attributed to Luther and others.

Articles VIII and IX drew many distinctions, most of them concerned with the advisability of permitting Communion under both Species at least in some cases. Others thought the Council must be careful not to condemn the practice of the early Church, which did communicate children.

X. Faith alone is sufficient preparation for receiving the Eucharist, nor is confession necessary for it. Rather it is a free decision, especially for the learned. Nor are people obliged to receive Communion at Paschal time.

This opinion is attributed to Luther.[60]

This was probably the article that evoked the greatest difference of opinions among the Tridentine theologians. The discussion centered on what kind of obligation existed in respect to the necessity of confessing mortal sins before receiving the Eucharist. Some outstanding Catholic theologians, notably Thomas de Vio, Cardinal Cajetan, had held that it was not always necessary to confess before receiving as long as one was duly repentant and had the intention to confess subsequently.[61] Some of the theologians and bishops at Trent agreed with Cajetan's position. Others strongly disagreed, saying that it was of divine law, or at least positive law of the Church, that all mortal sins had to be confessed before reception of the Eucharist. All agreed, nonetheless, that it was heretical to say that faith alone was sufficient preparation. As will be seen below, the discussion resulted in a careful wording of the final canon on this matter.

The discussions on the various errors of the reformers ultimately produced Trent's final Decree on the Eucharist as Sacrament. This teaching was expressed positively in the eight chapters and negatively in the canons that condemned the errors.

Decree and Canons of Council of Trent on Eucharist (Session XIII, October 1551)

Chapter I: On the Real Presence of Our Lord Jesus Christ in the Most Holy Sacrament of the Eucharist

The holy synod teaches and openly and simply professes that, in the nourishing Sacrament of the holy Eucharist, after the Consecration of the bread and wine, Our Lord Jesus Christ, true God and man, is truly, really, and substantially contained under the species

---

[60] The articles are found in *Concilium Tridentinum,* tome 7, pt. 4, vol. I, pp. III–14.

[61] Cf. *Concilium Tridentinum,* tome 7, pt. 4, vol. I, p. 126, n. 4.

of those sensible realities (cf. Canon I). For it is not contradictory to say that our Savior himself always sits at the right hand of the Father in heaven, according to his natural mode of existing, and that, nevertheless, he is in many other places present to us sacramentally in his own substance, by a manner of existing that is possible to God, even though we can hardly express it in words, but that we, by an understanding illuminated by faith, are able to perceive and ought most firmly believe.

All our forefathers—as many of them as belonged to the true Church of Christ, and who have treated of this most holy Sacrament—have most clearly professed that our Redeemer instituted this admirable Sacrament at the Last Supper, when, after the blessing of the bread and wine, he testified in explicit and clear words that he gave them his own very Body and his own Blood. These words that—recorded by the holy Evangelists and afterward repeated by St. Paul—bear that proper and most manifest meaning in which they were understood by the Fathers, have been distorted by certain contentious and wicked men to [become] fictitious and imaginary tropes [symbols], whereby the truth of the Flesh and Blood of Christ is denied, contrary to the universal sense of the Church, which, as the pillar and ground of truth (1 Tim 3:15), has detested as devilish these inventions devised by impious men. The Church, however, recognizes, with a mind ever grateful and ever mindful, this most excellent benefit of Christ.

Chapter II: On the Reason for the Institution of This Most Holy Sacrament

Therefore, our Savior, when about to depart out of this world to the Father, instituted this Sacrament, in which as it were he poured forth the riches of his divine love toward the human race, "making a memorial of his wonderful works" (Ps 111:4). He commanded us in the reception of this Sacrament to venerate his memory (1 Cor 11.24) and to announce his death until he comes to judge the world (1 Cor 11:26). He willed also that this Sacrament should be received as the spiritual food of souls (Mt 26:26) by which those may be fed and strengthened (cf. Canon V) who live with the life of him who said: "Whoever eats me shall live because of me" (Jn 6:58). He willed that it be an antidote by which we may be freed from daily faults and be preserved from mortal sins. He willed, furthermore, to have it be a pledge of our future glory and of everlasting happiness, and in this way be a symbol of that one Body of which he is the head (1 Cor 11:3) and to which he willed us to be joined as members united by the closest bonds of faith, hope, and charity, so that "we might all speak the same things, and there might be no schisms among us" (1 Cor 1:10).

Chapter III: On the Excellence of Most Holy Eucharist over the Other Sacraments

Indeed the most holy Eucharist has this in common with the rest of the sacraments, viz., that it is "a symbol of a sacred thing and is a visible form of an invisible grace" (cf. Augustine, *Questions on the Heptateuch,* bk. I, III, chap. 84). But there is found in the Eucharist this excellent and peculiar reality, viz., that the other sacraments first have the power of sanctifying when one uses them, whereas in the Eucharist, even before being used, there is present the very Author of sanctity (cf. Canon IV).

For the Apostles had not as yet received the Eucharist from the hand of the Lord (Mt 26:26; Mk 14:22), when he himself, nevertheless, truly affirmed that it was his own Body that he offered them. This has ever been the Faith of the Church of God: that immediately after the Consecration the true Body of our Lord and his true Blood, together with his soul and divinity, exist under the appearance [Lat. *species*] of bread and wine. By the power of the words the Body indeed exists under the appearance of bread, and the Blood under the appearance of wine. Nevertheless, by the power of their natural connection and concomitance—whereby the parts of Christ Our Lord, who has now risen from the dead to die no more, are united—the Body itself exists under the species of wine, and the Blood under the species of bread, and the soul under both. His divinity is present, furthermore, on account of the admirable hypostatic union of that divinity with his Body and Soul. Therefore it is most true that as much is contained under either species as is contained under both, because Christ whole and entire exists under the species of bread and under any and every part of that species; likewise the whole Christ exists under the species of wine and under the parts thereof (cf. Canon III).

Chapter IV: On Transubstantiation

Because Christ our Redeemer declared that what he offered under the appearance of bread was truly his own Body (cf. Mt 26:26ff.; Mk 14:22ff.; Lk 22:19; Jn 6:48; 1 Cor 11:24), it has, therefore, ever been a firm belief in the Church of God—and this holy synod now declares it again—that through the Consecration of the bread and wine a conversion is made of the whole substance of the bread into the substance of the Body of Christ Our Lord, and of the whole substance of the wine into the substance of his Blood. This conversion is by the holy Catholic Church suitably and properly called transubstantiation (cf. Canon II).

Chapter V: On the Worship and Veneration to Be Shown to This Most Holy Sacrament

Therefore, there is no room left to doubt that all the faithful of Christ may, according to the custom ever received in the Catholic Church, venerate this most holy Sacrament with the cult of *latria,* which is due to the true God (cf. Canon VI). This Sacrament, therefore, is not the less to be adored on account of the fact that it was instituted by Christ the Lord in order to be eaten (cf. Mt 26: 26ff.). This is so because we believe that same God to be present therein, of whom the Eternal Father, when introducing him into the world, says: "And let all the angels of God adore him" (Heb 1:6), and whom the Magi falling down, adored (Mt 2:11), and who, finally, as the Scripture testifies, was adored by the Apostles in Galilee (Mt 28:17).

This holy synod declares, moreover, that very piously and religiously was the custom introduced into the Church according to which this sublime and venerable Sacrament is honored every year on a particular feast day with special veneration, and that it be carried reverently and with honor in processions through the streets and public places. For it is most just that there be established certain holy days on which all Christians may, with special and particular manifestations, testify that they are mindful and grateful to their common Lord and Redeemer for so ineffable and truly divine a benefit, whereby the victory and triumph of his death are represented.

Chapter VI: On Reserving the Holy Eucharist and Carrying It to the Sick

The custom of reserving the holy Eucharist in the tabernacle is so ancient that even the age of the Council of Nicaea recognized it. Moreover, as to carrying the Sacred Eucharist itself to the sick and carefully reserving it for this purpose in churches, apart from the fact that it is exceedingly conformable to justice and reason, it is also found to be prescribed in many councils and is a very ancient custom of the Catholic Church. Therefore, this holy synod ordains that this salutary and necessary custom is to be completely maintained (cf. Canon VII).

Chapter VII: On the Preparation to Be Made So That One May Receive the Holy Eucharist Worthily

If it is unsuitable for anyone to approach any of the sacred functions unless he approach in a holy manner, the more the holiness and divinity of this heavenly Sacrament are understood by a Christian, the more diligently should he see to it that he not approach it except with great reverence and holiness (cf. Canon XI), especially as we read in the Apostle those fearful words: "Whoever eats and drinks unworthily eats and drinks judgment upon oneself" (1 Cor 11:29). Therefore, whoever wishes to communicate should remember his command: "Let everyone examine himself" (1 Cor 11:28).

Now, Church custom declares that the necessary examination is that no one who is conscious of mortal sin, however contrite he may appear to himself, should approach the Sacred Eucharist without previous sacramental confession. This holy synod has decreed that this is to be invariably observed by all Christians, even by those priests whose duty it is to celebrate Mass, as long as there is not lacking the opportunity of a confessor. If, in an urgent necessity, a priest should celebrate without previous confession, let him confess as soon as possible.

Chapter VIII: On the Use of This Admirable Sacrament

As far as the reception of this holy Sacrament is concerned, our Fathers have rightly and wisely distinguished three ways of receiving it. For they have taught that sinners receive it only sacramentally;

others only receive spiritually, i.e., those who, eating in desire that heavenly bread that is set before them, by a lively faith that works by charity (Gal 5:6), experience its fruit and usefulness. The third type receive it both sacramentally and spiritually (cf. Canon VIII), and these are they who so prove and prepare themselves beforehand as to approach this divine table "clothed with the wedding garment" (cf. Mt 22:11). Now, as to the reception of this Sacrament, it was always the custom in the Church of God that laymen should receive the Communion from priests; but that priests who are celebrating should communicate themselves (cf. Canon XI). This custom, as coming down from an apostolic tradition, ought with justice and reason be retained. And finally this holy synod with true fatherly affection admonishes, exhorts, begs, and beseeches, through the bowels of the mercy of our God, that all and each of those who bear the Christian name would now at last agree and be of one mind in this "sign of unity", in this "bond of charity" (cf. Augustine, *On the Gospel of John*, 26, 13), in this symbol of concord, and that, mindful of the very great majesty and the exceeding love of Our Lord Jesus Christ, who gave his own beloved life as the price of our salvation and gave us his own Flesh to eat, they would believe and venerate these sacred Mysteries of his Body and Blood with such constancy and firmness of faith, with such devotion of soul, with such piety and worship, as to be able frequently to receive this supersubstantial bread (Mt 6:11), and that it may be to them truly the life of the soul and the perpetual health of mind. "Being comforted by its strength" (1 Kings 19:8), may they, after the journey of this miserable pilgrimage, be able to arrive at their heavenly fatherland, there to eat, without any veil, that same "bread of angels" (Ps 78:25) that they now eat under the sacred veils.[62]

---

[62] The reference to the "supersubstantial bread" refers to the Latin translation of Mt 6:11, the petition in the Lord's Prayer for "our daily bread". Several of the Fathers of the Church interpreted the petition as a reference to the Eucharist, among them most clearly St. Cyprian of Carthage who wrote:

When we say, "Give us this day our daily bread", we can understand the petition spiritually and simply. . . . Just as we say "Our Father" because he is the Father of those who know him and believe in him, so we say "our bread" because Christ is the bread of those who touch his Body. We ask that this bread be given to us daily lest we who are in Christ and receive the Eucharist daily as the food of salvation be kept from communicating

But inasmuch as it is not enough to declare the truth, if errors be not uncovered and refuted, it has pleased the holy synod to add these canons, so that all, having known the Catholic doctrine, may now also understand what the heresies are that they ought to guard against and avoid.

Canons

Canon I: If anyone deny that, in the Sacrament of the most holy Eucharist, are contained truly, really, and substantially the Body and Blood together with the soul and divinity of Our Lord Jesus Christ, and consequently the whole Christ; but says that he is only there as in a sign, or in figure, or virtue, *anathema sit.*

The discussion among the Fathers at Trent that preceded the final publication of the decree left this canon substantially unchanged from its first draft.

Canon II: If anyone say that, in the sacred and holy Sacrament of the Eucharist, the substance of the bread and wine remains together with the Body and Blood of Our Lord Jesus Christ and denies that wonderful and singular conversion of the whole substance of the bread into the Body, and of the whole substance of the wine into the Blood—the species only of the bread and wine remaining—which conversion indeed the Catholic Church most aptly calls transubstantiation, *anathema sit.*

We have seen sufficiently above how the discussion on Article III of the reformers proceeded at Trent. When the time came for formulating a canon on it, the first draft read:

---

in the heavenly bread because some grave sin has been committed and so we be separated from the Body of Christ. Christ taught us, "I am the bread of life who have come down from heaven. Anyone who eats my bread will live forever. The bread that I will give is my Flesh for the life of the world." When he says that anyone who eats his bread will live forever, he is clearly saying that those who touch his Body and receive the Eucharist of union will live. Thus, we must fear and pray against any abstention that will separate us from the Body of Christ and leave us far from salvation (Cyprian of Carthage, *Liber de Oratione Dominica,* 18; *PL,* 4, 531).

If anyone say that in the most holy Sacrament of the Eucharist, the substance of the bread and wine remains together with the Body and Blood of Our Lord Jesus Christ, or, according to a damnable and profane novelty of words, says that Christ is impanated, and denies that wonderful and singular conversion of the whole substance of bread into the Body and of the whole substance of wine into Blood, only the appearance of bread and wine remaining, which change our Fathers and the whole Catholic Church most suitably have named transubstantiation, *anathema sit.*[63]

There was almost unanimous agreement on the formulation of the canon. However, the Archbishop of Vienna, Frederick Nausea, thought that the canon as originally drafted should not say that all the Fathers had called this change transubstantiation,[64] and, having properly won that point, then said that the word itself should be dropped since the truth was already contained in the first canon,[65] a suggestion congruent with the remarks previously made by Bishop Thomas Campeggio.[66] This suggestion did not convince the others, and transubstantiation remained the matter for a special canon.

The Archbishop of Vienna's suggestion and its rejection are not without significance. It is often asserted that the doctrine propounded in Canon II concerning transubstantiation is really only another way of affirming the Real Presence, or that it is the consequence of taking literally the words of Christ at the Supper.[67] Undoubtedly there have always been Catholic theologians who have thought this to be the case. This position is certainly *similar* to that of St. Thomas, who claimed that, by intrinsic logic, the

[63] *Concilium Tridentinum,* tome 7, pt. 4, vol. I, p. 178.

[64] *Concilium Tridentinum,* tome 7, pt. 4, vol. I, p. 182.

[65] *Concilium Tridentinum,* tome 7, pt. 4, vol. I, p. 188.

[66] See above, p. 208.

[67] At times, J. Pelikan appears to equate the doctrines of the Real Presence and transubstantiation. Thus, he writes: "The Lutheran theory that the Body of Christ was present 'in, with, and under' the bread of the Supper, which Reformed polemics repeatedly attacked, was not significantly better than the theory of transubstantiation that it claimed to oppose—if, indeed, there was any real difference between the two doctrines of Presence" (4, p. 200); "Thus it [Trent]

Real Presence demands transubstantiation.[68] In this assertion Thomas is probably right, profound metaphysician that he was. It is also certain that many of the theologians and bishops at Trent thought this to be so. It is a view, however, difficult if not impossible to sustain historically. All of Christian history shows that there have existed those who were able to believe the literal truth of the Real Presence without seeing it as necessarily connected with transubstantiation, i.e., with a ceasing to be of the reality of bread and wine. Martin Luther's views were not a novelty. His position was very like the position that was, perhaps, held by Theodore of Mopsuestia and certainly held in the treatise attributed to Pope Gelasius. Nonetheless, the doctrine of these latter on the Presence was like "the Lutheran doctrine . . . as much a 'materialistic theology' as was the Roman Catholic doctrine of transubstantiation".[69] A mind as acute as that of Scotus, who firmly believed in both the Real Presence and transubstantiation, thought, nevertheless, that "consubstantiation" was apparently more logical, had God not revealed otherwise. Scotus' view even found a proponent at Trent.[70]

---

reaffirmed the reality of the Presence, and together with it the validity of transubstantiation as the Church's way of confessing that presence" (4, p. 299).

Karl Rahner, in the article "The Presence of Christ in the Sacrament of the Lord's Supper" (*Theo. Inves. 4*) makes a distinction between a *logical* explanation of a concept (i.e., an explanation "that makes the statement to be explained clear, that is, more definite and unmistakable . . . without appealing to matters distinct from the matter to be explained", p. 300) and an *ontic* explanation (i.e., an explanation "that asserts *something else* than the matter in question", p. 301). He then concludes: "I call the doctrine of transubstantiation logical on account of its relationship to the words of Christ, which are to be explained and guarded against all misunderstanding that would weaken or deny their sense. By this I mean that the doctrine of transubstantiation tells me no more than do the words of Christ, when I take them seriously" (p. 302).

[68] *S.Th.*, III, q. 75, a. 2. "Some have held that the substance of bread and wine remains in this Sacrament after the Consecration. But this position cannot stand. First of all it cannot stand because, by this position, the truth of this Sacrament—to which it pertains that the true Body of Christ exists in the Sacrament—is removed."

[69] Pelikan, 4, p. 201.

[70] Cf. above, p. 208.

The bishops at Trent, then, in rejecting the assertions of the Arch-bishop of Vienna, were in fact recognizing — at least implicitly — what history teaches: the doctrines of the Real Presence and transub-stantiation are *two* doctrines.[71] They They are intimately related, of course — probably even by metaphysical necessity as Thomas taught — but not identical. Luther's position was not that of either Zwingli or Calvin; the denial of transubstantiation has not always led to the denial of the Real Presence.

The doctrine of transubstantiation teaches, at least, that, for all the similarity between the Mysteries of the Incarnation and the Eucharist, there is a difference. In the Incarnation, a true human nature is preserved intact even while being created to exist in the Person of the Word. In the Eucharist, however, the nature of the bread and wine is not preserved intact. In full truth the bread and wine lose their natural reality and become what they were not. In the Incarnation and in the Eucharist God deals with material reality in different ways, preserving and elevating it in the case of the Incarnation, changing it totally in the case of the Eucharist.

> Canon III: If anyone deny that, in the venerable Sacrament of the Eucharist, the whole Christ is contained under each species and under every part of each species when separated, *anathema sit.*
>
> Canon IV: If anyone should say that, after the Consecration is completed, the Body and Blood of Our Lord Jesus Christ are not in the admirable Sacrament of the Eucharist but are there only in the use, while it is being received, and not before and after; and that, in the Hosts or consecrated particles, which are reserved or

---

[71] Schillebeeckx, *The Eucharist,* p. 46, n. 43, misses this point, apparently because of a historical error. He writes: "It would similarly be wrong to claim that some of the fathers of the Council wanted to delete the second canon (as implied in the first). Some authors have obviously been caught by the fact that, in some stages of the discussion, our 'canon 2' became 'canon 3' because an entirely different canon was inserted as 'canon 2' between our two canons." The assertion is certainly not correct. Apart from the numbering of the canons, the Archbishop of Vienna and Thomas Campeggio both said that transubstanti-ation need not be affirmed separately because it was already contained in the canon on the Real Presence. This historical mistake is what apparently led Schillebeeckx to assert that transubstantiation was affirmed at Trent "purely to

which remain after Communion, the true Body of the Lord does not remain, *anathema sit.*

Canons III and IV remained substantially the same from the time of their first formulation.

> Canon V: If anyone say either that the principal fruit of the most holy Eucharist is the remission of sins, or that other effects do not result from it, *anathema sit.*

This canon in the original draft read: "If anyone say that the most holy Eucharist was instituted only for the remission of sins, *anathema sit.*" It was reformulated because some thought that no reformer actually said what the first draft condemned and in order to make it more comprehensive.

> Canon VI: If anyone say that, in the holy Sacrament of the Eucharist, Christ, the only begotten Son of God, is not to be adored with the worship, even external, of latria; and that the Sacrament, consequently, is not to be venerated with a special festive solemnity, or to be solemnly carried in processions, according to the laudable and universal rite and custom of Holy Church; or is not to be proposed publicly to the people to be adored, and that the adorers thereof are idolaters, *anathema sit.*
>
> Canon VII: If anyone say that it is not lawful for the sacred Eucharist to be reserved in the tabernacle, but that, immediately after Consecration, it must necessarily be distributed among those present; or that it is not permitted to carry it honorably to the sick, *anathema sit.*

There was no substantial change in Canons VI and VII from the time of their first drafting. Canon VI is a firm reaffirmation of the truth that Christ is to be adored in the Eucharist, a truth already

---

explicate the first statement in a polemical context" (p. 48) and that, "because of what [the Real Presence] implied for them, they spoke, in the *second* place— that is, on the basis of theological reasoning—of a change of the substance of the bread. In comparison with the first dogmatic statement of *faith,* their affirmation of this change of substance is a *theologoumenon*" (p. 49). Despite these mistakes, he does see, however, that *two* things are being affirmed.

explicitly witnessed to by St. Augustine[72] and admirably expounded in the *Transiturus*. It is a truth, moreover, that underlies essential elements in Catholic devotional practices, manifested chiefly in the practices of Benediction of the Blessed Sacrament, and vigils, "holy hours", and other private periods of prayer before the Sacrament reserved in the tabernacle. Such practices are the inevitable result of the realization that the Sacrament is "Emmanuel", God with us.

Canon VIII: If anyone say that Christ, set forth in the Eucharist, is eaten spiritually only, and not also sacramentally and really, *anathema sit.*

In the first draft of the canons, this was originally Canon XI. The order and number of the canons changed in the final decree because some were made to coalesce, while others, mainly concerning Communion under both species, were removed pending further consideration.

Canon IX: If anyone deny that all and each of Christ's faithful of both sexes are bound, when they have reached the age of discretion, to communicate every year, at least at Easter, in accordance with the precept of Holy Mother Church, *anathema sit.*

This repetition of the decree of Lateran IV was originally Canon XII, and there was no substantial change from the time of its first formulation.

Canon X: If anyone say that it is not lawful for the celebrating priest to communicate himself, *anathema sit.*

This was originally part of Canon VIII, which also spoke of Communion under both kinds.

Canon XI: If anyone say that faith alone is a sufficient preparation for receiving the Sacrament of the most holy Eucharist, *anathema sit.* And lest so great a Sacrament be received unworthily, and thus unto death and condemnation, this holy synod ordains and declares that sacramental confession, when a confessor is

[72] Cf. above, p. 59.

available, must be made beforehand by those whose conscience is burdened with mortal sin, no matter how contrite they may think themselves. But if anyone shall presume to teach, preach, or obstinately to assert, or even in public disputation to defend the contrary, he shall be by that very fact be excommunicate.

The final formulation of this canon was the result of the previous discussion centering on the position of Cajetan. The Council takes no explicit position on the nature of the obligation (i.e., is it of divine positive law implied in 1 Cor 11:27–32 and in the Church's Tradition and practice, or is it positive law of the Church?) to confess mortal sins before reception of Communion. It merely confirms the Tradition and practice, with the recognition that a positive law, whether divine or human, does not oblige when it is impossible to fulfill. Such an impossibility would exist, in this case, were there no confessor available, and so the canon makes that condition explicit. This decree of Trent is expressed in the 1983 Code of Canon Law, Canon 916, which reads:

> Whoever is aware of being in grave sin may not celebrate Mass or receive the Body of the Lord without previously undertaking sacramental confession, unless there is present a grave reason for so doing and an opportunity for confessing is lacking. In such a case the person is reminded of the obligation to make an act of perfect contrition, which includes the resolution of confessing as soon as possible.[73]

The purpose of the canon—with the long history that precedes it, going back to St. Paul, as well as the stern injunctions of St. Cyprian of Carthage[74] and other Fathers of the Church—is to prevent the sin of sacrilege against Christ in the Eucharist. Speaking of such sacrilege and its sinfulness, Aquinas wrote:

---

[73] John Paul II has reiterated the teaching of Trent and of Canon 916 in the Apostolic Exhortation *Reconciliation and Penance* of 1984. Cf. *TPS,* 30, no. 1, p. 65.

[74] Cf. Cyprian, *De Lapsis,* nos. 25–29; *CCSL,* 3, pp. 234–37.

Something is said to be sacred because it is ordained for the worship of God. Moreover, just as something that is ordered to a good end is labeled good, so also something that is set aside for divine worship becomes, in a certain way, divine, and thus a certain reverence is owed to it and this reverence is referred to God. Therefore any irreverence pertaining to sacred things is in fact an irreverence to God and has the definition of sacrilege.[75]

Sacrilege that is committed against sacred things has different degrees according to the differences among the things themselves. Among these the highest place is held by the sacraments themselves, because by them a person is sanctified. And chief among these is the Eucharist, which contains Christ himself. Therefore a sacrilege committed against this Sacrament is most grave of all.[76]

The fear of committing the sin of sacrilege also extended from earliest times to the care to be taken in receiving the Sacrament and to the consecrated particles that might fall or remain from the Sacred Species. Already by 211 we find Tertullian writing:

We make offerings [Lat. *oblationes*] for the dead on the anniversary of their birth. We consider it a crime to fast or to worship on our knees on the Lord's Day. We rejoice in the same privilege from Easter Sunday until Pentecost. We suffer anxiously if anything of our chalice or bread should fall upon the ground.[77]

And Origen, writing around 245, said:

You who are accustomed to take part in the divine Mysteries know how, when you have received the Body of the Lord, you exercise every caution and reverence lest a particle of it fall and any of the consecrated gift perish. For you believe yourselves guilty—and you believe rightly—if any of it falls through your negligence. But if you use such caution in preserving his Body—and you do so rightly—how is it that you think it a lesser offense to neglect the Word of God than it is to neglect his Body?[78]

---

[75] *S. Th.*, II, IIae, q. 99, a. 1c.
[76] *S. Th.*, II, IIae, q. 99, a. 3c.
[77] Tertullian, *De Corona*, III, 3 to IV, 1; *CCSL*, 2, p. 1043.
[78] Origen, *Homily XIII on Exodus*, 3; *PG*, 12, 391.

The Eucharist as Sacrifice

As was the case with the theological treatises on the Eucharist in general, the Council of Trent only treated the Mystery of the Eucharist as sacrifice after it had completed its treatment on the Eucharist as Sacrament. During the pontificate of Clement VII (1523–34), however, two very brief works on the sacrifice of the Eucharist were published that were to influence the theologians and bishops at Trent when they came to treat of the theme. These treatises were the work of Thomas de Vio, Cardinal Cajetan (1469–1534), the renowned Dominican commentator on the works of Aquinas. Clement VII had asked Cajetan in 1525 to write a response to Zwingli's Eucharistic teaching as set forth in the *Commentary on True and False Religion.* This Cajetan did in his *Errors on a Booklet on the Lord's Supper — Instruction for the Nuncio.*[79] In this work Cajetan, after stating that John 6 — the interpretation of which was central to Zwingli's theology — does not speak of the *sacramental* eating of the Eucharist but rather only of the *spiritual* eating of the Eucharist, draws a significant distinction between the Presence of Christ's Flesh and Blood in the Eucharist and the Presence of Christ's sacrifice in the Eucharist. In the Eucharist Christ's Body and Blood are both *signified and contained;* his sacrifice is *signified but not contained.*

> For when one refers the sacrifice of the altar to the death of Christ, a sign is involved and not the reality, since neither the death of Christ nor Christ in death is present in itself. Since Christ lives and reigns in heaven, his death is consequently not contained in this sacrifice but is rather signified.
> Two things must be rightly understood: Christ himself is both signified and contained, while his death is indeed signified but not contained.[80]

---

[79] The work by Cajetan is translated in Jared Wicks' *Cajetan Responds,* pp. 153ff.

[80] Cajetan, *Errors on a Booklet,* in Wicks, p. 169.

In 1531, on his own initiative, Cajetan sent to the Pope a treatise specifically dedicated to the sacrificial aspect of the Eucharist, *The Sacrifice of the Mass and Its Rite—Against the Lutherans.*[81] It is a remarkable work of theological exegesis. Cajetan makes no appeal to Church Fathers, to councils, or to theologians (not even Aquinas) but rather sets out to answer from Scripture the objections brought by the reformers, especially as they used Hebrews 7–10 to defend their position that Christianity knows only one Priest (Christ himself) and one unrepeatable sacrifice (that of the Cross). Cajetan replies:

1.   There is only one sacrifice, that of the Cross.

2.   The Mass does not repeat the sacrifice of the Cross but is a sacramental and representative offering of that sacrifice where the victim and the One who offers are the same, namely, Christ Himself.

3.   The succession of priests offering the sacrifice of the Mass takes nothing away from the one priesthood of Christ, since they act in his person as he, through them, continues to offer himself.

4.   The sacrifice of the Cross is all-sufficient. Its sacramental offering in the Mass is done to apply to us the effects of that sacrifice.

5.   The Mass therefore is an unbloody sacrifice because in it the same Victim and same Priest who offers is present and his death is symbolically represented.

Trent and the Mass as Sacrifice

The discussions at Trent on the Mass as sacrifice began in 1547, but they were not completed. They were taken up again once the Council had been reconvened at Trent in 1552, and yet again after the reconvocation in 1562. The discussions reveal much common ground on the central questions.

---

[81] Cajetan, *The Sacrifice of the Mass and Its Rite—Against the Lutherans,* Jared Wicks, pp. 189ff.

It was clear to the theologians and bishops that the Mass is a sacramental or symbolic reenactment of the Cross. It is not a *re-presentation;* it is rather a representing of the sacrifice of the Cross. There is admittedly no destruction (Lat. *mactatio*) of the Victim at Mass, but many of the theologians and bishops pointed out that not all Old Testament sacrifices involved destruction of the offerings. This was especially true of the sacrifice of Melchizedek, which was held to be the ideal prefiguring of the Sacrifice of the Mass. Thus the Mass is no mere commemoration, but a sacrifice. Even though there was no destruction of the Victim, the Mass was truly an immolation because it was an image of the Passion that, by the intention of Christ, represented the sacrifice of the Cross.[82]

Following all Tradition, the discussions emphasized the identity of the Priest-Offerer and Victim of Calvary and the Mass. That thought was expressed by Alphonsus Salmeron, S.J.[83] And the

---

[82] The following comments are illustrative and representative of the discussion on these points. Riccardus of Vercelli said that the Eucharist is "the image of Christ who has suffered on the Cross" and is therefore a sacrifice. "The Eucharist represents [Lat. *repraesentare*] the Cross" (*Concilium Tridentinum,* tome 6, pt. 3, p. 325). It is quite clear that, for Riccardus, "image" and "represent" are synonymous concepts.

Fr. Thomas Maria Beccadellus, O.P., Fr. Nicholas Grandis, O.F.M., and Fr. Francis de Cesena all taught the same: by the institution of Christ the Eucharist represents the Passion and is therefore a sacrifice (cf. *Concilium Tridentinum,* tome 6, pt. 3, pp. 327, 330, 367).

Fr. Jerome d'Azambuja said: "As far as what the Lutherans say when they claim that Christ is not destroyed [Lat. *mactatur*] in the Mass and that therefore there is no sacrifice, let this be said. Even in the Old Law not all the animals that were offered for sins were destroyed" (*Concilium Tridentinum,* tome 6, pt. 3, p. 345).

Fr. Johannes Consilii: "In respect to the Lutheran charge that the Mass is only a commemoration of the sacrifice of the Cross and is not a sacrifice, let it be said that the oblation in the Mass is a certain commemoration of the sacrifice enacted on the Cross, but not only a commemoration. It is also a sacrifice because it is the memorial of the sacrifice enacted on the Cross. It is an oblation that represents the suffering of Christ, first of all by means of the fraction of the bread" (*Concilium Tridentinum,* tome 6, pt. 3, p. 350).

[83] Salmeron, *Concilium Tridentinum,* tome 6, pt. 3, pp. 376–77.

Dominican Fr. Placitus de Parma, O.P., drew upon St. Thomas to show how this was so. The "priest", he said, "offers *in persona Christi*".[84]

Under Julius III in 1551 the discussion on the Mass was taken up again. Following the procedure adopted in the discussion of the Eucharist as Sacrament, the following articles, excerpting the thought of the reformers, were drawn up to be considered.

> Article I: The Mass is not a sacrifice or an oblation for sins but only a commemoration of the sacrifice done on the Cross, and is called a sacrifice by the Fathers by a transposition of terminology. It is not truly and properly a sacrifice but only a testament and promise of the remission of sins.

This position is attributed to Luther and the Augsburg Confession.

> Article II: The Mass does not come from the Gospel, nor was it instituted by Christ, but rather is an invention of man. It is not a good and meritorious work; rather, there is committed in it manifest and multiple idolatry.

This view was said to represent the position of the Augsburg Confession, Calvin, and Melanchthon.

In the discussion of 1552 many of the bishops objected to the use of the word *meritorious,* since they thought it would appear then that Christ merited in the Mass, thus detracting from the fullness of what he merited on the Cross. Their thinking, in the words of Fr. Jerome Muzzarellus, O.P., was that the Mass is not a meritorious sacrifice but rather one of impetration or intercession.[85]

> Article III: Blasphemy is offered to the most holy sacrifice of Christ on the Cross if someone believes that the Son of God is offered again [*denuo*] to God the Father by the priests at Mass. To say that Christ is mystically immolated and offered for us is to

---

[84] Placitus de Parma, *Concilium Tridentinum,* tome 6, pt. 3, p. 387.
[85] Jermome Muzzarellus, O.P., *Concilium Tridentinum,* tome 6, pt. 3, p. 390.

say only that he is given to us to be eaten. And Christ, by the words "do this in memory of me", did not ordain that the Apostles offer his Body and Blood in the sacrifice of the Mass.

Article V: The Mass is of no value as a sacrifice for the living and the dead, and it is impious to apply it for sins, satisfactions, and other necessities.[86]

Much of the discussion on the articles repeated what had been previously said. Melchior Cano insisted that "Christ alone is the priest who offers himself; we indeed are his vicars and offer the sacrifice in his name".[87] And there were not a few of the theologians and bishops who stated that Christ was always a victim offering himself in heaven to the Father.[88]

Alfonsus de Contreras, O.F.M., Cap., located the sacramental sacrifice not in the *fractio,* as some would have it, but in the double Consecration, which represented the separation of Christ's Body and Blood on the Cross.[89]

The discussions on the articles led to the formation of a list of thirteen canons that set forth the theses to be condemned. These canons were presented to the bishops for discussion in January of 1552. They read in part:

I. If anyone say that in the Mass there is not a sacrifice or offering for sins but only a commemoration of the sacrifice per-

[86] The articles are found in *Concilium Tridentinum,* tome 7, pt. 4, vol. 1, pp. 375–77.

[87] *Concilium Tridentinum,* tome 7, pt. 4, vol. 1, p. 389.

[88] Cf., for example, Somnius, *Concilium Tridentinum,* vol. 8 Actorum, pt. 4, vol. 1, p. 396; Johannes Groepper, idem, p. 406; Marianus Feltrinus, idem, p. 423; Martin Pérez de Ayala (Bishop of Cadiz), idem, p. 454. This notion of a "heavenly sacrifice", already found in the Fathers (cf. Chrysostom above), was present as well in the theologians of the Middle Ages. Cf. Paschasius, *De Corp.,* 8, 1–2; *CCCM,* 16, p. 43; Alger of Liège, *De Sacramentis Corporis et Sanguinis Dominici,* Bk. I, chap. 14; *PL,* 180, 781; Aquinas, *S.Th.,* III, q. 83, a. 4, ad 9. The Roman Canon contained this truth ("May your holy angel take this sacrifice to your altar in heaven"), and all the discussion at Trent about the identity of Priest and Victim may be said to presume this truth.

[89] *Concilium Tridentinum,* tome 7, pt. 4, vol. 1, p. 418.

formed on the Cross, or that it is called a sacrifice by a transfer of terminology and not truly and properly, *anathema sit.*

II. If anyone say that the Mass is only a testament and promise of the remission of sins, *anathema sit.*

III. If anyone say that the sacrifice of the Mass does not come from the Gospels and was not instituted by Christ, but rather is the invention of man, and that to offer it is not a good and meritorious work but rather that in it there is committed a manifest and multiple idolatry, *anathema sit.*

IV. If anyone say that blasphemy is offered to the most holy sacrifice of Christ on the Cross by those who believe that the Son of God is offered to the Father by the priests in the Mass, *anathema sit.*

V. If anyone say that Christ is immolated and offered for us mystically in the Mass in no other way than being given to us to eat, or that by the words "do this in memory of me" he did not ordain that the Apostles and other priests offer his Body and Blood, *anathema sit.*

VII. If anyone say that the Mass is not of value as a sacrifice for the living and the dead, or that it is impious to apply it for sins, satisfactions, and other necessities, *anathema sit.*[90]

In April of 1552, the chapters on the Mass as sacrifice were also submitted to the bishops for discussion,[91] but the Council was adjourned the same year and did not meet again until 1562, after the deaths of both Paul IV (Carafa) and Emperor Charles V.

Pius IV (1559–65)

The man who succeeded the pious and very rigorous Paul IV did not appear to be a reformer. He was a Medici, native to Milan, and father of three illegitimate children before his election. "Sanctity then was not the principal characteristic of this man, to whom

[90] *Concilium Tridentinum,* tome 7, pt. 4, vol. 1, p. 460.

[91] The draft of the chapters on the Mass as Sacrifice are found in *Concilium Tridentinum,* tome 7, pt. 4, vol. 1, pp. 475ff.

[however] would belong the credit of having resumed and finally accomplished the indispensable work of reform, both with vigor and with greater ability than his forerunner"[92] bringing the Council to completion.

Further discussion on the draft of the chapters and canons on sacrifice resulted in only minor changes. Trent's Decree on the Eucharist as sacrifice was issued in September of 1562.

> Inasmuch as under the Old Covenant (according to the testimony of the Apostle Paul) there was no perfection because of the weakness of the Levitical priesthood, it was necessary (because God the Father of mercies so decreed) that another priest should arise "according to the order of Melchizedek" (Gen 14:18; Ps 110:4; Heb 7:11), namely, Our Lord Jesus Christ, who could make perfect as many as were to be sanctified and lead them to perfection (Heb 10:14). Therefore, our God and Lord, although he was about to offer himself to God the Father through death on the altar of the Cross in order to effect an eternal redemption, nevertheless, because his priesthood was not to be extinguished by his death (Heb 7:24, 27), at the Last Supper, the "night on which he was betrayed" (1 Cor 11:13), declared himself to be forever constituted a priest "according to the order of Melchizedek" and offered his Body and Blood to God the Father under the appearance of bread and wine. He did this in order to leave his beloved Bride the Church a visible sacrifice as the nature of the human race demands, a visible sacrifice by which that bloody sacrifice to be accomplished once and for all on the Cross might be represented [Lat. *repraesentaretur*] and its memorial remain until the end of the world, and so that its saving power might be applied to the remission of those sins that we commit daily. Under the signs of these same realities he gave them over to be eaten by the Apostles (whom he then constituted priests of the New Covenant) and ordered them and their successors in the priesthood to offer them, saying, "Do this in memory of me" (Lk 22:19; 1 Cor 11:24). All this the Catholic Church has always understood and taught (cf. Canon II).

Having celebrated the old Passover, which the multitude of the

---

[92] Henri Daniel-Rops, *The Catholic Reformation*, I, p. 133.

children of Israel immolated [Lat. *immolabat*] in memory of their exodus from Egypt, he instituted the new Passover, namely, himself who was to be immolated under visible signs by the Church through priests in memory of his departure from this world to the Father, when, by the shedding of his Blood, he redeemed us and "snatched us from the power of darkness and transferred us into his Kingdom" (Col 1:13).

This is that clean oblation that cannot be defiled by any unworthiness or evil of those who offer it, which the Lord predicted through Malachi would be offered as a clean sacrifice to his Name, which would be great among the Gentiles (Malachi 1:11), and which the Apostle Paul, writing to the Corinthians, indicated to us in a fashion that was not obscure when he says that it is not possible for those who have been defiled by sharing in the table of devils to be sharers of the table of the Lord (1 Cor 10:21), the word *table* meaning an altar in both cases. This, finally, is that oblation that was prefigured by various types of sacrifices at the time of nature and of the law (Gen 4:4; 8:20; 12:8, etc.), inasmuch that it, as their fulfillment and completion, includes all the good things signified by them.

Chapter II

Therefore, inasmuch as in this divine sacrifice that is celebrated in the Mass the same Christ is contained and immolated in an unbloody manner who "offered himself in a bloody way once and for all" (cf. Heb 9:27) on the altar of the Cross, this holy synod teaches that this sacrifice is truly propitiatory (cf. Canon III) and that by means of it—if we draw near to God with a sincere heart and right faith, with fear and reverence, with sorrow and repentance— "we receive mercy and find grace at the appropriate time" (Heb 4: 16). By the offering of this sacrifice the Lord is pleased and forgives crimes and even great sins, granting grace and the gift of penitence. For the victim is one and the same, the same who then offered himself on the Cross now offering by the ministry of priests, only the manner of offering being different. Indeed the fruits of this bloody oblation are abundantly received through this unbloody oblation. It does so in such a way that the unbloody oblation takes nothing away from the bloody oblation. Therefore it is properly offered, according to the Tradition of the Apostles, not only for the sins, satisfactions, and other necessities of the faithful who are living but also for the dead in Christ who are not yet fully purified (cf. Canon III).

[The technique of using "the same" and "one and the same" to signify the identity of the Victim of the Cross and the Victim of the Mass is the same as the procedure used by the Council of Chalcedon (451) when it wished to express that Christ, although of two natures, was but One Person.]

Canons

Canon I: If anyone say that in the Mass there is not offered to God a true and proper sacrifice or that to be offered means no more than that Christ is given to us to eat, *anathema sit*.

Canon II: If anyone say that, by these words, "Do this in memory of me" (Lk 22:19; I Cor 11:24), Christ did not institute the Apostles as priests or did not ordain that they and other priests offer his Body and Blood, *anathema sit*.

Canon III: If anyone say that the sacrifice of the Mass is only one of praise and thanksgiving or a mere commemoration of the sacrifice accomplished on the Cross, or that it is of benefit only to the one who receives, or that it should not be offered for the living and the dead, for sins, punishments, satisfactions, and other necessities, *anathema sit*.

Canon IV: If anyone say that, through the sacrifice of the Mass, a blasphemy is offered to the most holy sacrifice of Christ on the Cross, or that the Mass takes away from that sacrifice, *anathema sit*.

Canon V: If anyone says that it is a pretense to celebrate Masses in honor of the saints and to obtain their intercession with God as the Church intends, *anathema sit*.

Canon VIII: If anyone say that the Masses in which the priest alone communicates sacramentally are illicit and should therefore be abrogated, *anathema sit* (DS 1738–44, 1750–55, 1758).[93]

---

[93] A good and balanced account of the discussions at the Council of Trent in reference to the Mass as sacrifice is found in David Power's *The Sacrifice We Offer*, pp. 50–135. Strong objection would have to be taken, however, to his understanding of Trent's teaching on the role of the priest, the nature of propitiation, and the role of the Church in offering and being offered in the Eucharistic sacrifice.

The remaining canons (i.e., VI, VII, IX) are devoted to the defense of the Canon of the Mass and liturgical practices. It can be noted of all the canons that there is a difference in form but not in essential content between the final and the earlier drafts.

In many ways, the decree of Trent on the Mass as sacrifice is a model of conciliar teaching. It sedulously avoided taking a position on any of the theological opinions legitimately disputed by Catholic theologians and was content to formulate the common Tradition. The essentials of that Tradition, as restated by Trent, were: each Mass is itself a true sacrifice, a memorial sacrifice of the sacrifice of Christ. As such, Christ willed that it be left to the Church to offer, and thus Trent implicitly indicates that it is the Church's sacrifice, even though Christ himself is the Victim and Priest of each Mass, offering himself now in an unbloody manner through the ministry of priests. The Mass is truly propitiatory, i.e., it atones and makes satisfaction for sins and benefits in this regard both the living and the dead. The values inherent in each offering of the sacrifice of the Mass are available not only to those who communicate in the Mass but to others as well.

From Trent to Vatican Council II

The Tridentine Decree did not, however, resolve all the questions involved. This was by set purpose, since the Council wanted only to teach what was certain, leaving theology free to present a synthesis that would be consistent with what the Council had taught. Clearly implied, but not elaborated on, was the role of the Church in offering the sacrifice. The Patristic notion, particularly the Augustinian one, that the Church too is offered in the sacrifice of her Head is not explicitly mentioned. This lack of elaboration, however, left unexplained the *novum* (the new element) present in each Mass. In like manner, while the *fact* of the propitiatory nature of the Mass was taught, nothing was said explicitly about the *nature* of the "propitiation" in each Mass, except that it availed for pleasing God, atoning for sin, and making satisfaction. Passed over were the more subtle discussions about the relation between the Supper, the Cross, and the Mass. And it must be noted, finally, that the language used by Trent in respect to sacrifice, particularly the words *mactatio, oblatio, repraesentare*, was to lead, in the ages subsequent to the Council, to a variety of theories that sought to explain how the Eucharist is a sacrifice. These theories also sought to take into account the relationship that existed between the sacrifice of the Cross, the institution of the Eucharist at the Supper, and the Mass, as well as the other elements left undecided or unelaborated on by Trent. The specifics of the theories differed greatly from author to author, but some modern writers of manuals of theology have conveniently grouped the multiform approaches into three general tendencies.[94]

First tendency: For the Mass to be a true sacrifice there is required an offering (*oblatio*) and some type of real destruction (*mactatio*) of the Victim. Those usually cited as proponents of this thesis are St. Robert Bellarmine and Cardinal Franzelin.

1. Bellarmine (1542–1621) thought that some form of *physical* destruction of the Victim was necessary, and such a destruction he saw as existing in the act of Eucharistic reception made by the priest who offers the Mass. In the act of receiving the Host, the Victim, already dedicated to God at the Consecration, was "destroyed" in the sense that, through the consumption of the Sacred Species by the priest, Christ lost his form of sacramental existence, i.e., was equivalently "destroyed". He wrote:

> Sacrifice is an eternal offering, made to God alone, in which some sensible and permanent thing is consecrated and changed in a mystical rite by a legitimate minister and done as a recognition of human dependence and a profession of the Divine Majesty.[95]

---

[94] Cf. especially, Aldama, *De SS. Eucharistia,* pp. 326–32, and Piolanti, *De Sacramentis,* pp. 287–97.

[95] Bellarmine, *De Missa,* 1, chap. 2, *Opera Omnia,* vol. 3, p. 477.

Bellarmine then explained each part of the definition in detail. When he came to explain the "and changed", he wrote:

> For a true sacrifice it is required that what is offered to God be fully destroyed, i.e., that it be changed in such a way that it ceases to be that which it was previously. . . . A reason for this is that sacrifice is the highest profession of our dependence on God and the supreme external act of worship by which such dependence can be shown. Such a supreme profession demands not only that there be offered to God the use of the thing, but even its very substance. Therefore, not only its use but its substance is consumed.[96]

> The Eucharistic Consecration pertains to the essence of sacrifice. . . . In the Eucharistic Consecration there occur three things in which the real definition of a true sacrifice is found. First, something profane [the bread and wine] becomes sacred. Bread, an earthly and common thing, is changed, by the Consecration, into the Body of Christ, the Most Holy of all things. Second, in the Consecration this sacred thing, which has been effected from the profane, is offered to God when it is placed on the altar. To place a victim on an altar is really to offer it to God, and, by the power of the Consecration, it comes about that the Body and Blood of Christ begin to be on the altar through the medium of the priest's hands. . . . Third, through the Consecration, the things that are offered are ordained toward a true, real, and eternal change and destruction, which destruction is required by the definition of sacrifice. Through the Consecration the Body of Christ takes on the form of food, and of food to be eaten, and so is ordained to change and destruction. The fact that the Body of Christ in itself suffers no wound or loses its natural being when the Eucharist is eaten is no obstacle to the destruction required. For the Body of Christ loses its sacramental manner of being and therefore really ceases to be on the altar and ceases to be sensible food.[97]

Bellarmine is not saying that the essence of the sacrifice is found in the Communion, as some who summarize him seem to imply.

---

[96] Bellarmine, *De Missa,* I, chap. 2, *Opera Omnia,* vol. 3, p. 478.
[97] Bellarmine, *De Missa,* I, chap. 27, *Opera Omnia,* vol. 3, pp. 324–25.

For Bellarmine, the essence of the sacrifice is found in the Consecration, but in the Consecration that makes present the Victim destined to be eaten.

The opinion of St. Robert was followed—at least in general—by many theologians, among them St. Alphonsus Liguori,[98] thus bringing it about that moral theologians in particular thought that the reception of the Eucharist—at least by the priest—was necessary for the existence of the sacrifice.

2. Cardinal Franzelin, following Lugo, thought that the destruction was found in the fact that the Consecration of the bread and wine "reduced" Christ to a state of being in which he is not naturally. Thus he was not literally "destroyed" but, from a moral estimation, was "reduced" to a lower state of being.[99] The manualists often place Suarez[100] and Scheeben[101] in this category, but erroneously, I believe.

There appears to be no modern Catholic theologian who holds any of the above views on the nature of the sacrifice, although the idea concerning the immolation or destruction of the Victim reappears, in a different perspective, in the third tendency below.

Second tendency: This theory would hold that for the Mass to be a sacrifice there need not be an immolation or destruction but only an (new) offering. The most famous propounder of such a theory is Maurice de la Taille, S.J., (1872–1933), whose monumental work *The Mystery of Faith* undoubtedly influenced at least a generation of students for the priesthood on a worldwide scale. For de la Taille, "sacrifice, in its proper sense, has two factors; the (outward) act of offering and the immolation. The victim *is either offered to be immolated, or is offered by immolation, or is offered as immolated.* Neither the offering alone nor the immolation alone

---

[98] Alphonsus Liguori (*Theologia Moralis,* I. 5, t. 3, c.3, dub 1, no. 310).

[99] Cf. Aldama; Piolanti, pp. 287–88.

[100] Cf. Suarez, *In III Part. D. Thomae,* disp. LXXV, sec. V, *Opera Omnia,* vol. 21.

[101] Cf. Scheeben, *The Mysteries of Christianity,* p. 507.

suffices to confer victimhood; both are required."[102] At the Last Supper, Christ made the offering of himself as the Victim "to be immolated"; on Calvary he offered himself by immolation; in the Mass, the Church offers him "as immolated". The Church's offering of Christ as immolated must be seen, however, in light of the eternity of Christ's sacrifice.

> The sacrifice of Christ . . . continues: not of course the active sacrifice, for the sacrificial action has passed, it is not repeated, nor is it in continual process of completion . . . ; the passive sacrifice, however, remains, for the Victim remains in its state of being as accepted Victim.[103]

> Our offering, just like the offering of Christ, involves an *immolation* in symbol or representation. . . . The *offering,* however, in the Mass, just as in the Supper is real and present (not represented as past or future only, like the immolation). Very rightly, then, do we say that in the Eucharistic celebration we truly offer to God, in a bloodless representation or sacramental commemoration, the very death in Blood of Christ. For it is one and the same thing to offer the Body of Christ as having suffered and died in the Passion as to offer the Passion and death of the Body; it is the same to offer the Blood as shed as to offer its shedding; the same to offer Christ as Victim of a past immolation as to offer that immolation itself.[104]

De la Taille had achieved great depth of thought by linking the Mass to the continuance of Christ's sacrifice in heaven, an insight frequently overlooked by theologians prior to him, even though the idea is traditional. He also recognized that the offering of the Mass, made by the Church, was totally dependent on Christ and that "we now offer sacrifice by virtue of that one sacrificial act carried out long ago by Christ himself".[105] He appeared, however, to make the offering of the Mass by the Church totally dependent on a past act of Christ. "The subordination [of our

[102] De la Taille, I, p. 14.
[103] De la Taille, I, p. 202.
[104] De la Taille, 2, pp. 23–24.
[105] De la Taille, 2, p. 24.

offering at Mass to Christ's offering of his sacrifice at the Supper]
would not be safeguarded . . . if one taught that Christ mingles,
with each one of our sacrifices, a new, personal sacrificial action of
his own."[106] This assertion appeared, at least, to overlook the
Church's conviction that Christ himself is the principal priest in
each Mass, as well as to attenuate de la Taille's own teaching on
the link between the Mass and the continuance of Christ's sacrifice
in heaven.[107]

Third tendency: The approach favored by almost all recent
Catholic theologians, especially after the various magisterial teachings of Pope Pius XII, is that which says the Mass is a sacrifice
because, in it, in a sacramental and mystical manner, Christ's
offering, immolation, and priestly activity in heaven become
effectively present for us, while he simultaneously subsumes into
his unique sacrifice the sacrificial offerings of the Church. This
view, already implied in much Patristic writing and resting on the
principles set forth by Aquinas, was always present—at least
vaguely—in the writings of many of the post-Reformation Catholic theologians. For all who advocate this view, it is true to say
that "the Mass is therefore neither a new sacrifice or a part of the
one sacrifice; it *is* the one sacrifice in its totality, present under
a sign."[108] Among the many advocates of this view, the names
Vonier,[109] Masure,[110] and Journet[111] are among the most prominent. Vonier (1875–1938) writes:

> Christ, who gave his Body and Blood to the Apostles at the Last
> Supper, was whole and entire at the head of the festive board. The
> Christ whose Body and Blood is on the Catholic altar is whole and

[106] De la Taille, 2, p. 25.

[107] Cf. E. L. Mascall, *Corpus Christi*, pp. 126–31, for a further critique of the
consequences of de la Taille's theory.

[108] Mascall, p. 135.

[109] A. Vonier, O.S.B., *A Key to the Doctrine of the Eucharist.*

[110] Eugene Masure, *The Christian Sacrifice.*

[111] C. Journet, *La Messe, présence du sacrifice de la Croix,* and "Note sur la
théologie de la Messe", *Nova et Vetera* 39 (1959): 303–8.

entire in heaven. Now the Body and Blood of the Eucharist are representation of the Christ in the state in which he was not whole and entire, but when he was broken up into parts on the Cross at his death. The Eucharistic Body and the Eucharistic Blood, therefore, at the Last Supper, were the representation . . . of the Christ who would be broken up the day after, not of the Christ who was there at the head of the table. The Eucharistic Body and the Eucharistic Blood on our altars are the representation . . . not of the Christ who is in heaven but again of the Christ who was broken up on Calvary.[112]

It is truly the *Christus passus* of St. Thomas who is thus contained in the Eucharist. In virtue of the Sacrament, the Eucharist contains, not the mortal Christ, or even the dying Christ; nor does it contain the glorious Christ; but it contains the Christ directly after his death, though without any of the gaping wounds. . . .

From this we see that a very important distinction is necessary when we speak of Christ as being contained in the Eucharist. At the Last Supper, when the mortal Christ celebrated the Eucharistic Mystery, in virtue of his direct act he was contained in the Eucharist in the same phase of his existence that was to come about soon after on Calvary; but in virtue of the concomitance he was contained in the fullness of the mortal phase of his divine Personality. If Mass had been celebrated during the three days of Christ's death, the Eucharist would have contained the second phase of the Christ-Personality, and nothing more; there would have been no other concomitant personal quality. Today on our altar, again in virtue of the Sacrament, we have that second or middle phase of the Christ-Personality; but in virtue of concomitance we have also the whole third phase in the Christ-Personality, the glorious phase. But when treating of the sacrifice we need not think of any other rendering present except that of the second phase of the Christ-Personality.[113]

What Vonier and the others are stressing is the notion that the Sacraments effect what they signify. The double Consecration

[112] Vonier, pp. 121–22.
[113] Vonier, pp. 131–32.

signifies the separation of Christ's Body and Blood, and so what is present as *signified* and therefore as effective is the death of Christ. As Masure puts it: "The signs instituted by Christ contain and make real what they represent. The Eucharist was instituted by Christ as the sign of the sacrifice of the Cross. Thus the Eucharist contains and makes real the sacrifice of the Cross."[114] The general outlines of this view are also to be found in those theologians and liturgists who, seeking a more Biblical model, have developed the notions of *memorial/anamnesis*. Grounding their thought in the Jewish celebration of Passover, which is not simply a mere commemoration of a past event but also a lived experience here and now of God's saving action, they indicate how the memorial Passover celebrated at the Supper by Jesus helps us understand his own command to repeat what he did as memorial of his saving work. The Eucharist is therefore, like the Jewish celebration, an *effective* memorial that makes God's saving benefits present. There is much in this that enriches the theology of the Eucharist, but it must be remembered that there is a uniqueness to the Eucharist that goes far beyond the Old Testament concept of memorial. The Eucharist is an effective memorial of Christ's saving action because the Priest-Victim is himself actually and corporeally present, thus memorializing his own work in a manner not possible for other memorial celebrations.

An advantage of this third tendency is that it is capable of including—in a way that the second tendency does not—the notion of immolation. However, in some of its earlier advocates only peripheral reference was made to the continued sacrifice of Christ in heaven, while St. Thomas' *Christum passum* was interpreted as if the *passum* were a present and not a past participle. St. Thomas was not saying that the death of Christ is present, but rather that the Christ who has suffered is present.

In specifics, of course, there are differences among the theologians who favor this third tendency, just as there were differences among the individual theologians favoring one or another of the

[114] Masure, p. 15.

first two tendencies. Journet (1891–1975), for example, held that, in the Mass, the very Passion of Christ is present and operative. This, he said, was possible because the Passion is not simply a past event but in some mysterious but real way perdures eternally. In essence this view was a variation of that proposed by Dom Odo Casel (1886–1948), who held that "in the Mass not only was Christ present but also his Passion, numerically identical with the immolation on the Cross. In the Mass, the sacrifice of the Cross is *re-presented,* i.e., the same sacrificial action, numerically identical, although in a manner that is sacramental, viz., one that is completely singular and surpassing all rational laws."[115] Most theologians have found such specifics difficult to accept. How, it is asked, can a past historical act (as distinguished from the person who performed the act and the consequences of the act) be present to us now? Despite the criticism, the theory often manifests itself in the significance some theologians give to the word *repraesentare* as found in Aquinas, Trent, and the modern Magisterium. The word is frequently translated by many of those who favor this third tendency—not only Casel and Journet—as "re-present" in the sense of "making present again" rather than in its proper sense—as found in Thomas and Trent—of "signify".

Elements of this third tendency were found in Matthias Scheeben (1835–88), the great German theologian of the nineteenth century. He also managed to retain some of the thought set forth by Bellarmine, which came to him by way of Suarez. Scheeben approached the Mystery of the sacrifice from the Mystery of transubstantiation.

> In the opinion of many theologians, transubstantiation pertains to the Eucharistic act of sacrifice only with reference to its term; that is, it vividly presents Christ as the true sacrificial Lamb in the bosom of the Church, and represents him under the visible sym-

---

[115] Piolanti, p. 297, 2. For Journet, cf. his "Note sur la théologie de la Messe", pp. 303–8. For Casel, see his work *The Mystery of Christian Worship and Other Writings.* Presentations and critiques of his thesis are given by L. Bouyer, *The Early Liturgy,* pp. 153ff., and *Liturgical Piety,* pp. 86ff.; Mascall, pp. 150ff.

bols of the immolation once accomplished in him. In all truth these two factors are absolutely essential, since on the one hand it is not the bread but Christ that is properly the victim to be offered, and on the other hand Christ is not really to be immolated anew, but his former bloody sacrifice is to be offered in an unbloody manner by symbolic representation.

. . .

Not the bread, but the Body of Christ, is the proper sacrificial victim of the Church, as it is of Christ himself. But the Body of Christ truly becomes the sacrifice of the Church only on the condition that the Church makes an offering of that Body to God from its own midst by changing the bread into it, and by this conversion pledges and effects the surrender of itself to God. And if this oblation is to be more than a simple offering made to God in connection with a sacrificial act already accomplished, and is to be offered in a new, genuine act of sacrifice, the conversion of another gift [the bread and wine] into this gift [the Body and Blood of Christ] must be brought about.

. . .

. . . The proffered gift [bread and wine] is not merely altered in such a way that something is done to it, but its entire essence is changed into another gift, and in this gift is transferred to God and accepted by him. Hence the value of the sacrificial action is not gauged by the value of the gift undergoing change but by the value of the gift into which it is changed. But this latter gift, on which the value of the action depends, is not in any way to be altered by the sacrificial act. For there is no question of giving Christ anew to his Father as his own, but of exhibiting and ratifying the union of the Church with the gift of Christ that has already been handed over to God.

. . .

In the Mass the bread that represents the natural side of the mystical Body of Christ is changed into the hallowed and glorified Body of Christ; under the veil of the sacramental species the Holy Spirit reenacts the miracle that he once wrought in the womb of

Mary, and again in the darkness of the sepulcher. By the celebration of the sacrificial act that takes place on this earth, the Church is to enter directly into union with the heavenly sacrifice Christ offers in the Body that is glorified.... The Eucharistic act of sacrifice bears the stamp of the immolation consummated on the Cross, and reenacts it vividly in its form and power, only so far as in the heavenly holocaust the immolation of the Cross is exhibited and offered in God's eternal remembrance, and this remembrance is visibly depicted to us in the separation of the Blood from the Body in the Eucharist by the difference between the species.[116]

It seems to us that Scheeben has captured and synthesized the most valuable insights of all three tendencies. At any rate, there is much to be gained from all the theories and their various proponents. Each adds a piece or a perspective to a mosaic that is ultimately a great Mystery; the once-and-for-all sacrifice of the Lord is made effectively present in the sacrifice of the Mass, and each sacrifice of the Mass incorporates into Christ's all-sufficient sacrifice the sacrifices and offerings of the Church.

Venerable Pius IX (1846–78)

The only major teaching on the Eucharist that comes from the man who inaugurated the modern phase of the papacy is found in a decree of the Holy Office, July 7, 1875. The decree is presented in terms of a (apparently) hypothetical question about the nature of the change involved in transubstantiation. The hypothesis was as follows: a substance is something that exists in itself or stands alone without existence in another. Now, after the Consecration, the bread and wine exist not in themselves but are sustained by the Body and Blood of Christ. By that very fact and without any other change, the bread and wine no longer fulfill the definition of substance, and so there has been a substantial change. The matter and form of the elements of bread and wine remain what

[116] Scheeben, pp. 506–9.

they were, but, as sustained by the Body and Blood of Christ, they are no longer substances. The Holy Office replied that, expounded in this fashion, the thesis "cannot be tolerated" (DS 3121–24).

The theory was propounded in the terminology of Aristotelian and Scholastic philosophy, and the answer must be understood in that context. What the answer is saying, nevertheless, is part of the perennial teaching of the Church. The elements of bread and wine do not remain "untouched" at the Consecration; they are not left as they were while being taken up into, or brought into a new relationship with, or "undergirded" by the Body and Blood of Christ. Rather they are changed in such a way that, in all truth, they are no longer bread and wine except in those aspects that can be perceived by the human senses.

Pius IX also consecrated the world to the Sacred Heart of Jesus in 1875, having already made the feast universal in 1856. His successors Pius XI and Pius XII, through their encyclical letters *Miserentissimus Redemptor* (1928) and *Haurietis aquas* (1956), developed the theological significance of this devotion with its particular practice of Mass and Communion on the first Friday of each month, closely linking it to devotion to the Eucharistic Christ.

Leo XIII (1878–1903)

Leo is the only Pope of this century, apart from Paul VI, to have written an encyclical on the Eucharist. He published *Mirae Caritatis* on the eve of the Feast of Corpus Christi, 1902, almost at the end of his long pontificate. It is fundamentally a devotional treatise, in which the Pope repeats traditional doctrine on the Eucharist and draws application for the spiritual life of Christians.

Indeed, men and nations, since of necessity they come from God, are not able to live or move or do anything of good except in God through Jesus Christ. Through Christ have come and do come all the best and choicest gifts. But of these gifts the source and chief of them all is the august Eucharist, which both nourishes and sustains life ... and immensely enhances human dignity.[117]

According to the Fathers of the Church, the Eucharist must be thought of as a certain continuation and extension of the Incarnation. Through it, the substance of the incarnate Word is linked with individual men and women, and, in an admirable manner, the supreme sacrifice of Calvary is renewed, as was foretold by the prophet Malachi, "In every place a clean oblation is sacrificed and offered to my Name." This miracle, the very greatest of its kind, is accompanied by innumerable miracles, for here all the laws of nature are suspended. The whole substance of bread and wine is converted into the Body and Blood of Christ; the appearances of bread and wine, subjects of no reality, are sustained by divine power.[118]

The Eucharist is, as it were, the soul of the Church, to which is directed the very fullness of priestly grace in all its levels. From this Sacrament the Church draws and possesses all her strength and glory, all the graces of the divine charisms, indeed, all good things.[119]

As did the Council of Trent previously, Leo encouraged frequent reception of the Eucharist by all the faithful. Nor did the author of *Rerum Novarum* overlook the beneficial effects of this Sacrament in fostering social justice. Noting the "arrogance, hardness of heart, and fraud among the more powerful and the misery, envy, and strife among the more weak", he saw in the charity and equality that flow from the participation in the one Christ the radical cure for such social evils.[120]

---

[117] Leo XIII, *Mirae Caritatis, Acta Leonis XIII,* 8, p. 113. A full English translation of the encyclical is found in Wynne, *The Great Encyclical Letters of Pope Leo XIII,* pp. 517ff., and in Sr. Claudia Carlen, ed., *The Papal Encyclicals: 1878–1903,* pp. 499ff.

[118] *Mirae Caritatis, Acta Leonis XIII,* 8, p. 114.

[119] *Mirae Caritatis, Acta Leonis XIII,* 8, p. 119.

[120] *Mirae Caritatis, Acta Leonis XIII,* 8, pp. 116–18.

St. Pius X (1903–14)

The successor of Leo XIII is known as the "Pope of the Eucharist" because of his determined efforts to root out the remains of those Jansenistic tendencies that delayed the reception of First Communion for children and militated against frequent reception of the Sacrament by adults. A major initiative in his campaign was the decree *Quam Singulari,* published at his direction by the Congregation for the Sacraments in 1910.

> Mindful of [the love of Christ for children] the Catholic Church, even from the beginning, took care to bring the little ones to Christ through Eucharistic Communion, even being accustomed to administer the Sacrament to nursing infants. This, as was prescribed in almost all the ancient books of rites, was done at Baptism until the thirteenth century, and this custom prevailed in some places even later. It is still preserved in the Greek and Oriental churches. However, to remove the danger that nursing infants especially might eject the consecrated Host, it was the custom from the beginning to administer the Eucharist to them only under the species of wine.
>
> Not only at Baptism but frequently thereafter infants were refreshed at the sacred meal. It was the custom of some Churches to give the Eucharist to the children immediately after the clergy; in other places, after the Communion of the adults, the remaining fragments were given to the children.
>
> Presently this practice died out in the Latin Church, and children were not permitted to be participants at the Sacred Table until they had come to the use of reason and had some knowledge of the august Sacrament. This new practice, already accepted by certain local synods, was solemnly confirmed by the Fourth Lateran Council in 1215, when it promulgated its celebrated Canon XXI [the *Omnis untriusque sexus*]. . . .
>
> The Council of Trent, in no way condemning the ancient discipline of administering the Eucharist to children before they had attained the use of reason, confirmed the decree of the Lateran Council. . . .
>
> Therefore, according to the still effective decree of the Lateran Council, the faithful are obliged, as soon as they arrive at the age

of discretion, to receive the Sacraments of Penance and the Eucharist at least once a year.

It is true that, in establishing the age of reason or discretion, not a few errors and deplorable abuses have been introduced during the course of time. There were some who thought that one age of discretion should be assigned for reception of the Sacrament of Penance and another for the Eucharist. For Penance they held that the age of discretion is reached when one can distinguish right from wrong, and thus be able to sin; for the Eucharist, however, there was required a greater age, one in which a fuller knowledge of the Faith and a more mature preparation of the soul could be had. As a result, because of various local customs and the opinions of men, the age established for the first reception of the Eucharist was placed at ten years or twelve, and in some places fourteen years or even more were required. . . .

This custom, under the appearance of safeguarding the august Sacrament, has kept the faithful from the Eucharist and been the cause of many evils. . . .

No less worthy of condemnation is the custom that prevails in many places of keeping from sacramental confession children who have not yet been admitted to the Eucharistic table, or of not granting them absolution.

. . .

Pope Pius IX, of happy memory, by means of a letter of Cardinal Antonelli to the bishops of France, March 12, 1866, severely condemned the growing custom existing in some dioceses of postponing the first Communion of children until more mature years along with the ages fixed for this.

. . .

[Therefore the following is decreed:]

I. The age of discretion, both for Confession and for Holy Communion, is that at which a child begins to reason, that is, about the seventh year, perhaps a little above or even a little below. From that time begins the obligation of fulfilling the precept of both confession and Communion.

II. For first confession and first Communion there is not necessary a full and perfect knowledge of Christian doctrine.

. . .

III. The knowledge of religion that is required in a child in order to be properly prepared for first Communion is that by which the child will understand according to his capacity those Mysteries of Faith that are necessary as a means of salvation and can distinguish between the Eucharistic bread and ordinary, bodily bread. . . .

. . .

VII. The custom of not admitting children to confession or of not absolving them even when they have already reached the use of reason must be totally disapproved. The Ordinary of the diocese shall see to it that this custom is completely done away with, even by using the remedies of canon law.[121]

Pius XII (1939–58)

The pontificate of Eugenio Pacelli was of great importance for the theological and liturgical life of the Church. He began the liturgical reforms that would be completed by the Second Vatican Council and its postconciliar commissions; he mitigated the Eucharistic fast that previously had involved abstinence from food and water from the midnight preceding Communion; he renewed reflection on the Church as Body of Christ, thus eventually giving ecclesiology a Eucharistic orientation. Particularly notable are the contributions of his encyclical letters *Mystici Corporis Christi* and *Mediator Dei.*

Mystici Corporis Christi (On the Mystical Body of Christ) (June 29, 1943)

The things we have proposed up to this point about the intimate union of the mystical Body of Christ with its Head would be incomplete—so it seems to us—if at this point we did not add at least something about the most holy Eucharist by which this union is led to its culminating point, as it were, in this life.

---

[121] Pius X, *Quam singulari; AAS,* 2 (1910), pp. 577–83.

Christ the Lord willed, indeed, that this union—to be marveled at and never sufficiently honored with praise—be manifested to the faithful in a particular manner through the Eucharistic sacrifice. In this sacrifice the ministers of the sacred things act not only in the place of Our Savior but also in the place of each of the members of the whole Mystical Body. In the Eucharistic sacrifice the faithful themselves, joined together in common offerings and prayers, offer the immaculate Lamb, made present on the altar by the voice of the priest alone, to the eternal Father. They do so through the hands of the same priest, offering the most pleasing victim of praise and satisfaction for the needs of the entire Church. Just as the divine Redeemer, dying on the Cross, offered himself as Head of the whole human race to the eternal Father, so also in "this clean oblation" (Malachi 1:11), he, as Head of the Church, offers not only himself but, in himself, all his mystical members.[122]

Mediator Dei (November 20, 1947)

The Church, therefore, faithfully obeying the command she has received from her Founder, effects the priestly office of Jesus Christ especially through the sacred liturgy. And she does this in the first place at the altars where the sacrifice of the Cross is perpetually represented [Lat. *repraesentatur*] and renewed, only the manner of offering being different.[123]

In every liturgical action her divine Founder is present with the Church; Christ is present in the august sacrifice of the altar both in the person of his minister and especially under the Eucharistic species; he is present in the Sacraments by his power, which he pours into them as instruments for effecting holiness; he is present finally in the prayers and supplications lifted up to God, as he said, "Where two or three are gathered in my Name, there am I in the midst of them" (Mt 18:20).[124]

The head and center, as it were, of the Christian religion is the Mystery of the most holy Eucharist, which Christ the high priest

[122] Pius XII, *Mystici Corporis Christi; AAS,* 35 (1943), p. 232.
[123] Pius XII, *Mediator Dei; AAS,* 39 (1947), p. 522.
[124] *Mediator Dei; AAS,* 39, p. 528.

once instituted and which he ordered to be perpetually renewed [Lat. *renovari*] through his ministers. . . .

. . .

Therefore the august sacrifice of the altar is no mere and simple commemoration of the Crucifixion and death of Jesus Christ but rather a true and proper act of sacrifice [Lat. *sacrificatio*] by which, through an unbloody immolation, the High Priest does that which he already did on the Cross, offering himself as a most acceptable victim to the eternal Father. . . .

It is the same priest, whose sacred Person his minister bears. . . .

It like manner, it is the same Victim, namely, the divine Redeemer according to his human nature and in the truth of his Body and Blood. Nevertheless, the manner in which Christ is offered is different. On the Cross he offered himself and all his sufferings completely to God, and the immolation of the Victim was effected through a bloody death, undertaken with a free will. On the altar, however, because of the glorious state of his human nature, "death has no more dominion over him" (Rom 6:9), and therefore a shedding of Blood is not possible. Nevertheless, according to the plan of divine wisdom, the sacrificial act of our Redeemer is shown forth in a manner to be marveled at by means of external signs that are indications [Lat. *indices*] of his death. Indeed, through the transubstantiation of the bread into his Body and the wine into the Blood of Christ, just as his Body is really present, so is his Blood. Moreover, the Eucharistic species, under which he is present, signify [Lat. *figurant*] the bloody separation of his Body and Blood. Therefore the memorial showing forth [Lat. *memorialis demonstratio*] of his death, which really took place on Calvary, is repeated in every sacrifice of the altar, as often as, through the distinct indications, Jesus Christ in the state of victim is signified and shown forth.[125]

---

[125] *Mediator Dei; AAS,* 39, pp. 547–48. He repeats the same idea succinctly later in the encyclical when he writes: "It must be noticed again and again that the Eucharistic sacrifice is by its nature the unbloody immolation of the divine Victim which is clear in a mystical manner from the separation of the species" (*AAS,* 39, p. 563).

Moreover the august sacrifice of the altar is, as it were, the very special [Lat. *eximium*] instrument by which the merits originating from the Cross of the divine Redeemer are distributed to believers. ... This sacrifice in no way diminishes the dignity of the bloody sacrifice; rather it declares and makes evident its greatness and necessity, as the Council of Trent taught. While it is offered daily, it teaches us that there is no other salvation except in the Cross of Our Lord Jesus Christ, and that God himself has willed that the continuation of that sacrifice be effected from the "rising of the sun to its setting" (Malachi 1:11).[126]

Moreover it is clear that the faithful offer the sacrifice through the hands of the priest from the fact that the minister of the altar bears the person of Christ as Head of the Body, offering in the name of all the members of the Body. Thus it comes about that the whole Church is rightly said to make the oblation of the Victim through Christ.[127]

And it is not to be said that, by Eucharistic adoration, the historical Christ who once lived on earth and the Christ present in the august Sacrament of the altar and the Christ who triumphs gloriously in heaven are simultaneously mixed together in some false manner. Rather it is to be asserted that, in this manner [viz., Eucharistic adoration], the faithful testify to and solemnly make evident the Faith of the Church according to which the Word of God and the Son of the Virgin Mary who suffered on the Cross, who lies present hidden in the Eucharist, and who reigns in heaven are believed to be identical.[128]

Pius XII's efforts were directed at a renewal that was faithful to Tradition. While he was Pope there began those theological discussions on the Eucharist and especially on the nature of transubstantiation whose full effect would be seen in later years. That the Pope considered some of the discussion to have passed acceptable

---

[126] *Mediator Dei; AAS,* 39, pp. 551–52.
[127] *Mediator Dei; AAS,* 39, p. 556.
[128] *Mediator Dei; AAS,* 39, p. 570.

bounds is evident from the words of warning he included in the encyclical *Humani Generis* in 1950.

> Nor are there wanting those who contend that the doctrine of transubstantiation, as founded upon an antiquated notion of substance, should be corrected in order that the Real Presence of Christ in the most holy Eucharist be reduced to a certain kind of symbolism so that the consecrated species would be only efficacious signs of the spiritual Presence of Christ and of his intimate union with his faithful members in the mystical Body (DS 3891).

Other important items of theological discussion during the reign of Pius XII centered on the value to be attached to the celebration of the Mass, and the nature and value of a priest celebrating a "private" Mass as opposed to the same priest, with greater devotion, attending a Mass and communicating. Much of the discussion centered on various positions taken by Karl Rahner.

In 1949 Rahner published a work entitled "The Many Masses and the One Sacrifice".[129] Rahner asked whether it was true to say that the offering of many Masses gave more glory to God than the offering of one Mass. In an effort to answer that question he pointed to a truth accepted by all of Catholic theology: the sacrifice of the Cross is all-sufficient. What is new in every Mass is not primarily the self-offering of Christ but the liturgical offering made by the Church of Christ's one sacrifice. In this, Rahner was fundamentally following the position set forth by de la Taille. He concluded, however, that, although "the sacrifice of the Mass remains primarily and chiefly Christ's act",[130] "from the point of

---

[129] The original work by Rahner was republished, with the cooperation of Angelus Haussling, in an updated edition as *The Celebration of the Eucharist.* This edition takes into account the many criticisms aimed at the original and attempts to answer them. The book basically maintains the original thesis, even asserting it to be in conformity with the teaching of Pius XII and Paul VI in *Mysterium Fidei* (cf. pp. 104–5). This assertion, however, does not seem tenable in any way. A fine study of Rahner's thesis is that of H. Francis Davis, "The Pope and Private Masses".

[130] Rahner and Haussling, p. 95.

view of increasing the honor of God . . . Mass is to be said as often as is necessary or useful for the human beings (the Church) actually taking part in each particular Mass actually to share as intimately and personally as possible in Christ's sacrifice on the Cross".[131] This is so because the honor offered to God as well as the benefits or fruits derived from the Mass—aside from its purely cultic value as an offering of the Church—depends on the faith and devotion of those participating. As consequent conclusions, Rahner wrote:

> We should probably be right in saying nowadays that personal union with Christ's sacrifice on the Cross will be less if a greater number of Masses is celebrated than it would be if, instead of celebrating themselves, the various priests were to assist at one Mass in as close a manner as possible.[132]

> The celebrant as such . . . does not receive more of the fruit of the Mass than one of the faithful who hears Mass or than he himself does when he simply assists at Mass, if we assume the *devotio* in each case to be the same.[133]

> As regards the measure of its fruits, it does not in itself matter (i.e., leaving out of account whether one or other way of taking part in the Mass is more favorable to the degree of *devotio*) in which of the possible ways a person takes part in the Mass (celebration as priest, participation as layman, concelebration, making the Mass possible by providing the materials of the offering by the stipend). . . . Therefore if the disposition is assumed to be the same in each, each can receive the same benefit from the Mass, quite without regard to the particular way in which each takes part.[134]

---

[131] Rahner and Haussling, p. 36.

[132] Rahner and Haussling, pp. 100–101.

[133] Rahner and Haussling, p. 84. In this work, Rahner refers to the question of gradated fruits of the Mass (a "general fruit, a special fruit, a most special fruit" referring to the Church, the person(s) who take part or for whom it is offered, the priest, respectively) and says, "It is impossible to trace the distinction further back than Duns Scotus" (p. 54). As seen above, this is not accurate. The distinction (without the specifics of "general-special–most special") is found in Aquinas and, in some form, probably even earlier in Lombard.

[134] Rahner and Haussling, pp. 83–84. This aspect of the Rahnerian thesis is

Pius XII responded negatively to the central concerns of the Rahnerian thesis in an allocution of November 2, 1954.[135] He returned to critique the thesis even more strongly the following year, repeating and amplifying much of what he said in the earlier talk.

[In our previous talk we said the following:] The celebrating priest, acting in the person of Christ, sacrifices—and he alone, not the people or clerics or even priests who piously and religiously assist the priest who performs the rite, even though all of these are able to have and do have certain active parts in the sacrifice. We stressed that, failing to distinguish between the question about the celebrant's participation in the fruits of the sacrifice of the Mass and the nature of the action that he performs, one arrives at the conclusion that "the celebration of one Mass that one hundred priests assist at with religious devotion is the same thing as Masses celebrated by a hundred priests". About that affirmation, we said: "It should be rejected as erroneous." We added by way of explanation: "As far as the offering of the Eucharistic sacrifice is concerned, there are as many actions of Christ the High Priest as there are celebrating priests; in no way are there as many actions of Christ as there are priests piously assisting at a Mass celebrated by a bishop or priest. Those who are present at Mass in no way bear or act in the person of Christ offering sacrifice but

---

not, in all aspects, a new theory. It appears to be at least similar to the position held by Cajetan, who, commenting on the *S.Th.*, III, 8. 79, a. 5 (a text of Aquinas often cited by Rahner, although only partially, since he omits the first paragraph), wrote: "Therefore people who ignorantly seek or demand that, for their offering, the entire Mass be offered for them or for their dead are to be both challenged and instructed. For a person will have no less if a thousand others seek the same Mass for themselves and their dead than if it is said to be celebrated for one person only" (*S.Th.* [Leonine, ed., vol. 12] commentary on III, 8. 79, a. 5). Cajetan, however, did not hold that the offering of one Mass could be the same, because of devotion, as the offering of a hundred. Cf. de la Taille, 2, Thesis XXVIII, pp. 269–89, esp. p. 275, for a good, although complex, study of the fruits of the Mass and of stipends.

[135] Cf. Pius XII, "Allocution of November 2, 1954"; *AAS,* 46 (1954), pp. 668ff.

rather are to be compared to the Christian laity who are present at the sacrifice."

. . .

The central element of the Eucharistic sacrifice is that in which Christ intervenes as "offering himself"—to use the very terms of the Council of Trent. This happens at the Consecration where, in the act of transubstantiation worked by the Lord, the celebrating priest "acts in the person of Christ". If the Consecration takes place in simplicity, without festivity, it is the central point of the whole liturgy of sacrifice, the central point of the "action of Christ in whose person the celebrant acts"—or the "concelebrants act", in the case of a true concelebration. . . . When the Consecration of the bread and wine is validly effected, the whole action of Christ himself is accomplished. If all that remains could not be accomplished, nothing essential would still be lacking in the Lord's offering.

. . .

Thus, it is not permitted to affirm that "the only decisive question in the last analysis is to know in what measure personal participation, sustained by the grace one receives in that cultic offering, increases the participation in the Cross and in the grace of Christ who unites us with himself and with each other." We have already rejected this inexact manner of posing the question in the allocution of November 2, 1954, but certain theologians are still not able to accept it. And so we repeat: the decisive question (for concelebration as well as for the Mass of one priest) does not consist in knowing what fruit the soul receives but rather in the nature of the act that is effected. Does the priest, as minister of Christ, perform "the action of Christ sacrificing and offering himself" or does he not? . . . In celebration and concelebration, it is necessary to see whether, along with the necessary interior intention, the celebrant accomplishes the external action and above all pronounces the words that constitute "the action of Christ sacrificing and offering himself". This is not verified when the priest does not pronounce over the bread and wine the words of the Lord "This is my Body", "This is my Blood."[136]

[136] Pius XII, "Allocution *Vous Nous avez demandé*" to the International

In summary what the Pope was saying was this:

1. One must carefully distinguish between the objective value of each Mass and the question that concerns the effects of each Mass on those who offer or participate in it. Although Pius makes no reference to it, this was the distinction already made by Aquinas.[137] The value of the Mass ultimately depends upon the fact and nature of Christ's own activity in and through it. In some real and valuable way Christ himself acts each time his minister consecrates. The question of how much good is done to and for the celebrating priest, the community present, the person who offered the stipend, etc., is an important question—and one that the Pope does not treat directly. What he does say, however, is that Christ's work, the Mass, is not measured in value by its effects (immediate or remote) on those celebrating or participating.

2. Furthermore, in Christ the entire Church is somehow present and offering at each Mass, i.e., the Church in heaven, here on earth, and in Purgatory.[138] Even apart from subjective dispositions, the whole Mystical Body is engaged in the mystery of Christ's sacrifice and expresses that engagement in each Mass, even the so-called private ones. The Pope did not spell out the nature of

Congress on Pastoral Liturgy, Sept. 1956; *AAS*, 48 (1956), pp. 716–18. An English translation is found in *TPS*, Winter 1956–57, pp. 273ff.

[137] See above, pp. 197–200, for Aquinas on the distinction between Eucharist as Sacrament and sacrifice and the "gradated level" of participation in the fruits. Rahner, who frequently cites the *Summa* article (III, q. 79, a. 5), never refers to the first paragraph, which contains the distinction, nor does he refer to the above-cited quotation from question 7 of the same question.

[138] As Pius XII noted in the excerpt cited, Trent had already taught, at least implicitly, that the Mass is always a public act since it is offered by the priest who acts as the representative for the whole Mystical Body. In its chapter 6, which treats of those Masses in which the priest alone communicates, it said: "These Masses are to be considered truly public because . . . they are celebrated by the public minister of the Church, not for himself alone, but for all the faithful who belong to the Body of Christ" (DS 1747). It is true that Trent is not speaking here of a Mass where a congregation is not present but only of one where the congregation does not communicate, but the principle applied for the one situation is equally valid for the other.

this engagement and its effects, and they must be left for further discussion.

3. The essential and sacrificial aspects of the Mass are completed in the Consecration, said the Pope. As a consequence it must be said that Communion by the priest himself, or concelebrants, or the faithful—however important they be for other reasons or for the proper integrity of the Mass—cannot be said to be required for a valid offering of the sacrifice.

4. From all this it follows that—apparently by the institution of Christ himself or, at least, by determination of the Church—a valid concelebration by priests is effected only when all the concelebrants actually say the words of Consecration.[139]

Paul VI (1963–78)

Having succeeded John XXIII, who had convoked the Second Vatican Council on October 11, 1962, Giovanni Battista Montini inherited the difficult task of completing the work that had been started and of guiding the Church during the postconciliar years, which were often theologically and pastorally turbulent. Under Paul VI, Vatican II's *Constitution on the Sacred Liturgy* (*Sacrosanctum Concilium*) was published (1963). Its teaching was implemented through numerous papal directives issued over the years subsequent to the Council's close (December 8, 1965) and constituted the most sweeping changes in the Eucharistic liturgy of the Roman Rite since the reforms of Pius V after the Council of Trent. A new

---

[139] It is disputed whether historically it was always the case in concelebrations that all the concelebrants actually pronounced the consecratory words. Whatever the historical question, it is clear that such pronouncement of the words is now necessary for a valid concelebration. That is to say: if a concelebrating priest does not pronounce the words of Consecration, he is not in fact offering the Mass. A year following Pius XII's talk there was issued a declaration of the Holy Office, which said that "by the institution of Christ, only one who pronounces the consecratory words validly celebrates" (*AAS,* 49 [1957], p. 370). This decision is still the effective norm, although it appears that even as late as 1966 Rahner and Haussling (pp. 107–9) considered it questionable.

Sacramentary was published and ultimately included several Eucharistic Prayers as alternatives to the venerable Roman Canon. A revised *Lectionary* was issued that expanded the number and variety of the readings from Sacred Scripture. Celebration of Mass in the vernacular languages was permitted, as was a change in the position of the altar of sacrifice so that the priest made the offering facing the congregation. Provision was made for reception of the Eucharist by the faithful under both Species. The Order of Diaconate was restored as a permanent body. The laity, under certain conditions, were allowed to serve as Extraordinary Ministers of the Eucharist, administering the Eucharist both at Mass and to the sick at home and in hospitals.[140]

The scope and the rapidity of the many changes occasioned strong opposition in some parts of the Western Church and were accompanied by widespread abuses in others. The difficulties were compounded by the theological discussions and writings about the Eucharist that have been described in the previous section.[141] Even before the close of the Council, Paul VI found it

[140] The norms for the exercise of such an extraordinary ministry are found in the 1983 Code of Canon Law. They read: "Where the need of the Church urges it due to a lack of ministers, even the laity who may not be lectors or acolytes may exercise certain of their functions, namely, that of exercising a ministry of the word, presiding at liturgical prayers, conferring Baptism and distributing Communion in accordance with the provisions of the law" (Canon 230, 3).

"The ordinary minister of Holy Communion is the bishop, priest and deacon.

"The extraordinary minister of Holy Communion is the acolyte or another member of the faithful who is deputized according to the norms of Canon 230, 2." (Canon (910, 1–2).

Because of certain abuses in the use of the extraordinary ministers, the Pontifical Commission for the Interpretation of the Code of Canon Law, in a decision of Feb. 20, 1987, stated that, when the ordinary ministers are present in sufficient numbers, even if they are not celebrating, and are not impeded by other obligations, the extraordinary ministers are not permitted to distribute Holy Communion.

[141] Cf. above, p. 152ff.

necessary to respond to the theological issues being raised by publishing the encyclical *Mysterium Fidei.*

The encyclical, published on the Feast of Pius X, September 3, 1965, begins by referring to the Constitution on the Sacred Liturgy of Vatican II with its reaffirmation of the Eucharist, Sacrament and sacrifice, as the center of the Church's life. The Pope then notes what he calls "causes for pastoral concern and anxiety", among which he lists a lack of appreciation for the so-called private Mass (i.e., a Mass said by a priest without a congregation in attendance), an excessive concern with Eucharistic "symbolism", theological writings that seemed to say or imply that transubstantiation means no more than "transignification" or "transfinalization", and the proposal and even putting into practice of the idea that, after the celebration of the Mass, Christ no longer remains in the consecrated Species. Of all such concerns, Paul VI writes: "Everyone can see how these and similar opinions, once spread, do great harm to faith in and devotion to the Eucharist."[142]

Paul VI then recalls various truths to be remembered when one is dealing with the Eucharist. It is, first of all, "the mystery of faith", containing, he says quoting Leo XIII's *Mirae Caritatis,* a singular abundance of miracles. Because it is a mystery in the strict sense, one cannot rely simply on human reason but needs to cling to divine revelation. As examples of a proper approach to the Eucharist, the Pope cites Sts. Peter, John Chrysostom, Aquinas, and Bonaventure. Then, in a presentation that was subsequently made more precise by the declaration *Mysterium Ecclesiae,* he indicated that, in order to preserve divine revelation, one must be cautious in the use of language. It is true that theological formulations can be rendered clearer and more precise as our understandings of the revealed Mysteries develop, but no one is permitted to

---

[142] Paul VI, *Mysterium Fidei; AAS,* 57 (1965), p. 755 (nos. 10–12). English translation of the encyclical can be found in *TPS,* 10, no. 4, pp. 309ff., and in Sr. Claudia Carlen, etc. The Latin original in the *AAS* is not subdivided into numbered paragraphs. Therefore, after the *AAS* citation I have included the paragraph references in the *TPS* translation.

change on one's own authority the theological formulations made by the Magisterium of the Church.[143]

The Pope then proceeds to recall the chief truths connected with the Eucharist. First of all, he writes, it is "through the Eucharistic Mystery that the sacrifice of the Cross, completed once and for all on Calvary, is represented [Lat. *repraesentari*] in a wonderful manner, is always called to mind, and its saving power is applied for the forgiveness of the sins that we commit daily."[144] It is, furthermore, a sacrifice that avails the souls in Purgatory as well as the living, and a sacrifice in which Christ associates with himself as Priest and Victim all the members of the Church, priests and victims in and through him.[145]

Because of its very nature as the sacrifice of Christ and the Church, no Mass is "private", even when the priest celebrates alone with a server. "From such a Mass comes a most ample supply of special graces for the salvation of the priest himself, as well as for all the faithful, the whole Church, and the entire world, and this same supply of graces is not obtained through Holy Communion alone."[146] Here the Pope has taken up the question already addressed by Pius XII in the dispute over the significance of the so-called private Mass, and, in taking it up, reaffirmed the teaching of his predecessor. A priest who communicates without himself offering the Mass is not effecting for the Church what is effected by his celebration of the Mass. Therefore, because of the objective value of every Mass—even the so-called private Mass—the priest is urged to celebrate Mass daily.

[143] *Mysterium Fidei; AAS,* 57, pp. 757–58 (nos. 23–25).

[144] *Mysterium Fidei; AAS,* 57, p. 759. The *TPS* translation renders *repraesentarti* as "reenacted" (no. 27).

[145] *Mysterium Fidei; AAS,* 57, pp. 760–61 (nos. 30–31).

[146] *Mysterium Fidei; AAS,* 57, p. 762 (no. 32). It is to be noted that the requirement of having at least one server at such "private" Masses is a positive liturgical norm of the Church that does not oblige when a server is not available. The truth of the public nature of every Mass was, as seen above, already taught by Pius XII and rests, at least implicitly, on the teaching of the Council of Trent (DS 1747).

The Pope then turns to the nature of Christ's Presence in the Mass, which was, in fact, the central issue involved in the debates of theologians at the time.[147] Elaborating on paragraph 7 of Vatican II's *Sacrosanctum Concilium,* Paul mentions the various ways in which Christ is present in his Church. He is present in his Church as she prays, performs works of mercy, and moves on her pilgrimage through history—indeed, wherever two or three are gathered in his Name (cf. Mt 18:20). Christ is present in the Church as she preaches—not just in the liturgical celebrations but as she proclaims the gospel everywhere—and as the Church is governed through the bishops. The Lord is present, in a more sublime manner, as the Church offers (Lat. *immolanti*) the sacrifice of the Mass in his Name. At Mass, as the Pope has already indicated, Christ is present in the people at prayer, in the proclamation and preaching of the word, and, as the Council had already said, "in the person of the minister".[148] All these manners of Christ's Presence, says Paul VI, are "real" and "fill the mind with wonder and offer the Church a Mystery to contemplate. But there is another type [of Presence], indeed the outstanding one, according to which Christ is present to his Church in the Sacrament of the Eucharist ... which is, as it were, the consummation of the spiritual life and the goal of all the sacraments. This Presence is called 'real'—not by way of exclusion as if the others were not 'real'—because of its excellence, i.e., it is substantial Presence by which Christ, God and man, becomes present whole and entire."[149]

Therefore it is wrong for anyone to explain this type of presence by inventing a so-called pneumatic nature for Christ's glorious Body, according to which it would be everywhere present, or to restrict this Presence within the limits of symbolism as if this august Sacrament is nothing other than an efficacious sign "of the

[147] Cf. above, p. 157ff.
[148] *Sacrosanctum Concilium,* 7.
[149] *Mysterium Fidei; AAS,* 57, pp. 763–64 (nos. 38–39).

spiritual Presence of Christ and his intimate union with the faithful members in his mystical Body."[150]

There is much rich symbolism in the Eucharistic Mystery, writes Paul VI, but symbolism is not sufficient to explain the unique Eucharistic Presence of the Lord. Among those who have borne witness to the inadequacy of symbolism, the Pope cites the writings of Ignatius of Antioch, Theodore of Mopsuestia, and the Council of Trent.

Symbolism is not sufficient, of course, because of the nature of the change that takes place in the elements of bread and wine. Citing Leo XIII again and calling the Eucharist the "greatest miracle of all in its kind",[151] Paul VI situates "transfinalization" and "transignification" within the context of transubstantiation.

> The voice [of the Church], which always echoes the voice of Christ, makes us certain that Christ becomes present in this Sacrament in no other way than through the change of the whole substance of bread into his Body and the whole substance of wine into his Blood, which change, truly marvelous and unique, the Catholic Church suitably and properly calls transubstantiation. When transubstantiation has taken place, the appearances [Lat. *species*] of bread and wine undoubtedly take on a new signification and a new finality since they are no longer common bread and common drink but rather the sign of a sacred reality and a sign of spiritual food; but they take on this new signification and new finality because they contain a new "reality", which we rightly call "ontological". Under those appearances [*species*] there now lies hidden not what was there previously but something completely different. And it is different not only according to the judgment of the Church's Faith but rather in reality itself because, once the substance or nature of bread and wine has been changed into the Body and Blood of Christ, nothing remains of the bread and wine except the appearances [*species*] alone. Under these appearances [*species*], the whole and entire Christ is present in his physical

---

[150] *Mysterium Fidei; AAS,* 57, p. 764 (no. 39). The citation within the text is to Pius XII's encyclical *Humani Generis* (*AAS,* 42, p. 578).

[151] *Mysterium Fidei; AAS,* 57, p. 766 (no. 46).

"reality", indeed, is bodily [Lat. *corporaliter*] present, although not in the way in which bodies are present in place.[152]

The Pope then cites abundant Patristic and Magisterial evidence to the teaching just set forth and cites St. Augustine on the consequent duty the Christian has to offer adoration to the Sacrament of the Lord's Flesh.[153] This adoration of the Sacrament is shown in a special way on the Feast of Corpus Christi and in the visits paid by the faithful to their churches where the Blessed Sacrament is to be reserved in a "most noble place", such visits being the "proof of a soul filled with gratitude, a pledge of love, and the carrying out of the adoration that is due [to the Sacrament]".[154] Reserved in the tabernacle, "Christ is truly Emmanuel, God with us."

> For day and night he is in our midst, dwelling among us full of grace and truth. He establishes good morals, nourishes virtues, consoles the sorrowing, strengthens the weak, and calls to all who approach him to imitate him so that, from his example, they may learn to be meek and humble of heart, seeking not their own interests but those of God.[155]

> [Such visits will lead a person to experience] what great value there is in conversing with Christ. Here on earth there is nothing more pleasant, nothing more efficacious for advancing on the road to holiness.[156]

[152] *Mysterium Fidei; AAS,* 57, p. 766 (no. 46).

[153] The citation from Augustine is the one cited above on p. 59.

[154] *Mysterium Fidei; AAS,* 57, p. 771 (no. 66). The reference to "a most noble place" was later carried into Church legislation. Canon 938, secs. 2 and 3, of the 1983 Code of Canon Law reads: "The tabernacle in which the most Blessed Sacrament is reserved must be situated in a distinguished part of the church or oratory, a part of the church or oratory that is conspicuous, properly adorned, and suitable for prayer. The tabernacle in which the most holy Eucharist is habitually reserved is to be immovable, made out of solid and nontransparent material, and closed in such a way as to avoid, as much as is possible, any danger of being profaned."

[155] *Mysterium Fidei; AAS,* 57, p. 771 (no. 67).

[156] *Mysterium Fidei; AAS,* 57, pp. 771–72 (no. 67).

The worship of the divine Eucharist greatly promotes the culti-
vation of a "social" love, by which we place the common good
ahead of our personal good, taking up the cause of the community,
the parish, the universal Church and extending our charity to the
whole world, since we know that the members of Christ are
present everywhere.[157]

Paul VI ends the encyclical by recalling that truth that runs as a
constant theme throughout the whole history of the Church's
teaching on the Eucharist. He invokes the prayers of Mary, "from
whom Christ the Lord assumed that Flesh that in this Sacrament
'is contained, offered, and received' under the appearances of
bread and wine".[158]

The *Creed of the People of God*

The profession of faith made by St. Peter at Capernaum has been
made to echo in our own age by means of the inclusion of the
Eucharist, for the second time in the history of the Church, in a
Creed, a solemn profession of faith. Paul VI may be said to have
completed his defense of the Eucharistic Mystery by his publication of the *Creed of the People of God* on June 30, 1968. There, in
the name of the entire Church, he proclaimed:

We believe that the Mass, which is celebrated by a priest acting
in persona Christi, by the power received through the Sacrament
of Orders, and which is offered by the priest in the name of Christ
and of the members of his Mystical Body, is truly the sacrifice of
Calvary that is made sacramentally present on our altars. We
believe that the bread and wine consecrated by the Lord at his Last
Supper were changed into his Body and Blood, which were to be
offered for us on the Cross. Likewise the bread and wine consecrated by the priest are changed into the Body and Blood of
Christ, now gloriously seated in heaven. And we believe that the
Presence of the Lord—hidden under the appearance of these realities,

---

[157] *Mysterium Fidei; AAS,* 57, p. 772 (no. 69).
[158] *Mysterium Fidei; AAS,* 57, p. 774 (no. 75).

which continue to appear to our senses as they were before—is truly, really, and substantially present.

Therefore in this Sacrament, Christ is not able to be present other than through a change of the whole substance of bread into his Body and a change of the whole substance of wine into his Blood, while the properties of bread and wine that appear to our senses remain intact. This hidden change is fittingly and properly called transubstantiation by the Church. Thus, if it is to be in harmony with Catholic Faith, any interpretation of theologians that seeks some understanding of this Mystery, must preserve the truth that, in the very nature of the things themselves, that is, as separate from our mind, the bread and wine cease to exist after the Consecration. After the Consecration, under the sacramental species of bread and wine, there are present for our adoration the Body and Blood of the Lord Jesus, just as he himself wished, so that he might offer himself to us as food and associate us in the unity of his Mystical Body.

The one and individual existence of Christ the Lord, glorious in heaven, is not multiplied but is made present in this Sacrament in the various places throughout the world where the Eucharistic sacrifice is enacted. Moreover, the same existence remains present in the most Blessed Sacrament after the sacrifice has been celebrated. In the tabernacle on the altar this most holy Sacrament is the living heart of our churches. Because of this, we have the pleasant duty of offering honor and adoration in the Sacred Host upon which our eyes gaze, to the Word Incarnate himself, whom our eyes are not able to see and who has become present before us without leaving heaven.[159]

---

[159] Paul VI, *Creed of the People of God; AAS,* 60, pp. 442–43.

IV

Mysterium Fidei

The Real Presence and Transubstantiation

A certain disdain for the flesh has always run as a minor but not insignificant theme through human history, its religions, its philosophies, its activities. For some persons, matter and the flesh, the body and its activities have been seen as an impediment to the spirit, or as having no moral significance for the person apart from the orientation given by the spirit or mind or intention. In propounding its Eucharistic doctrine from the beginning, Christianity has had to combat this view of reality, and evidence of that struggle can be found from the times of Ignatius of Antioch through Innocent III and in the teachings of Paul VI against the "spiritualizing" tendencies found in the notion of transfinalization. Robert Browning's Rabbi Ben Ezra echoed the views of Christian saints and orthodox theologians when he said:

> *Let us not always say*
> *"Spite of this flesh to-day*
> *I strove, made head,*
> *gained ground upon the whole!"*
> *As the bird wings and sings,*
> *Let us cry "All good things*
> *Are ours, nor soul helps flesh more,*
> *now, than flesh helps soul."*[1]

---

[1] Robert Browning, *Rabbi Ben Ezra,* in *Major British Poets,* Oscar Williams, ed., p. 276.

"Nor soul helps flesh more, now, than flesh helps soul." The line is a strong affirmation of the value of matter, not of the insignificance of soul. And it expresses what appears to be the view of God as well. It is always a source of wonder for a Christian to contemplate God's dealings with matter. The Creator of "all things visible and invisible" appears to enjoy working with matter and has given it a wonderful multiformity. Consider some of its variety: from the smallest atom of inorganic material to the puzzle of a protein cell, to an amoeba; from water and air to a blade of grass, and trees, and the immensity of planets, stars and galaxies; the many species of animals; the human body in all its stages from conception to death; human faces—so similar yet so different because each reflects or can reflect a personality that, even if it differs ever so slightly from another, is nonetheless unique. All of these show us something of God's extravagant use of matter. And all the aspects and phases of matter—if we could only view it as a whole while seeing all its parts—are, of course, only a reflection of his beauty—and of only a fraction of that since we may surmise that the spiritual order of creation is at least as varied, intricate and as astounding as the material creation.

God delights in matter. One might say that he surpasses every scientist in his fascination for its potentialities, its capacities for change, the varieties of its use. While so often in history the human race, which is matter and spirit, has renounced the former while pretending to seek the latter in its "pure" form, the Creator has sought to ennoble matter. He leaves the Gnostics, the dualists, the Idealists, the transcendentalists, the Cathari to deal with "spirit" and "Reason" and "ideas". God himself deals in clay.

A great thing was being done when God constructed [man] from matter [i.e., clay]. It was honored as often as it experienced the hand of God, when he touched it, when he pulled at it, when he formed and shaped it. Reflect on God, totally occupied and given over to it, with his hand, his senses, his work, his counsel and wisdom, his providence, and especially his affection, which guided its features. For, whatever was expressed in clay, it was Christ, the future man, that was thought of, for he, the Word made Flesh, was then clay and earth.[2]

So much then does God love matter that he has made it his own, in the Incarnation, in an inseparable union that will never end, a union that left his material Body, its chemicals and functions, all that they were by "nature", even while making that Body the "hinge of salvation"[3] through which the divine power operates. In God's love for matter, he appears like a child playing with wet sand at a beach, making and unmaking, forming and changing, blotting out what is made only to fashion it anew. But, in all the changes, he respects the matter he created, which is always clay to its Potter. At times he leaves it integrally unchanged despite appearances. Thus he made a woman his Mother while preserving her virginal integrity. At times, he refashions its very being and appearances, as at Cana, changing water to wine. And, at the Mass, he touches matter in order to leave nothing but the appearances, since in the Eucharist, even materially, it has become Another, himself in his own materiality of Flesh and Blood.

Taking insights from the Fathers of the Church, especially from Tertullian, St. Cyril of Alexandria, and St. John of Damascus, Aquinas taught that Flesh has become the instrument of salvation. This is true because in the humanity of the Son of God, human flesh has, in St. Thomas' words, become the "conjoined instrument" of the Divinity. In the human nature he created for himself God worked our salvation. Now, raised in glory, it is through that human nature that God communicates to us the effects of the salvation he has won. Not by some remote action at a distance, but by person-to-person, even body-to-body, contact has God willed to save us in Christ. In a general sense this person-to-person

---

[2] Tertullian, *De Resurrectione Mortuorum*, VI, 2–4; CCSL, 2, p. 928. Cf. Vagaggini's fine book *The Flesh*, p. 77, when he uses a variant form of this citation as he studies the Patristic tradition on the value of matter-Flesh.

[3] Tertullian, *De Resurrectione Mortuorum*, VIII, 2; CCSL, 2, p. 931. Tertullian writes there: "The flesh is the hinge of salvation. . . . The flesh is fed on the Body and Blood of Christ, so that the soul may grow fat on God."

contact is a spiritual reality; it operates through grace and faith's response to grace. It is a spiritual contact made concrete in word and sign through the sacraments. In them matter is charged with the power of Christ's activity upon us. In the Eucharist, however, which among the sacraments is the most noble, this person-to-person contact with Christ's humanity occurs *through touch.*

> Because we find different sacramental actions distributed among the different sacraments, all of them operative by virtue of the incarnate Word, it is necessary that there be some sacramental action that is attributed to the Principal Agent himself, viz., to the incarnate Word. Therefore it was necessary that there exist the Sacrament of the Eucharist to contain the incarnate Word himself, the other sacraments acting in virtue of this One. So it was fitting that this Sacrament was instituted under the figure of food. Among the senses it is only the sense of touch that is really joined with its sensible object. . . . Taste is a form of touch; and among the other things that pertain to touch, it is only in eating that there is a union between the food and what is eaten, because the food and the one eating it become one; other tangible things act only by making a sensible impression on what touches them. Therefore, although every sacrament must be set forth under the likeness of some sensible reality, it is fitting that this Sacrament, in which the incarnate Word himself is contained in order to be joined to us, be given to us in the likeness of food. He is joined to us, not by changing into us but by changing us into him, as St. Augustine says in *Confessions,* 7, 10.[4]

Eucharistic reception, then, is a touch that assimilates our own bodies to the Body of Christ. By a paradox, it is the food that absorbs the eater and not vice versa. This happens, of course, because in the conjunction of our bodies through Communion, the life-giving touch of Christ, as instrument of divinity, is the stronger. It is true to say that in the process of receiving him, he receives us.

---

[4] Aquinas, *In Quatuor Libros Sententiarum,* bk. IV, dist. VIII, a. 3, quaest. III.

Visus, tactus, gustus   *Sight, touch, and taste*
in Te fallitur;   *In you are deceived;*
sed auditu solo   *only hearing is safely*
tuto creditur.   *believed.*

Like all the senses except hearing, touch too is deceived in the Eucharist. What is touched is not bread and wine but the Body of Christ, hidden by the appearances that properly belong to other matter than Christ's Body.

The importance of contact with Christ's Flesh may be said to be the very reason for the mystery of the Real Presence in the Eucharist. And that Real Presence comes about through transubstantiation so that the contact may be direct, not mediated through independent material realities as it is in the other sacraments. Using his Aristotelian terminology, St. Thomas, describing what is meant by transubstantiation, said that the "matter and form" of the bread and wine are changed into the "matter and form" of the Body and Blood of Christ. In this terminology, "matter" means not ordinary matter as we perceive it but rather what we might call the "pliable" or transformable aspect of material reality, that aspect that makes it susceptible to being molded and shaped, changed and solidified, distended or rarefied, etc. "Form" is that aspect that effects any concrete realization of this pliability. In this sense, matter is not different from the material structures (such as atoms, molecules, etc.) revealed to us by the natural sciences, but it is not identical with them either. It is those elements viewed in their aspect of pliability. It is this pliable aspect that allows grain to be shaped and fashioned in such a way that it becomes the edible we know as bread. When one asks, from a philosophical point of view, what has changed *materially* in the atoms that were grain and have become bread, one can respond that the pliability aspect has been touched and determined in a new way. When one asks this question from the point of view of natural science, there is no certain answer. The nature and properties of atoms and the laws that govern atomic action are, to a large extent, a natural mystery to us.[5] This opaqueness about the being of material reality affects, of course, not only the natural scientist but also the philosopher. We deceive ourselves when we think that the full identity of any being is an open book. This being so, some of the criticisms often brought against St. Thomas' use of the hylomorphic concepts and terminology of Aristotle to describe (and one must emphasize "describe", not "explain") transubstantiation are really wide of the mark. That which constitutes the "essence" of bread, viz., its matter and form, was to Thomas—and still is to us—a relative unknown. He took it as meaning that the factor of indetermination present in matter had been so structured or "informed" that it was now bread and not simply an amalgam of particles of grain. He had admittedly no real awareness of the structure of either the grain or the bread as probed ever more diligently by the physical sciences. We, with that awareness, are still left with the basic question: What allows the same atoms to be the physical substrate of different realities? He answered that it was "matter", i.e., the element of pliability or malleability inherent in physical realities. As yet, physics has revealed to us nothing that directly contradicts such an understanding. With that understanding, then, Thomas said that the essence of bread and wine, i.e., their matter (element of pliability) and form (that which fixed the pliable in a specific way), were changed into the matter and form of Christ's Body and Blood. He rejected the theory of the annihilation of the substance of bread and wine; they did not cease to be, having been

[5] The mysteries of matter continue to amaze even physicists, as the current discussions of the "string theory" or "superstring theory" make evident. Among the postulates of this theory is the hypothesis that, in addition to the normal three dimensions of space and the one which is time, there are at least six invisible dimensions of reality that must be taken account of when dealing with material reality (cf., for example, James Trefil, *The Dark Side of the Universe,* esp. pp. 150ff.). Whatever may ultimately be decided about the truth of such a theorem, the very existence of such discussions must be sobering to those theologians and philosophers who long since have rejected the traditional philosophical understanding of material reality because it postulated a "substance" not directly accessible to the senses.

replaced by something else. Rather they themselves were transformed, molded into that which they had not been before. In
itself such a change is not miraculous. Indeed, it is an everyday
occurrence, since matter constantly changes in its configurations,
as even the Fathers of the Church indicated when speaking of the
process of digestion and the human assimilation of food. The
miraculous in the Eucharistic change begins to be seen in the fact
that, once the change has taken place, there is no discernible
change in the properties of bread and wine as they reveal themselves to us, that which Thomas with Aristotle called "accidents".
By normal laws these properties should cease to exist in their
previous form and should manifest the new Reality that the bread
and wine have become. This does not happen. Rather they are
sustained by the power of God so as to become the symbolic
expression of the new Food that in reality the bread and wine
have become, the physical Body of Christ. Such a possibility was
unforeseen by Aristotle. Wyclif, following Aristotle, thought
it impossible and so concluded, as others had and would, that
the bread and wine in their proper reality remain even while
the Body of Christ is present in some way. Aquinas, however,
working from the Faith that said this was no longer bread and
wine in any true sense, and respecting the natural mysteries
involved in matter, held that the properties or accidents could be
and are so subservient to the power of God that they continue to
exist as material *signs* of what they had become and not as the
visible and measurable aspects of the realities that they had ceased
to be.

The official teaching of the Church on this matter, as we have
seen, has never employed the concepts and terminology of Aristotle to the extent that Aquinas did. It has even generally abstained
from using the word *accidents,* preferring the more traditional
appearances (species). Indeed, the focus of the Church's teaching—as
would be expected—has been on the Reality present in the Eucharist and not on the earthly realities (bread and wine) that have
become this Reality. These elements, says the Church, are not,
despite appearances, bread and wine at all. They are Christ.

Furthermore, they are not just a spiritual Presence of the Lord. He is physically present in his actual Flesh and Blood as our food, and as Priest and Victim. He is present in such a way that he has intimately, profoundly, and totally changed into himself that which was there before the Consecration, not just in the estimation of faith but in themselves. Adhering to those truths, one may speculate as one sees fit. This does not mean, however, that the Church has rejected the conclusions of Aquinas and his predecessors. Indeed, some of their conclusions have given the Church insights to the Mystery that she has declared as true, although they were never *explicitly* revealed. One such conclusion gives us a deeper insight into the Mystery of transubstantiation. We return to Aquinas to guide us in consideration of that conclusion. Two of the most provocative aspects of St. Thomas' treatment of the Blessed Sacrament are found in articles 5 and 6 of the *Summa Theologiae,* q. 76. In these articles, Thomas reflected on the questions: "Is the Body of Christ in this Sacrament as though it were fixed in one place?" and "Is the Body of Christ in this Sacrament capable of being moved?" Part of his thought on those questions follows:

It must be said that the Body of Christ is not in this Sacrament according to the manner proper to extended material quantity but rather according to the manner of substance itself.

Therefore it must be said that the Body of Christ is not in this Sacrament as definitively located, because if this were so it would not be able to be anywhere else than on the altar where the Sacrament is being brought about, whereas in reality the Body of Christ is in heaven in its proper form and on many other altars in its sacramental form. Likewise it is clear that the Body of Christ is not "enclosed" in this Sacrament because it is not there in a manner commensurate with its own proper quantity. The fact that his Body is not present outside of the dimensions of the Sacrament or present on another part of the altar outside of the Host does not militate against the position that his Body is not definitively located in or circumscribed by the Host. Rather this simply indicates that his Body begins to be there on the altar through the

Consecration and through the change that takes place in the bread and wine.[6]

> When we say that he is present under the sacramental appearances, we do this to signify a certain relationship [*habitudo*] between him and the sacramental sign. Therefore, according to this mode of being, Christ is not moved about properly speaking, but only *per accidens*. As we have said, Christ is not present in this Sacrament in the manner of being contained in a place, and that which is not contained in place is not moved locally in respect to itself but rather is moved only according to the movement of that in which it is present.[7]

This teaching of Aquinas has been taught by the Magisterium in the documents of Clement IV, teaching that Christ's Body is locally in heaven,[8] and Paul VI, teaching that the Lord has become present in the Eucharist without leaving heaven.[9]

What is at stake here centers on two Articles of Faith and the human mind's efforts to integrate and understand them to the (limited) extent possible. The Articles of Faith are these: (1) the bodily Presence of Christ in its proper form is only present in heaven, "at the right hand of the Father", as we say in the Creed. Even as transformed at the Resurrection—such that we speak of his "glorified" Body—Christ's Body is still a real human body of Flesh and Blood, with its own material dimensions and characteristics. As such, it is localized; it cannot be "spread out" everywhere throughout the universe in some kind of vaguely "spiritualized" condition. In this the Mystery of his Resurrection and glorification is like the Mystery of the Incarnation itself, in which the immensity of God takes on the littleness of the human condition without becoming little. The very question of God's immensity and transcendence is a Mystery in itself, as Solomon already

---

[6] *S. Th.* III, q. 76, a. 5c, and ad 1.
[7] Idem, q. 76, a. 6c.
[8] Cf. above, p. 202.
[9] Cf. above, pp. 265, 267.

indicated on the occasion of the dedication of his temple to the Lord in Jerusalem. On that occasion he prayed:

> But will God really dwell on earth? The heavens, even the highest heavens, cannot contain you. How much less this temple I have built" (1 Kings 8:27).

Augustine, too, pointed out this truth in that beautiful series of questions at the beginning of the *Confessions.*

> Do heaven and earth, then, contain the whole of you, since you fill them? Or, when once you have filled them, is some part of you left over because they are too small to hold you? If this is so, when you have filled heaven and earth, does that part of you that remains flow over into some other place? . . . You fill all things, but do you fill them with your whole self? or is it that the whole of creation is too small to hold you and therefore holds only a part of you? And is this same part of you present in all things at once, or do different things contain different parts of you, greater or smaller according to their size? Does this mean that one part of you is greater and another smaller? Or are you present entirely everywhere at once, and no single thing contains the whole of you?[10]

In Christ the immensity and transcendence of God are contained in a way that Solomon could never have imagined, for the humanity of the Lord is the temple not built by human hands. Here there is present a greater than both Solomon and his temple; indeed the Lord of the temple himself is present in the Messiah. Nonetheless, when he became man, taking for himself a human body and soul, God the Word did not "enclose" his divinity within the limited dimensions of his humanity. For, as the Faith of the Church proclaims and as Pope Leo the Great wrote in his famous *Tome to Flavian,* "The Son of God entered the lowliness of this world, descending from his heavenly throne yet not leaving the glory of the Father."[11] While he was carried in his humanity

---

[10] Augustine, *Confessions,* I, 3. Translation by R. S. Pine-Coffin, London; Penguin Books, 1961, pp. 22–23.

[11] DS 294.

in Mary's womb, or was teaching in Galilee and Jerusalem, or was dying on the Cross, the eternal Word in his divinity was also governing the universe with the Father and Holy Spirit, thereby present in regions of creation where his humanity was not. "Not leaving the glory of the Father", said Leo. This is true even though that humanity was, from the time of the Incarnation, *inseparably* his own, so that the one Divine Person who was governing the universe was also truly present in the restricted temporal and geographic circumstances of Palestine. Part of the great "emptying out" of which St. Paul speaks when referring to the Incarnation (cf. Phil 2:7) is simply that: his humanity was limited in a way his divinity was not. So, too, now, after the Resurrection. In his humanity he has been marked out as Son of God in power (cf. Rom 1:3–4) and been given all power in heaven and on earth (cf. Mt 28:18), but that human body and soul are still limited by comparison with his divinity. Being everywhere present is proper to divinity alone; it is not, and cannot become, an attribute of humanity, even when the humanity in question is the very humanity of God. As a result, in his humanity—his human body, blood, soul, etc.—the Son of God can properly be in only one place at one time. There is no actual "ubiquity" of Christ's human nature.

The second Article of Faith in question is the nature of the Eucharistic Mystery itself. For in the Eucharist, Christ is truly contained, Body (with all the physical dimensions and members proper to his Body,[12] Blood, Soul, and Divinity, the same Body

---

[12] Aquinas states this truth in very realistic language when he writes: "By the power of the Sacrament there is contained in this Sacrament—as far as the species of bread is concerned—not only the Flesh but the whole Body of Christ, that is, his bones, nerves, and other such things" (*S. Th.,* III, q. 76, a. 1, ad 2). He repeats the truth in a subsequent article of the same question. "There is in this Sacrament the whole dimensive quantity of the Body of Christ and all the other accidents of that Body" (*S. Th.,* III, q. 76, a. 4c).

How it is possible for the quantity and other dimensions of Christ's Body to be present without also being extended in space and therefore visible, etc., is of the very essence of the Mystery of the Eucharist. Aquinas says that they are there *per modum substantiae,* i.e., operative in such a way *as if* only the substance of his Body were there (*S. Th.,* III, q. 76, a. 1, ad 3, and a. 4c and a.4, ad 2).

born of Mary, dead on the Cross, raised gloriously from the tomb. It is not a different Body from the one that "sits at the right hand of the Father", nor is it a part of that Body, nor some kind of amorphous extension of that Body. The Eucharist is the identically one, risen Body of the Lord, only the mode or manner of Presence differing from that which it exhibits in heaven.

How are these two truths interrelated and to be understood? To this question the Church has given no definitive answer. She defends both truths, leaving the questions that flow from those truths to be means of nourishing the meditation and theological speculation of the faithful, who, in living awe at the Mystery, are left to ask: What is it that takes place at the Consecration of the Mass? What is it that occurs when the reality of bread and wine are changed into the very reality of the risen Christ—the Mystery of transubstantiation?

It must be remembered, first of all, that the manner or mode of the Lord's Presence in the Eucharist is unique. "It is correctly said that the mode [of presence] is proper to this Sacrament: not only because of its difference from the other sacraments but also because in all the universe there does not appear to be any mode of presence similar to this one. Therefore, with admiration and veneration, we must admit our lack of knowledge concerning this type of presence."[13] The truth of Cajetan's comment also helps to situate the remarks of St. Thomas and Popes Clement and Paul on the "local Presence" of the Lord in the Eucharist. It should be obvious that neither is attempting to mitigate in any way the corporeal reality present to us in the Blessed Sacrament. They are, rather, striving to highlight its uniqueness.

Jesus is present and contained in many Hosts in the same ciborium; he is bodily present in many ciboria in many churches of the world at the same time. What is more, he is fully and completely bodily present in each part of each Host, so that when the Host is broken, Christ is wholly present in each part, as well as in each

---

[13] Cardinal Cajetan, *Commentary on III, q. 75, a. 1,* in the *Opera Omnia Sancti Thomae Aquinatis,* vol. 12 (Leonine Edition), Rome, 1906, p. 160.

recognizable particle. This last is the fact expressed by Aquinas in that stanza of the *Lauda Sion* that reads:

Fracto demum Sacramento
Ne vacilles, sed memento,
Tantum esse sub fragmento,
Quantum toto tegitur.
Nulla rei fit scissura:
Signi tantum fit fractura:
Qua nec status nec statura
Signati minuitur.

When the sacramental sign is broken
Have no doubts, rather remember that
All is contained in the part as in the whole.
For there is no dividing the reality,
Only the sacramental sign is broken. The One signified is not affected in any way.

It is the Presence of the Body of Christ in each broken part, of course, that necessitates equal respect for a recognizable fragment of the Host or for drops of the Precious Blood as for the entire Host or the contents of a full chalice.[14]

What is clear is that, despite the number of Hosts entire or broken, it is only the one Body of the Lord present. In one ciborium of many Hosts, there is only one Christ bodily present. What is multiplied is the sacramental sign, not the Lord's Body. And yet, his Body and Blood "are truly contained" (as the *Firmiter,* Trent, and other documents teach) in each of the different

---

[14] We say "recognizable" fragment or drop of the Precious Blood because, as Aquinas long ago wrote (*S.Th.*, III, q. 77, a. 4), Christ is bodily present as long as the appearances of bread and wine have not decomposed or been diminished into a state in which they are no longer recognizable as being the species of bread and wine. Cf. also K. Rahner, "On Developing Eucharistic Devotion", in *Mission and Grace,* vol. 1 (London and New York: Sheed and Ward, 1963), pp. 290ff., although he pushes this point beyond just limits. Rahner seems to hold that, *once eaten and even before decomposition of the species,* the bodily Presence of the Lord ceases in order to give way to his Presence in the Spirit. His distinction between the Host as existing "to be eaten" and the Host as "having been eaten" is too philosophic and too little biblical. The Lord is bodily present until the Eucharistic elements have decomposed.

species. And so we return to the question already asked: How are we to envision (not *explain,* since that cannot be done) what happens?

Throughout Christian history some theologians have attempted to envision this Mystery by an appeal to the qualities of the glorified state of Christ's risen Body. As seen above, St. Jerome already gave indications of such an approach, as did Hildebert of Lavardin and Alan of Lille after him. Surely such attempts are legitimate. They seem to me, however, to "spiritualize" the resurrected Body to such an extent that its material element no longer bears real similarity to matter as we know it now (admittedly with a very limited awareness). Furthermore, some explanations along this line would appear almost to fall into the problem of defending what amounts to at least a practical (as opposed to a theoretical) "ubiquity" of Christ's human nature, thereby leaving them open to the many objections leveled against Luther's position. I think, therefore, it is better to envision the Mystery in a way that approaches it from a perspective different from what may be offered by the notion of a glorified Body.

In a beautiful essay on the Eucharist, written in 1916 during the First World War, Teilhard de Chardin gives us the fruit of a meditation made in front of the Blessed Sacrament. Entitled "The Monstrance", the essay describes how, while kneeling in prayer, a person (probably the author himself) suddenly had the sensation that the Host began "to expand and grow bigger". The white Host soon enveloped not only the one in prayer but all reality as it continued to grow. Soon "through the mysterious expansion of the Host the whole world had become incandescent, had itself become like a single giant Host. . . . It had penetrated, through the channels of matter, into the inmost depths of all hearts and had dilated them to breaking point, only in order to take back into itself the substance of their affections and passions."[15]

---

[15] Pierre Teilhard de Chardin, "Christ in the World of Matter: Three Stories in the style of Benson: The Monstrance", in *Hymn of the Universe,* pp.

It is truly a magnificent picture, revealing in graphic form the power of the Eucharistic Lord to reach out and embrace and transform all things. It is, moreover, a perception of a great truth and one that corrects the unreflecting accusation made at times by those who have little experience of the true nature of Eucharistic adoration. For it has frequently been said that the Eucharist has been given to us as our food, not (at least not primarily) to be adored, and that adoration in a silent church or before a monstrance is a devotion that flows from a "static" view of the Eucharist, one, that is, that emphasizes the Lord's Presence as opposed to his action of self-giving or sacrificial self-surrender, etc. What is erroneous in such a view is, at least in part, its failure to appreciate how much can be happening when nothing *appears* to be happening. Two people sitting silently side by side, not physically contiguous, but nonetheless much in love with each other, are not unaware of how much can expressed when nothing appears to be expressed. There is in daily life a type of activity that transcends mere actions, and every true Christian is aware of how often the "passive" approach of prayer has been instrumental in solving a problem or providing for a need that no amount of frenetic activity had been able to achieve. What Teilhard's reflection indicates is that the very Presence of Christ is always dynamic, is indeed the very font of endless, though invisible, activity. Lifted up, he draws all things to himself (cf. Jn 12:32).

One can go beyond Teilhard's meditation, however, and consider not, first of all, the Eucharistic Lord but Christ the Lord risen in glory and seated in his natural Presence at the Father's right hand. Part of that glory, as he himself told the disciples at the last of his Resurrection appearances, is the fact that to him has

---

46–49. Teilhard's writings on the Eucharist are filled with beauty and great depth of thought and spirituality, although his erroneous opinions on original sin and the nature of actual sin left him incapable of appreciating the *redemptive* aspects of both Christ's death and the Eucharistic Mystery.

been given all authority or power in heaven and on earth (cf. Mt 28:18). God the Father has put everything under Christ's dominion, and he shall rule until all powers opposed to him have been subdued, the last of them being death itself (cf. 1 Cor 15:25–26). This present stage of Christ's rule is something we often profess in the liturgy (especially in the Feast of Christ the King) and in private devotion. The meaning of the Lord's subjection of all reality in its present stage is, however, something upon which most of us do not often reflect. It means that, in some mysterious but real way, the risen Jesus influences, shapes, and directs all things so that out of all persons and things he is shaping the future visage of creation as that creation moves toward his glorious return. Even the sinner—whose very sin is at least implicitly an attempt to thwart the sovereignty and dominion of Christ—operates now within the overall plan of the Lord for the establishment of his Kingdom. The ways in which Jesus exercises this dominion vary. Over creatures to whom he has given intelligence and free will, his action is such that it respects his natural gifts. Nonetheless, his power to move us by attraction, the arranging of circumstances, the example of others, the holy inspiration that comes from the reading of Scripture, interior grace that conveys the *delectatio* spoken of by Augustine—these and many other ways are some of the means by which he reigns efficaciously over intelligent creatures. As Vatican Council II said:

> Constituted Lord by his Resurrection, Christ, to whom all power in heaven and on earth has been given, already works in the hearts of men by virtue of his Holy Spirit, not only stirring up a desire for the age to come but by that very fact also animating, purifying, and strengthening the noble intentions by which the human family strives to make its life more human and to subject all the earth to that goal.[16]

Over the lesser beings of creation his power sometimes is not necessarily more powerful (for his attractiveness and inspirations

---

[16] Vatican Council II, *Gaudium et Spes,* 38.

are powerful indeed) but more direct and immediate. And such is the case with the elements of bread and wine, simultaneously products of his creation and of ours, "fruit of the earth and work of human hands". At the Consecration of the liturgy, the heavenly King touches these elements directly by and through the power of his Spirit. He touches them so mightily that—if we may put it this way—he extracts from them their very reality, dominating it and attracting it (forcefully pulling it even) toward himself, so subjecting it to himself that its own true being is lost to it as it becomes the very Lord who has mastered it.

The mystery of transubstantiation is a totally marvelous change but not one wherein the Lord descends from heavenly glory to "enter" under the appearances of bread and wine. Rather it is one in which he, not coming down, lifts the creaturely realities to himself, drawing them up to where he is now with the Father. He draws them to himself in such a fashion that he subjugates them and so transforms their own being that it becomes identical with his. The very being of bread and wine is lifted out of itself in a mighty spiral of ascent, is subsumed by and converted into the reality of Jesus seated in glory. By drawing the reality of all the elements scattered throughout the world unto and into himself, Jesus maintains his own bodily unity. The elements are changed into him, not he into them. If he did to the appearances, the species, what he does to the very reality of the bread and wine, then, once the Consecration of the Mass was finished, the priest would be left with nothing before him on the paten or in the cup, and Christ would appear in glory. For then not only the being but the very appearances that manifest that being to the world would have been subsumed into the exalted Lord, and human history on earth would have reached its conclusion.[17]

Myles Connolly has caught this truth well in his little book *Mr. Blue*. There the book's hero, Blue, gives an imaginative scenario

[17] St. Thomas (*Summa Contra Gentes,* IV, 63, 12) appears to contradict this opinion. His remarks, however, are predicated on the presumption that Christ would not will the end of the world at such a moment.

of the kingdom of the Antichrist. The last priest on earth, hunted by a universal dictatorial government, has determined to offer the Mass one last time. He goes to the roof of a building, vests, and begins the liturgy. His treason discovered, a plane is sent to bomb the building on top of which he is celebrating. The target sighted, the bomb is prepared for deployment just as the priest reaches the consecratory words of the Roman Canon: *Hoc est enim corpus meum.*

> There was a moment of awful silence. Then, a burst of light beside which day itself is dark. . . . The earth burst asunder. And through this unspeakably luminous new day, through the vault of the sky ribbed with lightning, came Christ as he had come after the Resurrection. It was the end of the world![18]

It is fantasy, of course, but it is also real in that it is founded on a truth. Were Christ to let happen to the sacramental Species or appearances what should follow from the change of reality in which they formally had their being, it would be the Parousia, the Second Coming in bodily appearance of the Lord. If, developing the imagery of St. John Chrysostom,[19] we may use yet another fantasy, one created by Lewis Carroll, to help with an analogy to illustrate what is being said, then let us imagine what it would be like not to have the Sacred Host or the Precious Blood pass into our mouths but rather to have us be enabled to pass directly into them. To have us pass, that is, *through* what remains of the bread and wine, viz., their appearances. Were we able to do this, we should find that, having passed through the appearances, we would be standing with Christ in heaven itself, at the Father's right hand. And not only would we be standing there, but everyone who, anywhere in the world, was capable of doing the same thing would be standing there with us united in Christ. This would be so because the Eucharistic appearances are themselves the boundary between the visible and invisible orders of creation, the horizon at which earthly time and the everlasting aeon of the

---

[18] Myles Connolly, *Mr. Blue,* pp. 63–64.
[19] Cf. above, Section I, pp. 47–49.

blessed touch. The appearances are the window whose far side holds "what God has prepared for those who love him" (1 Cor 2:9).

The analogy may appear to contain more of Lewis Carroll than of reality. In fact, however, the reality of the Eucharistic Presence is in itself and in its consequences (for time, geography, spatiotemporal relationships, and interpersonal relationships) more fantastic than fantasy. It is more true, more real than the narrow, almost one-dimensional view of reality from which we often suffer because of contracted intellectual vision. It was a wideness of vision vis-à-vis reality that nourished the imaginations of a Leonardo da Vinci, a Jules Verne, and so much of yesterday's "science fiction". The first glimpse may at times have distorted the reality, but so much of yesterday's fantasy is, in essence, the quickly superseded "fact" of today. The potentialities latent in God's universe have only begun to be realized by mankind. Indeed, one of the "side benefits" of his revelation of some aspects of his Mysteries is that it compels us to stretch our minds and imaginations to make room for the not-yet-experienced, the wonderful, the awesome. By the Christian Mysteries philosophy is enriched and experiential science is challenged. And certainly this is preeminently true of the Mystery of the Eucharist. By its very nature, this Mystery touches upon the natural and philosophic "mysteries" of time, place, the nature of matter and of human bodies, their physical and metaphysical structures, the visible and invisible realms of the universe, their relatedness and compenetrability, etc. Just as he stretches the heart, so the Eucharistic Christ stretches the mind. The analogy given above limps, not because it is "fantastic" but simply because it is not daring enough.

By his power, then, as Universal Lord to attract all things to himself, Christ "lifts" the creaturely realities of bread and wine, draws them to himself, changes them into himself, leaving the appearance of the earthly realities as vehicles for the heavenly exchange by which he physically comes to us as our food while drawing us to himself through and in the Eucharistic species. In this way we can be helped to understand the affirmations of

Aquinas and Paul VI. The Lord himself is not moved locally, nor is he locally "in place"; what "happens" to the Sacrament happens to the appearances. It is they that are doubly consecrated, moved, broken, multiplied in many ciboria and churches throughout the world, etc. Having been, however, "destructured" of any real being of their own and preserved miraculously, the appearances of what were bread and wine mediate to all who touch them, receive them, worship before them the Person whose Flesh and Blood they contain and whose reality their own former reality has become. Thus, what happens to the appearances directly happens to the Lord's Body and Blood *per accidens,* since it is only through the sacramental species that he is physically accessible at all on this side of the divide that separates the visible and invisible dimensions of creation, both of which already contain spiritual and material-physical elements.

The Eucharist as Pledge and Foretaste of Heaven

Latent in what has already been said are truths concerning the eschatological aspect of the Eucharist and why it is called a "foretaste" of eternal life and Viaticum. When we speak of the "eschatological", we are generally speaking of the state of affairs and of reality that will exist at the conclusion of temporal history. It is what we pray for at the end of the Fourth Eucharistic Prayer when the priest says: "Heavenly Father, grant that all of us your children, together with the Blessed Virgin Mary the Mother of God and your Apostles and saints, may reach our heavenly inheritance in your Kingdom where, along with all creation, which has been liberated from the corruption of sin and death, we may glorify you through Christ Our Lord."[20] The eschaton is the

[20] The English translation of this part of Eucharistic Prayer IV in the *Sacramentary* is not quite accurate. The Latin reads: "Nobis omnibus, filiis tuis, clemens Pater, concede, ut caelestem hereditatem consequi valeamus cum beata Virgine, Dei Genetrice, Maria, cum Apostolis et Sancis tuis in regno tuo,

whole of creation redeemed and transformed. It is the bodies of the just risen and glorified. It is also the nonhuman ranks of material creation, which will, like the elements of bread and wine in the Eucharist, have been touched by the Spirit and thereafter serve Christ and all who belong to him in a new and more noble way than they do now. The constitution *Gaudium et Spes* of Vatican Council II refers to this work of Christ as he touches creation, drawing it toward its future through the Spirit and through his own Eucharistic Presence.

> The gifts of the Spirit are diverse: while he calls some to render a clear testimony to the desire for our heavenly dwelling and to keep this desire alive in the human family, he calls some to dedicate themselves to the earthly service of the human race, preparing by this service of theirs the material for the heavenly Kingdom. Nevertheless he liberates all so that, denying any selfish love and drawing all earthly forces into [the service of] human life, they may reach out to that future when humanity itself will become an offering acceptable to God (cf. Rom 15: 16).
>
> The Lord has left to his own a pledge of this hope [for the future] and a Viaticum for the journey in that Sacrament of faith in which the elements of nature as cultivated by man are changed into the glorious Body and Blood, that banquet of fraternal Communion and foretaste of the heavenly banquet.[21]

The Eucharistic elements are here-and-now signs of what the Lord's power can do—and is doing—to the material components

---

ubi cum universa creatura, a corruptione peccati et mortis liberata, te glorificemus per Christum Dominum nostrum."

The words "ubi cum universa creatura, a corruptione peccati et mortis liberata" are phrased in such a way that they refer to the Vulgate translation of Rom 8:19–24: "The creation waits in eager expectation for the sons of God to be revealed . . . in hope that the creation itself will be liberated from its bondage to decay, and brought into the glorious freedom of the children of God."

[21] *Gaudium et Spes*, 38.

of creation as he employs them to his service. Many reflections suggest themselves as we contemplate this great reality.

Created reality, part of which is the material constituents of this universe, even now groans, says St. Paul in the text from Romans cited above, for the liberation that will be its own future destiny. In the Eucharist, the material elements of this creation already participate in the glory that will belong to matter when the plenitude of liberation has been achieved. It is true that the material elements of the bread and wine that remain after the Eucharistic change still partake of the "present form of this world that is passing away" (cf. 1 Cor 7:31). Unlike the glorious Body and Blood of the Lord, whose medium the elements of what were bread and wine have become, the Eucharistic appearances are subject to the decay and change that all matter now undergoes until it, together with the children of God, is transformed. Nonetheless, more fully than any material body—except that of her as the medium by which he became Flesh and whose body he has already fully glorified—these products of God's creation and man's labors now share in the glory that will be the property of all matter. One might say that the appearances of bread and wine in this Sacrament are halfway between matter as we experience it and matter as it will become when, having made all things new, he will pour his new wine into new skins (cf. Mt 9:17).

Moreover, it is through these remnants of the present creation that the new breaks into the old, the future into the present. We have already seen that the Eucharistic elements can be compared to a window on the invisible dimensions of the universe. Hidden by the veil, nearly transparent to the eyes of a living Faith, having the appearances of earthly food, the heavenly banquet is present. This truth is expressed by the concluding words of so many of the Prefaces of the liturgy: "with all the choirs of angels in heaven", "together with all the angels and saints", "contemplating your glory they [the angels] incessantly praise you. With them we also, together with all creation under heaven, confess your Name in exultation, as we sing: Holy, Holy, Holy" (Eucharistic Prayer IV,

Preface). What is being said is that we are in fact *with* them in *their* liturgy as the One High Priest leads them in that worship that the very lives and activities of the citizens of heaven give to the heavenly Father.

By way of parenthesis it can be noted that we say "lives and activities" when speaking of the worship offered the Father by the citizens of heaven. We do this in order to remember that when we speak of a "liturgy" of heaven, we are using an analogy with the highest form of prayer that we know in this life. But it is only an analogy; the life of heaven is not a "prolonged Mass". There, because of the Beatific Vision, the blessed live in a state similar to what we call here "infused contemplation", except that in heaven faith and the gifts of wisdom and understanding, which are the sources and proximate causes for infused contemplation here, have given way to vision. Just as some who possess periods of infused contemplation in this life can maintain that special form of intimate union with God while carrying on at least some of the "ordinary" activities of daily life, so in heaven—but in a vastly superior way—do the blessed enjoy the uninterrupted vision of God. Their hearts are attentive to him in love and praise, even while they are engaged in those activities proper to that life. What those activities are has not been revealed to us—except the loving and familiar companionship that the blessed have one with another, as well as their intercessory concern for us. We do know, though, that human creativity and society will have been brought to the peak of their powers. That life is spent with and under the leadership of Christ himself so that, through him and with him and in him in the unity all will possess in the Spirit, everyone, in everything that is done, will glorify the Father. It is to all this we are joined when the Eucharist is celebrated.

This union of ours with the life and worship of heaven is also affirmed by the *Communicantes* prayer of the Roman Canon: *"Communicantes et memoriam venerantes, in primis gloriosae semper Virginis Mariae . . . sed et beati Joseph . . . et omnium Sanctorum tuorum";* ("Communicating with and venerating the memory of, in the first place, the glorious ever-Virgin Mary . . . but also of blessed Joseph

... and all your saints"). Even while venerating the memory of their lives here on earth, we are in communication with them, sharing mysteriously in their present manner of existence. With them we are made fellow partakers of the heavenly banquet here and now. With them we touch already the "hidden manna" (cf. Rev 2:17) that he has promised to those who overcome. How truly then is the Eucharist a *"praegustatum"*, a foretaste, a taste ahead of time of the heavenly banquet in which the saints already share fully. Their present, of course, is our future. It is a future that, both for them and us, will only reach its definitive form at the resurrection of the bodies of the dead. With them — Our Lady being the exception, since she is already risen in the flesh — we look forward to the resurrection of our flesh and do so above all in those moments when Christ through his sacramental Body and Blood draws creation into his own "sacrifice of praise".

Through the Sacrament of his Body and Blood, as through a vortex of tremendous energy, we who receive him in faith and cleansed of serious sin are being lifted into that future life where Christ, having subjected all creation to himself, will hand the Kingdom over to the Father so that God may be all in all (cf. 1 Cor 15:24–28). As Teilhard discerned in his meditation, it is through his Eucharistic Presence that Jesus now aggregates to himself the diverse elements of creation. He raises and draws to himself the bread and wine, completely changing their own being into his. He gives them life, the life that is his own life and being. This power to give life to matter flows ultimately, of course, from the fact that in the beginning "all things were made through him, and without him nothing was made that has been made" (Jn 1:3–4). Everything whatsoever stands related to him as the very source of its being, depends on him as keeping it from falling back into nothingness, and gravitates to him as the very source that perpetually activates it.[22] This supremacy over creation is his as the Eternal

---

[22] Cf. Augustine, *Tractatus in Jo.*, I, 16–17, where, working from a corrupted

Word, but it is a supremacy won for his humanity through the Mysteries of his Passion, death, and Resurrection. It is not only as God but as man, too, that all things have life through him. This life is primarily existence itself, but in the case of the Eucharistic elements he grasps the created existences of bread and wine and transforms them into his own being. Then, through the Sacrament, he draws to himself those who communicate, for in eating this Food we are changed into it, not it into us, as Augustine wrote. Even upon those who do not receive him sacramentally or receive him unworthily he works mysteriously, drawing them to repentance, to the Christian Faith, and to Catholic unity by means of the Spirit, which he mysteriously breathes forth in the Eucharist. The effectiveness and power of that mysterious attraction will be seen by us only at the Last Judgment, although even in this life one can discern at times wonderful effects of the attractive power of the Eucharist. J. R. R. Tolkien, reflecting on a time during which he had nearly ceased practicing his faith, wrote:

> I am one who came up out of Egypt, and pray God none of my seed shall return thither. . . . I fell in love with the Blessed Sacrament from the beginning—and by the mercy of God never have fallen out again. . . . Out of wickedness and sloth I almost ceased to practice my religion. . . . Not for me the Hound of Heaven, but the never-ceasing silent appeal of Tabernacle, and the sense of starving hunger.[23]

"I am one who came up out of Egypt." So much of the history of salvation is captured by those words. Freedom from servitude and misery and want, the Passover and the blood of the lamb, the miraculous manna and the water from the rock.

In the desert the whole community grumbled against Moses and Aaron. The Israelites said to them, "If only we had died by the

---

Latin text of the Prologue of John, he gives a wonderful explanation of how all things are life in Christ.

[23] J. R. R. Tolkien, *Letters of* J. R. R. Tolkien, p. 340.

Lord's hand in Egypt. There we sat around pots of meat and ate all the food we wanted. . . . " Then the Lord said to Moses, "I will rain down bread from heaven for you" (Ex 16:2–4).

But the people were thirsty for water there, and they grumbled against Moses. . . . The Lord answered Moses, "I will stand there before you by the rock at Horeb. Strike the rock, and water will come out of it for the people to drink." So Moses did this in the sight of the elders of Israel. And he called the place Massah and Meribah because the Israelites quarreled and because they tested the Lord saying, "Is the Lord among us or not?" (Ex 17:3–7).

The rabble with them began to crave other food, and again the Israelites started wailing and said, "If only we had meat to eat! We remember the fish we ate in Egypt at no cost—also the cucumbers, melons, leeks, onions and garlic. But now we have lost our appetite; we never see anything but this manna!" (Nb 11:4–6).

Why have you brought us out of Egypt to die in the desert? There is no bread! There is no water! And we detest this miserable food! (Nb 21:5)

Israel's grumbling never ceased. "Now these things occurred as types to keep us from setting our hearts on evil things as they did" (1 Cor. 10:6). It was then all a type of the Passover of the new Lamb, who has freed us from sin and misery, fed us with a more miraculous Food and Drink, and endured our grumbling.

"We never see anything but this manna! We detest this miserable food!" Even the miraculous wearied them, and they grumbled against it. Type that it was, it is sobering to reflect that we can say the same of the Eucharist: we are sick of it; it bores us; it does not satisfy. And we turn to other foods.

"Out of wickedness and sloth", wrote Tolkien. It is probably true of most Catholics that, at one time or another in their lives, they have experienced that same terrible distaste for the Eucharist. It is not only "the shadow of the Valois" who "is yawning at the Mass";[24] it is an affliction that has troubled many. Having tasted and seen that the Lord is good (cf. Ps 34:8), wickedness and sloth

---

[24] G. K. Chesterton, *Lepanto.*

(or perhaps some trial—one even permitted or caused by the Lord himself) can lead, if only for awhile, to what is even a contempt for the Bread of heaven. St. Thomas calls this *acedia,* a type of sloth and sadness that becomes a dislike or loathing of divine things. According to Aquinas it is an affliction that can come even to holy people: "Among holy people there are found some initial movements of spiritual sadness, initial because they do not reach the point of a deliberate consent."[25] Where it reaches a deliberated consent, however, says St. Thomas, it is a grave sin in itself and also very worrisome for the vices that accompany it. He lists some of those: bitterness, laziness, idle curiosity, verbosity, bodily restlessness, daydreaming, and instability of purpose.[26]

Elements of this spiritual sadness are quite natural, using "natural" here of the fallen state that at times so distorts and twists our emotions, passions, and better instincts. One can think of our relationships with those we love, how at times the very presence of the beloved will, for no apparent reason, stir up in us some emotion of annoyance or distaste or even revulsion. It is like the feeling of the husband who, although he loves his wife, looks across at her and feels regret at having pledged his life with her, or of the priest or religious who, fundamentally joyous in his or her vocation, awakes one day with the feeling, "I can't take forty more years of this type of life." Unlike the temptations that must be fought by running from them, spiritual sadness must be banished by a peaceful, steady reflection on the beauty of the divine realities. Running away is the answer indeed when continuous thinking will only increase the incentive to sin, as is the case in sexual matters. Meeting the challenge head on is the answer when persevering reflection will take away the incentive to sin. And the latter

[25] *S. Th.,* II–II, q. 35, a. 3, ad 3. We have translated *acedia* as spiritual sloth or sadness. Thomas R. Heath in *Summa Theologiae,* vol. 35 (New York: McGraw-Hill, 1972), p. 21, translates it as "spiritual apathy" and cites Urban Voll's translation of it as "disgust with the spiritual". All of these, I think, catch the idea present in *acedia.*

[26] Idem, q. 4, ad 3.

advice is that which is to be followed in the case of spiritual sadness, "because the more we reflect on spiritual things so much the more pleasing do they become, thus causing spiritual sloth or sadness to cease."[27]

"Not for me the Hound of Heaven, but the never-ceasing silent appeal of Tabernacle." Commenting on the words of Jesus as recorded in John 6:44 ("No one can come to me unless the Father who sent me draws him"), St. Augustine said: "There is a delight of the heart to which the Bread of heaven is sweet. If it was correct for the poet to say 'Every man is drawn by his own pleasure', not by necessity but by pleasure, not by obligation but by delight, then how much more should we say that a man is drawn to Christ when he delights in the truth, when he delights in blessedness, when he delights in righteousness, when he delights in eternal life—all of which Christ is? . . . Give me a person that longs, that hungers, that is on pilgrimage in this wilderness thirsting and panting after the fountain of his eternal home; give me such a one and he will know what I am talking about."[28] As St. Augustine never tired of repeating, we are drawn by what delights us, especially by beauty. And, for Tolkien, it was that special delight of friendship, the friendship of the One present in the tabernacle who did not follow "with unhurrying chase, and unperturbed pace, deliberate speed, majestic instancy" as did Francis Thompson's Hound of Heaven, but One rather who appealed by calling to that never-satiated hunger within us. It is the invitation of Wisdom to eat and drink.

> Wisdom has built her house; she has hewn out its seven pillars. She has prepared her meat and mixed her wine; she has also set her table. She has sent out her maids, and she calls from the highest point of the city. "Let all who are simple come in here!" she says to those who lack judgment. "Come, eat my food and drink the wine I have mixed. Leave your simple ways and you will live; walk in the way of understanding" (Prov 9:1–6).

[27] Idem, a. 1, ad 4.
[28] Augustine, *Tract. in Evangelium Johannis*, 26, 4.

Of that passage from the Book of Proverbs, St. Augustine has written:

> Here we certainly see that the Wisdom of God, namely, the coeternal Word of the Father, built for himself a home, that is, a human body, in a virginal womb, and to it, as members to the Head, joined the Church . . . and that he prepared a table of wine and loaves, at which table there also appears the priesthood according to the order of Melchizedek. We certainly see that he has called to it the foolish, those lacking in knowledge because, as the Apostle says, "He has chosen the weak things of this world to confound the strong" (1 Cor 1:27). To those weak persons he says the following: "Abandon foolishness so that you may live and seek prudence so that you may have life" (Prov 9:6). To become a sharer at this table is to begin to have life. And in another book, called *Ecclesiastes,* it says: "It is not good for a man unless he eats and drinks" (Qo 8:15). Is it not more credible to understand this as referring to participation at this table where the priest, the very mediator of the New Covenant according to the order of Melchizedek, sets forth his Body and Blood?"[29]

The eternal Wisdom of the Father, become Flesh, would invite mankind to partake of food and drink that would truly give life, understanding, and delight.

> Do not work for food that spoils, but for food that endures to eternal life, which the Son of Man will give you. On him God the Father has placed his seal of approval. . . . It is my Father who gives you the true bread from heaven. For the bread of God is he who comes down from heaven and gives life to the world (Jn 6:27, 32–33).

Rightly have many commentators on Sacred Scripture viewed the first part of the Lord's discourse (Jn 6:35–50) as having a sapiential theme. It is an invitation to faith in Wisdom incarnate

---

[29] Augustine, *City of God,* 17, 20; *CCSL,* 48, p. 588.

and to the understanding and life that such a faith will give. Even more profoundly have many noted the intimate connection between that sapiential theme and the remainder of the discourse (Jn 6:51–58). For Wisdom is not simply a spiritual abstraction or even a transcendent Divine Person; it is now, in Christ, a Person of Flesh and Blood who will offer that Flesh and Blood to the believer as the very embodiment of Wisdom. We grow wise, says the Lord, by eating. And in that eating there is a manifestation of the harmony that God has established between the human race's fall and its restoration. As Pope Urban IV wrote:

> Man fell by means of the food of the death-giving tree; man is raised up by means of the food of the life-giving tree. On the former hung the food of death, on the latter the nourishment of life. Eating of the former earned a wound; the taste of this latter restored health. Eating wounded us, and eating healed us.[30]

This is the eating of a meal prepared by the Begetter of Wisdom: it is the Father's gift. No one is able to partake, says Jesus, "unless it has been given to him by the Father" (Jn 6:65). And what the Father gives first of all is a realization of the starving hunger within us, and then the recognition of where that hunger is to be satisfied.

There is a beautiful foreshadowing of the Eucharist in 1 Kings 19. Ahab, the King of Israel, and his wife Jezebel, enraged at the prophet Elijah, seek to take his life. Elijah flees and enters the desert south of Judah. He is tired and despairing, and, having gone a day's journey, sits beneath a broom tree and prays, "I have had enough, Lord. Take my life." It is the prayer of so many in all ages who, having striven for the good and defended the truth, find themselves standing alone, friendless, and apparently without any hope for success in their efforts. But God strengthens Elijah at this point by sending an angel to provide the prophet with food (bread and water). "The angel . . . touched him and said, 'Get up

---

[30] Urban IV, encyclical letter *Transiturus.*

and eat, for the journey is too much for you.' So he got up and ate and drank. Strengthened by that food, he traveled forty days and forty nights until he reached Horeb, the mountain of God" (1 Kings 19:7–8). There God revealed to him his Presence and gave him the assurance that he was not alone, that a remnant in Israel, seven thousand in all, had not worshipped Baal. It is a foreshadowing of the Bread that strengthens us on the way, is Viaticum to us, companion on the journey of life, the Eucharistic Flesh of him who is the source of all life.

As Viaticum, of course, the Eucharist is also companion and source of strength for the final journey of life, the one that will end our exile and bring us to the mountain of God, where "the Lord Almighty will prepare a feast of rich food for all peoples . . . the best of meat and the finest of wines" and where "he will destroy the shroud that enfolds all peoples, the sheet that covers all nations; he will swallow up death forever" (Is 25:6–8). On that mountain we shall "enter into his rest" (Ps 95:11; 91:1). It is God himself who is our rest (Ps 62:5). In Jeremiah 6:16 we read: "This is what the Lord says: ' . . . Ask where the good way is and walk in it, and you will find rest for your souls.' " Of course, what happened is that God himself, who is the good way, as he declared to us when he came as man, saying, "I am the way, the truth, and the life", repeated the invitation he had made through Jeremiah, saying, "Come to me all you who are weary and burdened and I will give you rest" (Mt 11:28). That same Lord present in the Eucharist is our companion on the way to that rest where, journey done, we shall see him face to face. It is the gift we desire for all the dead: "Eternal rest grant unto them, O Lord." It is not the rest of sleep. It is the rest of God, the rest of the Lord, the rest promised to those who do not harden their hearts, who do not have hearts of stone but hearts of flesh, since it is a heart of flesh that is required in that rest whose activity is love.

So essential does the Church consider the necessity of Viaticum for this final journey that she has legislated as follows in the 1983 Code of Canon Law:

Christ's faithful who are in danger of death, from whatever cause it may proceed, are to be refreshed by Sacred Communion in the form of Viaticum.[31]

Sacred Viaticum for the sick is not to be put off too long; those who have the care of souls are to be sedulously vigilant that the sick are to be refreshed by Viaticum while in full possession of their faculties.[32]

It is through Viaticum, the passageway to the future, that we shall finally pass beyond the appearances and behold the Lord face to face. "Your face, Lord, I will seek. Do not hide your face from me", we pray in Psalm 27:8–9. Implicit in that request is the desire for our eternal home, where we shall see the house of God, Jesus himself, face to face. "In the house of God there is endless festivity. There something is not celebrated only to have it pass away. There the choirs of angels keep endless festival because the face of God, present to them, gives a joy that has no defects."[33] It is there that we shall fully receive the Manna, hidden now under the appearances of bread (cf. Rev 2:17).

The Eucharist as Sacrifice

It was not by some aberration that so much controversy on the Eucharist has centered on the Real Presence, or that so many great theologians made the Eucharist as sacramental Presence the focal point for their treatment of the Mystery's sacrificial aspects. For the Mystery of the Eucharist as sacrifice is encompassed within the doctrine of the Real Presence. Jaroslav Pelikan has this insight when he writes:

[31] Canon 921, 1.
[32] Canon 922.
[33] Augustine, *Ennar. in Psalmos,* 42, 9; *CCSL,* 38, p. 467.

Although the doctrine of a substantial presence and the interpretation of the Lord's Supper as a sacrifice logically belonged together and those who defended the presence had difficulty refuting the sacrificial interpretation . . . [34]

When Christ, at the Consecration of the Mass, acts through his minister and sends his Spirit to transform the gifts, the Lord himself as he is now in heaven becomes present. Under the appearances of the bread and wine, Jesus is present as the "One who has suffered." Emile Mersch wrote:

Christ is undoubtedly no longer on the cross but in glory. On the altar, however, he is present neither as historical nor as glorious. He is present as the body delivered up for us and as blood poured forth for us, as dying and communicating his death to his followers. Death is assuredly his passage to glory, and is therefore a glory, but from the standpoint of earth, this glory is manifest only in the immolation leading to it. On the human level, the glory of this immolation consists in the fact that the immolation is diffused among men; it is a passing to God that contains mystically and procures sacramentally the passing of all humanity to God. [35]

Christ lives now in the Father's Presence as the "Lamb who was slain" making intercession for us (cf. Rev 5:6 and Rom 8:34). In that heavenly intercession, it is himself that he presents or offers to the Father. He offers himself as man and as Calvary's Victim. In his resurrected and glorified Body he is the human race reconciled to God. He, who "had no sin" and was "made sin for our sake" (2 Cor 5:21), merited, by his Passion and death, his own glorification and, in that, through his own humanity, the reconciliation of mankind with God.

Depending on the aspect from which one views it, a sacrifice includes several things. It is the consecration and offering to God of some material reality intended to signify the internal dispositions of the one who offers it. Sacrifice comes about as the

[34] Pelikan, 4, p. 200.
[35] Emile Mersch, *The Theology of the Mystical Body,* pp. 587–88.

necessary consequence of the recognition that we, as creatures, are totally dependent on God, whose help we need in all things; that he is infinitely good and worthy of adoration and praise; and that, as sinners, we have offended him and alienated ourselves from him. Thus, as expressed in theological terminology, sacrifice is latreutic (rendering adoration and praise), propitiatory (giving satisfaction for offenses), and deprecatory (asking God's help).

Because of sin, the human race was totally incapable of achieving any of these values in a proper way. So God himself became a man to do, as one of us, what we could not previously do on our own. As the Church prays at Mass:

> *We see your infinite power*
> *in your loving plan of salvation.*
> *You came to our rescue by your power as God,*
> *but you wanted us to be saved by one like us.*
> *Man refused your friendship,*
> *but man himself was to restore it*
> *through Jesus Christ Our Lord.*[36]

The sacrifice of Jesus, the total and voluntary giving over of his human life to the Father, achieved all the values inherent in every true sacrifice offered throughout time by our race to the Supreme Being. In offering his life in obedience to the Father's Will, he offered praise and adoration. In accepting death, which had come to our race as a consequence of sin, he propitiated for all sin and called forth from the Father what that Father of mercies was always disposed to give and had arranged for us to have through Christ: every good grace and heavenly blessing. Drawing examples from the sacrifices of the Old Covenant, the author of the Epistle to the Hebrews wrote:

> The blood of goats and bulls and the ashes of a heifer sprinkled on those who are ceremonially unclean sanctify them so that they are outwardly clean. How much more, then, will the blood of

---

[36] The *Sacramentary:* Preface III for Sundays in Ordinary Time.

> Christ, who through the eternal Spirit offered himself unblemished
> to God, cleanse our consciences from acts that lead to death, so
> that we may serve the living God.
>
> For this reason Christ is the mediator of a new covenant, that
> those who are called may receive the promised eternal inheritance—
> now that he has died as a ransom to set them free from sins
> committed under the first covenant.... By one sacrifice he has
> made perfect forever those who are being made holy (Heb 9:13-15;
> 10:14).

When Christ becomes present at Mass he does so not in order to
repeat the sacrifice of the Cross but to draw us into it, to make us
participants in his one sacrifice, priests and victims along with
himself. The Last Supper and Calvary and the Mass are all the
same sacrifice, not because the historical acts of the past are
repeated or re-presented but because of the intrinsic unity that all
these actions, past and present, possess in the one Priest and
Victim. The twofold Consecration symbolically represents what
is past, but it makes actually present Christ who is what he is now
because of those past actions. The killing and offering of the
Victim has passed; the Victim who was killed and offered remains,
now alive but Victim still. The past is irretrievable, but it always
lives on in those it has affected. Any Jewish man or woman who
lived through the concentration camps is marked forever with
victimhood, even though the actual persecution is over. So, too,
with the Victim of *the* Holocaust, the God-Man. And what is
properly his he makes ours through the Eucharist. St. Augustine,
a man who deeply recognized his own need for a sacrificial
victim, meditated on the sacrifice of Christ on Calvary and in the
Eucharist when he wrote his *Confessions:*

> How much you have loved us, Good Father, who did not spare
> your only Son but handed him over for us (cf. Rom 8:32)! How
> much you have loved us . . . ! For us he became in your sight both
> victor and victim, and victor, indeed, because he was victim; for
> us, too, he became before you both priest and sacrifice, and priest,
> indeed, because he was sacrifice, making us who were servants to
> be your sons, being born from you and serving you.

Rightly my firm hope is that, in him, you will heal all my infirmities through him who sits at your right hand and intercedes for us (cf. Rom 8:34). Otherwise I would despair. For many and great are my infirmities, many and great indeed, but your medicine is more extensive than my infirmities.

. . .

Behold, Lord, I cast my cares upon you so that I may live. . . . You know my ignorance and my weakness; teach me and heal me. Your only Son, in whom are hidden all the treasures of wisdom and knowledge (cf. Col 2:3), redeemed me with his Blood. . . . I ponder the price [of my salvation], and I eat it and drink it and share it with others. Poor man that I am, I want to be filled with it in the company of those who eat and are satisfied.[37]

"I eat the price of my salvation, I drink it, I share it with others"—the sacrificed Body and Blood of Christ. These are the words of an ordained priest who acts in the person of the one eternal Priest. All orthodox Tradition teaches us that it is Christ himself who is the principal Priest and Offerer at each Eucharist.

Therefore the august sacrifice of the altar is no mere and simple commemoration of the Crucifixion and death of Jesus Christ but rather true and proper act of sacrifice [Lat. *sacrificatio*] by which, through an unbloody immolation, the High Priest does that which he already did on the Cross, offering himself as a most acceptable victim to the eternal Father.[38]

Some have thought that Christ, as principal Offerer at each Mass, must make an explicit and individual act of his will so that the sacramental sacrifice of each Eucharist may be accomplished.[39] The difficulties inherent in such a position are evident, however, when one considers the numbers of Masses offered throughout

---

[37] Augustine, *Confessions,* 10, 43; *CSEL,* 33, pp. 278–80.

[38] *Mediator Dei;* cf. above, p. 252.

[39] Cf. Piolanti, p. 285; R. Garrigou-Lagrange, "An Christus non solum virtualiter sed actualiter offerat Missas quae cotidie celebrantur", *Angelicum* (1942): pp. 105ff.

the world on any given day. The Lord would be required to make many thousands of individual acts of his will to effect daily each one of the sacrificial offerings. It would appear better to say that the Lord's action in each Mass consists essentially of two elements: his own unending giving or offering of himself to the Father in heaven and his decision to send the Holy Spirit to effect the Consecration through the ministry of the ordained priests who act for Christ, act, that is, *in persona Christi*. In this way it is the individual acts of will of the ministerial priests that bring about the action of the Spirit of Christ to transform the elements so that they become the veil for the actual sacrificial Presence of the Lord as he is now in heaven. With that act what is being enacted here on earth in sign is truly, although invisibly, united with the Person and actions of the Lord in heaven, where he exists always as Priest and Victim.

From this point of view one is also able to see something of the necessity, the function, and the dignity of the ordained ministerial priest. It is an act of his will that effects the offering of the sacramental sacrifice. It is, of course, an act of will wholly subordinate to Christ and totally dependent on him. It must be an act of will elicited by one who has been given the authority to act in this way by Christ; it must be expressed by using Christ's own words; and its effect is achieved not by the minister's own authority and power and moral goodness but by the power of the Spirit of Christ. Nonetheless, it is a truly human and personal act of the priest, an act, moreover, upon which Christ has made himself dependent in a certain way since it is by the will of the ministerial priests that the faithful of the Church on earth and in Purgatory are sacramentally brought into the presence of heaven's Victim and Priest in order to become effectively united with all that Christ achieved for us by his unique sacrifice. In this way it can be correctly said that the ministerial priest has been given the right and duty to determine or direct in a certain measure the power that flows from the sacrifice of Christ. Since it is the priest's human will that will determine whether and when the sacramental sacrifice will be offered, so it is given to him, in a certain measure, to determine or direct the flow of graces with which his human will puts the faithful in contact when he acts as the minister for transubstantiation. It is ultimately upon this unique place of the ministerial priest and his human decisions in effecting the sacramental sacrifice that one must begin an explanation of the "fruits of the Mass" and their distribution.

Traditional theology, speaking of the benefits and graces that flow from the Mass, has categorized these "fruits" or effects in a threefold manner. First of all there are the "general fruits or effects", which flow directly to the entire Church and, indirectly, to all men and women of goodwill. There is, secondly, a particular or "special" fruit or value, which is directed to those for whom the Mass is specifically offered. And, finally, there is what the theologians call the "most special" fruit or effect, which pertains to the celebrating ministerial priest. The latter two, the "special" and "most special" fruits, directly depend on the role and will of the ministerial priest. Constituted a channel of grace by his ordination and willingly serving as such a channel each time that he offers the sacramental sacrifice, special graces are offered the priest so that, by a growth in his own holiness, he may be ever better conformed to the High Priest whose minister he is. As the Second Vatican Council taught:

> God, who alone is the Holy One and Sanctifier, willed to raise up for himself as companions and helpers men who would humbly serve the work of sanctification. Hence, priests are consecrated by God through the ministry of the bishop so that they [are made] by a special title sharers in the priesthood of Christ.[40]
>
> Therefore, since every priest in his own way bears the person of Christ, he is also enriched with special grace.[41]
>
> Thus, by acting as the Good Shepherd, they will find in the very exercise of pastoral charity the bond of priestly perfection, which will unify their life and activity. Indeed this pastoral charity flows especially from the Eucharistic sacrifice, which is therefore

[40] *Presbyterorum Ordinis,* 5.
[41] *Presbyterorum Ordinis,* 12.

the center and root of the whole life of the priest so that his priestly soul must study to apply to itself that which is enacted on the altar of sacrifice.[42]

Not only do his role and vocation make the priest the recipient of special graces that flow from the Eucharistic sacrifice, but it also is given to the priest to direct, by his will, particular graces of the sacrifice to others, those, that is, for whom he, acting in the person of Christ, offers the Mass. Perhaps nowhere else—apart from the unique privilege of consecrating the elements of bread and wine— does the special mediatorial role of the priest more manifest itself. In willing to offer the Mass for a particular intention, the priest is an instrument not merely of some specific sacramental grace (he is that in any of the sacraments he administers) but of the universal fullness of graces that flows from Christ's sacrifice, from which all the other sacraments draw. In this case, furthermore, not only are such graces made available by his ministry, but he, by his own will, is able to direct them for the benefit of specific persons and inten- tions—and direct them in a way that, in itself, offers greater benefit to the direct objects of his intention than is offered to all those Christian faithful whom the sacrifice always benefits in general.[43] It is upon this prerogative of the ministerial priest that the

---

[42] *Presbyterorum Ordinis,* 14.

[43] The considerations given here on the role of the priest are in fundamen- tal disagreement with the position presented by D. Power (cf., for example, pp. 163–64, 172ff.). Power's reflections are closely tied up with his ecumenical concerns and his recognition that the role of the priest acting *in persona Christi* and offering the sacrifice of *propitiation* are still difficulties in the ecumenical dialogue. He recognizes, however, that the Magisterium continues to insist on both the unique role of the ministerial priest and the notion of propitiation. Power writes: "Inasmuch as this Roman magisterial teaching highlights the nature of the Mass as a sacrifice of propitiation, and inasmuch as it associates this belief with the sacramental action and words of the ordained priest, it offers another interpretation of Trent than that of the ecumenical documents. ... There are ways, however, in which this Magisterium may modify the Tridentine teaching" (p. 24). We think that his own efforts at reinterpretation are not sufficient to maintain the fullness of Catholic doctrine. His conclusions

notion of the "Mass stipend" rests and finds its significance. Like all privileges in life, however, it is open to abuse and therefore is carefully regulated by the Church.[44] It must be noted, as well, that what is spoken of here in respect to the application of special fruits or graces of the Mass is spoken of in the *objective* order. That is to say that we are speaking of the special graces *offered* to the priest and to those people or intentions for whom he will offer the Eucharist. The extent to which that offer is received, the way it bears fruit, will depend on the dispositions of those for whom the graces are intended. Those dispositions, whether on the part of the priest or the part of those living or dead for whom the Mass is offered, will never be adequate to receive all that is offered. Only the Mother of the Savior was fully disposed to receive all the good coming to the human race from her Son's sacrifice. For the rest of us—men and women of all times, no matter what the degree of personal holiness—our hearts are too small to appropriate all that is offered. By receiving what we can at any given time, we work to expand those hearts, and by its example and its power the

---

on the fruits of the Mass ("The theology of fruits, which seemed to speak of the Mass as an offering of the Body and Blood of Christ made by the Church, in subordination to, but over and above, the sacrifice of Christ on the Cross, was not the majority opinion of theologians or bishops at the Council [of Trent]" (p. 130) fails to take into account the long Tradition, extending to the Fathers, that sees the Church as offering the sacrifice in and with and through Christ. His defense of the *Lima Text* (the *BEM* document) in its seeming equation of the Catholic notion of propitiation with "intercession" (p. 131) does not appear to preserve adequately what Trent meant by "propitiation", even when one grants that Trent did not make explicit what it meant by the word. The Vatican Response to the *Lima Text* (*Baptism, Eucharist and Ministry: An Appraisal*), issued too late to receive consideration in Power's book, questions whether "it is sufficient to describe the role of Christ in the 'application of the propitiatory effects of the Cross' as 'intercessor' " (*Origins*, 17, no. 23, p. 410). Propitiation, as Power notes, was, at Trent, and still is linked in some way with the notion of making satisfaction for sin. It is therefore also linked with the questions of merit and the Church's role in offering and meriting, in the accomplishing of which realities the Church views the ministerial priest's; role in offering the Mass as essential.

[44] Cf. 1983 Code of Canon Law, Canons 945–58.

sacramental reenactment of Christ's sacrifice is the instrument for that expansion. It is certainly true that our own sins and the sin of a fallen world make us incapable of appropriating for ourselves all the effects of Christ's sacrifice at any given time. Were the opposite true, our participation in one sacramental offering of that sacrifice would be sufficient. We are, however, clay that is shaped and molded slowly, so slowly indeed that we may presume that Purgatory is necessary for many of us in order to render our offering of self in and with Christ perfect. That fact—as well as the necessity of extending the effects of his sacrifice to all peoples to the end of time—helps explain the multiple sacramental repetitions of the one sacrifice of Calvary. Each Mass offered is like the yeast which must be mixed and spread until it has worked its way through all the dough (cf. Mt 13:33). By repeated offerings, some small part of a recalcitrant world is daily prepared to become "an everlasting gift" to God the Father as we pray in Eucharistic Prayer III.

In considering the intention made by the ministerial priest, some find it difficult to understand the benefit which accrues to a person or persons who are not present at the Mass when it is offered. Perhaps an analogy will help. St. Peter was not present when the sacrifice for his own redemption was offered. He was away from Calvary living through the after effects of his treason. Yet he was saved by that act from which he was absent in every way except in the will and intention of the One who gave his life as ransom for the many. Indeed, the effects of Christ's sacrifice benefited not only Peter, who was absent, but all others who, according to God's plan, are called to salvation. For there has been no favor God has given to our race since the fall of Adam and Eve which he has not given either by anticipation of or as a consequence of Christ's sacrifice. All who are saved or ever will be saved are such because knowingly or unknowingly (in the case of those of good will who know no better) they are drawn up into Christ and his sacrifice.

The prerogatives of the priest as minister of the graces of the Eucharistic sacrifice must not lead to the conclusion that the Mass "belongs" in some unique way to the ministerial priest. Such is not the case for several reasons. As already noted, the minister does not act in his own person. He acts in the person of Christ who, as priest and victim, unites to himself and includes within his own sacrificial offering his entire Mystical Body, the Church. As Augustine wrote: "In the sacrifice she offers, the Church herself is offered."[45] The ministerial priest also acts ecclesially; he is a public person representing the entire Church. It is from the Church, through the bishop, that the priest has received ordination. It is for the Church that he has been ordained. It is as the Church's representative that he offers the sacrifice. Indeed, in bearing the person of Christ, he represents not only the Lord but the entire Church. As so often emphasized in Tradition and in the teachings of the Magisterium, the Mass is the sacrifice of Christ and his Body, the Church.[46]

The realization that the Mass is the sacrifice of Christ and of the Church also helps toward an understanding of how each Mass is itself a sacrifice and not just an effective memorial of Calvary. To say that the Mass adds nothing to the sacrifice of the Cross is an imperfect understanding of how Christ effects our redemption. Jesus offered his sacrifice to the Father as a man, and as mankind's priest and representative. That sacrifice was sufficient for the reconciliation of the entire world. Nonetheless, Christ willed and wills to associate us with that sacrifice. St. Paul expresses this truth very strongly when he writes: "Now I rejoice in what was suffered for you, and I fill up in my flesh what is still lacking in regard to Christ's afflictions, for the sake of his Body, which is the Church" (Col 1:24). By Christ's will, we bring more than Christ and his offering to the Father. As sacrificial offerings we also bring ourselves, and our own lives with their joys and sufferings. Taken up into the sacrifice of Christ, these too become part of the sacrifice of

[45] Augustine, *City of God,* 10, 6; *CCSL,* 47, p. 279.

[46] Henri de Lubac has well explained the relationship and different functions of the priestly people and the ministerial priesthood in offering the Eucharist in his *The Splendor of the Church,* chap. 4, pp. 134ff.

praise and propitiation presented to the Father. Thus, each Mass is a sacrifice in which something new is being offered, the constant accumulation of what the members of Christ offer with and in him. In this way, in each sacrifice, the members of the Body add their own merits to the merits of Christ. These merits are indeed totally dependent on Christ and come to us because of him and the work of his Spirit in us. As the Preface for Holy Men and Women says: "You are glorified in your saints, for their glory is the crowning of your gifts." They are his gifts, but in truth he has made them properly our own. We stand before the Father, in Christ, with something of our own to offer. We are recipients whom he has not left beggars. What is ours, of course, is Christ's, as what is his is ours. Such is the nature of our union with him. Because of that union, what is ours to offer back to the Father is present in each offering of the Mass where, however small the congregation—even if it be the priest alone as representative—the whole Body of Christ is engaged in sacrifice. Scheeben puts all this very succinctly:

> Christ's entire mystical body is to be sacrificed through his power and according to the model of his real body. As his sacrifice is by no means purely symbolic in character, but is utterly real, so too, when considered as the sacrifice of the community, it must not merely represent what the community of itself could and should achieve for the honor of God, but should be the efficacious ideal of the real sacrifice which the community ought actually to offer.
>
> . . .
>
> In this sense Christ suffers and sacrifices in all the faithful who endure their sufferings in his spirit, and especially in the martyrs who, in the form and cause of their suffering and death, are most of all like their head. By the immolation of their bodies and their earthly life, effected in all the sufferings, mortifications, and toils of this life and crowned in death, by the immolation which takes place in Christ's members in the spirit and power of Christ, the members are made ready as a fragrant holocaust to enter with Christ into the presence of God in their glorified bodies and to be

received by God. After the general resurrection the whole Christ, head and body, will be a perfect holocaust offered to God for all eternity, since Christ himself, not only in his personal being, body and Soul, but also in his entire mystical body will be a truly universal, total holocaust offered to God through the transforming fire of the Holy Spirit.[47]

Since all this is so, it is true to say that *there are many sacrifices in the one sacrifice.* The "once-and-for-all" nature of Christ's sacrifice (cf. Heb 10) is a truth in no way mitigated by confessing the truth of the many sacrifices in the one sacrifice. Had God wanted us to be but passive recipients of his bounty, he would not have determined that we should be saved by a man like us in all things except sin. He would rather have pardoned us without demanding satisfaction. Instead, he willed to dignify and ennoble us, inserting into our own race the ability to satisfy for our evils. This he did by becoming man himself and saving us as man. Our redemption goes beyond a merely juridical imputation of pardon to us because of Christ's work. Christ actively associates us with himself, mediators in the one Mediator, priests in the one Priest. What Vatican Council II says of the mediation of Mary is a universal principle, true for all.

> No creature can ever be ranked with the Word Incarnate and Redeemer; but just as the priesthood of Christ is shared in by the ministers and the faithful in various degrees, and just as the one goodness of God is really poured out on his creatures in diverse degrees, so the unique mediation of the Redeemer does not exclude but rather raises up various forms of cooperation which participate in the unique font.[48]

It is in the sacrifice of the whole Church that the royal priesthood of all the faithful fully manifests itself. This common priesthood is immediately tied up with sacrifice, for it is the offering of sacrifice that constitutes the priest. The teaching of *Lumen Gentium,*

[47] Scheeben, p. 439.
[48] *Lumen Gentium,* 62.

10, links the priesthood of the faithful to the offering of "spiritual sacrifices" and "living sacrifices", and, of course, the Eucharist. That same section notes the difference in kind, not merely in degree, between the common and the ministerial priesthood. It is the ministerial priest who brings about the sacrifice of Christ and offers it in the name of all. "Nevertheless the faithful, by the power of their royal priesthood, join [Lat. *concurrunt*] in the offering of the Eucharist."[49]

We do not think sufficiently of this role of the laity. Not everyone belongs to the people of God, yet everyone who will be saved is saved by the sacrifice of Christ. It is the whole priestly people who offers this sacrifice, as Canon IV says, "with them and in the name of every creature under heaven". It is by the common priesthood of all that our world has a priesthood, capacitated to offer sacrifice. In that sense the whole priestly people is to the world what the ministerial priesthood is for the priestly people. This truth imposes on all the faithful, as well as upon the priest, the duty of imitating what they offer. This effort to imitate the sacrifice of the Eucharist —a notion already present in the theology of St. Ignatius of Antioch—was expressed beautifully by St. Augustine.

> On the Cross, the Lord effected a great exchange; there the purse that contained the price of our redemption was opened. When his side was opened by the lance of the soldier, there flowed forth from it the price that redeemed the whole world. The faithful and the martyrs were bought by it, and the faith of the martyrs has been tested. Their blood is witness. They have given back what was paid for them, and fulfilled what St. John said, "As Christ laid down his life for us, so should we lay down our lives for the brethren." It is said elsewhere, "You have sat down at a great table. Diligently consider what is set before you because it is necessary for you to prepare the same things." The great table is that at which the Lord of the table is himself the food. Now no one feeds the guests with his very self, but that is what the Lord Christ does. He is the One who invites, and he is the food and

---

[49] *Lumen Gentium*, 10.

drink. Therefore the martyrs recognized what they ate and drank so that they might give back the same, viz. [their own lives].[50]

In this way, the Mass becomes for us our union with Christ's sacrifice, source of all our good, power through which our offerings are made an agreeable holocaust to the Father, and the effective sign by which we are enabled, in the words of Ignatius, "to imitate the passion of our God".

The Sacrament of Sacraments

The seven realities that bear the name "sacraments" existed and were operative in the Christian community long before that particular word was used to describe them. The gradual emergence of the one word to categorize all seven sacred things was a long process, and not always consistent in its development. In respect to the Eucharist, it was even common for a long time to speak not of one, but of two sacraments, viz., the Sacrament of the Lord's Body and the Sacrament of his Blood. This usage is still reflected in some of the prayers of the Roman Rite, as, for example, when the priest speaks, in the Prayers after Communion for the feast of the Guardian Angels or St. Thérèse of the Child Jesus, of the "sacraments that we have received".

The application of the one word *sacrament* to denominate all seven sacred rites was not without danger. It was easy enough to understand the word in a univocal way, i.e., as having the identical meaning in each of the instances in which it is used. Such in fact is not the case. When applied to the seven sacred realities, the word *sacrament* is used in an analogous sense, i.e., bearing a meaning that points out the similarities among them but leaving room for the differences as well. That the use of the word *sacrament* when applied to the Eucharist and the other six was analogous was recognized relatively early in the Scholastic period.[51] Indeed,

[50] Augustine, *Sermon 329; PL*, 38, 1454–55.
[51] Cf. Pelikan, 3, pp. 204ff.

the differences between the Eucharist and the other six are great, and Aquinas, drawing upon his predecessors, wrote as follows in his commentary on the *Sentences* of Peter Lombard.

> It must be said that the Eucharist is a sacrament, but in a different way from the other sacraments. . . . A thing is said to be holy in two ways. One way, simply and per se, inasmuch as it is the subject of holiness, as when we say a man is holy. In a secondary and conditioned way, we say something is holy from the fact that it has some relationship to such holiness, either as having the power of sanctifying (as, for example, the chrism), or as having been set aside for some sacred function. . . . In the Eucharist, that which sanctifies a person is holy in the first sense, namely, as the subject of holiness because it is Christ himself. Therefore the Sacrament consists in the very sanctification of the matter [the bread and wine], and the effect of the Sacrament is the sanctification of man. Therefore, considered in itself, this Sacrament is more noble than all the other sacraments because it possesses absolute holiness, even when it is not being received. This Sacrament is the perfection of the other sacraments. . . . The source of the whole Christian life is Christ, and so in this way the Eucharist perfects the others, by joining us to Christ. Therefore this Sacrament is the perfection of all perfections.[52]

The Eucharist is holiness itself, says St. Thomas, because it is Christ. The other sacraments produce holiness in us since Christ acts through them; they are holy themselves because they are things set aside for sacred purposes. They are not, however, in themselves, subjects of holiness as is the Eucharist. This teaching on the superiority of the Eucharist in relation to the other sacraments was, as seen above,[53] formally taught by the Council of Trent. But the difference between the Eucharist and the other sacraments goes beyond that; the former is the Author of Grace, the others his actions. Since the Eucharist is Christ, the "source of the whole Christian life", the Eucharist is both the source of the

---

[52] Aquinas, *In Quatuor Libros Sententiarum,* Bk. IV, dist. VIII, quaest. I, art. I, quaest. III.

[53] Cf. above, p. 214 for Trent on the Eucharist.

other sacraments and their perfection. Indeed, it is the "perfection of perfections". Quoting Aquinas, the Second Vatican Council teaches the same truths:

> The other sacraments and also all ecclesial ministries and all the works of the apostolate are linked with the holy Eucharist and are directed to it. For in the most holy Eucharist, the entire spiritual good of the Church is contained, namely, Christ himself, our Passover and living Bread. Through his Flesh, vivified and vivifying through the Holy Spirit, he offers life to men and women who are invited and led to offer up, with him, themselves, their works, and all created things. Thus, the Eucharist stands forth as the source and culmination of the whole work of evangelization.[54]

Or, as the Dogmatic Constitution on the Church succinctly states:

> The Eucharistic sacrifice is the font and culmination of the whole Christian life.[55]

Not only is the Eucharist Christ, apart from whom there is no salvation (cf. St. Peter in Acts 4:12), it is also the "perfect sacrament of the Lord's Passion, since it contains the Christ who has suffered".[56] "Therefore the effect that the Passion of Christ realized for the world, this Sacrament realizes for the individual."[57] This Sacrament contains in itself all the graces and effects of the other sacraments, and is indeed the cause of the other sacraments.

When one has properly understood the relationship of the Eucharist to the other sacraments, it is easier to answer the question concerning the necessity of receiving the Eucharist in order to be saved. Traditionally this question has been posed in such a way that it is seen only within the perspective of the necessity of the Sacrament of Baptism for salvation because, through it, original sin is remitted and the grace of justification is bestowed. When

---

[54] *Presbyterorum Ordinis,* 5.
[55] *Lumen Gentium,* 11.
[56] *S. Th.,* III, q. 73, a. 5, ad 2.
[57] *S. Th.,* III, q. 79, a. 1c.

viewed in that perspective, the answer given normally runs as follows. Baptism is the absolutely necessary means for salvation, either in fact (i.e., actual Baptism) or in desire. When Baptism is not had in fact, through no fault of one's own, the desire to receive it may even be implicit. An implicit desire means that a person, acting under the influence of grace and cooperating with that grace (even if not aware of such cooperation), strives to lead a good life, following the dictates of conscience.[58] Aquinas taught that this implicit desire becomes operative in the first moral act performed by a person since, cooperating with grace, a person at that point can opt for that objective good that his reason is capable of perceiving. "If the person at that point directs himself to his proper end, the remission of original sin is obtained through grace. If, however, the person does not direct himself to his proper end, according to his capacity for discernment at that age, then he sins mortally, for not doing what he is capable of doing."[59] This teaching concerning an implied desire for Baptism rests, of course, on the notion that, were the person to be aware or become aware of how God has actually arranged for our salvation, the person would then embrace what God wills and seek actual Baptism. The Council of Trent (cf. DS 1524) and Pope Pius XII (cf. DS 3869–70) both dealt with this matter basically within the framework of the necessity of Baptism for justification, and thus do not speak of the necessity of receiving the Eucharist.

When the question was asked concerning the necessity of Eucharistic reception, it was too frequently dealt with in the perspective set by the questions concerning Baptism and justification, and to it various answers were given. In his *Commentary on the Sentences of Peter Lombard,* Aquinas wrote:

> Grace is the cause of salvation. Therefore nothing can be necessary for salvation if grace is able to be had without it. But the Eucharist

[58] For the Church's teaching on the possibility of salvation for those who are invincibly ignorant of all or part of God's actual will in this regard, cf. *Lumen Gentium,* 16.

[59] S.Th., I, IIae, q. 89, a.6c.

presupposes grace, because it presupposes Baptism, in which grace is given.... Therefore, in and of itself, the Eucharist is not necessary for salvation. "In and of itself" because, by command of the Church, people are obligated to communicate at least once a year.[60]

This immature opinion of Aquinas is followed even in our own day. A notable manual on theology, for example, could state: "The Sacrament of the Eucharist is not necessary as a necessary means—either in reality or in desire—to obtain salvation."[61]

The opinion is not without apparent merit. What one needs to be saved is grace; grace can and does come to us apart from the reception of the Eucharist. Therefore, the Eucharist is not, in itself, necessary for salvation. Baptized infants are a good example. They are in the state of grace but have not received the Eucharist in fact or in desire since they are incapable at their age of having any intention, either explicit or implicit. Thus, Baptism is necessary, in fact or desire, by an absolute necessity of means, and this is what Jesus meant when he said to Nicodemus, "I tell you the truth, no one can enter the Kingdom of God unless he is born of water and the Spirit" (Jn 3:5). The Eucharist, although not absolutely necessary in itself, is necessary by a "necessity of precept", since Jesus said, "I tell you the truth, unless you eat the Flesh of the Son of Man and drink his Blood, you have no life in you" (Jn 6:53) and since the Church has specified that by giving us the commandment of yearly Communion.

A major difficulty with this position, however, is that it reduces the preeminence of the Eucharist among the sacraments to one of dignity, not of effectiveness. For it makes Baptism the truly necessary sacrament, the one that is effectively the cause of justification. And such, in fact, is the way the matter is often viewed even yet. The difficulty is corrected only if one follows Aquinas in the maturing of his own views. This maturation took place as St. Thomas shifted his perspective from the *things* (grace and sacraments) that led to salvation to the *Person* who causes salvation, the one

---

[60] Aquinas, *Commentum I Quatuor Libros Sententiarum*, Book IV, dist. 9, q. I, a. I.
[61] Aldama, p. 372.

Mediator between God and man, the man Jesus Christ. It is Christ who saves, and it is union with him that effects salvation. Baptism itself is but the means to such a union with Christ, and grace the cause and consequence of such a union. It is with Christ that one must be united, either actually or in desire (explicit or implicit), in order to be saved. And, since the Eucharist is Christ, it is with the Eucharist that one must be united, actually or in desire, in order to be saved. Baptism is but a step to such a union, and its reception, either in fact or desire, directs one to the full union that comes in Eucharistic reception. Aquinas indicated this deeper insight in his approach to the two sacraments when he treated them in his *Summa.* He wrote: "Even though the Eucharist is received after Baptism, it is nevertheless first in the intention of Christ."[62]

Thus, Baptism or a desire for Baptism directs one to the Eucharist. Even infants, who can apparently have no desires, explicit or implicit, of their own, are nonetheless directed by desire to the Eucharist.

> This Sacrament of itself has the power of conferring grace, and no one has grace before the reception of this Sacrament unless there is some desire [*votum*] for the Eucharist, either on the part of persons themselves in the case of adults, or, in the case of infants, a desire supplied by the Church.[63]

> The reception of Baptism is necessary for beginning a spiritual life; the reception of the Eucharist is necessary for its completion. The reception of the Eucharist need not be had in fact. It is sufficient that it be had in desire, just as the goal is had in one's desire or intention.

> By the very fact that children are baptized they are directed, through the Church, to the Eucharist. Just as they believe through the Faith of the Church, so, by the intention of the Church, they desire the Eucharist, and as a result receive what the Eucharist effects [unity in the mystical Body of Christ].[64]

---

[62] *S. Th.,* III, q. 73, a. 5, ad 3.
[63] *S. Th.,* III, q. 79, a. 1, ad 1.
[64] *S. Th.,* III, q. 73, a. 3c.

Thus, the mature position of Aquinas is the absolute statement: no one has grace before the reception of this Sacrament, either in reality or desire. In the case of baptized infants, God has given the Church, as a parent, the right to act for them: expressing their faith and directing them to the Eucharist. In the case of adults, this faith and intention are either explicit, leading to actual reception of the sacraments, or are implied in the way they live cooperating with God's grace. The liturgical practice of the Church confirms this view. Baptism, Confirmation, and first Eucharist are called the Sacraments of Initiation. This initiation is a process, and it is progressive. The three sacraments, received in the order that is traditional (first Baptism, then Confirmation, then Eucharist), culminate in the Eucharistic union with Christ. Baptism and Confirmation are directed to that union. Even where, for pastoral reasons, Confirmation has been separated in time and received outside of the traditional order, its role as an initiatory rite is not completely forgotten, although other aspects of its significance are stressed.

It is important to realize that St. Thomas does not separate membership in the Church or the desire for membership in the Church from what he teaches concerning the necessity of the Eucharist. For Aquinas, following St. Paul and so many of the Fathers, it is the Eucharist that creates the Church. Indeed, the *res sacramenti,* the effect of the Eucharist, is the union of the Mystical Body. Thus, desire for the Eucharist (explicit or implied) is also desire for the reality created by the Eucharist, union in Christ's Mystical Body, the Church. Indeed, Aquinas begins his *Summa* article on the necessity of the Eucharist by writing:

> It must be said that the reality effected by this Sacrament [*res sacramenti*] is the unity of the mystical Body, without which one cannot be saved, since the entrance to salvation does not exist for anyone outside the Church. . . . As I have already said, though, the effect of a sacrament can be had before the actual reception of the sacrament if one has the desire for receiving it.[65]

[65] *S.Th.,* III, q. 73, a. 3c.

To summarize, then, Aquinas' teaching on what is necessary for salvation:

To be saved:

1. A person must live in union with Christ and with the Church, which is his Mystical Body.

2. This union with Christ and the Church is fully achieved here on earth through the Eucharist.

3. The reception of Baptism begins a person's union with Christ but is directed to the Eucharist as its completion and perfection.

4. For those who, through no fault of their own, are ignorant of all or part of God's salvific plan in Christ, their efforts to live a good life in cooperation with grace and according to the dictates of conscience is to be seen as an implied desire for union with Christ, and therefore for the Eucharist, which is Christ.

Some have raised an objection to the position of Aquinas, saying that it appears from what he teaches about the possibility of being justified in one's first moral act, without actually receiving Baptism, and about being united to the Eucharistic Christ by desire, even without actual reception of the Eucharist, that the sacraments are of only *relative* importance and their actual reception is unnecessary. That it relativizes the importance of the sacraments (at least of six of them) cannot be denied—but it does so only by relating them more explicitly to Christ. It reminds us that we are never to give absolute importance to *things*, even things as sacred as the sacraments. The Eucharist, however, is not a thing, or even a sacred thing. It is not simply a holy sacrifice; it is "this holy and *living* sacrifice", as Eucharistic Prayer III indicates. Unlike the other six, the Eucharist bears the aspect of "thing" or "sacred thing" only in appearances; the reality is personal, the incarnate Word, to whom all things have been made subject until he restores them to the Father and God is all in all (cf. 1 Cor 15:25–28). Moreover, to claim that, since one can attain the reality or effect of Baptism and Eucharist through an explicit or implicit desire, the actual reception of them is unnecessary, is an erroneous and dangerous misunderstanding for several reasons. First of all, it must not be thought that the remission of original sin through a good first moral act is the equivalent of Baptism in all respects. Such was not the thought of Aquinas, nor is it the teaching of the Church. Only through actual Baptism is the *character* received that conforms a person in a special way to Christ. Nor does the person justified through an implicit desire have access to the fullness of truth and grace accessible to a person fully incorporated into the Church. The teaching concerning the possibility of salvation, through actual or implied desire for Baptism and the Eucharist, does not in any way say that the opportunities for salvation are equal in any religion. Such would be a conclusion that equates the conditional with the actual, i.e., it tends to presume that because one *can* receive the grace of the sacraments without actually receiving the sacraments themselves that one *in fact* does receive that grace. This may not be—and perhaps very often is not—the case. There are an objectivity and efficacy in the actual reception of the sacraments that are not present in a desire, especially when it is only implicit, for the sacramental reality. This special objectivity and efficacy—what are technically called the *ex opere operato* nature of the sacramental rites—are based on the fact that the sacramental actions are concrete gestures of Christ himself and engage him in a way that cannot be true, at least normally, when the contact with him is initiated by a graced desire on our part. To put it another way: in God's plan, salvation and grace are meant to come to us through contact and union with Jesus Christ. This contact—like all contact among men—is normally deepest and most effective when it occurs through material or physical immediacy or proximity and is not merely that type of "spiritual" contact that occurs when humans are "attuned" to one another by intention and desire. Christ's bodily Presence to us—whether through an action or gesture in the case of the six sacraments or through his complete and bodily bestowal of self in the Eucharist—unites us effectively to him in a way that human relations both need and long for. It is such contact that helps us to know him explicitly, more intimately, and to come under his influence in a

way that a union with him by desire—especially when the desire
is only implicit—can, at least in ordinary circumstances, never
hope to achieve. Indeed, it is our ultimate ability to achieve a
personal, bodily proximity with him that makes any union with
him by desire possible. And as far as salvation itself goes, it is his
very Presence in our lives that makes that salvation possible. The
deeper, more personal, and more intimate the union, the better
our own hope for salvation. The weaker and more distant such
union is, the greater the difficulties we will have in attaining what
he offers us. Indeed, when put on the personal level where it
ultimately rests, it is inconceivable how anyone could equate
actual reception of the sacraments with a desire for the same,
especially if that desire be only implicit. It would be the same as to
say that knowing and loving Christ explicitly is of no greater
advantage to us than having no explicit knowledge or love of him.

In line with the above reflections one is also able to understand
the significance of what has come to be called a "spiritual Communion". The idea follows from the distinction already found in
the Fathers of the Church who distinguished a sacramental reception from a spiritual reception. Their emphasis in making that
distinction was on the importance of what later theology would
call a worthy and fruitful reception of Christ, wherein we not
only receive the Sacrament in a "bodily" manner but also have
our souls properly prepared and desirous of being joined to
Christ. The Sacrament was instituted so that we might become
one with the Lord in mind, heart, and affection, not merely in
body. For them, "spiritual Communion" was to accompany sacramental reception. For later theology, however, "spiritual Communion" came to mean that union with Christ that was achieved
by worthiness, desire, and affection *when sacramental reception was
not possible.* Such a spiritual reception was seen to effect a true union
with the Lord—and to enable the recipient to receive the effects of
Eucharistic Communion—even though it was a union not consummated in sacramental reception. It has become a common and
important practice of Catholic spirituality. It is not, however, to
be viewed as "receiving Communion without actually receiving

Communion". The values of a "spiritual Communion" flow from the Sacrament, since the person explicitly directs himself to the Eucharist by a desire to receive the sacramental Lord, even though, for various possible reasons, that is not possible at the moment.

> As was said above, the effects of a sacrament can be received when the sacrament is received in desire even though not received in reality. Thus, some are baptized by a baptism of fire—because of a desire for Baptism—before they are baptized with water. So, too, some eat the Eucharist spiritually before eating sacramentally. And this happens in two ways. The first way is through a desire to receive the Sacrament itself. Thus those who are baptized and who desire to receive this Sacrament, already in existence, thereby eat spiritually and not sacramentally. The other way is when one eats it figuratively, as was the case spoken of by the Apostle in 1 Corinthians 2ff. Nevertheless, sacramental eating is not thereby emptied of meaning because the actual reception of the Sacrament brings with it a fuller effect of the Sacrament than does the desire alone.[66]

Just as Baptism is the beginning of a process that is directed toward the Eucharist and draws its efficacy from it, so too the other sacraments. Each of them may be said to render concrete particular aspects of the Eucharist, in which alone the "entire spiritual good of the Church is contained". The Eucharist itself is the covenant of reconciliation, the "cup of my Blood shed for all so that sins might be forgiven". It is, therefore, the cause for the remission of all sins. From the Eucharist, through the Sacrament of Penance, the grace of reconciliation comes to all who confess the evils that separate them from the Eucharist, that is, from him who is "the atoning sacrifice for our sins" (1 Jn 2:2). The Sacrament of Penance is thus both a preparation for Eucharistic reception and a fruit of the Eucharist. The history of the penitential practice of the early Church, especially the practices associated with the public or canonical Penance, reveals how intimately bound together are the two sacraments. Only a modern catechesis that has lost sight of its roots could desire to give Penance a

---

[66] *S. Th.*, III, q. 80, a. 1, ad 3.

significance of its own apart from the Eucharist. Penance is a preparation for the Eucharist; it is Christ coming to us with pardon so that he may join himself to us in the Flesh. However, the Sacrament of Penance is not merely preparation *for* the Eucharist. An ever greater conformity to the sacrifice that takes away the sin of the world can only leave the communicant more deeply aware of the need for the virtue of Penance, an ongoing death to sin and conversion to God. That virtue is both practiced and deepened in us by the Sacrament of Penance, thus making our more frequent and fruitful use of this sacrament an essential part of our response to the Eucharistic Lord who, aware of our inconstancy, constantly enjoins us to "repent and believe the good news" (Mk 1:15). Penance, virtue and sacrament, flows from that cup of his Blood, shed for forgiveness and healing.

Writing of the work of Jesus, St. Matthew said: "When evening came, men who were demon-possessed were brought to him, and he drove out the spirits with a word and healed all the sick. This was to fulfill what was spoken through the prophet Isaiah, 'He took up our infirmities and carried our diseases' " (Mt 8:16–17). The healing ministry of Jesus to our spirits and flesh is carried on by the Eucharistic Lord. Like Penance, but directed more immediately to physical infirmity and its consequences, the Anointing of the Sick is the sacramental manifestation of that ministry. In his poem *Felix Randall,* Hopkins depicts the thoughts of a priest who has just heard of the death of one of his parishioners whom he had been attending in his sickness. The priest reflects on how the Anointing had changed the man, although in fact the change had begun before with the man's return to the Eucharist.

> Sickness broke him. Impatient, he cursed at first, but mended
> Being anointed and all; though a heavenlier heart began some
> Months earlier, since I had our sweet reprieve and ransom
> Tendered to him. Ah well, God rest him all road ever he
> offended![67]

[67] Gerard Manley Hopkins, *Felix Randall,* in *A Hopkins Reader,* John Pick, ed., Garden City, N.Y.: Image Books-Doubleday, 1966, p. 64.

"Our sweet reprieve and ransom" is, of course, the Eucharist, which is itself the ordinary Sacrament of the sick. Jesus is the Healer. His very Presence is our consolation and cure. If but to touch his garment with faith is sufficient to heal (cf. Lk 8:42–48), how much more curative is actual union with his Flesh! For those seriously ill, however, from sickness or old age, and rendered subject to the miseries, trials, and temptations that accompany such serious sickness, he further symbolizes his power and concern through the rite of anointing. It is the gesture of our Healer and Restorer by which he ministers to the whole person. By it (when previous reception of the Sacrament of Penance is not possible) he pardons sin, the ultimate cause of sickness and death; he comforts mind and body in their trials, and even restores them to the degree of health appropriate to the time allotted for our pilgrimage. The anointing is his gesture, effected by his action and his power, through the hands of a minister. But to show that it is a gesture that flows from him, the sacramental rite is to be completed, when possible, by Communion so that he who has touched us spiritually may be with us in the Flesh.

The links between the Eucharist and Confirmation are intrinsic and manifold. The humanity of the risen Christ is the "conjoined instrument" of salvation; from that sacred humanity flow all the good things that come to our race. Raised to heaven, Christ's human nature is, above all, the medium by and through which we receive the Holy Spirit, who is now and forever the Spirit of Christ. As the Second Vatican Council said:

> The Son of God, in the human nature united to himself, redeemed the human race and transformed it into a new creature (cf. Gal 6:15; 2 Cor 5:17) by overcoming death through his own death and Resurrection. Communicating his Spirit, he has made his brothers and sisters, called together from all nations, in a mystical way his own Body.
>
> . . .
>
> In order that we may be unceasingly renewed in him (cf. Eph 4:23), Christ has given us of his Spirit, who, being one and the

same in head and members, so vivifies, unifies, and moves the whole Body that his function was able to be compared by the holy Fathers with the function that the principle of life, the soul, fulfills in the human body.[68]

Meditating on the Mystery of the communication of the Holy Spirit by the humanity of Christ, Emile Mersch wrote:

The God-Man, because of what he is, possesses the fullness of the Spirit and has it in his humanity, not assuredly by reason of this humanity but by reason of him to whom the humanity belongs; and he pours out this fullness over the whole human race. This mysterious communication, this participation in Christ's humanity, is an earnest of what our own humanity is to become.[69]

As the citations make clear, the role of the Holy Spirit is to bind us to Christ, making us live by his Spirit, exercising a life that has his Spirit as activating principle. And this Spirit is communicated to us through the Eucharist. With profound insight, Aquinas wrote:

That person has eternal life who eats and drinks not only sacramentally but also spiritually. Indeed, whoever eats and drinks sacramentally receives this Sacrament. The one who eats and drinks spiritually, however, is the one who reaches the reality of the Sacrament which is twofold: (1) the reality contained and signified, namely, the whole Christ who is contained under the species of bread and wine; (2) the reality signified but not contained, namely, the mystical Body of Christ, which exists in the predestined, the called, and the chosen.

Whoever eats and drinks spiritually becomes a sharer in the Holy Spirit, through whom we are united to Christ by a union of faith and charity and through whom we are made members of the Church.[70]

---

[68] *Lumen Gentium,* 7.

[69] Mersch, p. 427.

[70] Aquinas, *Super Evangelium S. Joannis,* chap. 6, lec. VII, nos. III and IV, p. 183.

It was by the power of the Holy Spirit that Mary conceived as God created a human nature for his Word. It is by the invoked Presence of the Holy Spirit, sent now by the risen Lord, that the words of Consecration change the bread and wine into the resurrected Flesh and Blood of Christ. And it is the Holy Spirit, breathed into the communicant by the Eucharistic Lord, that binds the members of the Church to Jesus and to each other. Indeed, it can be said that Christ feeds us with his very Flesh and Blood *in order* to give or deepen our share in his Spirit. Through the Sacrament, the physical Presence of Christ remains with us for only a brief time; it perdures only as long as the sacramental species of bread and wine remain. This union in Flesh is intended, however, to bind us to him in the Spirit, the Lord's Flesh serving as instrument for the bestowal of the Spirit. One can see here both the humility of the incarnate Word and the mediatorial role of his Flesh. God the Son uses his very humanity for a purpose beyond itself, namely, to unite us to the divinity and, in him, to each other so that our fellowship may be with the Father as well as with the Son (cf. 1 Jn 1:3). It was to establish this fellowship that the Son became incarnate and still uses his humanity as an instrument for a good even beyond itself. For in him we too are subjected to the Father so God can be all in all (cf. 1 Cor 15:28). The reception of the Eucharistic Flesh of Christ and our share in the offering of the sacrifice is intensely Trinitarian. By the Flesh of Christ, we are united to and in his Spirit so that we might be a pleasing offering to the Father.

As is true of Baptism, the Sacrament of Confirmation is meant to anticipate the completion of Christian initiation that comes with Eucharistic reception. In both Baptism and Confirmation the Spirit comes and works by anticipation of the gift that will temporally come later, the sacramental reception of him who bestows the Spirit. In this, both sacraments are like the many workings of the Spirit—most notably the Immaculate Conception of Mary—which anticipated the Redemption of Christ, which is now memorialized and made effective for us in the Eucharist. Like all the sacraments, Confirmation effectively symbolizes an aspect of the fullness of grace present in Christ. In the case of Confirmation, that aspect is a deepened conformity to Christ the priest, and especially to the prophetic office of the Lord. The one confirmed is indelibly marked by the prophetic office of Jesus and thus "prepared to give an answer to everyone who asks you to give a reason for the hope that you have" (1 Pet 3:15).

On the Sacrament of Orders we need not repeat what has been said already. It may suffice to note that each of its three degrees, diaconate, priesthood, episcopacy, makes concrete particular aspects of the person and work of the Lord who is personally present and operative in the Eucharist. Each of them conforms the man ordained more intimately to Christ the priest, bestowing through the sacramental character a depth of conformity that differs from the royal priesthood of all the faithful "in essence and not only in degree".[71] Christ as servant-minister to others is manifest in the role of deacon; Christ the priest-offerer of sacrifice is manifest in the presbyterate; Christ as authoritative teacher is manifest in the episcopate.

> The other sacraments make men members of the Church; holy Orders makes a man a representative of the whole Church. The other sacraments join members to the Body that they may perform the actions of members. . . . Holy Orders joins a member to the Body that he may perform the actions of the Body. . . .
>
> This fact reveals its excellence, and also what we may call its inferior quality: its excellence in the order of the function it gives, its inferiority in the order of the holiness it confers. In other words, the sacrament confers the power to administer all the sacraments but does not confer a holiness proportionate to this universal power. . . . This is beyond question; for such a holiness would have to be a holiness of God, the total holiness of Christ, holiness itself.[72]

In other words, the holiness proportionate to the sacrament that enables men to represent the entire Church and administer

---

[71] *Lumen Gentium,* 10.
[72] Mersch, p. 578.

the other sacraments would have to be the holiness of him from whom all the sacraments and all grace flow, the Eucharistic Lord himself. That is not possible, but it adds, nevertheless, a new demand upon the ordained. More than all others they must strive to imitate what they handle and celebrate. Furthermore, as noted above, the fruits of Christ's sacrifice are directed in the first place to them so that, by their free cooperation, God, who has begun the good work in them, may bring it to completion.

The Eucharist is the Sacrament of sacraments. If the statement is properly understood, it may be said that there is but one Sacrament, and six derivatives of it. Such an observation is certainly true, but it runs the risk of a "Eucharistic monism", i.e., an attitude in which the six are depreciated since all that they "have to offer" is contained in fullness in the Eucharist. This attitude already appears at times in respect to the Sacrament of Penance. Someone—perhaps from a dislike of confessing to the priest, perhaps from some other motive—will say or write: "The Eucharist itself forgives sin when I am sorry. There is no strict need of going to Confession." There is much truth in the statement. The Eucharist is the source and cause for forgiveness of sins. Indeed, it is even true to say that the Eucharist will itself cause pardon and sanctifying grace for a repentant sinner—even original sin—if the person is *not conscious of being in serious sin and is repentant of all his sins.* This truth was intended in the theological texts that spoke of "receiving first grace *per accidens*". However, such an approach to the sacraments errs on many accounts. Although the Eucharist is indeed the source and cause of all grace and all the sacraments, it has been the intention of Christ to specify and direct certain aspects of his own work through the other sacramental rites. For the sincere Christian, the will of the Lord is normative. One will approach him, in whom all riches are contained, in the manner appropriately decided by him. The various sacramental rites are intended to highlight the different ways he touches our lives. As a rite, the Eucharist alone is unable to signify all these aspects, and human nature needs the various symbolic and expressive gestures if it is to be led to contemplate and appreciate all that the Eucharistic

Lord is for us and offers to us. What is more, so normative is his will in this matter that certain things—even when good faith is present—cannot be imparted by the Eucharist. The sacramental characters of Baptism, Confirmation, and Orders cannot be received without the actual reception of those sacraments. Orders and Marriage cannot be validly entered into simply by a reception of the Eucharist. Thus, while the particular graces peculiar to each sacrament are present in the Eucharist as an effect is present in its cause, Eucharistic participation cannot supplant the other six sacraments. In the case, of course, where such a supplanting was attempted in bad faith (e.g., a person who, knowing the injunctions of St. Paul and the Church vis-à-vis the type of examination needed before Eucharistic reception), not only are such graces not received but also one commits the grave sin of sacrilege. Our oneness with him must be a unity of mind, heart, and affection that means, minimally, the effort to do what he wants as he wants it. Without that effort, our union with him in the Eucharist is like a marriage whose only bond is the flesh.

The Eucharist and the Church

Our union with him in the Eucharist is like a marriage. This marriage imagery is but an extension of that used to describe the relationship between God and his people as depicted in the Bible. As Pope John Paul II has not tired of pointing out, God's relationship to his people is nuptial, spousal. He makes a covenant of marriage with his people. This is a truth evidenced long ago by the prophets of the Old Testament, Hosea and Ezekiel in particular. In a special way this love was praised and meditated upon in the Old Testament's Song of Songs, the Canticle of Canticles. Today, it is true, it has become more common to interpret the Canticle as a poem about human love, but such an approach is one that has not been advanced without protest. One of the outstanding Catholic theologians of the twentieth century has written:

Exegetes are still discussing the antecedents of this enigmatic little composition and its original meaning. We may note that those who will not admit any "mystical" interpretation do not merely strike at "the most sacred fibers of the heart and the deepest theological roots of our faith"; their naturalist exegesis, even when it does not stop short at the incredibly platitudinous, is no more able than any other to avoid all use of allegory.... Interpretations of this kind, and many others whose more modern and more scientific nature still clothe a similar arbitrariness, are really not worth forsaking the traditional paths for.[73]

In reality a conflict between a "mystical" and "realistic" interpretation of the Song of Songs should not arise. The love of man and woman, covenanted in the fruitful union of marriage, was ordained by God from the beginning as a sacred and "mystical" reality. It is noble and holy in itself but, as the prophets testify, it was meant to point beyond itself. It is the earthly pattern of a holier and more intimate love, the union of God with Israel. Symbolism is inherent in the covenant of marriage as God established it. To deny that symbolism is not the enrichment of human love but its impoverishment.

The Old Testament affirmations concerning a covenanted love must be viewed as only a courtship or betrothal, however, in light of the Mystery of the Incarnation. For it is at the Annunciation that God and man become two in one Flesh. On this point, Aquinas, again summarizing Tradition, wrote:

> There is a certain spiritual marriage between the Son of God and human nature. And therefore through the Annunciation there was awaited the consent of the Virgin acting in the place of all of human nature.[74]

[73] Henri de Lubac, *The Splendor of the Church*, p. 354. St. Paschasius Radbertus, the first systematist of Eucharistic theology, also interpreted the Canticle as expressive of Christ's union with the Church. Cf. his *Expositio in Mattheo Libri XII; CCCM*, 56, pp. 116–20.

[74] *S.Th.*, III, q. 30, a. 1c.

This nuptial relationship between the Son of God and those he came to save was indicated by the Savior himself when he described himself as the "bridegroom" in the midst of his followers (cf. Mt 9:15). St. Paul, following the Master, expounded the same teaching in his classic text on marriage in Ephesians 5:22–33. " 'For this reason a man will leave his father and mother and be united to his wife, and the two will become one flesh.' This is a profound mystery—but I am talking about Christ and the Church." For Paul, this truth is not empty imagery. Just as it is "through the Eucharist [that] the Church not only receives her name (Body of Christ) but also her mission to extend Christ's salvation to the world",[75] so, too, is it through the Eucharist that the marriage covenant between the Lord and his Bride is established. The Covenant sealed in blood between Israel and God (cf. Ex 24) was a betrothal of lovers, a love that longed for its consummation. Therefore, much of the beloved's words in the *Canticle* are expressions of longed-for fulfillment. "I arose to open for my lover . . . I opened the door for my lover but my lover had left; he was gone. My heart sank at his departure. I looked for him but did not find him. I called him but he did not answer" (Song 5:5–6). That search is answered when the lover, in his human Flesh, consummates the union, sealing the Covenant "not by means of the blood of goats and calves, but by his own Blood" (cf. Heb 9:12). "This cup is the New Covenant in my Blood" (Lk 22:20). This is the marriage covenant that rests on the reality of the Eucharistic Flesh that we receive. "Let him kiss me with the kisses of his mouth— for your love is more delightful than wine. . . . I am my lover's and my lover is mine; he browses among the lilies" (Song 1:2; 6:3). The Eucharist accordingly becomes the prolongation of what the Word promised to Israel and begins in Mary: the process of taking Flesh to himself—Flesh for himself in Mary; Flesh to himself by uniting his Flesh to ours in Eucharistic Communion. The Eucharist is also, in this way, the literal fulfillment of the promise that, when lifted

[75] *Vatican Response to WCC Document Baptism, Eucharist and Ministry: An Appraisal,* in *Origins,* 17, no. 23, p. 411.

up, he would draw all things to himself (cf. Jn 12:32). This union of two (and many) in one Flesh is mirrored by the Sacrament of Marriage and reveals the grandeur of the marriage union. Of all the sacraments, it is the one that most fully reflects the reality of the Eucharist.

> Indeed, by means of baptism, man and woman are definitively placed within the new and eternal covenant, in the spousal covenant of Christ with the Church. And it is because of this indestructible insertion that the intimate community of conjugal life and love, founded by the Creator, is elevated and assumed into the spousal charity of Christ, sustained and enriched by his redeeming power.
>
> By virtue of the sacramentality of their marriage, spouses are bound to one another in the most profoundly indissoluble manner. Their belonging to each other is the real representation, by means of the sacramental sign, of the very relationship of Christ with the Church.
>
> Spouses are therefore the permanent reminder to the Church of what happened on the Cross.[76]

"The permanent reminder of what happened on the Cross." For all its greatness, however, it is only a sign, a reminder. The union of flesh and heart and affections that it achieves and sanctifies is but an image of the intimacy realized between Christ and his Bride, the Church, between Christ and those joined to him in the Flesh. As the love of husband and wife is "singularly expressed and perfected" by the marital act, "which signifies and fosters the mutual self-giving by which the spouses enrich each other with a joyful and grateful heart",[77] so Eucharistic Communion singularly expresses and perfects union with the Lord. Truly, the union of Christ and those united to him is like the union of husband and wife but is of a transcendent order. As was true in Mary, so for us, it is a union of flesh and flesh achieved virginally.

Christ's spousal union with the Church and with each individual member is achieved in the Flesh but is expressed and nourished

---

[76] John Paul II, *Familiaris Consortio*, 13. Boston: St. Paul Editions, p. 26.
[77] *Gaudium et Spes*, 49.

in word. The Bridegroom speaks; the Spouse listens and responds in reflection and prayer. The Father's Word who feeds us with his Flesh is the Word who speaks through the Scriptures. The relation between the Eucharist and Scripture is therefore intrinsic, rooted in the identity of the One who is our food and inspires, through his Spirit, the "divine words".[78] Thomas à Kempis wrote:

> In this life there are two things I particularly need, without which this miserable life would be unbearable. While detained in the prison of my body, I confess my need for two things: food and light. Knowing my weakness, you have given me your holy Body for the nourishment of my soul and body and your word as a lamp to my feet.
> Without these two I cannot live well; for the word of God is the light of my soul, and your Sacrament is the Bread of life.[79]

Undoubtedly the Eucharistic Christ is always in intimate colloquy with those who receive him or who nourish their love for him in adoration before the Blessed Sacrament. Untold millions have grown in intimacy with him and been made saints with at times only the most minimal knowledge of the Sacred Scriptures. In doing so, however, they have profited from that compassion of his that supplies for our defects and our involuntary ignorance of his will. For his will is that we who feed on his Flesh drink also of his every word from Genesis through Revelation. That is the lesson that his Bride the Church gives us in the way she structures the Eucharistic liturgy, which she teaches must be the norm for our personal devotion.

> The Bride of the incarnate Word, the Church, strives to advance to an understanding of the Sacred Scriptures that is each day more profound.[80]

---

[78] *Dei Verbum*, 23.
[79] *Imitation of Christ*, Bk. 4, 4, p. 266.
[80] *Dei Verbum*, 23.

What is true of the Church must be true of each of her children so that, in receiving him, each may pray: "How sweet are your words to my taste, sweeter than honey to my mouth" (Ps 119:103).

The marriage imagery, founded on a deep and mysterious reality, can be developed further by reflecting on an unfaithful relationship to the Eucharistic Lord. So often in the Old Testament the unfaithfulness of the espoused Israel was called adultery. So, too, with more reason in the New Covenant, and, especially so, in the case of sacrilegious reception of the Eucharist.

Sacrilege is adultery. In his powerful account of the destruction of a marriage through adultery, Tolstoy gives us the reactions of the faithless spouse and her lover after they have first consummated their sinful relationship.

> Looking at him, she had a physical sense of her degradation and could not utter another word. He felt what a murderer must feel when he looks at the body he has robbed of life. The body he had robbed of life was their love, the first state of their love. There was something frightful and revolting in the recollection of what had been paid for by this terrible price of shame. Shame at her spiritual nakedness crushed her and infected him. But in spite of the murderer's horror before the body of his victim, that body must be hacked to pieces and hidden, and the murderer must make use of what he has obtained by his crime.[81]

Thus, says Tolstoy, adultery is a type of murder. So, too, the marital union with Christ in the Eucharist when he is received unfaithfully.[82] It renders the faithless one, in St. Paul's words, "guilty of the Body and Blood of the Lord" (1 COR 11:27). For this reason the Church prays:

---

[81] Leo Tolstoy, *Anna Karenin,* translated by Rosemary Edmonds, England: Penguin Classics, 1978, p. 165.

[82] Aquinas expresses similar thoughts in *S. Th.,* III, q. 80, a. 5, ad 2.

In accepting these gifts, O our God, purify us from every stain of body and soul. Teach us how to perfect our holiness through reverence for you, so that, receiving a portion of your hallowed gifts without any reproach from our conscience, we may be united to the holy Body and Blood of your Christ. Having received them worthily, may we have Christ living in our hearts and may we become the temple of your Holy Spirit.

Especially, O God, let none of us become guilty regarding these awesome and heavenly Mysteries of yours, or let us become weakened in spirit or body by partaking of them unworthily. O Lord, grant that we, even until our last breath, may worthily receive a portion of your holy gifts as a provision for the journey to eternal life and for an acceptable defense before the dread tribunal of your Christ. Then, together with the saints who have been pleasing to you at all times, may we become partakers of your eternal blessings that you have prepared for those who love you.[83]

"Marriage", wrote Pope Paul VI beautifully in the encyclical *Humanae Vitae,* "is a special form of friendship", and, from the same Pope, the Church has been taught that "prayer, contemplation, love, and friendship" are the higher values of life.[84] As marriage reflects the Church's union with Christ and is itself solidified and enriched by the spouses' union with Christ in the Eucharist, so all our earthly friendships are intended to find their support in the Eucharist and be indescribably enriched by it. Writing to his son about marriage, Tolkien said:

Out of the darkness of my life, so much frustrated, I put before you the one great thing to love on earth: the Blessed Sacrament. . . . There you will find romance, glory, honor, fidelity, and the true way of all your loves upon earth, and more than that: death: by the divine paradox, that which ends life, and demands the surrender of all, and yet by the taste (or foretaste) of which alone can what you seek in your earthly relationships (love, faithfulness, joy)

[83] *The Liturgy of St. Basil: Prayer of the Litany,* in *Byzantine Book of Prayer,* Pittsburgh, Pa.: Byzantine Seminary Press, 1976, pp. 205–6.

[84] Paul VI, *Populorum Progressio,* 20.

be maintained, or take on that complexion of reality, of eternal endurance, that every man's heart desires.[85]

The taste of the Eucharist is that alone by which all our earthly relationships are maintained and take on that complexion of reality, of eternal endurance that our hearts desire. The words are, in effect, a commentary on the First Commandment. Love of God above all things leads to a right order and harmony in all other relationships, thereby strengthening them in anticipation of the companionship of heaven. Indeed, it is the Eucharist that is the pledge of a future for friendship when our journey here ends.

> Comradeship and serious joy are not interludes in our travel; but ... our travels are interludes in comradeship and joy, which through God shall endure forever. The inn does not point to the road; the road points to the inn. And all roads point at last to an ultimate inn where we shall meet Dickens and all his characters; and when we drink again it shall be from the great flagons in the tavern at the end of the world.[86]

Heaven as a tavern may seem a typical Chestertonian remark, but the imagery was created by God himself inspiring his prophets.

> On this mountain the Lord Almighty will prepare a feast of rich food for all peoples, a banquet of aged wine, the best of meat, and the finest of wines (Is 25:6).

And the words of the Savior confirm the promise of table-fellowship in the communion of saints with Christ himself to serve his guests.

> Here I am! I stand at the door and knock. If anyone hears my voice and opens the door, I will come in and eat with him and he with me (Rev 3:20). I tell you the truth, [the master] will dress himself to serve, will have them recline at the table, and will come and wait on them (Lk 12:37).

---

[85] J. R. R. Tolkien, pp. 53–54.
[86] G. K. Chesterton, *Charles Dickens, The Last of the Great Men,* New York: Press of the Readers Club, 1942, p. 212.

For a Christian, of course, our table-fellowship here must yield a love directed to all those Christ invites to eat of his Flesh. In a special way, the love that flows from the table must encompass the poor and lowly. As Aquinas wrote:

Panis angelicus fit panis hominum;	*The Bread of angels has*
Dat panis caelicus figuris	*become the Bread of mankind;*
terminum;	*This heavenly Bread puts an*
O res mirabilis; manducat	*end to all images;*
Dominum	*O wonderful reality! The*
Pauper, servus, et humilis.	*poor, the slave, and the*
	humble eat the Lord.

The Eucharistic Christ, who feeds the poor, the slave, and the humble, is both the model and cause of the Church's love of preference for the poor.

> Christ Jesus, although he was rich, became poor in order to make us rich by means of his poverty. St. Paul is speaking here of the Mystery of the Incarnation of the eternal Son, who came to take on mortal human nature in order to save man from the misery into which sin had plunged him. Furthermore, in the human condition Christ chose a state of poverty and deprivation in order to show in what consists the true wealth that ought to be sought, that of communion of life with God. He taught detachment from earthly riches so that we might desire the riches of heaven. . . . Therefore the beatitude of poverty that he proclaimed can never signify that Christians are permitted to ignore the poor who lack what is necessary for human life in this world.[87]

The measure of our fruitful reception of the Eucharistic Lord is charity in thought, word, and deed. This is a truth always taught in the Church from the beginning, as the texts cited earlier from Ss. Ignatius and Justin, Leo XIII, and Paul VI indicate.[88] It must be also a charity that, according to the abilities and situation of each communicant, effectively reflects the Church's love of prefer-

---

[87] Congregation for the Doctrine of the Faith, *Instruction on Christian Freedom and Liberation,* March 22, 1986, nos. 66–67, Boston: St. Paul Publications.

[88] See above, pp. 16, 20, 245, 264f.

ence for the poor. Even the man who is not able to say that he has kept all the Commandments from his youth but comes rather to the Eucharist as a repentant sinner is looked upon and embraced by the Lord with love. But that same Lord, always consistent, still says: Go, sell, give to the poor (cf. Mk 10:17–21). The One Bread that feeds the multitudes is a constant reminder that "the duty of every person, the urgent duty of the Christian, is to consider what is superfluous to them according to the measure of others' needs."[89] Thus, the Eucharist ever remains the force that impels the Church's apostolate for social, political, and economic justice. The bond of solidarity established by our participation in the One Bread and the evangelical imperative to lead all mankind to share that Bread is the same bond of solidarity that must unite all the Church's members to struggle against the structural and institutionalized forms of sin that oppress so many of the world's peoples. A participation in the Eucharist that fails to stimulate a "social consciousness" is a defective participation. This is one of the fine themes stressed by some of the various "theologies of liberation". It is true, indeed, that some of those same theologies have "disputed that the participation of Christians who belong to opposing classes at the same Eucharistic table still makes any sense". For them, the Eucharist "becomes a celebration of the people in their struggle. As a consequence, the unity of the Church is radically denied", and "unity, reconciliation, and Communion in love are no longer seen as a gift we receive from Christ".[90] Such excesses, however, must not be allowed to obscure the fact: Communion demands liberation.

Communion, which unites us with the saints in glory and with the members of the Church being purified, and which is the impelling motive for the whole range of the Church's contributions to the social, economic, and political development of mankind, is

[89] John XXIII, cited in n. 10 of sec. 69 of *Gaudium et Spes*.

[90] Congregation for the Doctrine of the Faith, *Libertatis nuntius: An Instruction on the Theology of Liberation*, Aug. 1984, nos. IX and X; *TPS*, 29, no. 4, pp. 302, 306.

also, of course, the most apt description of the organization of the Church Universal. Just as it is the Eucharist that gives the Church her existence and name as Body of Christ, so it is Communion that links the individual local Churches in the one Catholic Community. Such is the explicit teaching of the Second Vatican Council.

> The bishop, marked with the plentitude of the Sacrament of Orders, is the "steward of the grace of the Supreme priesthood". This is especially true in the Eucharist, which the bishop himself offers or causes to be offered and by which the Church continually lives and grows. This Church of Christ is truly present in all legitimate local congregations of the faithful, which, adhering to their shepherds, are themselves called churches in the New Testament. For, in their own territory, these churches are the New People, called by God in the Holy Spirit and in much fullness (cf. 1 Th 1:5). In these congregations, through the preaching of the gospel of Christ, the faithful are gathered together and the Mystery of the Lord's Supper is celebrated "so that through the food and Blood of the Lord's Body the whole brotherhood may be linked together".
>
> . . . In these communities, frequently small and poor as they may be, even living among non-Christians [lit., "or living in the dispersion"], Christ is present and, by his power, the one, holy, catholic, and apostolic Church is joined together. This is so because "participation in the Body and Blood of Christ brings it about that we pass into that which we receive".[91]

The model for the Church, therefore, is not to be found in some transnational conglomerate or business corporation, or in the political linking of independent states in a federal or world union, which would have its central executive in Rome. Nor can the Universal Church "be conceived as the sum of the particular Churches, or as a federation of particular Churches".[92] Rather,

[91] *Lumen Gentium*, 26.

[92] John Paul II, *Address to the U.S. Catholic Bishops:* September 16, 1987, *Pope John Paul II: "Building up the Body of Christ", Pastoral Visit to the United States,* ed. National Catholic News Service, San Francisco: Ignatius Press, 1987, p. 183.

the Church's model is Eucharistic Communion. As the individual members enter into communion with one another by passing into him whom they receive, so the local congregations are drawn out of their own isolation by a kind of "ecclesial circumincession", a living in and for one another through Eucharistic Communion. It is this living in and for one another, through the Eucharist, that makes the Petrine ministry of the bishop of the local Church of Rome a ministry intrinsic to each community.

> We must see the ministry of the Successor of Peter not only as a "global" service reaching each particular Church from "outside", as it were, but as belonging already to the essence of each particular Church from "within".[93]

The truth of the intrinsic nature of the Petrine ministry in each local Church is specifically witnessed to at each offering of the Mass when the Pope is prayed for. This is the Eucharistic Communion in life, faith, and prayer that was already described by St. Luke when he wrote: "They devoted themselves to the Apostles' teaching and to the fellowship, to the breaking of the bread, and to prayer" (Acts 2:42). It is this Eucharistic Communion that stimulates their concern for one another and for all who are called to be of their number. "All the believers were together and had everything in common. Selling their possessions and goods, they gave to anyone as he had need" (Acts 2:44-45). It is this Eucharistic Communion that unites them as well with those who have gone before them, and especially with her whom they invoke collectively as Mother.

The Eucharist and Our Lady

In her devotion to the Eucharistic Lord the Church has long sung the *Ave verum*. The thoughts of this hymn are far older than the

---

[93] John Paul II, *Address to the U.S. Catholic Bishops:* September 16, 1987, *Pope John Paul II: "Building up the Body of Christ"*, p. 183.

fourteenth century, which saw its publication. Already in 107, St.
Ignatius of Antioch, as seen above, noted that the heretics "abstain
from the Eucharist and from prayer, because they do not confess that
the Eucharist is the Flesh of our Savior Jesus Christ, which suffered
for our sins and which, in his goodness, the Father raised".[94]
Following Ignatius, the Church's Magisterium repeated against
Berengarius that the Eucharist "is the true Body of Christ, which
was born of the Virgin, which hung on the Cross as an offering
for the salvation of the world and which sits at the right hand of
the Father". Aquinas, too, following St. Ambrose, taught the
same truth when he wrote:

> The change that takes place in this Sacrament is not like any
> natural change but is, rather, completely supernatural, effected by
> God's power alone. Therefore Ambrose says: "It is clear that the
> Virgin gave birth to Christ beyond the order of nature. And that
> which we consecrate is the Body born from the Virgin."[95]

Ave verum corpus natum de Maria Virgine. Here we have recalled
for us the first link of Mary with the Eucharist. It is she who has
provided Flesh for our bread. "The bread that I will give", he
would say, "is my Flesh for the life of the world" (Jn 6:15).
Reflecting on that truth, Augustine preached: "She gave milk to
our bread."[96] Mary's consent to the Incarnation of the Word is
the condition that makes our eating possible.

The *Ave verum* serves to remind us of two other aspects of
Mary's relationship to the Eucharist. She is, in the first place, the
great defender of Eucharistic truth. All symbolism and false spiri-
tualism are excluded when one recognizes in the Eucharistic
species the very Flesh that God has taken from her. Whatever must
be said correctly about the qualities of the risen Body of the Lord,
one truth remains intact. What has risen from the tomb and what
is in truth now our food is the *verum corpus natum de Maria Virgine,*

---

[94] Smyrna, 7. Cf. above, p. 16.

[95] *S.Th.,* III, q. 75, a. 4a, 4c.

[96] Augustine, *Sermon 184: On Christmas; PL,* 38, 997.

the very Body born of Mary. It is not by accident that the Catholic Church and the separated churches of the East, which have best maintained that truth intact, are marked by a fervent love for the one who gave him our flesh.

In combating the Eucharistic errors of our own day, Pope Paul VI taught this truth when he closed his encyclical *Mysterium Fidei* with the prayer:

> May the most Blessed Virgin Mary from whom Christ the Lord assumed that Flesh that in this Sacrament "is contained, offered, and received" under the appearances of bread and wine intercede before the Father of mercies for us.[97]

In the second place, as the *Ave verum* helps to recall and as Pope Paul made explicit in the prayer just cited, Mary is the model of devotion for all who are called, imitating her, to receive the enfleshed Word. In an age of frequent Communion on the part of nearly all practicing Catholics, it is more than ever necessary to remember the required conditions for a worthy reception of the Most High. Those conditions have never changed substantially, and what the decree *Sacra Tridentina Synodus* said of them in summary form is still valid.

> No one who is in the state of grace, and who approaches the holy table with a right and devout intention, can be prohibited therefrom. A right intention consists in this: that whoever approaches the holy table should do so, not out of routine, or vainglory, or human respect, but rather wishing to please God, to be more closely united with him by charity....
>
> Although it is especially fitting that those who receive Communion frequently or daily should be free from venial sin, at least from such as are fully deliberate, and from every affection thereto, nevertheless, it is sufficient that they be free from mortal sin, with the purpose of never sinning in the future; and if they have this sincere purpose, it is impossible but that daily communicants

[97] *Mysterium Fidei; AAS,* 57, p. 774 (no. 75).

should gradually free themselves even from venial sins, and from all affection thereto.[98]

As reflective of Patristic thought, Augustine wrote that "what the Lord magnified in Mary was that she did the will of the Father, not that flesh begot flesh" (*In Jo.,* X, 3). She desired and trusted him before she gave him our Flesh. She, by his grace, merited to bear him, as we say in the *Regina Coeli.* So, too, must we merit to bear him if our union with him is to make us one in mind, in heart, and in affection with him. As model and teacher, Mary reminds us that spiritual communion must precede our union with him in the Flesh.

"In communion with and venerating the memory in the first place of the ever-Virgin Mary, Mother of God ... " With these words of the Roman Canon we can be guided to another aspect of the mystery of Mary and the Eucharist. The communion spoken of in this prayer is, of course, a reference to the communion of saints, "whereby", as Paul VI wrote, "the life of each individual child of God in Christ and through Christ is joined by a wonderful link to the life of all his other Christian brothers and sisters in the supernatural unity of the mystical Body of Christ, until, as it were, a single person is formed."[99] One of the implications of this communion is the exchange of spiritual goods that takes place among all the members of the Church. Traditionally, this exchange has been expressed in the teaching about the "treasury of merit", a doctrine well described by Paul VI.

> This "treasury" of the Church is the infinite and inexhaustible value that the expiation and the merits of Christ Our Lord have before God, offered as they were so that all of mankind could be set free from sin and attain communion with the Father. It is Christ the Redeemer himself in whom the satisfactions and merits of his redemption exist and find their force. This treasury also includes

---

[98] *Sacra Tridentina Synodus,* trans., *Living and Growing Through the Eucharist,* Boston: St. Paul Editions, p. 39.

[99] Paul VI, *Apostolic Constitution Indulgentiarum Doctrina,* no. 5, Washington, D.C.: U.S. Catholic Press Conference, 1967.

the truly immense, unfathomable, and ever pristine value before God of all the prayers and good works of the Blessed Virgin Mary and all the saints.[100]

We would be wrong to presume that this holy exchange takes place only through the acquisition of indulgences. It is a sharing of life and benefits that is constant for those in the state of grace and, here on earth, finds its root and culmination in the sacramental sacrifice of the Mass, which "contains the total spiritual good of the Church".[101] This truth can only be fully appreciated when we remember that it is the whole Church that offers the Eucharist, thereby involving the whole "treasury of merit" in the Eucharistic action. This fact was pointed out by Pius XII in *Mediator Dei* when he wrote:

> The sacred liturgy is consequently the public worship that our Redeemer as Head of the Church renders to the Father as well as the worship that the community of the faithful renders to its Founder, and through him, to the heavenly Father. It is, in short, the worship rendered by the mystical Body of Christ in the entirety of its Head and members.[102]

It is a truth repeated by the same Pope in *Mystici Corporis Christi,* no. 82, and by the Second Vatican Council in its *Constitution on the Liturgy,* no. 8. The clearest expression, however, is probably that given by Vatican II in *Lumen Gentium,* no. 50.

> Our union with the heavenly Church in heaven is actuated in its noblest manner especially in the sacred liturgy in which the power of the Holy Spirit acts upon us through the sacred signs and we celebrate together the praise of the divine Majesty with common rejoicing, and when all those who have been redeemed by the Blood of Christ from every tribe and language and people and nation (cf. Rev 5:9) and gathered together into one Church, praise the one and triune God with one canticle of praise. Celebrating

---

[100] Idem.
[101] *Presbyterorum Ordinis,* 5.
[102] *Mediator Dei,* 20; Washington, D.C.: NCWC Publications, 1947.

> the Eucharistic sacrifice, therefore, we are most closely united to the worship of the heavenly Church as we communicate with and venerate the memory first of all of the glorious ever-Virgin Mary, of Blessed Joseph and the blessed Apostles and martyrs, and of all the saints.[103]

As offering of the whole Church, there is included in the Eucharistic sacrifice all that "treasury of merits" of the saints and of Our Lady in a unique degree. Thus, in the Eucharist we share their merits and hers, ever mindful that all of this comes from God in Christ, *de tuis donis ac datis,* as the *Unde et memores* of the Roman Canon says.

It is clear from such teaching that our Eucharist is a participation, a share in the liturgy of heaven (cf. *Sacrosanctum Concilium,* no. 8), and that the praise offered to the Father in heaven is, like our own, hierarchical, in a hierarchy not determined by the Sacrament of Orders but by one's proximity in charity to Christ the One Priest. In this hierarchy, Mary's place is unique.

> Redeemed in a more sublime manner in light of the merits of her Son, and united to him by an intimate and indissoluble bond, she is endowed with the supreme office and dignity of being the Mother of God and therefore the beloved daughter of the Father and the temple of the Holy Spirit, by which gift of sublime grace she far surpasses all other creatures, both in heaven and on earth.[104]

The role played by each member of the Body in that worship offered to God in heaven is a role congruent with that which each fulfilled here on earth in charity. The Lord's own role in that worship is essentially linked with his perfect and all-sufficient offering made on the Cross. It is that which the earthly Eucharist makes sacramentally present. But Christ has associated others with that Mystery, and Mary especially so. "Suffering with her Son as

---

[103] *Lumen Gentium,* 50.
[104] *Lumen Gentium,* 53.

he died on the Cross, she cooperated in a totally singular way by her obedience, faith, hope, and ardent charity in restoring supernatural life to souls."[105] And because the bond between Son and Mother is "intimate and indissoluble", as the Council teaches, she remains with him—and because of him and after him—the chief offerer of that sacrifice that is made present in our earthly Eucharist. As it is the Lord who offers and is offered in every Eucharist, and who, in and with himself, offers the sacrifice of praise of his entire Body, so, in him and with him, Mary offers and is offered in each Eucharistic celebration in that utterly unique way that reflects her role in the redemption her Son achieved for her and for all of us. This, I think, is the meaning of the *communicantes in primis* of the Roman Canon. The whole Church in heaven and on earth offers with and in Christ. "It is our mystery that is present on the paten and in the cup", as Augustine said—and uniquely it is Mary's.

It can be seen from the above that this offering by Mary totally transcends that of the ministerial priesthood. Indeed, the ministerial priesthood exists to make this transcendent offering sacramentally present. Therefore, it is quite useless to attempt to describe Mary's role in the Eucharist in terms of ministerial priesthood. The ministerial priest, acting *in persona Christi*, operates in the order of the sacramental effectuation of the Eucharistic Mystery. Mary operates on the level of the *realities* that are made sacramentally present in the earthly Eucharistic celebration.

Something of Mary's role as chief offerer of the Eucharist after the High Priest himself is captured by the prayer that the Church invites the priest and faithful to say as a thanksgiving after Mass. As we find it in Appendix I of the *Sacramentary,* it reads:

> *Mary, holy virgin Mother,*
> *I have received your Son, Jesus Christ.*
> *With love you became his Mother,*
> *gave birth to him, nursed him,*
> *and helped him grow to manhood.*
> *With love I return him to you*

---

[105] *Lumen Gentium,* 61.

> *to hold once more,*
> *to love with all your heart,*
> *and to offer to the Holy Trinity*
> *as our supreme act of worship*
> *for your honor and for the good*
> *of all your pilgrim brothers and sisters.*

"She is Mother to us in the order of grace."

These words of *Lumen Gentium,* no. 61, illuminated by Pope Paul VI's proclamation of Mary as Mother of the Church at the end of the third session of Vatican Council II, must serve to guide our consideration of another aspect of Mary's relation to the Eucharist. We say *must* because it is as Mother that Mary's dignity and role must always find their ultimate explanation. It is in her as Mother that the eternal Word, by the power of the Spirit, takes his human origins, becoming her Son. It is in her, made fruitful again by the Spirit, that the members of Christ come to birth. All those who are children of God, "children born not of natural descent, or of human decision or a husband's will, but born of God" (Jn 1:13), are such only because they are members of Christ and, like him, are conceived by the Holy Spirit and born of the Virgin Mary.

We have already referred to the teaching of St. Thomas, which sees a certain mystical marriage as having taken place at the Annunciation—a marriage between God and humanity in Mary. As Aquinas saw it, this nuptial union is progressive; it did not end with the Incarnation. He makes this clear in his commentary on St. John's account of the marriage at Cana.

> Through this marriage there is spiritually understood the union between Christ and the Church, as the Apostle says in Ephesians 5:32. . . .
>
> This marriage was initiated in the virginal womb when God the Father united human nature to the Son in a unity of Person. The bridal chamber of this union was the womb of the Virgin. . . . The marriage will be consummated when the Bride, that is, the Church,

is introduced into the bridal chamber of the Spouse, that is, into heavenly glory.[106]

That Mary's role in this nuptial union does not end with her cooperation in the Incarnation, Aquinas makes clear from what follows.

> In this spiritual marriage, the Mother of Jesus, the Blessed Virgin, is present as the go-between of the nuptial rites, because by her intercession, [the Church] is joined to Christ through grace.[107]

Several things are to be noted in these remarkable passages of Aquinas as exegete. First, he refrains from calling Mary herself the bride. She is the bridal chamber, the Mother. That she can be described as Mother and Bride of Christ, as Scheeben and others wished, is probably correct, but Aquinas—and the Second Vatican Council—both avoid such terminology. Second, Thomas calls Mary the "go-between", the *conciliatrix,* of the spiritual union that Christ progressively achieves with all those who will become one Flesh with him. I think it is fair to develop his notion of progressive union and Mary's role in that ongoing espousal by applying it to Mary's role in the Eucharist.

As containing the "total spiritual good of the Church", namely, Christ himself and, in him, the plenitude of merits of Mary and the saints, the Eucharist is the all-sufficient and chief means by which his members are joined to Christ.

Even there, then, Mary acts as "go-between" or *conciliatrix,* and thus her relationship with our Eucharistic celebrations is never sufficiently explained by her role in giving Flesh to Christ, nor to the exemplary aspect of her faith and devotion, nor even to her role as offered and offering in and with her Son. She must be seen, as well, as exercising a continuing role—or causality, if we would introduce the technical word—in all that concerns the ongoing marriage of the Word and humanity. In a general way this truth is

[106] Aquinas, *Lectura super Evangelium S. Ioannis,* caput II, lect. 1.
[107] Aquinas, *Lectura super Evangelium S. Ioannis,* caput II, lect. 2.

a fixed part of Catholic doctrine and is taught by the Second
Vatican Council.

> This maternity of Mary in the economy of grace unceasingly
> perdures, beginning with the consent that she faithfully offered at
> the Annunciation and sustained unhesitatingly beneath the Cross,
> and lasting until the perpetual fulfillment of all the elect. For,
> assumed into heaven, she did not lay aside this saving role but by
> her multifold intercession continues to obtain for us gifts of eternal
> salvation.[108]

How is one to explain this role in relation to the Mass? In part,
we think, by employing the idea of nourishing, which is surely
one of the functions of a mother. Mary nourishes her own. As she
nourished the Child of her womb, "giving milk to our Bread", as
St. Augustine said, so she nourishes those who are being born of
her spiritually by providing them with the fruit of her womb. It
is, of course, a subordinate role. It is Christ who is our food; it is
he who gives himself as our daily nourishment. But, as he associated
her with himself in giving himself to the world and in giving
himself to the Father on the Cross, he likewise associates her with
himself in bestowing himself to the Father and to us in the
Eucharistic action.

If such is the case, the question arises: What kind of presence of
Mary in the Eucharistic action makes such a role possible? Speaking of Mary's Assumption into heaven, Bishop Austin Vaughan
has written:

> Maybe the presence of her body in heaven now, when those of
> the other saints are not, has a special meaning of its own. Jesus'
> bodily Presence in heaven makes possible the unique Presence that
> brings him into our tabernacles and onto our altars. That is a
> matter of faith for us. Perhaps, and this is a matter of pure speculation,
> the presence of Mary's body in heaven is tied in with the unique
> role that God has given her as Mother of the Church.

. . .

---

[108] *Lumen Gentium,* 62.

To put it in a more pointed form: Is there a presence of Mary as mystery in all salvific acts? I know many people might find that a little bit repelling, too strong. Yet, we have lived with centuries of writers, many of them saints, who maintained that all grace comes through Mary. Does that mean anything beyond intercession, in terms of her direct and immediate contact with us?[109]

If we may rephrase the question with specific reference to our own theme, we may ask: In her role as *conciliatrix nuptiarum*, which finds its chief expression in the sacramental sacrifice of the Eucharist, can we speak of a direct and immediate contact of Mary with us? I think the answer is "yes", even though one cannot have the assurance that a clear doctrine of the Faith gives on such matters.

On this question, Fr. Garrigou-Lagrange, citing a commentary of Fr. Hugon on a text of St. Louis de Montfort, wrote:

> The exterior fecundity of the Divine Paraclete is the production of grace, not in the order of moral causality — for the Holy Ghost is not a meritorious cause or impetratory cause — but in the order of physical causality. To reduce this fecundity to act is to produce physically grace and the other works of holiness that are appropriated to the third Divine Person. From this it follows that the Holy Ghost produces grace physically in souls by Mary.[110]

In an extended Note, Garrigou-Lagrange attempts to explain the nature of this contact. It is certain, he wrote, that it is at the least what may be called "affective contact" by which a lover and beloved are present one to another even though spatially distant. As mysterious as this is, we are all aware of this type of contact and of its reality, evidenced in those cases of those who love deeply and who share true intimacy. On this reality rest, in part, St. Thomas' theory of knowledge by connaturality and those unusual premonitions that lovers can have of each other, even when separated by great distances.

---

[109] Austin Vaughan, "The Assumption and Eschatology", *Marian Studies* 33 (1982): 159–61.

[110] R. Garrigou-Lagrange, *The Mother of the Savior*, pp. 210–11.

Normally, this contact must be nourished by at least occasional "contiguous" contact, that is, by the immediate contiguous presence of person to person. Between "affective" and "contiguous" contact, there can be inserted that form of contact called "virtual" whereby one acts on another without being physically contiguous. This can be seen in the case of the angels who, not having bodies, are nonetheless present where they act, thus virtually present.

According to Thomistic teaching, the humanity of Christ has a direct physical influence on us as conjoined instrument of the Divinity. Through that humanity, all grace comes to us. According to Garrigou-Lagrange, Christ's humanity acts on us virtually. "It does not touch us", he wrote, "because it is in heaven."[111] His statement, however, is not completely accurate, because it does not allow sufficiently for the unique contact achieved with the Lord in the Eucharist. Although not a contiguous contact in the usual sense of the word, it is more than the virtual contact that Jesus has with us in the other sacraments; it is, indeed, quasi-contiguous because of his Real Presence in the Sacrament of the Eucharist.

Mary's presence in the Eucharistic action, on the other hand, is what would be called virtual contact. As offered and offerer—the principal one in and after her Son, as Mother who endlessly bestows to us what God has given her, as "go-between" in the nuptial union of Christ and his Church, Mary acts and is present through her actions. How she is capable of acting in so many places at the same time is partially explained by considering the nature of the Eucharistic celebration itself, as we have attempted to do above. Its exterior, sacramental aspect—the level of the *sacramentum tantum*—is multiform, happening in many places and at different times. But in the reality of the Eucharistic action, the sacrifice of praise offered to the Father does not, properly speaking, come down to us. Rather, we are taken up into it. The sacramental action carried out here on earth is the very threshold of heaven. The temporal and the everlasting converge and meet. In what

[111] Garrigou-Lagrange, p. 213.

used to be called the *Infra actionem* of the Eucharist, we are actually *communicantes* with Christ, Mary, and the angels and saints in a reality that is not earthly. At that point, more than at any other time, our lives are already "hidden with Christ in God" (Col 3:3). Such is the truth perceived by all those who insist that there is only one Eucharist, although the appearances are many. In that sense, Mary's presence in each Eucharistic action is real, physical (because she has been bodily assumed into heaven), and unique (as Mother and associate) in this memorial of our redemption.

The Sacramentary's Prayer to the Virgin Mary in preparation for Mass reflects this truth.

> Mother of mercy and love ... you stood by your Son as he hung dying on the Cross. Stand also by me, a poor sinner, and by all the priests who are offering Mass today here and through the entire Church.

I think we can have the assurance that this prayer is answered affirmatively. The Mother of God stands by us and with us in each Eucharist, offering to the Father and to us the fruit of her womb, the Price of our redemption. She will be our guide until her Son, our Manna now hidden, calls us to himself. As Aquinas sang in his *Verbum supernum:*

Se nascens dedit socium,	*Being born he gave himself as*
Convescens in edulium	*our Companion,*
Se moriens in pretium,	*Eating with us he gave himself*
Se regnans dat in praemium.	*as Food,*
	Dying He became our Ransom,
	Reigning he gives himself as
	our Reward.

BIBLIOGRAPHY

Since the bibliography on the Eucharist is so vast, I have limited the following, for the most part, to works actually cited in the text.

Aland, Kurt. *Four Reformers.* Minneapolis: Augsburg Publishing House, 1979.

Aldama, Joseph A., S.J. *De SS. Eucharistia,* in *Sacrae Theologiae Summa* IV. Madrid: Biblioteca de autores Cristianos, 1962.

Ambrose, St. *De Fide. CSEL,* vol. 78. Otto Faller, ed. Vienna, 1962.

_____. *De Mysteriis. CSEL,* vol. 73. Otto Faller, ed. Vienna, 1955.

Aquinas, St. Thomas. *In IV Libros Sententiarum, Opera Omnia.* Parma, 1852–73.

_____. *Lectura super Evangelium S. Ioannis.* Romek: Marietti, 1952.

_____. *Summa Theologiae.* Leonine ed. Rome, 1888–1906.

Auer, Johann. *Allgemeine Sakramentenlehre und das Mysterium der Eucharistie.* Regensburg: Verlag Friedrich Pustet, 1971. A translation of this is to appear in English as *The Mystery of the Eucharist,* Washington, D.C.: Catholic University of America Press.

Bellarmine, St. Robert. *Opera Omnia.* Naples, 1872.

Berengarius. *De Sacra Coena Adversus Lanfrancum.* A. F. Vischer and F. T. Vischer, eds. Hildesheim: Georg Olms Verlag, 1975 (reprint).

_____. *Epistola Contra Almannum,* J. de Montclos, ed., in J. de Montclos, *Lanfranc et Bérenger* (q.v.), pp. 531–38.

Berkouwer, G. C. *The Sacraments.* Grand Rapids, Mich.: Eerdmans, 1969.

Betz, Johannes. "La Eucharistía, Misterio Central", in *Mysterium Salutis* (Spanish edition, IV/2), Madrid: Ediciones Cristiandad, 1975.

Boff, Leonardo. *Ecclesiogenesis.* Maryknoll, N.Y.: Orbis Books, 1986.

Bouyer, Louis. *The Early Liturgy to the Time of Gregory the Great.* South Bend, Ind.: University of Notre Dame Press, 1959.

_____. *Eucharist.* South Bend, Ind.: University of Notre Dame Press, 1968.

_____. *Liturgical Piety.* South Bend, Ind.: University of Notre Dame Press, 1957.

Brooks, Peter. *Thomas Cranmer's Doctrine of the Eucharist.* New York: Seabury Press, 1965.

Browne, Edward H. *An Exposition of the Thirty-Nine Articles.* London: Longmans, Green, and Co., 1894.

Burgess, Joseph A., ed. *The Role of the Augsburg Confession: Catholic and Lutheran Views.* Philadelphia: Fortress Press, 1980.

Cajetan, Thomas de Vio. "The Sacrifice of the Mass". In Jared Wicks. *Cajetan Responds.* Washington, D.C.: Catholic University of America Press, 1978.

Calvin, John. *Institutes of the Christian Religion,* vol. 2. John T. McNeill, ed., Ford Lewis Battles, trans. and indexer. In *The*

Library of Christian Classics, vol. 21. Philadelphia: Westminster Press, 1977.

Carlen, Sr. Claudia, I.H.M., ed. *The Papal Encyclicals.* 4 vols. Wilmington, N.C.: McGrath Publishing Co., n.d.

Casel, Odo. *The Mystery of Christian Worship and Other Writings.* Burkhard Neunheuser, O.S.B., ed. Westminster, Md.: Newman Press, 1962.

CCCM (Corpus Christianorum Continuatio Mediaevalis). Belgium: Turnhout, 1953–.

CCSL (Corpus Christianorum, Series Latina). Belgium: Turnhout, 1953–.

Chrysostom, St. John. *On the Priesthood.* W.A. Jurgens, trans. In *The Priesthood.* New York: Macmillan Co., 1955.

Concilium Tridentinum: Diariorum Actorum Epostularum Tractatuum Nova Collectio. Societas Goerresiana, ed. (Postina, Ehses, Birkner, Freudenberger et al.) Freiburg: Herder, 1901–.

Connolly, Myles. *Mr. Blue.* Garden City, N.Y.: Doubleday-Image, 1955.

CSEL (Corpus Scriptorum ecclesiasticorum latinorum). Vienna, 1866–.

Daniel-Rops, Henri. *The Catholic Reformation.* 2 vols. Garden City, N.Y.: Doubleday-Image, 1961.

Davies, Horton. *Worship and Theology in England,* vol. 1. Princeton, N.J.: Princeton University Press, 1970.

Davis, Charles. "Understanding the Real Presence". T. Patrick Burke, ed., *The Word in History.* New York: Sheed and Ward, 1966.

Davis, H. Francis. "The Pope and Private Masses". *Clergy Review* 42 (1957): 2–14.

de Baciocchi, J. *L'Eucharistie.* Tournai, Belgium: Desclée and Co., 1964.

————————. "Présence Eucharistique et Transsubstantiation". *Irenikon* 32 (1959): 139–64.

de la Taille, Maurice. *The Mystery of Faith.* 2 vols. New York: Sheed and Ward, 1940. Originally published 1919, with revised editions in 1923 and 1929.

de Lubac, Henri, S.J. *Corpus Mysticum.* Paris: Aubier, 1949.

————————. *The Splendor of the Church.* San Francisco: Ignatius Press, 1986.

Emminghaus, Johannes H. *The Eucharist.* Collegeville, Minn: Liturgical Press, 1978.

Funk, F. X. *Patres Apostolici.* 2nd ed. Tübingen, 1901.

Garrigou-Lagrange, Reginald. *The Mother of the Savior.* St. Louis: Herder Book Co., 1959.

GCS (Die griechischen christlichen Schriftsteller der ersten drei Jahrhunderte). Berlin, 1897–.

Geiselmann, Joseph. *Die Eucharistielehre der Vorscholastik.* Paderborn: Druck und Verlag von F. Schonigh, 1926.

Gelasius. *Tractatus de Duabus Naturis Adversus Eutychen et Nestorium. PL,* 224, Supplementum 3, pp. 763–87.

Gerrish, B. A., ed. *Reformers in Profile.* Philadelphia: Fortress Press, 1967.

Gregory of Nyssa. *Catechetical Discourse.* In Louis Meridier, ed., *Grégoire de Nysse: Discours Catéchètique.* Paris: Éditions du Cerf, 1908. The critical text used here is that of Srawley, *The Catechetical Oration of Gregory of Nyssa.* Cambridge: University Press, 1903.

Grillmeier, Aloys, S.J. *Christ in Christian Tradition,* vol. 2, pt. 1. Atlanta, Ga.: John Knox Press, 1987.

Hall, John Brewer. *The Perilous Vision of John Wyclif.* Chicago: Nelson-Hall, 1983.

Hart, Charles A. *Thomistic Metaphysics.* Englewood Cliffs, N.J.: Prentice Hall, 1959.

Herron, Thomas J. *The Dating of the First Epistle of Clement to the Corinthians.* Dissertation for the Faculty of Biblical Theology. Rome: Pontifical Gregorian University, 1988.

Irenaeus, St. Cf. *Sources Chrétiennes,* vols. 100, 152, 153.

Johanny, Raymond. *L'Eucharistie: Centre de L'Histoire du Salut chez Saint Ambroise de Milan.* Paris: Beauchesne et Fils, 1968.

Jorissen, Hans. *Die Entfaltung der Transsubstantiationslehre bis zum Beginn der Hochscholastik.* Munster: Münsterische Beitrage zur Theologie, 28/I, 1965.

Journet, C. *La Messe, présence du sacrifice de la Croix.* Paris: Desclée de Brouwer, 1957.

Jungmann, Joseph, S.J. *The Mass of the Roman Rite.* 2 vols. New York: Benziger Bros., 1955.

_____. *The Sacrifice of the Church.* London: Challoner, 1956.

Jurgens, William. *The Faith of the Early Fathers.* 3 vols. Collegeville, Minn.: Liturgical Press, 1979.

Justin, St. *Justini, Phil. et Mar., Opera.* J. T. Eques de Otto, ed. Vaduz, Lichtenstein: Sandig, 1969.

Kelly, J. N. D. *Early Christian Doctrines.* 5th ed. London: Adam and Charles Black, 1980.

_____. *The Oxford Dictionary of Popes.* Oxford: Oxford University Press, 1986.

Kempis, Thomas à. *The Imitation of Christ*. Clare L. Fitzpatrick, trans. New York: Catholic Book Publishing Co., 1977.

Kidd, B. J. *The Later Medieval Doctrine of the Eucharistic Sacrifice*. London: SPCK Press, 1958.

Klauser, Theodor. *A Short History of the Western Liturgy*. 2nd ed. Oxford: Oxford University Press, 1979.

Kleist, James, trans. and ed. *The Epistles of St. Clement of Rome and St. Ignatius of Antioch*. Ancient Christian Writers Series, Westminster, Md.: Newman Press, 1946.

Küng, Hans. *On Being a Christian*. Garden City, N.Y.: Doubleday and Co., 1976.

_____. *The Church*. New York: Sheed and Ward, 1967.

Lambert, Malcolm. *Medieval Heresy*. New York: Holmes and Meier Publishers, 1976.

Lanfranc. *Liber de Corpore et Sanguine Domini*. PL, 150.

Leenhardt, Franz. "La présence eucharistique". *Irenikon* 33 (1960): 146–72.

_____. "This Is My Body". In *Essays on the Lord's Supper*. London: Butterworth Press, 1959.

Lightfoot, J. B. *The Apostolic Fathers, I–II*. Revised texts. New York: Macmillan and Co., 1893.

_____. *The Apostolic Fathers*. English translations only. Grand Rapids, Mich.: Baker Book House, 1980.

Luther, Martin. *Luther's Works*. 55 vols. General eds., Jaroslav Pelikan (vols. 1–30); Helmut Lehmann (vols. 31–55). Philadelphia: Concordia Press.

_____. Vol. 36, *Word and Sacrament II*. Abdel Ross Wentz, ed., 1959.

_____. Vol. 37, *Word and Sacrament III.* Robert Fischer, ed., 1961.

McCauley, Leo, and Anthony Stephenson, eds. *The Works of Saint Cyril of Jerusalem,* vol. 2. Washington, D.C.: Catholic University of America Press, 1970.

Macy, Gary. *The Theologies of the Eucharist in the Early Scholastic Period.* Oxford: Clarendon Press, 1984.

_____. "Influence of Exegesis on The Theology of the Eucharist in the Eleventh and Twelfth Centuries". *Recherches de Théologie Ancienne et Médiévale* 52 (1985): 64–77.

Mansi. *Sacrorum conciliorum nova et amplissima collectio.* Florence, 1759–98.

Mascall, E. L. *Corpus Christi.* London: Longmans, 1965.

Masure, Eugene. *The Christian Sacrifice.* New York: P. J. Kenedy and Sons, 1943.

Mersch, Emile. *The Theology of the Mystical Body.* St. Louis, Mo.: B. Herder Book Co., 1958.

Montclos, Jean de. *Lanfranc et Bérenger: La Controverse Eucharistique du XIᵉ Siècle.* Louvain, Belgium: Spicilegium Sacrum Lovaniense, 1971.

Moore, R. I. *The Birth of Popular Heresy.* New York: St. Martin's Press, 1975.

Morin, Dom G., O.S.B. *Miscellanea Agostiniana.* Vatican, Rome: Polyglot Press, 1930.

O'Carroll, Michael. *Corpus Christi: A Theological Encyclopedia of the Eucharist.* Wilmington, Del.: Michael Glazier, 1988.

Ochoa, Xaverius. *Index Verborum Cum Documentis Concilii Vaticani Secundi.* Rome: Commenatrium pro Religiosis, 1967.

O'Connor, Flannery. *The Habit of Being.* New York: Farrar-Straus-Giroux, 1979.

Origen. *Homilies on the Canticle of Canticles. Sources Chrétiennes,* vol. 37. Dom O. Rousseau, O.S.B., trans. and notes. Paris: Éditions du Cerf, 1953.

Pelikan, Jaroslav. *The Christian Tradition: A History of the Development of Doctrine.* Chicago: University of Chicago Press, vol. 1, 1971; vol. 2, 1974; vol. 3, 1978; vol. 4, 1984.

Piolanti, Antonius. *De Sacramentis.* Italy: Marietti, 1962.

PG (Patrologia graeca). Migne. Paris, 1857–66.

PL (Patrologia latina). Migne. Paris, 1878–90.

Portalie, Eugene, S.J. *A Guide to the Thought of St. Augustine.* Chicago: Regnery, 1960.

Power, David N., O.M.I. *The Sacrifice We Offer.* New York: Crossroad Publishing Co., 1987.

Powers, Joseph. *Eucharistic Theology.* New York: Herder and Herder, 1967.

Quasten, Johannes. "The Liturgical Mysticism of Theodore of Mopsuestia". *Theological Studies* 15: 431–39.

——————. *Monumenta Eucharistica et Liturgica Vetustissima.* Vol. 8, part I, of *Florilegium Patristicum,* Geyer and Zellinger, eds. Bonn: Peter Hanstein, 1935.

——————. *Patrology.* 3 vols. Westminster, Md.: Newman Press, 1960.

Radbertus, St. Paschasius. *De Corpore et Sanguine Domini. CCCM,* XVI. Pede Paulus, O.S.B., ed., 1969.

_____. *Expositio in Mattheo Libri XII. CCCM,* LVI. Pede Paulus, O.S.B., ed., 1984.

Rahner, Karl. "The Presence of Christ in the Sacrament of the Lord's Supper". *Theological Investigation,* vol. 4. Baltimore: Helicon Press, 1966.

Rahner, Karl and Angelus Haussling. *The Celebration of the Eucharist.* Montreal: Herder-Palm, 1967.

Ratramnus. *De Corpore et Sanguine Domini. PL,* 121.

_____. *De Corpore et Sanguine Domini: Texte Établi d'après les Manuscrits et Notice Bibliographique.* J. N. Bakhuizen van den Brink, ed. Amsterdam: Holland Publishing Co., 1954.

Ratzinger, Joseph. *Feast of Faith.* San Francisco: Ignatius Press, 1986.

_____. "El Problema de la transustanciación y la cuestíon sobre el sentido de la Eucaristía". In Ratzinger and Beinert, *Transustanciacion y Eucharistia.* Madrid: Ediciones Paulinas, 1969.

Richardson, Cyril C., ed. *Early Christian Fathers.* New York: Macmillan Company, 1970.

Rouet De Journel, S.J. *Enchiridion Patristicum.* New York: Herder, 1953.

Sasse, Hermann. *This Is My Body.* Minneapolis: Augsburg Publishing House, 1959.

Scheeben, Matthias. *The Mysteries of Christianity.* St. Louis: B. Herder, 1964.

Schillebeeckx, E. *The Eucharist.* New York: Sheed and Ward, 1968.

_____. *Ministry.* New York: Crossroad Publishing Co., 1981.

_____. "Transubstantiation, Transfinalization, Transfiguration". *Worship* 40 (1966): 324–38.

Schmemann, Alexander. *The Eucharist.* Crestwood, N.Y.: St. Vladimir's Seminary Press, 1988.

Schoedel, William. *Athenagoras, Legatio and De Resurrectione.* Oxford: Clarendon Press, 1972.

Schoonenberg, Piet, S.J. "Transubstantiation". *Concilium,* vol. 24. New York: Paulist Press, 1967, pp. 78ff.

Sheerin, Daniel J., ed. *The Eucharist.* Wilmington, Del.: Glazier, 1986.

Solano, Jesús, S.J. *La Eucaristía: Textos del Vaticano II y de Pablo VI.* Madrid: Biblioteca de Autores Cristianos, 1969.

_____. *Textos Eucarísticos Primitivos.* 2 vols. Madrid: Biblioteca de Autores Cristianos, 1954–69.

Sources Chrétiennes. Paris: Éditions du Cerf.

_____. Vol. 100, *Irenée de Lyon: Contre les Hérésies,* Livre IV. A. Rousseau, 1965.

_____. Vol. 126, *Cyrille de Jérusalem: Catéchèses Mystagogiques.* Auguste Piedagnel and Pierre Paris, 1966.

_____. Vol. 152, *Irenée de Lyon: Contre les Hérésies.* Livre V. A. Rousseau, 1969.

_____. Vol. 153, *Irenée de Lyon: Contre les Hérésies.* A. Rousseau, 1969.

_____. Vol. 167, *Clément de Rome: Epître aux Corinthiens.* Annie Jaubert, 1971.

_____. Vol. 248, *Didache.* W. Rordorf and A. Tuilier, 1978.

Spinka, Matthew. *John Hus.* Princeton, N.J.: Princeton University Press, 1968.

Staniforth, Maxwell. *Early Christian Writings: The Apostolic Fathers.* London: Penguin Books, 1981.

Stephens, W. P. *The Theology of Huldrych Zwingli.* Oxford: Clarendon Press, 1986.

Stone, Darwell. *A History of the Doctrine of the Holy Eucharist.* 2 vols. New York: Longmans, Green, and Co., 1909.

Suarez, Francisco, S.J. *Opera Omnia.* Paris: Vives, 1877.

Tanner, J. R., et al. *The Cambridge Medieval History,* vol. 6. Cambridge: University Press, 1964.

Teilhard de Chardin, Pierre. *Hymn of the Universe.* Simon Bartholomew, trans. New York: Harper and Row, 1961,

Tennyson, Alfred Lord. *The Poems and Plays of Alfred Lord Tennyson.* New York: Modern Library, Random House, 1938.

Tertullian. *Adversus Praxaen. CCSL,* vol. 11. Brepols: Turnholt, 1954.

Theodore of Mopsuestia. *Homily XV (First on the Mass).* In *Studi e Testi,* vols. 144–45. Rome: Polyglot Press, 1949.

——————. *On the Eucharist.* In *Woodbrooke Studies,* vol. 6. A. Mingana, ed. Cambridge, 1933.

Thurian, Max, ed. *Churches Respond to BEM: Official Responses to the "Baptism, Eucharist and Ministry" Text 2–3.* Geneva: World Council of Churches, 1986–87.

Tolkien, J. R. R. *The Letters of J. R. R. Tolkien.* Selected and edited by H. Carpenter with assistance of C. Tolkien. Boston: Houghton Mifflin Co., 1981.

TPS (The Pope Speaks). A quarterly of Church documents. Huntington, Ind.: Our Sunday Visitor.

Trefil, James. *The Dark Side of the Universe.* New York: Charles Scribner's Sons, 1988.

Vagaggini, Cipriano. *The Flesh: Instrument of Salvation.* Staten Island, N.Y.: Alba House, 1968.

van der Meer, F. *Augustine the Bishop.* London and New York: Sheed and Ward, 1961.

Vonier, Anscar, O.S.B. *A Key to the Doctrine of the Eucharist.* New York: Benziger Brothers, 1925.

Wicks, Jared, S.J. *Catjetan Responds.* Washington, D.C.: Catholic University of America Press, 1978.

Williams, Oscar, ed. *Major British Poets.* New York: New American Library, 1963.

Wyclif, John. *De Eucharistia Tractatus Maior.* London: Wyclif Society, 1892.

————. *Wyclif's Latin Works.* Vol. 1, *Sermons.* London: Wyclif Society, 1887.

Wynne, John J., S.J., trans. and ed. *The Great Encyclical Letters of Pope Leo XIII.* New York: Benziger Brothers, 1908.

Zwingli, Huldrych. *Commentary on True and False Religion.* Samuel Macauley Jackson, ed. Durham, N.C., Labyrinth Press, Durham, 1981.

INDEX